The Collector's Guide to 3rd Reich Tableware

by

James A. Yannes

Order this book online at www.trafford.com
or email orders@trafford.com

Most Trafford titles are also available at major online book retailers.

Printed in the United States of America.

ISBN: 978-1-4269-8193-7 (sc)
ISBN: 978-1-4669-0242-8 (hc)
ISBN: 978-1-4269-8194-4 (e)

Trafford rev. 12/14/2011

www.trafford.com

North America & International
toll-free: 1 888 232 4444 (USA & Canada)
phone: 250 383 6864 • fax: 812 355 4082

Table of Contents

Preface

On 16 October 2010, a Wall Street Journal article headline read, "Germany Mounts Hitler Exhibit, a First". We learn that the German Historical Museum in Berlin (the most important public institution on the nation's history) opened the exhibit "Hitler and the Germans"! This in a country that does not allow the UPS "Men in Brown" to wear their trademark color but instead must wear green. The times are a changing. We are slowly moving into the "historic" view of the 3rd Reich, a time for a new level of reflection.

This book is my third addressing 3rd Reich tableware. The first, *Collectible Spoons of the 3rd Reich* ran 224 pages leading to *A Guide to 3rd Reich Cutlery* with 374 pages. This edition is a further expansion of the history of the 3rd Reich as abundantly reflected in its cutlery (besteck). Its diversity reflects subtle Government policy as does the quality. Military attitudes regarding the Nazi's is reflected in their cutlery. So much to learn but so little surviving documentation. No list of manufacturers trade marks has survived. Even manufacturers catalogs of the period are very difficult to locate. My focus with my books has been to document, as best I can, this very interesting microcosm from the surviving debris and to encourage the collection and further research so as to throw more light on this dark threat that could have destroyed our civilization.

This book primarily explores German BESTECK, defined as knives, spoons and forks, its English translation is cutlery. English has a number of descriptors for besteck including cutlery, silverware, tableware and flatware. Although I've included a small number of Service pieces, such as a coffee pot or a can opener, my focus remains on metal tableware and metal service items.

Fundamental Types of 3rd Reich Tableware

There are 3 major cutlery types defined by their basic material for which devices are required and which normally appear on the cutlery's reverse.

First is the 'silver' tableware (Silberbesteck). Here the tableware is composed of a mixture of silver and copper. The most common German decimal silver standard marks are 800 and 925 and attest to the proportion of the silver as 80% and 92.5% (sterling) with the remainder copper. German laws required the stamp of either 800 or 925. There are also 830, 835, 900, and 935 to be found.
Note: Some dealers will incorrectly identify 800 as sterling

Second is silver plated or clad tableware (Versilbertes Besteck). Here the basic tableware is typically made of 'German Silver' (see pp 37) with a plating of pure silver. The plating number will appear on the reverse of the spoon or fork and typically on the neck of the knife handle. Per contemporary Wellner & WMF inputs, silver plating is only done using pure silver. The most popular plating indicator is the number 90. If, as an example, a '90' appears, it indicates, per Wellner, that 90 grams (3.2 oz) of silver is applied per a surface area of 24 quadradezimeters, equivalent to 24 cutlery pieces (6 each: teaspoons, forks, tablespoons, and knives). WMF states the '90' is 90 grams of silver plate on 24 square decimeters = 372 square inches which corresponds to the surface of 24 menu spoons. A third explanation comes from Beata Waliczak's book *Firmenstempel auf Besteck*: "These numbers indicate the thickness of coating in microns." Plating numbers may go as low as 30 for hotel ware and up. When alone, can be in either a circle, a square or a stand alone. Both Wellner and WMF attested to this marking scheme. There are plated cutlery with not only silver plating signs but also gram weight signs. In this case, the silver plate is typically listed inside a circle. The gram weight number follows and is inside a Wellner square or WMF lozenge, see page 475.

Third is tableware which is neither 'silver' nor silver plated. Their base material is typically aluminum, stainless steel or Alpacca Silver - Also known in English as German Silver or Nickel Silver. The vast majority of service pieces will be of alpacca and some will have silver plating.

Typical markings / materials include:

Alpacca - see page 37
Aluminium = aluminum
Rustfrei = Rust Free (Stainless Steel)
Nicht Rostend = None Rusting
Gusstahl Solingen = Cast Steel
Tomback = an alloy of copper and zinc. Replaced during the late war with pure zinc
Cupal: Aluminum between two thin sheets of copper. Usually surface plated with silver.
Leichtmetall or Lightweight alloy
Kriegsmetall or War Metal, a poor quality alloy of zinc, copper and lead. Commonly called 'Pot Metal' by collectors.

Almost all cutlery will carry a Herstellerkennzeichen or Makers Mark or Manufacturers ID on the reverse. This can be the name of the manufacturer: "Bruckmann" or the manufacturers initials or a mark such as Wellner's die (cube) in a circle. Unfortunately, many makers marks remain a mystery as the original registries have been lost or destroyed. Surprisingly, for a nation famous for its organization, there does not appear to be a directory of 3rd Reich era makers marks!

Collector Alert; If you do not find your favorite collectible in this book, it is due to the fact that I do not own one.

German Law regarding Silver Marks

In 1884 a law was enacted making .800 the minimum national standard in Germany for silver. In 1886 the use of individual city marks was abolished and replaced by the national mark (Reichsmark or RM) of a crescent moon (silver symbol) & crown (symbol of empire) representing the entire German state. These marks became compulsory by 1888. The Crescent Moon & Crown (Halbmond und Krone), are used in conjunction with a decimal silver standard mark, usually .800 or .925 and a maker's mark. Due to the large number of manufacturers and an apparent lack of centralized records, many maker's marks can no longer be identified.

This Prussian eagle is a Bruckmann & Sohne maker's mark, manufacturers ID, hallmark, herstellerkennzeichen or herstellerpunzierungen. A Schutzzeichen is a proof mark; trade mark.

The tableware is organized into sections

Section I - Personalities

Tableware associated with specific personalities. In some cases the flatware carries the initials of the owner and in others, a pattern strictly associated with a specific person and is typically applied to the obverse. The easy examples are the Adolf Hitler spoons marked with his personal eagle straddled with his initials “A” and “H”. In the absence of initials, at times the Eagle is the key, von Ribbontrop’s eagle is very similar to Hitler’s but unique as is Bormann’s. Another identifier would be a Hans Frank spoon which carries the / his official state pattern of the Governor General of Poland. These pieces are usually listed by the associated owners name as per below in order acquired:

Adolf Hitler
Eva Braun
Hermann Goering
Heinrich Himmler
Albert Speer
Helmut Weidling
Bernard Rust
Dr. Robert Ley
Ernst Kaltenbrunner
Fritz Sauckel
Hans Frank
Bishop Ludwig Mueller
Martin Bormann
Joachim von Ribbentrop
Rudolf Hess
Reinhard Heydrich
Dr. Gustav Scheel
General Hermann Breiht

Section II - Other Government

Under the 3rd Reich, all organizations were either in the government or were eliminated. Organizational cutlery typically carries the Logo of the organization on the obverse.

N.S.D.A.P. - NS Deutsche Arbeiterpartei, (National Socialist German Worker's Party)
SA - Sturmabtellung - Storm troopers
DJV - Deutsche Jungvolk - German Youth
HJ - Hitler Jugend - Hitler Youth
DAF - Deutsche Arbeitfront - German Labor Front
DLV - Deutscher Luftfahrt Verband - German Aviation League
DR - Deutsche Reichsbahn - German National Railways
DRK - Deutsches Rotes Kreuz - German Red Cross
NSDStB - National Socialistische Studenten Bund - National Socialist Student Association
NSKK - NS Kraftfahrkorps - NS Motor Corps
NSKOV - NS-Kriegsopferversorgung - NS War Victims Welfare Service (WWI)
NSRL - NS Reichsbund für Leibesübungen - NS Physical Fitness
NSV - NS Volkswohlfahrt - NS People's Welfare
RAD - Reichs Arbeitsdienst - National Labor Service,
RDB - Reichsbund der Deutschen Beamten - Federation of German Civil Servants
RK - (Neu) Reichkanzlei - New National Chancellery, Berlin
RKB - Reichskolonialbund - Colonial League
RLB - Reichs Luftschutzbund - National Air Raid Protection League
RMJ - Reichministerium der Justiz - Ministry of Justice
RNS - Reichs Nahrstand - Food Estate

Section III - Wehrmacht

Section IV - SS:

Section V - Miscellaneous

Berghof 'House' Service
Fuhrerbau's Italian Service
Reichswerke Hermann Goering
Gastehaus Reichsparteitag
Hotel Deutsche Hof
Der Deutscher Hof Hotel
Bayerischer Hof Hotel
Hotel Post, Berchtesgaden
Platterhof Hotel, Obersalzberg, Creamer
Dietrich Eckart Krankenhaus
U-47 commemorative
Danziger Werf
Haus der Deutschen Arbeit 1933
House of German Art, 1937
    Cutlery, Goblet, Coffee Pot, Creamer
Staatskasino
Kasino Lamsdorf
Rabbit Breeders Association
Danzig Andenken
Nurnberg Andenken
AVRO Tempelhof
German Embassy - Paris
Gau Posen Welfare Office
LZ 129 Hindenburg
Danish Mystery
Wellner of East Germany
America's Swastikas
Hitler's Favorite Monogram?
NPEA - National Political Educational Institute
Platterhof Hotel, Tray

INTRODUCTION

In a recent visit to Munich, we came across a “Third Reich Tour”. This was a walking tour which “covers all important facts and sites that played a role in the origin of this black chapter, that ended with the beautiful city of Munich in ruins.” With a sub title, “Hitler’s Munich.”. When we asked the tour guide if he was comfortable with the subject matter, he explained that he had been born in the mid 1960’s and that for him, the Second World War was history. He said his grand parents and his parents wanted nothing to do with memories of the war. We even have a German friend who was born in the late 1930’s and baptized ‘Adolf’ who had his name changed out of revulsion for what had occurred. This encounter brought to mind the changed opinion of Napoleon who had caused the deaths of millions and was condemned by the world in the mid 19th century only to now be a hero of France. This is not to say that Hitler and the 3rd Reich will ever be revered like Napoleon but that as time passes, perceptions dim and places and items take on a historical patina. As a current example of this trend, the German Historical Museum in Berlin, the most important public institution on the nation’s history, opened the first ever Hitler exhibition “Hitler and the Germans” on 14 Oct 2010!. Curator Hans-Ulrich Thamer described the Fuhrer as “a medium for contemporary expectations” a screen onto which a crisis-battered society projected its yearning for salvation.

There are a number of very interesting Third Reich locations available to anyone with an interest in the historical aspects of what will undoubtedly be the defining military effort in history. My wife and I have visited all the sites mentioned but unfortunately when we made our visits, I had no intention of writing about them so the descriptions will be from memory and with little detail. In my earlier book, *A Guide to*

3rd Reich Cutlery; Dresden, Wewelsburg, Quedlinburg, and Wunsdorf were mentioned. I will expand upon:

Munich Area: This is a good place to start as Hitler called Munich the "Capital of the Movement". There are two walking tours, the two and one half hour "Third Reich Tour" and a 5 hour "Extended Third Reich Tour". I highly recommend a down town hotel so you can walk to the start point in the Marienplatz. Much of the "Nazi" architecture has survived such as the The Fuhrerbau which is now a music school but no longer open to the public - the place where Chamberlin received his 'Peace in our time' paper from Hitler and its mirror image, the Administration building. Also the Feldherrnhalle (Field Marshals' Hall) where the 9 Nov 1923 "Beer Hall Putsch" was put down. The early NSDAP office was on Schillingstr which accounts for Hitler's favorite restaurant at Schellingstr 54, now a billiard hall with a small snack corner (when we visited they had only one type of Kucken!). Still in operation is another favorite - Osteria Italiana at 62 Schellingstr, (3 doors from NSDAP's HQ) which remains popular - dinner reservations recommended. A one day side trip to Bad Wiessee to visit the site of Hitler's arrest of SA leader Ernst Rohm as depicted in a History Channel episode. The hotel has been renamed 'Hotel Lederer am See' on Tegernseer Tal. The staff is not interested in discussing the matter but there is a very pleasant bar overlooking the lake for cake and coffee. And as you will note later, I have taken a fancy to the Art Museum.

Bad Toelz - SS Officers Training Facility. The famous arch between the main entry towers was removed shortly after the U.S. Army vacated. The chapel outside the formal grounds, remains due to the refusal of the contractor to destroy it along with the arch. The indoor swimming pool and bowling ally remain in use today!

Landsberg Prison: Some 40KM North of Munich, the Prison is closed to the public but understood to be open to the public 2 days a year.

So much for travel suggestions.

My first disclaimer: I am not an expert on 3rd Reich cutlery! In fact, I am not really a collector. I am an accumulator. My interests change with time and several years ago I bought a Hitler spoon and used it for several years in my morning coffee. Then I saw an Eva Braun spoon and it seemed appropriate to join them together. This led to picking up various spoons over the years. As it is obvious, my collection is a type collection, with emphasis on breadth rather than depth. As a rank amateur, I have relied on my sources to deliver correct material and to date have had only one catastrophe from a Florida dealer. So I challenge the reader to point out the inevitable fakes. The intent of the book is to broaden the coverage of this interesting area. Why tableware? My first book entitled, "*Collectible Spoons of the 3rd Reich*" which was published in 2009 was focused on spoons. It later dawned on me that the book should focus on the variety of markings / monograms on the cutlery and to limit the scope to spoons would leave out many variations that may be only available in forks and knives. Therefore, forks and knives were added as well as service pieces. To summarize, spoons and forks are friendly, non threatening utensils and easily displayed. They also entice their collection, both obvious and clandestine. Thomas Breyette, the author of the definitive book on German Tank Destruction Badges told me the story of one of the recipients of the TDB purloining one of Adolf Hitler's spoons as he (the most junior officer in attendance) was the last to retire from his award luncheon hosted by the Fuehrer.

Regarding "Hitler's" personal flatware variations: The only reference books I have are, *Treasure Trove - The Looting of the Third Reich* by Charles E. Snyder, Jr. Major USAF (Retired) and *"Liberated" Adolf Hitler Memorabilia* by Mark D. Griffith, M.D. In the Griffith book on page 15 he illustrates and states "close-up of the handles illustrating five of the six different patterns of silverware." Whereas Snyder illustrates 16 different patterns on pages 37 to 41. As always, these types of inquiries will remain somewhat of a mystery as the records no longer exist. The AH 'formal' pattern (PS-1) is well known, documented and high priced. Estimates of total number struck top out at 6,000 pieces. The similarly priced AH 'informal' (PS-3) is rather a mystery as no one seems to know how many were produced with guesses at 1,000, why they were produced and most interesting - where they were used. This matter is explored later in the book.

Where are the records? - as an example, I bought a Kriegsmarine binocular, maker marked 'beh' for the manufacturer Leitz. After the war Leitz became Leica who in turn destroyed all W.W.II. Leitz records. Even inquiries to the U.S. Government and Corning Glass proved unsuccessful so that determining the production history is apparently lost forever. You may ask, why Corning - After the war, the U.S. Government sent teams to Germany to retrieve all technical advancements that Germany had made during the war and to bring all the technology back to the U.S. for evaluation and to make use of anything of value. The team from Corning got the optics advancements. You may recall that during the Carter administration, tons of W.W.II German material related to the manufacture of petroleum products from coal were pored over in an effort to find some economic solution to the "energy crises' of that period.

Common Markings, Terms and General Comments

Hoheitszeichen (German national emblem) during the period 1933 to 1945 was the combination Eagle and Swastika.

Although the swastika officially became the emblem for the Nazi Party on August 7, 1920, at the Salzburg Congress; per USM Books, "There was absolutely no mandatory use of a swastika on silverware or silver service items that we are aware of."

The German Silver Makers Guild mandated that at least part of all cutlery sets carry the silver designation. This explains why some pieces of broken sets turn up with no designation.

RZM = Reichzeugmeisterei (National Equipment Quartermaster) founded in 1934 by the NSDAP as a Reich Hauptamt (State Central Office) The RZM procured and distributed items, approved designs, insured quality, supervised standardization and compliance to specifications.

RB = (Reichsbetrieb nummer) RB numbers replaced Manufacturer's names on products in 1942 to conceal the manufacturers name and therefore location from allied bombing.

Heer

W.H. = Wehrmacht Heeres (Armed Forces Army) Army field, folding cutlery sets (Essbesteck) of either Knife/Spoon/Fork or Spoon/ Fork combinations are typically of aluminum for weight considerations

Kriegsmarine

An "M" indicates Kriegsmarine and can appear either above or below the eagle The eagles vary from simple 3 lined wings to 5 full feathered wings Or no 'M' but the eagle and swastika remain recognizable as Kriegsmarine.

Luftwaffe

Fl.U.V. = Flieger Unterkunft Verwaltung = Flight Barracks Administration

Eagles come in two variations: Early version with "Drooped Tail" on items marked up through 1937 Later version with "Straight Tail" on items dated 1938 and later

SS

Allgemeine SS = General / Universal SS
SS-VT (Verfugungstruppe) or Political Troops.
SS-TV = (Totenkopfverbande) or SS-Death's Head Units)
SS-WB = SS-Wachverbande (SS-Guard Units)
Waffen SS = Armed SS / Weapons SS

D.R.P.

Deutsche Reichs Patent / German National Patent

LOOTED?

Was the tableware looted? The obvious answer would appear to be 'yes', (Referring to PS-33, the original source for this item was PFC Jack Greene, 86th Infantry Div who stated he "immediately filled his pockets with silverware" while searching the Scheel residence in Salzburg May 45. Also see PS-30 and M-165. but the precedent in international law provides that, "any moveable property of an enemy becomes the property of the capturing power."

The post Nazi German Government's directions regarding 3rd Reich material: Relevant sections of German Law summary of section § 86, 86a:

> "Items that are used for making propaganda for a party or group which is classed as unconstitutional or forbidden, even if they act outside Germany, may not be spread inside Germany. This applies for items made to propagate ideas that correspond with the ideas of the "Third Reich". They might not be made, kept, imported or exported. The punishment may be prison (up to three years) or a fine.
> This does not apply if those items are used in order to inform others, repel actions that are aimed against the constitution, if they are used in art, science, research, teaching, or to report about historical events or similar purposes.
> If you use or show symbols or signs used by parties or groups that can be classified as unconstitutional, or if you manufacture, keep, export or import those, you may be punished (three years imprisonment or fine). You may not use or spread items that display or contain those signs or symbols, e.g. flags, insignia, uniforms (or parts of uniforms), mottos and forms of greeting. You may also not use or spread signs or symbols that look similar to those. This does not apply if those items are used in order to inform others, repel actions that are aimed against the constitution, if they are used in art, science, research, teaching, or to report about historical events or similar purposes."

Detailed Locations of Photos & Text

Personal

Other Government

Wehrmacht

SS

Note: All knife blades are in the 'modern' style unless otherwise noted.

Miscellaneous

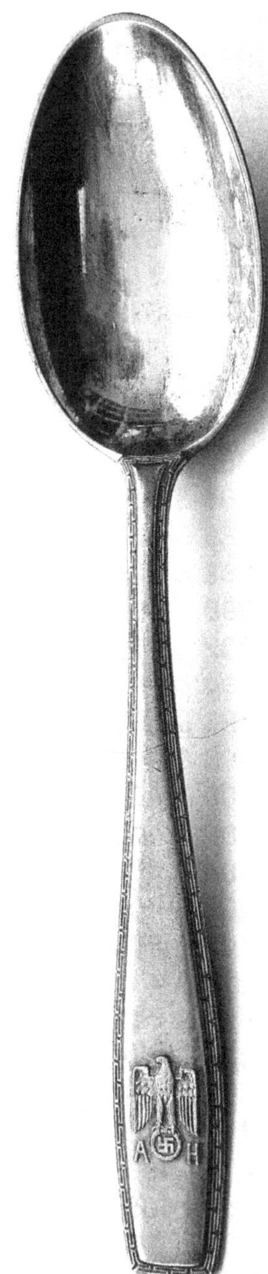

PS-1
L = 146 mm / 5 3/4"

PERSONALITY CUTLERY

PS-1 Hitler, Adolf "Formal" Pattern
(1889 - 1945)

Tea spoon: Teeloffel: Obverse carries Hitler's personal eagle with static swastika straddled with A & H.. Reverse carries Reichsmark / RM, 800 and Bruckmann's Prussian eagle.

This is the most recognizable and available, likewise the most sought after of the Hitler memorabilia. As per Billy Price's, *Hitler, the Unknown Artist* "it is well known that the Fuhrer had personally designed these formal pieces featuring the "Fuhrer Adler" (the Leaders Eagle) with "A" and "H" to either side of the wreathed, static swastika in its talons." Much of Hitler's silver flatware was manufactured by the firm of P. Bruckmann & Sohne of Heilbronn an ancient town on the Neckar River in Wurttemberg. Bruckmann, (1805 - 1973), was one of the leading silver manufacturers in Germany. As a gift for Hitler's 50th birthday on 20 April 1939, Bruckmann presented some 3,000 pieces made up of six complete sets of 500 pieces, one set each for his 'Berghof' (Mountain Home), the Obersalzberg guest house and the 'Adlerhorst' (the Eagles Nest) nearby; the Nazi Party's 'Braune Haus' (Brown House) in Munich; his Prinzregertenplatz apartment in Munich and the 'Reichschancellery' Chancellery in Berlin. The tableware, needing to be harder and more durable, were made of .800 silver while the matching service pieces were made of .925 silver. The state formal pattern has a Greek Key "Meander" pattern, (representing the Greek river Meander as Hitler was an admirer of ancient Greece). Design assistance is sometimes attributed to Frau Professor and Architect Gerdy Troost (wife of Hitler's foremost architect - Paul Ludwig Troost) in any case, Hitler oversaw the effort.

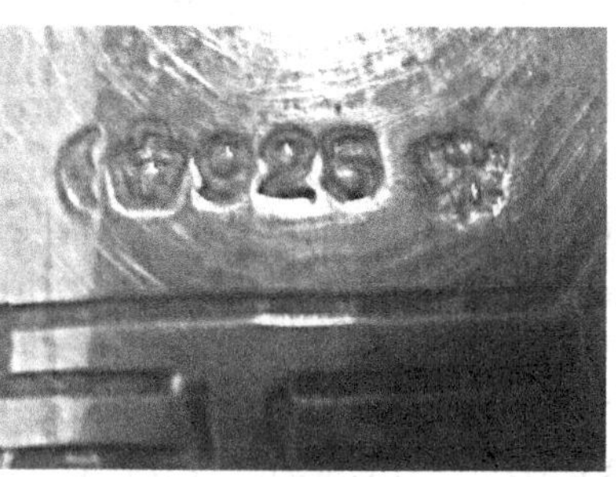

Measures: 1 3/4” H X 1 5/ 8” Diameter.

PS-2 Hitler's Napkin Ring (Serviettenring)

In Hitler's State 'Formal' (Bruckmann) pattern. The upper and lower edges have a border in a Greek Key geometric "Meander" pattern attributed to Frau Professor Gerdy Troost. Hall marked with the Reichsmark composed of a crescent moon and a crown mark indicating silver made in Germany, followed by the silver content of 925 (sterling) and then a spread eagle (Maker Mark of Bruckmann of Heilbronn). This napkin ring reportedly from the Obersalzberg residence near Bertesgaden in the Alps via a 101st Airborne veteran.

Hitler Trivia: His uniforms are divided into 3 periods / styles:

1. Kampfzeit: The brown shirt with Sam Brown cross belt 1920's - 1933
2. Statesman: Fine brown tunic with white shirt 1933 - 1939
3. Victory or Death: Field Gray tunic and white shirt 1939 - 1945 (with SS sleeve eagle in Gold)

.

(Kampfzeit = Period of struggle)

or

(Der Kampfseit = The Struggle for Power)

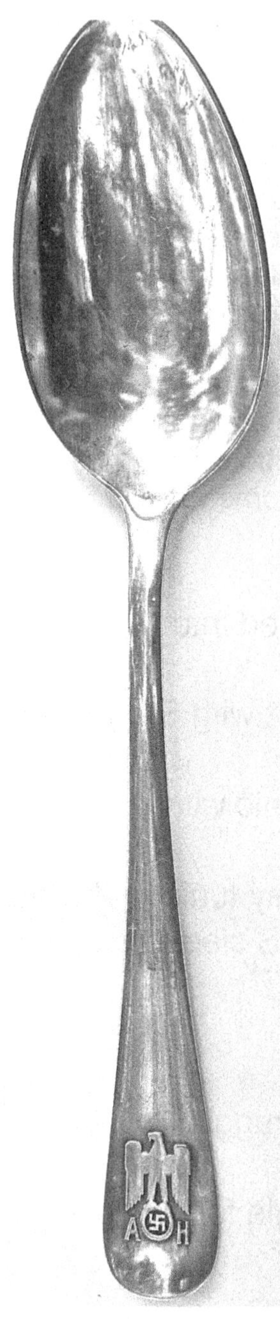

PS-3
L = 185 mm / 7 5/16"

Note: There is a very shallow scratch across the otherwise smooth breast.

PS-3 Hitler's "Informal"

Dinner spoon: Obverse with Fuhrer Adler (the Leader's Eagle). Reverse with RM, 800 and Bruckmann's MM.

Fellow collector (Br.) James Teets BSG, Canon was the provocateur that pushed me into adding this last piece to my collection, even though it remains a mystery as to why it was created, where it was used and the quantity fielded. Various guesses include a projected quantity of 1,000, It is thought to have been possibly used as a "luncheon" pattern, The origin of the terms "formal" and "informal' is also unknown. From James Teets again, "German sources indicate that there was no such thing as formal or informal and that the difference in patterns was to distinguish services belonging to one dining room or another." The terms 'formal' and 'informal' have been retained, despite their inaccuracy, due to widespread collector acceptance.

My analysis, based on my research, is that this treatment of the Fuehrer Eagle came as a complete surprise to Hitler although the two presentations (formal and informal) were fielded in the same time frame of his 50th birthday. The 'informal' was purchased for his 50th birthday and fielded to the Eagles Nest under the coordination of Bormann who would have been well aware of the Bruckmann "formal" present and who took the opportunity to have a complimentary, simplified tableware present at the Eagles Nest for Hitler's arrival. Original quantity 854. More details in the appendix.

Note: Although the eagle is identical to the 'formal' eagle, it has no detail and gives the appearance of being worn until the swastika and AH are noted.

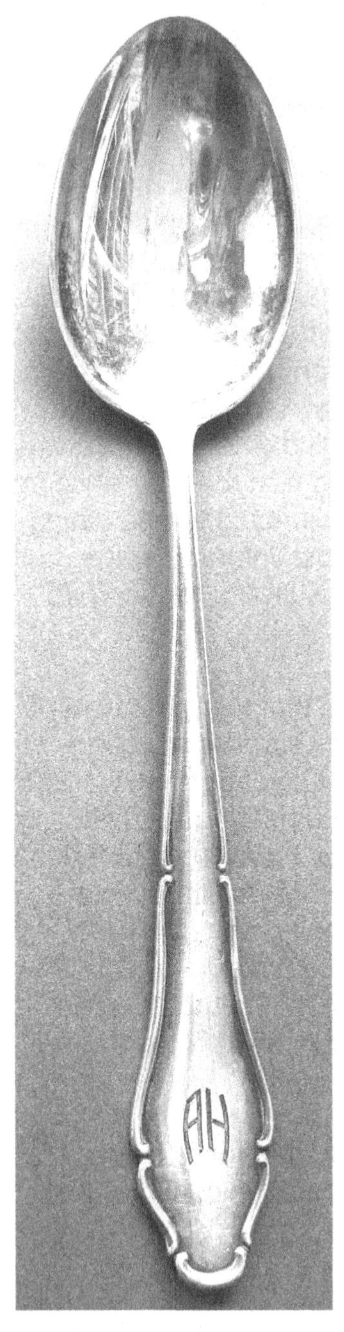

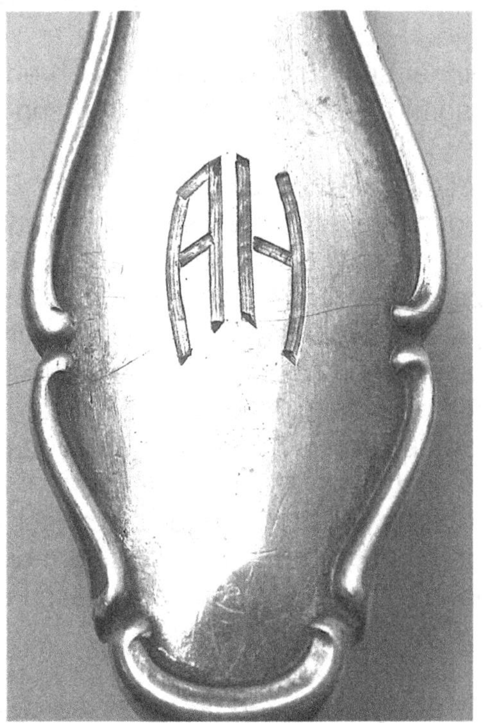

PS-4
L = 148 mm / 5 13/16"

PS-4 Hitler's Curved

Teaspoon: Obverse with curved AH monogram. Reverse with 'Reichsmark' RM, 800 and the maker's mark of Lutz & Weiss of Pforzheim, founded 1882. (a stylized L over W inside a shield)

The curved monogram was also used on his crystal ware in the Obersalzberg area. Distinctive and unique to the Berghof, Hitler's mountain retreat in the Alps per Mark D. Griffith's *Liberated - Adolf Hitler Memorabilia*, published 1985, page 14. "The 'AH' is side by side with outer edges curved convex (outward). The top centers of the letters form a peak in the middle and the bottoms of the letters are proportionally indented. This spoon has the "flattop A" and is executed in 4 strokes, one for the convex outer side, one for the interior vertical, one for the top of the A and one for the middle. The H is virtually a mirror image of the "A" without the top stroke and is executed in three strokes."

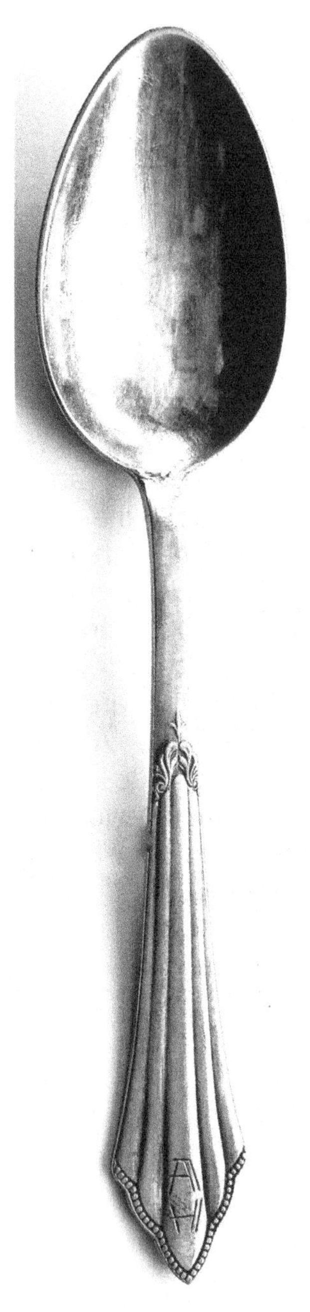

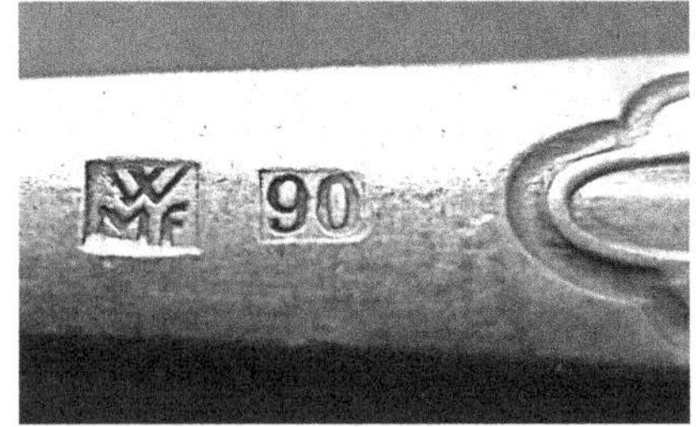

PS-5 L = 139 mm / 5 1/2”

PS-5 Hitler's Runic

Teaspoon: Obverse monogram; A over H, struck on the center-wave of five from 1/ 2 of length, terminated with 41 dots pattern. Reverse. Maker mark of a W over MF (Wurttembergische Metallwarenfabrik, Geislingen 1853 to the present) and 90.

Note: Hitler's complimentary silver service pieces and heavier items such as coffee & tea services, trays, coasters, gravy boats, etc. typically came from August Wellner & Sohne, of Aue (1854 - 1992) Germany's other leading silver manufacturer. Hitler's silverware patterns have the following observed characteristics, in general: they are relatively plain and utilitarian, symmetrical, well balanced, and display very little - if any - ornamentation.

Fact: Hitler became a millionaire in 1931. On his 1933 tax return he declared an income of 1,232,335 Reichmark, subsequently he arranged to have himself exempted from taxes for life. By 1944, some 12.5 million copies of Mein Kampf had been printed with royalties to Hitler. He also collected royalties on the use of his likeness on postage stamps making him very wealthy. In 2000, his assets, still held by the Bavarian State were estimated to be worth $ 22 million.

Hitler trivia: His favorite part of the meal was desert. He relished cakes, pies and ice cream with strawberries drowned in mounds of whipped cream. He drowned his coffee and tea with sugar and cream. He favored Fachingen Heilwasser mineral water which is still available in Germany and is not to my taste!

PS-6
L = 134 mm / 5 1/4”

PS-6 Hitler's Block / Alpacca*

Teaspoon: Obverse: Block A over H with triple raised ribs on front, 3 pair of matched ribbons. Reverse: Wellner with their trade mark elephant over 'alpacca'.

> Although he was originally party member number 55, to make the party appear larger than it actually was, his membership number was registered as 555. Later after he had assumed control, he gave himself party number 7 to appear as a founder and mentioned same at the 1934 Nurnberg party meeting.

Alpacca Silver - Also known in English as German Silver or Nickel Silver and in French as Maillechort is an alloy composed of nickel, copper and zinc - contains NO silver. The Alpacca alloy was created in 1823 by the German chemist Dr. Ernst August Geitner (1783-1852). It is very similar in its appearance to silver, but significantly cheaper. This new alloy was first called "Argentan", French for nickel silver. It consisted of 20% nickel, 55% copper and 25% zinc. The new silver-imitating alloy soon became very popular. The Gebrueder Henninger (Henninger Bros.) proposed a similar alloy (5-30% nickel, 45-70% copper and 8-45% zinc with trace amounts of lead, tin and iron) which they called "Neusilber". Later both Argentan and Neusilber were used under the trade name of Alpacca (or Alpakka). The great advantage of the use of Alpacca alloy as the base metal for silver plating is that the appearance of the objects does not change significantly with the wearing away of the silver layer.
Wellner's Alpaca formulation: Copper 65%, Zinc 23% and Nickel 12%.
Note: the French term Argenta indicates silver plated.
Trivia: The SS used Alpacca at many of its facilities and this service may have been a gift from the SS or to be used at SS functions.

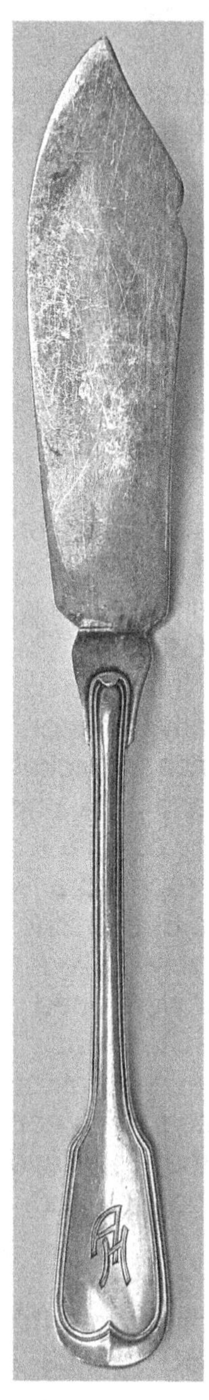

PS-7
L = 210 mm / 8 5/16”

PS-7 Hitler's Curved Linked Pointed A

Master Butter Knife. Obverse with outlined curved linked 'AH" with pointed 'A' above and linked to the "H". Obverse with "Die" icon with '4' showing, Wellner, 90 and the per piece gram weight of silver of 30 (see pp 475 for complete explanation). Compare this monogram's style with Speer's PS-16.

This monogram also appears on cutlery supplied by BSF, Gebrueder Reiner and M. H. Wilkens although all manufacturers have their own patterns, the monograms are identical. This is the first time I have seen multiple sources using the same monogram (See V-196 to V-200). Even more interesting is the fact that Wellner has three patterns. Note: Some sources have attributed this style to Adolf Hitler's trains.

Obviously, Adolf Hitler had a number of specially engraved monogram patterns. The Curved separated flat top (PS-4) monogram is also seen on some of his glassware and several of AH's cufflinks as is the 'pointed' top version. The "Runic" 'A over H' pattern (PS-5) was reportedly prevalent in the Obersalzberg at the Berghof. The Outline 'AH' Pattern (PS-6) was machine impressed by Wellner and seen in silver from the Reichskanzlei in Berlin, and other government locations. The same monogram was also hand engraved and noted on sets made by Berndorf Krupp recovered from the Obersalzberg in 1945.

See 'Hitler's Favorite?' at the end of the book pp 480.

PS-8
L = 142 mm / 5 10/16”

PS-8 Braun, Eva
(1912 - 1945)

Teaspoon: Obverse in high relief, asymmetrical Baroque pattern, with the engraved 'EB' butterfly pattern monogram. Reverse carries the maker mark: 46 Jurst 50. Jurst was a high end, luxury jewelry shop in Berlin and in this case, a designer/retailer. Actual manufacturer remains unknown The EB Butterfly monogram was designed by Albert Speer, perhaps her best friend and closest confidant while at the Obersalzberg.

In the 16 years of the Braun-Hitler relationship, Eva, spent the last ten years of her life virtually sequestered in the Berghof where Hitler provided everything for her. He even assigned her the monetary rights to some of his photos, taken by Hoffmann, which made her financially independent.

Two of her surviving quotes from 1945 - "I want to be a beautiful corpse" and after the wedding, "You may safely call me Frau Hitler."

She practiced Yoga.

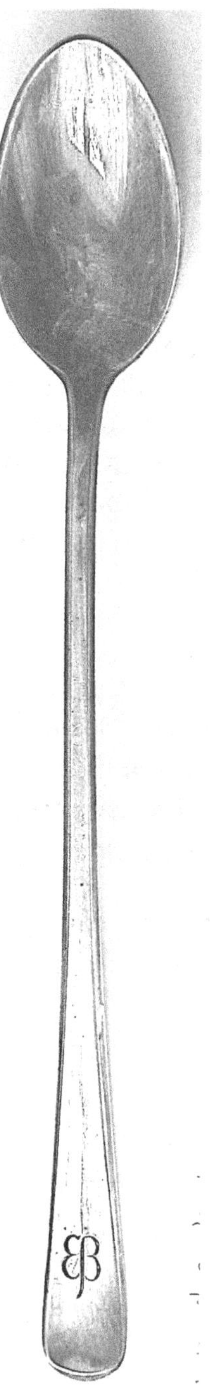

PS-9
L = 212 mm / 8 3/8"

PS-9 Braun, Eva

Iced Tea Spoon (Limonadeloffel): Obverse carries the **"EB"** butterfly monogram, a very plain symmetrical design with single line engraving. Reverse carries the maker mark: 'EKA' of Otto Kaltenbach, Nagold and silver plate of '90 - 1 1/4'.

Per Albert Speer, "Eva Braun especially delighted in showing off her new patterns at any opportunity, frequently using a different pattern at each place of the table and asking her guests which patterns they preferred."

Braun Trivia: She was 23 years Hitler's junior and first met him when she was 17 in 1929. For my movie buffs, Loren Bacall was 17 when she met Humphrey Bogart.

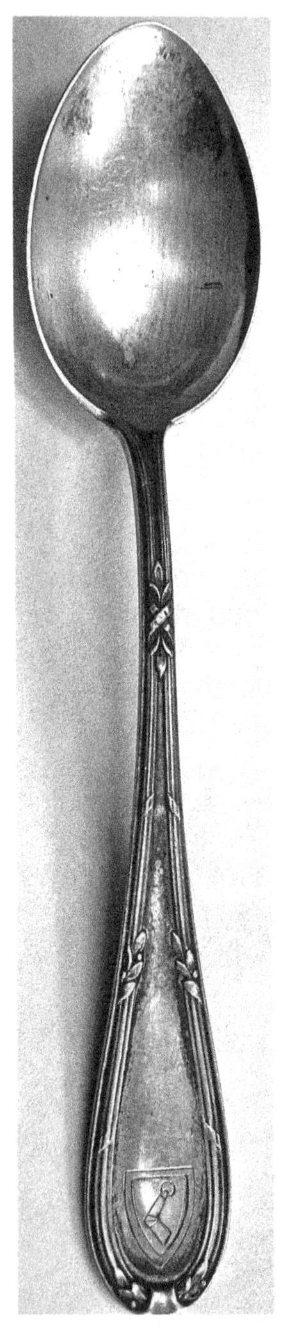

PS-10
L = 137 mm / 5 7/8”

PS-10 Goering, Hermann
(1893 - 1946)

Teaspoon: Obverse with the Goering Coat-of-Arms, a right arm raised, facing right, grasping a ring. Pattern: Triple raised ribs, both sides, front and rear wheat pattern. Reverse: 800, RM and the torch of Bremer Silberwarenfabrik 1905 - 1981 and KOPPEN. This Goring coat of arms logo is called the 'un-ribbed' variant.

From Charles Hamilton's "*Leaders & Personalities of the Third Reich*" - Reich Marshal and Commander in Chief of the Luftwaffe, Prime Minister of Prussia, Goering began his career as a fighter pilot in WWI and scored 22 kills, received the Pour le Merite, and was the last commander of Richthofen's squadron. In 1922 he joined the Nazi party and in 1923 was wounded in the unsuccessful Beer-Hall Putsch. After three years of exile in Sweden (Goering was later to talk Hitler out of invading this nation which gave him sanctuary), he returned to Germany and was one of the first Nazis elected to the Reichstag. On August 30 1932 he became president of the Reichstag.

He now focused on building up the Nazi police state, established the first concentration camps, and made Himmler chief of the Gestapo. By 1933, Goering was the second man in Germany and in 1935 was appointed by Hitler to command the Luftwaffe.

Luftwaffe failures in the Battle of Britain and the supply of Stalingrad cost Goering his standing with Hitler. He was semi retired for the last 2 years of the war. Tried at Nuremberg, found guilty - swallowed poison the morning of the execution 15Oct1946.

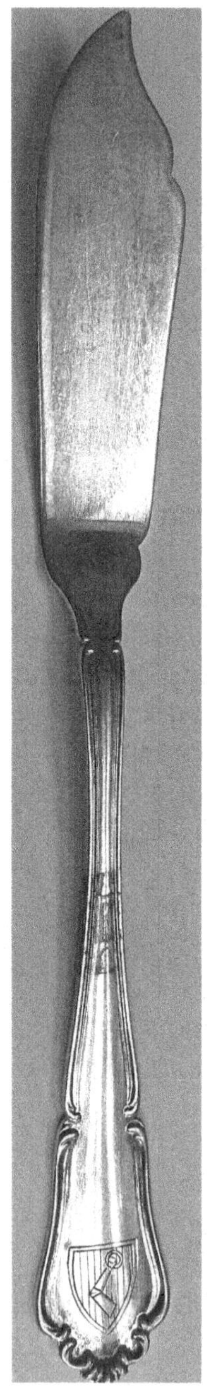

PS-11
L = 214 mm / 8 3/8”

PS-11 Goering Ribbed

Master Butter Knife: Obverse carries the Goering 'ribbed' Coat-of-Arms. Reverse 800, RM, HULSE. Hulse was a high end, luxury jewelry shop in Berlin.

With four stately homes: Carin Hall, two castles, Mauterndorf and Veldenstein and his palace in the Leipziger Platz plus the hunting lodge at Rominten Goering had literally dozens of sets of silver and thousands of individual pieces of Besteck (cutlery). He was given sets from France, England and numerous German districts. The Reichsmarschal did not favor Hitler's Wellner or Bruckmann but was partial to others such as Hulse. In the early years of Nazi power, Goering was the chief procurement officer of the military, the leader of the four-year plan, director of the 700,000 workers in the Goering Works (see M-167) and for all intents and purposes - a Head of State.

It was Goering who fined the German Jewish community a billion marks and ordered the elimination of Jews from the German economy, the 'Aryanization' of their property and businesses.

On Goering's 45th birthday - 12 Jan 1938, He accepted an exquisite Serves centerpiece from all the workers in his Four-Year Plan, who, at Goering's behest and most cheerfully he was sure, had received their last month's salaries deducted of 5% for the purchase of the gift.

> Note: Master Butter knives are scarce as they are meant to sit in the middle of the table or near the butter dish for cutting the butter and is passed around the table with the butter dish. Thus, only one to a table!

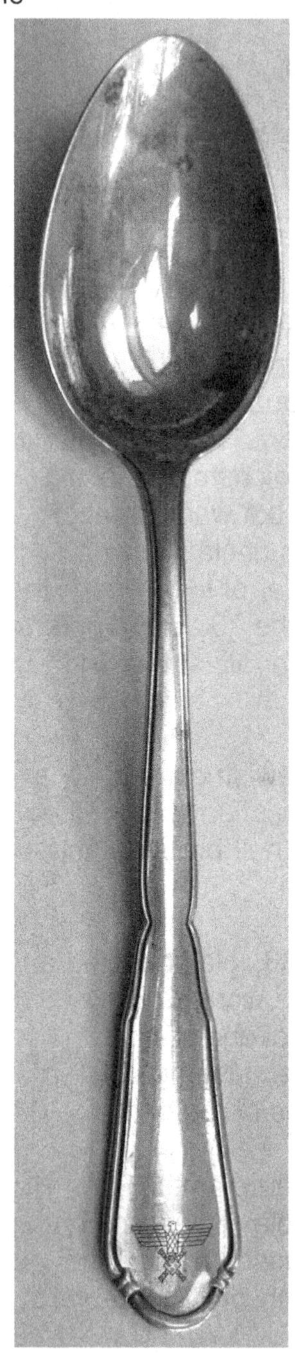

PS-12
L = 145 mm / 5 11/16”

PS-12 Goering Reichsmarshall

Teaspoon: The obverse carries his Reichsmarshall Coat of Arms: recessed rib, both sides, full length of handle. Reverse: RM, 800 unidentified hallmark. This Monogram is the Type 3 Reichsmarschall Eagle (5 wing feathers).

Goring Trivia: As Reich Minister of the Hunt, he outlawed: Horse-and-hound hunting, shooting from cars, claw and wire traps, artificial lights to attract quarry and the issuance of hunting licenses to poor marksman. On the other hand, he Introduced American raccoons into Europe's forests.

As Reich Forestry Minister, lighting cigarettes in a forest area was punishable by jail. Pushed scientific research to come up with a spray to do away with parasitic grubs. Passed special laws to protect endangered ferns, bushes and trees. Put irrigation schemes into effect. Had planted green recreational belts around industrial cities. Had 1,000 square miles of new trees planted from the Baltic to Austria. Created jobs for hundreds of thousands of unemployed building hutments and barracks, making roads, digging dikes, learning woodcraft and lumbering.

He favored a blue pencil for signing orders and documents,

Goering Trivia: He famously stated that, "I intend to plunder, and to do it thoroughly."

His IQ was 138!

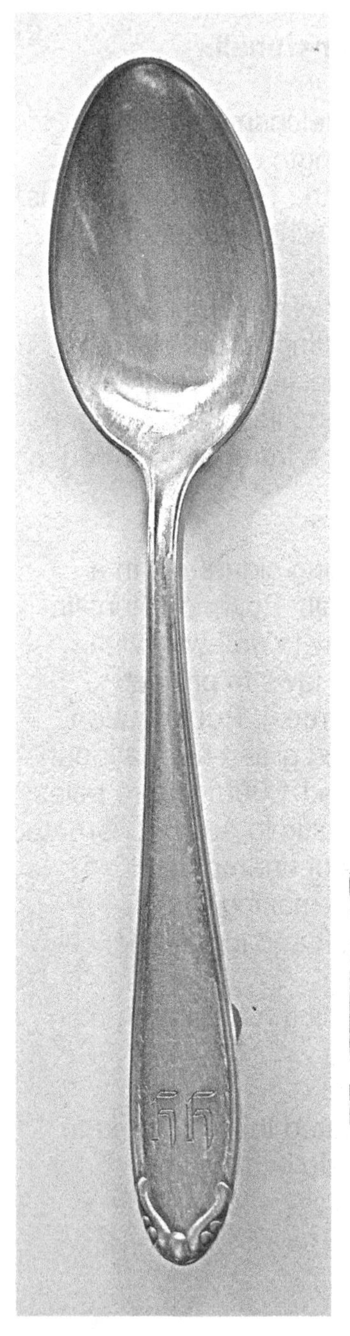

PS-13
L = 141 mm / 5 1/2”

PS-13 Himmler, Heinrich
(1900 - 1945)

Teaspoon: Obverse with the runic **HH** Monogram in block letters. Smooth art deco with raised rib, full length of handle. Reverse: Maker Mark: B (Bruckmann), a locomotive engine and 90 indicating silver plate.

Reichsfuhrer-SS / RfSS, Head of the Gestapo and the Waffen-SS and later Minister of Interior from 1943 to 1945. After Hitler, the most powerful man in Nazi Germany during 1944 & 1945.

As a leading Nazis vegetarian, Himmler launched programs to stop the SS from eating artificial honey, was against food companies using refined flour and white sugar and banned cigarettes in the Allgemeine-SS based on Nazi medical research in the early 1930's linking both cigarettes and asbestos to lung cancer. Interestingly, the Schwarzes Corps sold tobacco during the Kampfzeit period to raise money.

Trivia: Himmler's private trains: His Feldkommandostab RfSS (Field HQ of the Rf-SS) was organized like a military Hq and accompanied Himmler on his numerous tours. His first, named "Sonderzug Heinrich" had fourteen carriages to accommodate his staff, attached SS units including signals section, escort battalion and flak detachment, reportedly, at times up to 3,000 men accompanied the chief on his tours.. Later names were Steiermark and in 1944, temporarily named Transport 44.

PS-14
L = 138 mm / 5 7/16"

PS-14 Himmler

Teaspoon: Obverse with **HH,** a hand engraved script monogram of partially intertwined, vertical HH. Triple raised ribs on front only, Reverse with raised plain rib, Ostrich (emu?) in diamond cartouche with maker mark of 'WMF 18' (Wurttembergische Metallwarenfabrik, Geislingen founded in 1853 as the result of the merger of Schweizer and A. Ritter & Co. and still in operation).

Trivia - This failed chicken farmer actually received a diploma in agricultural chemistry from Munich Technical in 1922. His Nazi party number: 14,303. He joined the SS in 1925 with a membership number of 168. He held Blood Order #3.

During the 1930's, he is quoted. "I'm Party member number 2." ie after Hitler!

In 1934, Kurt Daluege, leader of SS-Gruppe Ost, refused to deal with "that Bavarian chicken breeder Himmler."

Himmler required medicinal herb gardens at all concentration camps for inmate herbal remedies, his wife being a qualified homoeopath.

Himmler favored a green pencil for signing orders and documents, green ink being a prerogative of government ministers.

PS-15 L = 140 mm / 5 1/2"

PS-15. Speer, Albert

(1905 - 1981)

Teaspoon: Obverse with intertwined 'AS': Reverse: Wellner trade mark 'die' 'WELLNER' '60' in a circle and unreadable gram weight of silver number in a square. He personally designed the monogram of the Intertwined, block AS.

As Hitler's architect he designed and supervised the construction of both the new Reich Chancellery in Berlin (arguably the most profound statement of 'NAZI" architecture and referred to as the most beautiful building ever built) and the Party palace in Nuremberg. Reich Minister for Armaments and War Production from February 1942 to 1945. On 1 November 1944, Speer instituted the Notprogramm (emergency program) virtually halting all aircraft manufacture except that of jets and single engine fighters. He reorganized war production and in spite of massive allied bombing attacks raised 1941 production.

Germany manufactured	1941	1944
Tanks	3,790	19,002
Aircraft	11,776	39,807
Heavy Guns	11,200	70,700

Also In 1944, produced more aluminum, synthetic rubber and coal. Slightly less synthetic oil as well as raising overall fighter aircraft production to 3,000 a month. FW-190's reaching 1,000 per month with some 20,000+ having been produced. Speer's efforts probably prolonging the war by at least 2 years.

His NAZI party number was 474,481 and his IQ was 128.

He favored a red pencil for signing orders and documents,

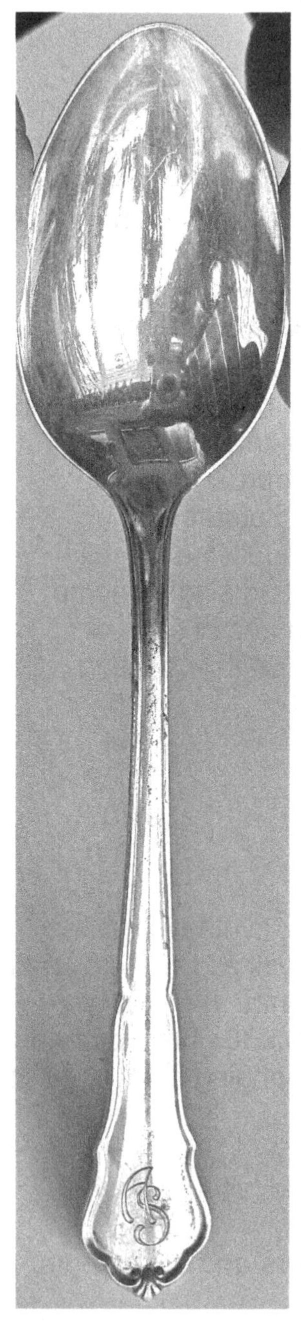

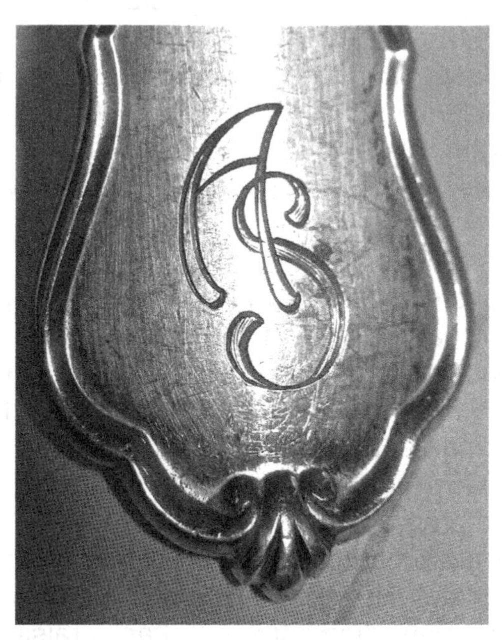

PS-16
L = 181 mm / 7 1/8"

PS-16 Speer, Albert

Tablespoon: Obverse carries stylishly engraved 'A' over 'S'. Reverse with RM, 800 and maker mark of 'HTB" for Hanseatishe Silberwarenfabrik, Bremen.

Speer supported the German invasion of Poland and the subsequent war though he recognized that it would lead to the postponement, at the least, of his architectural dreams. In his later years, Speer, talking with his biographer-to-be Gitta Sereny, explained how he felt in 1939: "Of course I was perfectly aware that [Hitler] sought world domination ... At that time I asked for nothing better. That was the whole point of my buildings. They would have looked grotesque if Hitler had sat still in Germany. All I wanted was for this great man to dominate the globe."

Speer placed his department at the disposal of the Wehrmacht. When Hitler remonstrated, and said it was not for Speer to decide how his workers should be used, Speer simply ignored him. Among Speer's innovations were quick-reaction squads to construct roads or clear away debris; before long, these units would be used to clear bomb sites developing a considerable organization to deal with this work.

In 1940, Joseph Stalin proposed that Speer pay a visit to Moscow. Stalin wished to meet the "Architect of the Reich". Hitler, alternating between amusement and anger, did not allow Speer to go, fearing that Stalin would put Speer in a "rat hole" until a new Moscow arose. When Germany invaded the Soviet Union in 1941, Speer came to doubt, despite Hitler's reassurances, that his projects for Berlin would ever be completed.

PS-17
L = 143 mm / 5 5/8"

PS-17 Weiding, Helmut

(1891 - 1955)

(General of the Artillery - 2nd highest regular Army rank)

Teaspoon: The obverse carries his personal pattern of 'HW'. The HW monogram has the letters intertwined and outlined in block style. Reverse maker marked: 'die - 4 & 2 showing, '"Wellner" and plating mark of '90' and the gram silver weight number of '21'

In 1944 he was awarded the Knights Cross with Oak Leaves and Swords. In 1945, he was appointed defense commandant of Berlin and the General in Command of the LXI Panzer Group. The Soviet forces under Marshall Zukhov had 2,500,000 troops, 6,000 tanks and 40,000 artillery pieces facing 300,000 men, many of them Hitler Youth down to the age of 12! The Soviets lost 400,000+ vs 300,000 German civilian and military casualties. He surrendered Berlin on 2 May 1945, was captured by the Soviets, condemned to 25 years in prison and died in Russian captivity in 1955.

During the Battle of Berlin, The Reich Youth Leader (Reichsjugenfuhrer), Artur Axmann formed the HJ into a major part of the defense commencing at the Seelow Heights. General Weidling ordered Axmann to disband the HJ combat formations but in all the confusion his order was never carried out. During the April 1945 defense of Berlin, General Weiding is quoted regarding the use of Hitler Youth, "You cannot sacrifice these children for a cause that is already lost."

PS-18T
L = 210 mm / 8 1/4"

PS-18 Rust, Bernard
(1883 - 1945)

Tablespoon & Demitasse spoon: 'Dh' for Deutsche-Hochschule, short-form for German Higher Education. This is his Ministry's official state pattern. Table spoon has an unmarked obverse while the "DH" below the national eagle appears on the reverse of the spoon. Maker Marked: BR. HENNEBERG BM, a scale in a circle followed by '90' in a square.

Prior to WWI, he was a senior master at a secondary school. A WWI Lieutenant, he suffered a serious head wound, receiving the Iron Cross 1st class. During April 1934 he was appointed Reich Minister of Science, Education and Popular Culture till 1945. Purged all Jews from the universities. Dismissed over 1,000 professors including a number of Nobel Prize winners thus hindering German science studies. Rust reported that he had "liquidated the school as an institution of intellectual acrobatics." Committed suicide on 8 May 1945 by gunshot.

PS-19D
L = 109 mm / 4 5/16”

PS-19 cont. Rust, Bernard

Small silver demitasse spoon (Moccaloffel) marked "Dh" below the national eagle on the obverse. Dh for "Deutsche-Hochschule" or German Higher Education, his official state pattern. Maker marked on the reverse: 'Br Henneberg BM' a scale in a circle, and '90' in a square.

Among the Nobel prize winners he had dismissed were Albert Einstein, James Franck - Physics, Fritz Haber - Chemistry, Otto Warburg - Medicine and Otto Meyerhof - Medicine. His comment, "We must have a new Aryan generation at the universities, or else we will lose the future."

Special note regarding Fritz Haber: The world was facing an agricultural catastrophe with the impending exhaustion of natural nitrate fertilizer (required for the production of wheat) primarily the 2.5M tons of bird droppings annually exported from Chile at a price of $45 per ton employing 60,000 workers. Haber's process for synthesizing ammonia created an endless supply of nitrates with the result that by 1934, Chile was exporting only 800,000 tons from 14,133 workers at $ 19 per ton! and the World's production of wheat was assured.

Note: One dealer ascribed the 'Dh' monogram to the Deutscher Hof Hotel although most hotels mark their full name on their cutlery as on the Hotel Deutscher Hof master butter knife M-169 and the Der Deutsche Hof salad fork M-170.

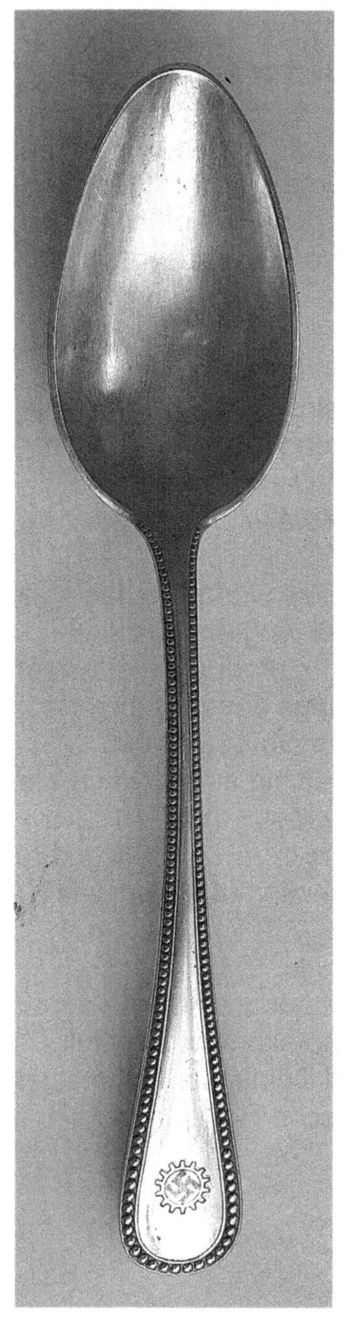

PS-20
L = 216 mm / 8 1/2"

PS-20 Ley, Dr. Robert

(1890 - 1945)

Tablespoon: **'DAF'** for Deutsche Arbeitsfront - German Labour Front, owned by DAF leader Dr. Robert Ley and carries his Ministry's official state pattern on the obverse. Other patterns: Beaded ribs. both sides, front and back, the length of the handle. Maker marked: a Die in a circle, "WELLNER", "90" in a circle, "45" in a square. By far, much more rare than Hitler's flatware pieces.

With the 10 May 1933 founding of DAF, through the 'coordination' (gleichschaltung) of all trade unions, DAF with 25 Million members was composed of all trade unions, corporate and professional associations and might better be translated as "Work Force" since the organization included both employers and employees. This accomplished Hitler's direction for "all who create with head and hand" to be under a single Nazi controller. He also headed the Kraft Durch Freude - 'Strength through Joy' & the Volkswagen factory (no VW's were ever delivered). The DAF emblem was a cogged wheel (Zahnrad) with 14 teeth encompassing a mobile swastika. Dr. Ley commented on the trade unions, "Ideologically speaking, the class war was anchored in the trade unions. and the trade unions lived off this." Dr. Ley committed suicide on 24 October 1945.

Note: A sub organization of DAF, the SdA - Schonheit der Arbeit (Beauty of Labor) which was established in 1934 and headed by Albert Speer, supplied canteens with flatware and cutlery. Initial production was of minimal quality reflecting the general poor economic conditions. The Farben spoon OG-50 exhibits the early period. Later cutlery exhibit better material and much better appearance.

Nicknamed: "Reich Drunk Master."

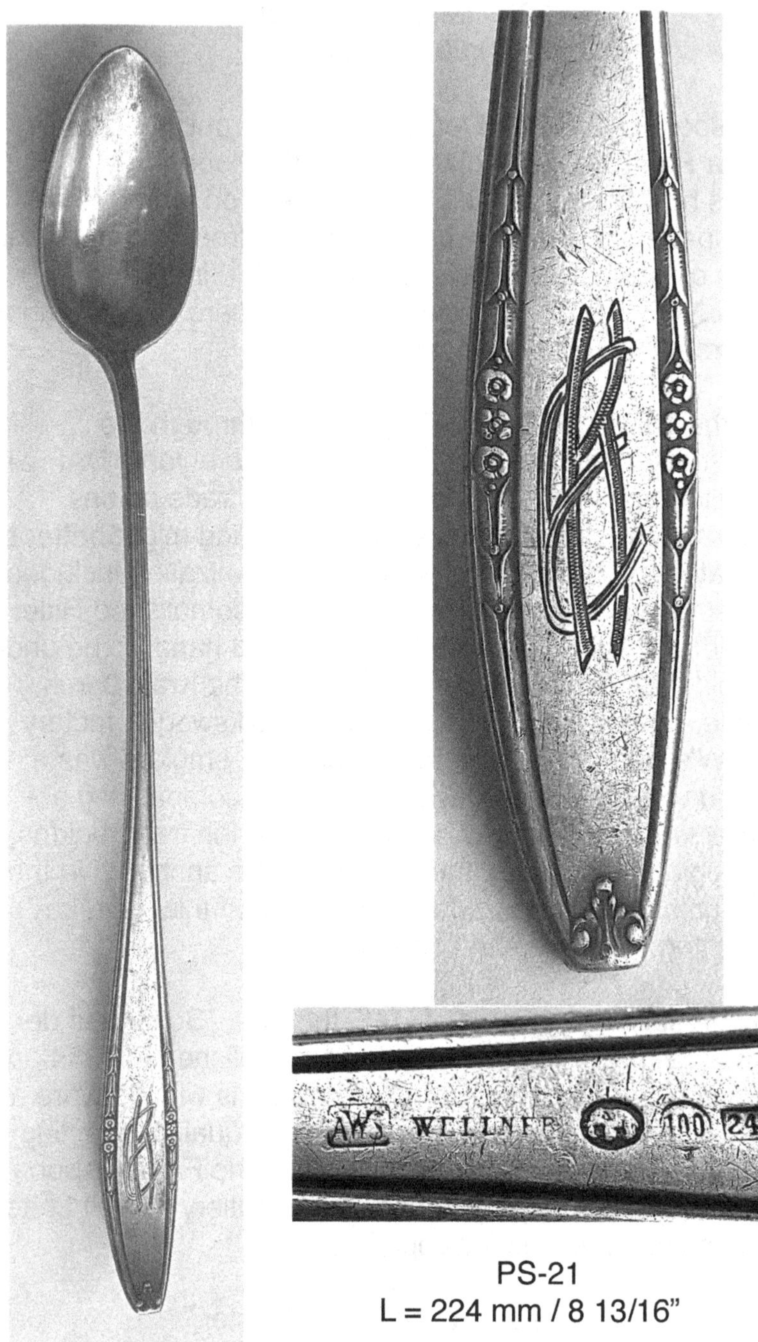

PS-21
L = 224 mm / 8 13/16”

PS-21 Kaltenbrunner, Dr. Ernst
(1903 - 1946)

Ice tea / parfait spoon: The obverse carries his personal 'EK' monogram, double lined with highlights between. Front and back symmetrical with 3 flowers straddling the initials. Maker marked: 'AWS' in a square box (August Wellner & Sohne), Wellner, an elephant, '100' silver plate in a circle and '24' silver gram weight in a square box. The AWS maker mark was used by Wellner from 1928 to 1938.

A lawyer and fanatical Austrian Nazi with an IQ of 113, he along with Seyes-Inquart (IQ 141) were the leaders of the Austrian SS from 1934, prior to Anschluss in 1938. In January 1943 he became the 2nd and last Chief of the Reich Main Security Office, (RSHA) succeeding Heydrich with a rank of SS-Obergruppenfuhrer, equivalent to a U.S. Army rank of Lt. General (3 stars). Under his tireless direction, the RSHA was responsible for hunting down and exterminating several million civilians, primarily Jews in the East. Hanged in Nuremberg on 16 October 1946.

Nicknamed "The Callous Ox". NAZI party number 300,179.

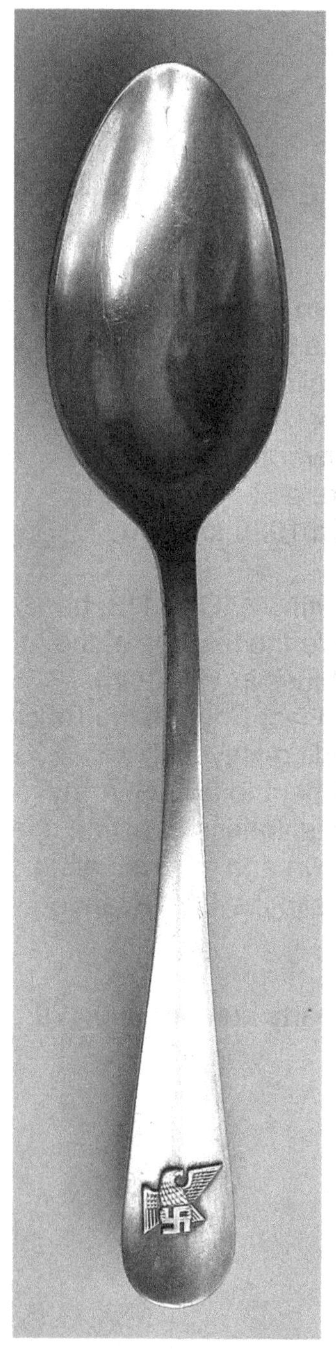

PS-22
L = 213 mm / 8 7/16"

PS-22 Sauckel, Fritz
(1894 - 1946)

Tablespoon: obverse carries his State pattern of the 'Thuringian Eagle', with its broken wing. Maker marked: "Bruckmann 90" on the reverse.

As the General Plenipotentiary for the Distribution of Labour (Generalbevollmächtigter für den Arbeitseinsatz), 1942 - 1945 he was responsible for directing the deportation of some 5 million slave laborers from the occupied territories, primarily Poland, Ukraine and other eastern countries, to work in German war related industries. With an IQ of 118, he rose from Thuringia's district manager in 1925 to Governor in 1933. He was also both an honorary SA and SS General. At Nuremberg he was "shocked in his innermost soul" to find out about the Nazi atrocities. His most remembered defense, "just following orders".

> Trivia: Sauckel's worker quotas were set by Albert Speer. Speer's labor shortage was primarily due to the prohibition on using German women in industrial jobs. During the Nuremberg trial in 1946 Sauckel pointed at Albert Speer and said, "There is a man you should hang." Speer was sentenced to 20 years. Sauckel was hanged on 16 Oct 1946.

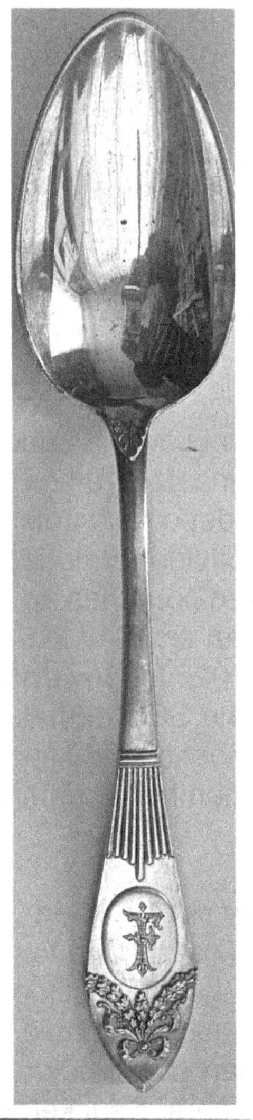

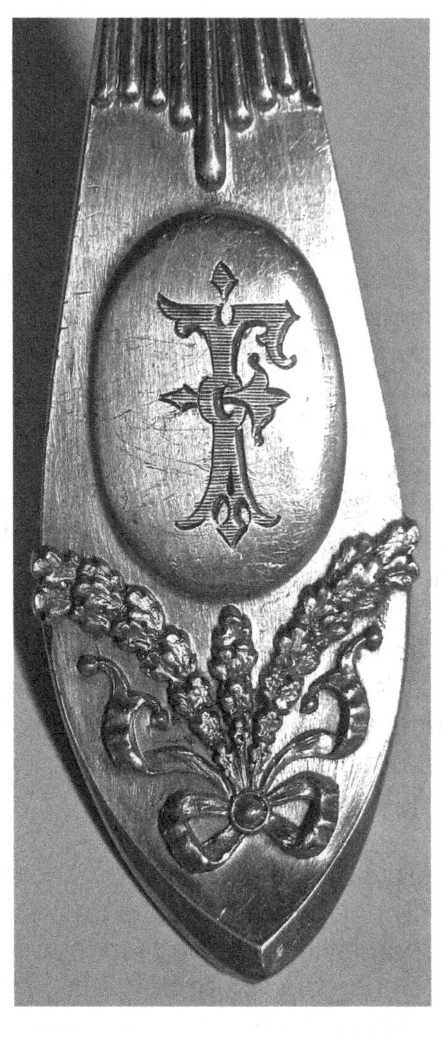

PS-23
L = 214 mm / 8 7/16”

PS-23 Frank, Dr. Hans
(1900 - 1946)

Serving spoon: Obverse carries the personal engraved pattern of the Governor-General of Poland, Hans Frank. The pattern is by T. H. STRUBE & SOHN, (the firm Strube & Son, was active in Leipzig, Germany from 1819 until WWII. Although the firm did manufacture silver in the 19th century, by the time this piece was made they were primarily luxury retailers) with the maker mark of Koch & Bergfeld, Bremen, founded 1929, 800, RM. The monogram is an elaborate engraved "F". The back is also embellished.

With an IQ of 130, he was the Nazi Party's leading jurist and Governor General of Poland. Prior to 1933, as Hitler's lawyer, he successfully defended Hitler in several hundred actions and afterwards become Reich Minister of Justice. Out of favor with Hitler, he was sent to Poland in 1939 as punishment, where he earned the unofficial title of 'Slayer of Poles'. Hitler's direction to Frank, "The task which I give you is a devilish one, other people to who territories are entrusted would ask, 'What will you construct?' I shall ask the opposite." In October 1939 Frank said, "The Poles shall be the slaves of the German Reich." and in 1944, "I have not hesitated to declare that when a German is shot, up to 100 Poles shall be shot too." In 1939, there were some 3 million Jews in Poland. Hanged as a war criminal in Nuremberg 16 Oct 1946.

At Nuremberg in 1946, Speer commented that, "As for Frank, he is a little wacky."

Nickname: Stanislaus the Little. (At 5'10" little to do with his height.)

PS-24
L = 217 mm / 8 9/16"

PS-24 Frank, Dr. Hans

Tablespoon: The obverse carries his machine incised, official state pattern of the Governor General of Poland. Maker marked on the reverse with: '45' in a square, '90' in a circle, "ART. KRUPP", their trademark 'Bear with 'ART KRUPP' over and "BERNDORF" under" followed by 'BERNDORF'.

In 1939, as a result of the combined invasions by Germany and the Soviet Union, Poland was partitioned with the Soviet Union acquiring 52.1% of the territory with 13.7M population (only 38% Polish) and Germany the remaining territory with 10M (predominantly Polish) population. The German's divided their territory into three administrative units. The two on Germany's Eastern border including reclaimed parts of Prussia lost under the Treaty of Versailles were incorporated into Germany. Some 1M poles were dispossessed and 1M Reich and East European Germans brought in to replace them. The Eastern territory or 'General Government' (per Hitler - 'Occupied Poland' and 'Vandal Gau') was headed by Hans Frank and the destination of the 1M displaced Poles. Frank managed out of an old royal palace in Cracow. In 1942, after a close friend was executed, he called for the return to constitutional rule. As a result, he was stripped of all Party honors and returned to his post as Governor-General of Poland, regarded by Hitler as the most unpleasant position he could award him.

Note: Identical tableware has been represented (by the same dealer as had commented on the Rust's spoon) as from the 'Castle Klessheim' located near Salzburg, Austria, a luxurious government guest residence maintained to house dignitaries waiting to see Hitler at the Burghof. This was vigorously denied by my source.

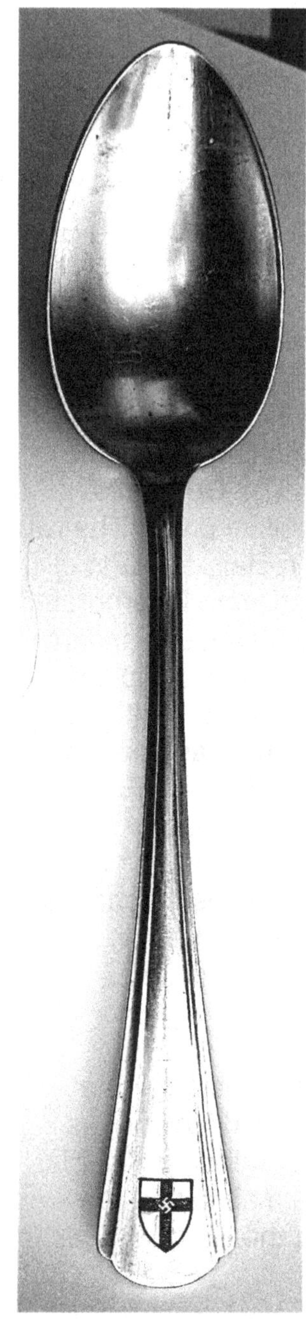

PS-25
L = 218 mm / 8 9/16"

PS-25 Mueller, Bishop Ludwig
(1883 - 1945)

Tablespoon: The obverse carries the Deutsche Christen symbol of a Christian cross with a mobile swastika in the middle encompassed by a shield. Reverse maker marked Koch & Bergfeld of Bremen, (founded 1829), 800, and RM. From Bishop Ludwig Mueller's service.

In 1932 the Protestant church came under the influence of a Nazi movement called "German Christians", (also called "Stormtroopers of Jesus"). The Deutsche Christen (DC) became the voice of Nazi ideology within the Evangelical Church and approved by Hitler, they proposed a church "Aryan paragraph" to prevent "non-Aryans" from becoming ministers or religious teachers. Only a very few Christians opposed Nazism such as the "Confessing Christians". The German Christian Movement was strongly nationalistic and adopted Luther's anti Semitism (ref his 1543 book, "On Jews and Their Lies") as well as his respect for authority (see Romans 13). Composed of the radical wing of German Lutheranism, the main Protestant branch supported the Nazi ideology, reconciling Christian doctrine with German nationalism and anti semitism. This movement represented Hitler's "Positive Christianity" views as lawfully encoded into the Nazi "constitution."

In the 1933 church elections, Hitler made a radio appeal in support of the German Christian movement and later appointed Ludwig Mueller, Reich Bishop of the Protestant Church. Bishop Mueller committed suicide in 1945!

> Fact: In 1925, of the German population of 65 million, some 40 million were Evangelical Lutherans and 21 million Roman Catholics.

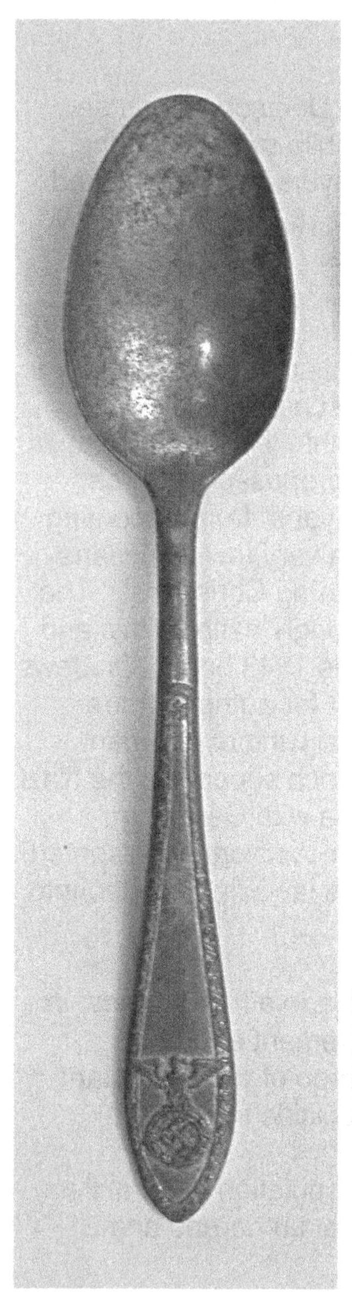

PS-26
L = 112 mm / 4 7/16”

PS-26 Bormann, Martin
(1900 - 1945)

Egg spoon: Carries the Bormann Eagle (the NSDAP 1929 pattern) on the obverse. Reverse carries 'Aluminium Germany'. Dealer states: "the Martin Bormann egg spoon came directly from Bormann's house wreckage at the Obersalzberg! (He had bought the Berghof for Hitler and ran the Obersalzberg complex of properties.) a very rare and extremely difficult to locate pattern."

Born in 1900 he joined the party in 1927 and became chief of staff for Rudolf Hess. Described as brutal, coarse and lacking culture. Made head of the Party chancellery in 1941 and Hitler's personal secretary in April 1943. Party # 60,508 acquired after his rise to power and qualified him for a Golden Party Badge. He was a major advocate of Gleichschaltung (coordination). This was the umbrella term under which virtually all major civilian organizations in the political, economic and social life of the German nation were placed under Nazi control By the end of WWII he had become second only to Hitler in terms of real political power and an SS General to boot. At Nuremberg in 1946, he was tried as a war criminal and sentenced to death in absentia as his death on 2 May 1945 while attempting to escape Berlin after Hitler's suicide was unknown at the time.

Nickname: The Brown Eminence"

A second opinion identified the spoon as a typical souvenir (Andenkens) offered at the prewar, annual NSDAP Nuremberg rally (Reichsparteitag) held in early September and focused on strengthening Hitler's position as Germany's savior. This spoon has no characteristics of German andenkens as exhibited by real andenkens M-187 & M-188.

PS-27
L = 250 mm / 9 3/16”

PS-27 Bormann, Martin?

Table Knife: Obverse carries the initials MB, upside down. Having seen Luftwaffe and Eva Braun items so marked - it is possible this knife is legitimate - but I have my doubts. Reverse Art Krupp, Bear and Berndorf. Blade with stick figures of Henkels, Solingen

In October 1933, Bormann became a Reich Leader of the NSDAP, and in November, a member of the Reichstag. From July 1933 until 1941, Bormann served as the personal secretary for Rudolf Hess. During this period, Bormann also managed Hitler's finances through various schemes such as royalties collected on Hitler's book, his image on postage stamps, as well as setting up an "Adolf Hitler Endowment Fund of German Industry", which was really a thinly veiled extortion attempt on the behalf of Hitler to collect more money from German industrialists. In May 1941, the flight of Hess to Britain cleared the way for Bormann to become Head of the Party Chancellery. Bormann took charge of all Hitler's paperwork, appointments and personal finances. Hitler came to have complete trust in Bormann and the view of reality he presented. During a meeting, Hitler was said to have screamed, "To win this war, I need Bormann!". (He acted as a witness to AH's marriage with Eva Braun)
An arch fanatic of racial policy, anti-semitism and Kirchenkampf (war against the churches). On 9Oct42 he signed a decree for the "permanent elimination of the jews from Greater German territory by the use of ruthless force in the camps of the East"'. Faced with the imminent demise of the Third Reich, he systematically went about the organizing of German corporate flight capital, and set up off-shore holding companies and business interests in close coordination with the same Ruhr industrialists and German bankers who, although often not Nazis, had helped to facilitate Hitler's explosive rise to power 10 years before.

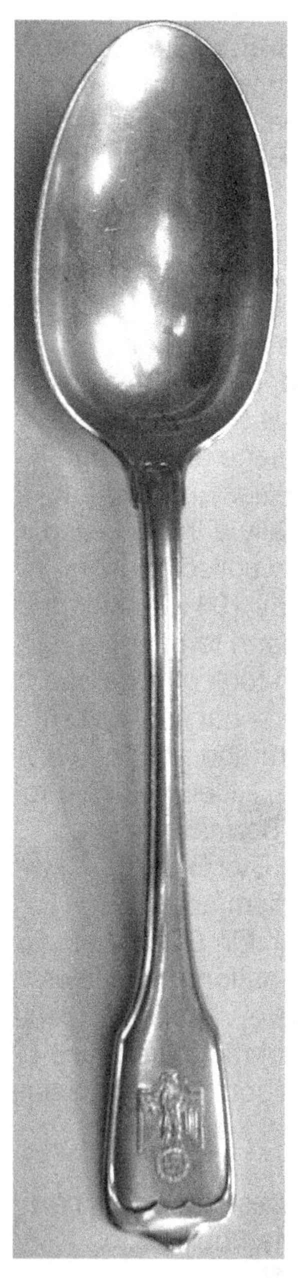

PS-28
L = 208 mm / 8 2/16”

PS-28 von Ribbentrop, Joachim
(1893 - 1946)

Tablespoon, official service: The obverse features a raised Reich eagle and swastika, the same type as used on the formal pattern AH flatware but with subtle differences in the Eagle and without the AH monogram. The reverse marked RM, 925 and the dot inside circle of Gebrueder Sauerland, Berlin. The 925 (sterling silver) is unusual for cutlery.

As Hitler's Minister of Foreign Affairs (1938-1945), IQ of 129 this pristine flatware piece may have been used by Hitler and by von Ribbentrop as a special setting for the highest Foreign Ministry / Diplomatic dinners or functions.

A truly controversial personality. Wounded and winner of the Iron Cross 1st Class in WWI. Joined the Party on 1 May 1932, member 1,119,927 and Winner? of the Nazi Golden Party Badge. Ambassador to England 1936-1938. Negotiated the treaty with Russia. On 11 August 1939 Ribbentrop stated, "We want war." He was blamed for convincing Hitler that Britain would not react to an attack on Poland and thus starting WWII. In August 1939, Goring said, "Now you've got your @%#* war. It's all your doing!" In 1943 Hitler said, "He is greater than Bismarck". The other prominent members of Hitler's inner circle saw him as arrogant, vain, touchy, humorless and contemptible for his haughty incompetence. One German diplomat, Herbert Richter, in an interview later recalled "Ribbentrop didn't understand anything about foreign policy. His sole wish was to please Hitler." He testified at Nuremberg: "Do any of us look like murderers" and "There are lots of things I did not know" he was tried, convicted and hung at Nuremberg,

Nicknames: "Ribbensnob", "Iago"

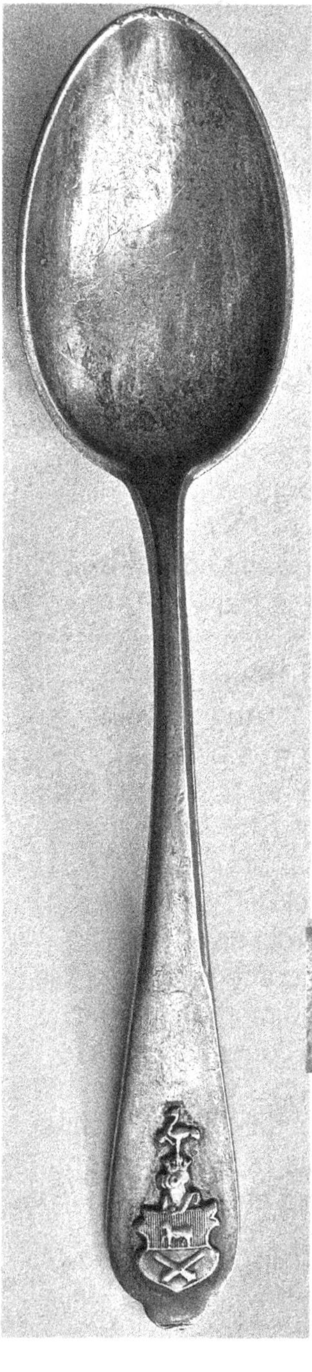

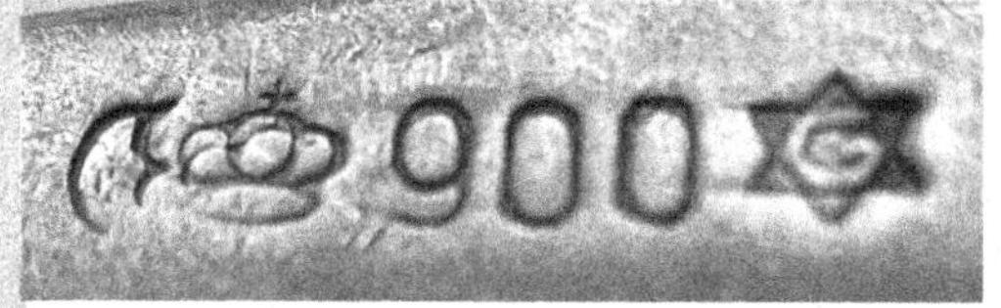

PS-29
L = 130 mm / 5 1/8”

PS-29 von Ribbentrop, Joachim

Coat-of-Arms

Relish Spoon: Obverse with Coat-of Arms, reverse with 900 and Maker Mark of J. Grimminger, Schwaebisch Gmuend.

One of his teachers at Metz later recalled that Ribbentrop "was the most stupid in his class, full of vanity and very pushy". In 1919 Ribbentrop met Anna Elisabeth Henkell, daughter of a wealthy champagne producer from Wiesbaden. They married on 5 July 1920, Ribbentrop travelled across Europe as a wine salesman. He and his wife had five children. He persuaded his aunt Gertrud von Ribbentrop to adopt him on 15 May 1925, which allowed him to add the aristocratic von to his name. Goebbels remarked: "He bought his name, he married his money and he swindled his way into office."
In 1928, Ribbentrop was introduced to Hitler as a man who "gets the same price for German champagne as others get for French champagne" as well as a businessman with foreign connections. Goering referred to him publicly as that "dirty little champagne pedlar." He joined the NSDAP on 1 May 1932 at the urging of his wife, who herself joined at the same time. In the summer of 1932, Ribbentrop began his political career when he offered to be a secret emissary between the Chancellor, Ribbentrop's old war buddy Franz von Papen and Hitler. Ribbentrop's offer was refused at the time, but six months later, in January 1933, Ribbentrop's offer was taken up by Hitler and von Papen.

The Allies' International Military Tribunal found him guilty of all charges brought against him. Even in prison, Ribbentrop remained loyal to Hitler, stating "Even with all I know, if in this cell Hitler should come to me and say 'Do this!', I would still do it."

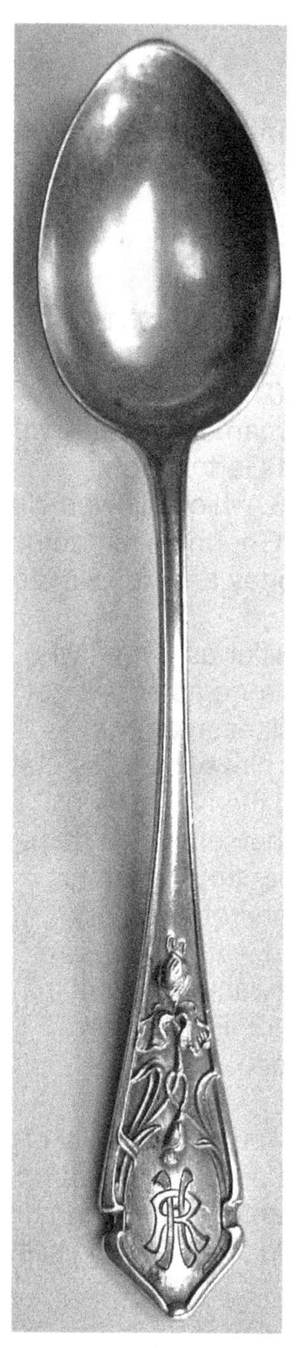

PS-30 L = 112 mm / 4 6/16"

PS-30 Hess, Rudolf

(1894 - 1987)

Demitasse spoon: Obverse bears the Rudolf Hess "R.H." monogram in art nouveau pattern. The reverse bears 800 RM, and the most likely maker's mark of Vereinigte Silberwarenfabriken of Dusseldorf.

Hess joined the party in 1920, wrote Mein Kampf as dictated by Hitler where he was able to introduce his own ideas regarding *lebensraum.* As Deputy Leader of the Nazi Party, in 1939 he became the No. 3 man in Nazi Germany when he was made successor designate to Hitler and Goering. He embarked on a self-appointed secret peace mission to Britain on 10 May 1941 and was imprisoned and treated as a prisoner of war. Sentenced to life imprisonment at Nuremberg. He died, the only inmate in Spandau prison, on 17 Aug 1987. His son quotes his father's statement uttered at the Nuremberg trial: "I regret nothing!" IQ 120 est

Hess, the man, had a strong interest in astrology, the occult. and a deep interest in herbal and homeopathic medicine, as well as organic gardening and biodynamic agriculture. Hess was a vegetarian who strongly advocated animal welfare. He oversaw recycling programs and was an ardent conservationist. Hess ordered a mapping of all the ley lines in the Third Reich which defined the Externsteine rock formation in Lower Saxony as the center of Germany.

Dealer states that the piece came from Sergeant Richard Cowling, the GI looter who stole the silverware from the Hess estate at Reicholdsgrün in lower Bavaria. This is supported by a sworn statement from Phyllis Orsi dating from July 2, 2005, where she certifies before a Michigan notary public as to the authenticity of the item.

Nicknamed: "The Brown Mouse"

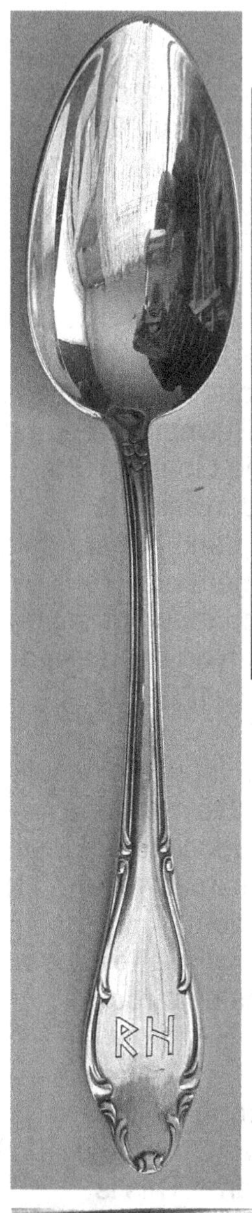

PS-31
L = 215 mm / 8 1/2"

PS-31 Heydrich, Reinhard
(1904 - 1942)

Serving spoon: Obverse engraved with bold, modern 'RH'. Reverse WELLNER PATENT silver plate 90 and silver weight 45.

Tall, slim, blond with blue eyes, a first class fencer, excellent horseman, pilot and violin player (he joined Mrs. Himmler in duets) he was the epitome of the Nordic-Aryan type. Became Commander of the Security Police, the Security Service (SD) and Gestapo. Joined the SS in 1931, became a Major in December, a Colonel in July 1932, Brig General March 1933. As Heinrich Himmler's number two he secured control of the Munich and Bavarian police in 1933. For his role in "The Night of the Long Knives" he became a Lt. General in July 1934. In 1936 he directed the forging of documents that convinced Stalin that his 35,000 man officer corp was plotting against him resulting in Stalin obliterating half of the corps. In 1939 he provided Hitler with the justification for the invasion of Poland. Focused on the Jewish question, in 1941 he stated, "The Fuhrer has ordered the physical extermination of the Jews." The code word for the extermination of Polish Jewry was 'Operation Reinhard'. In September 1941 he moved to Prague as Deputy Reich Protector of Bohemia and Moravia. Personally convened the Wannsee Conference on 20 Jan 1942 to effect the "Final Solution". On 27 May 1942 he was wounded by Free Czech agents and died on 4 June 1942. In reprisal, the German's killed some 15,000 Czechs.

Nicknames: "The Blond Beast", "The Butcher"

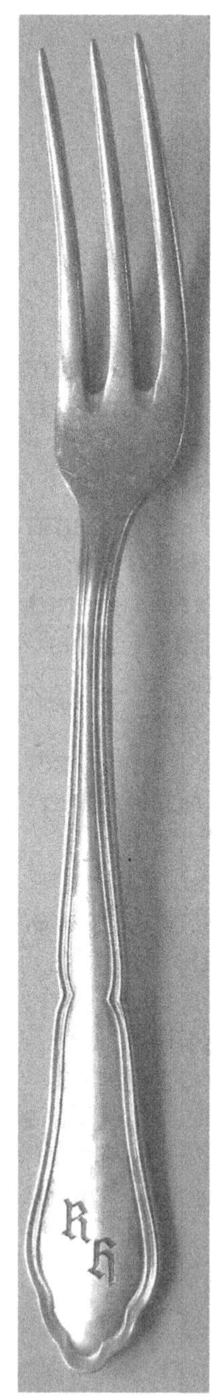

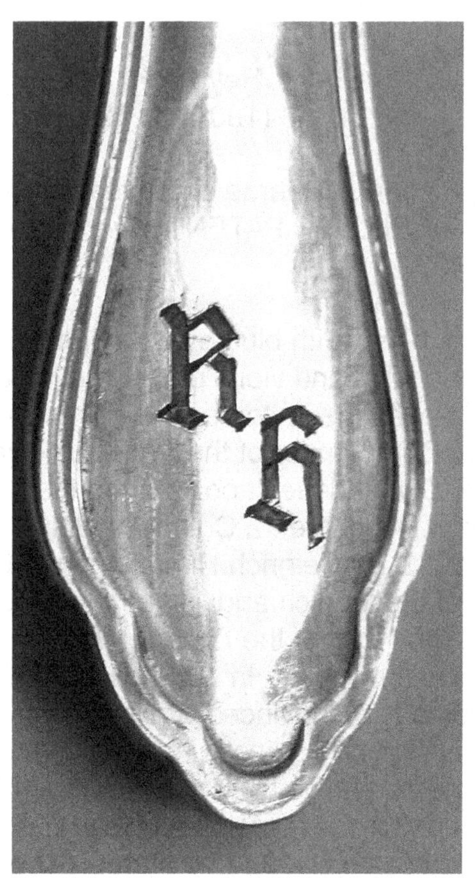

PS-32
L = 144 mm / 5 11/16”

PS-32 Heydrich, Reinhard

Cocktail Fork: The obverse carries his personal, hand engraved, monogram of a staggered 'RH'. Reverse: Wellner die, WELLNER 100 in a circle and 18 in a square.

He became an S.S. General and Protector of Czechoslovakia and attempted to use tact and diplomacy to gain the confidence of the Czechs and to encourage more production. The British feared he would be successful and sent in the assassination team. The German reprisals cemented Czech resistance.

Himmler commented, "It will interest you to know that Heydrich was a very good violinist. He played a serenade in my honor, it was really excellent - a pity he did not do more in this field." and in June 1942 shortly after Heydrich's funeral, "Yes, as the Fuehrer said at the funeral, he was indeed a man with an iron heart."

After the war, Walter Schellenberg, SS-Brigadefuehrer, Heydrich's personal aide described him as. "He was a tall, impressive figure with a broad, unusually high forehead, small restless eyes as crafty as an animal's and an uncanny power, a long predatory nose and a wide full lipped mouth. His hands were slender and rather too long - they made one think of the legs of a spider. His unusual intellect was matched by the ever-watchful instincts of a predatory animal, always alert to danger and ready to act swiftly and ruthlessly."

Other nickname: The Hangman.

Note: Regarding the forks provenance: Dealer states, "It came back from WWII with a 506th PIR 101st A/B officer"

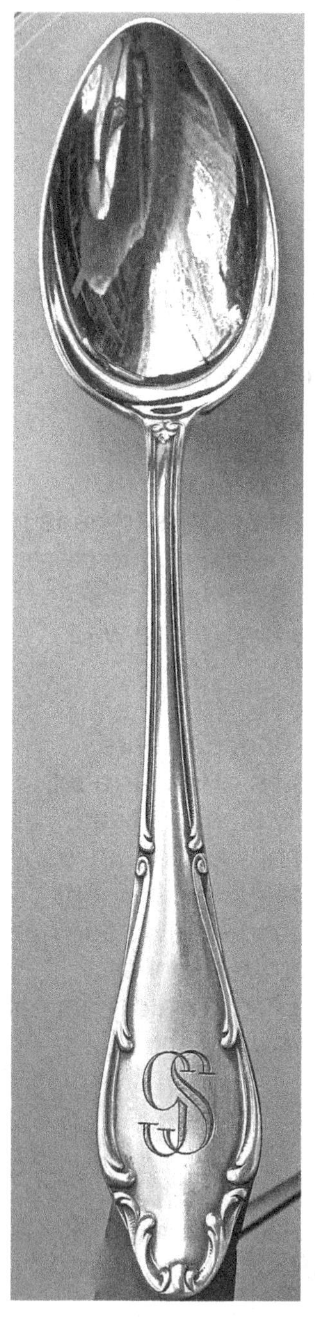

PS-33
L = 215 mm / 8 7/16"

PS-33 Scheel, General Gustav Adolf MD
(1907 - 1979)

Tablespoon/serving spoon: Obverse intertwined G and S. Reverse Maker Mark of WELLNER, "100" plating and silver gram weight number "50".

Initially a physician, later a "multi-functionary" (see below) during the 3rd Reich. Initial involvement with the Nazi student movement in the early 1930's, became Leader of the Heidelberg Student Body then Honorary Senator of the University of Heidelberg. In 1936 he became both the Reich Student Leader and the Leader of the National Socialist Students' Bund (University Students) see OG-62 & 63.

Organizer of the SD in the Southwest, Superior SS and Police Leader in Salzburg and Gauleiter in Salzburg from November 1941. When commander of the security police and SD he organized the deportation of Karlsruhe's Jews to the death camps in the East. Police Major General; (SA and SS member), Leader of the Berlin SD School; Inspector of the Security Police and the SD in Stuttgart; Leader of the Nazi Old Gentlemen's Federation; Chairman of the Reich Student Works; President of the German Study Works for Foreigners; Member of the Reich Labour Chamber; Commander of the Security Police and the SD under Chief of the civil administration in Alsace; Member of the Reichstag; Leader of the SD Upper Division South (Munich); Inspector of the Security Police and the SD under the higher SS and Police leaders South and Main; Higher SS and Police leader; Leader of the SS Upper Division Alpenland (Salzburg); Volksturm Leader.

Appointed Minister of Culture in Hitler's will. Released early from a five year sentence by a de-Nazification court.

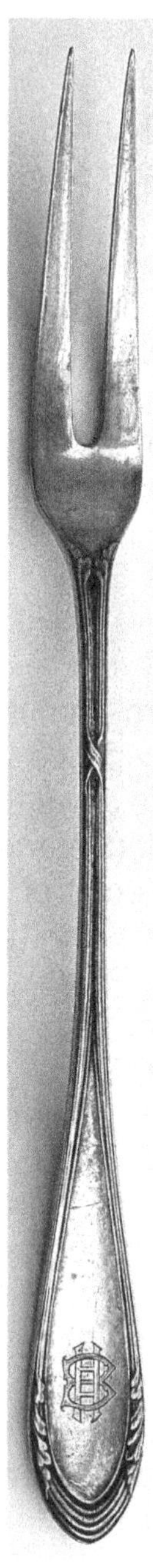

PS-34
L = 191 mm / 7 1/2”

PS-34 Breith, Hermann Albert - Panzertruppe General
(1892 - 1964)

Meat serving Fork: Obverse carries engraved B over H. Reverse: P. Exner (retailer pattern '1929'), Maker Mark of Koch & Bergfeld, Bremen founded 1829, 800, RM.

Hermann Breith enlisted in the German army as a cadet (infantry) in 1910. He ended WWI as a lieutenant having won the Knight's Cross of the Hohenzollern. Promoted to the rank of Generalmajor on 1Aug1941 and Generalleutnant (3 star) on 1Nov1942 and finally General of Panzer Corps (General der Panzertruppe) on 1Mar1943 .

He was recipient of the Knight's Cross of the Iron Cross with Oak Leaves and Swords awarded to recognize extreme battlefield bravery or successful military leadership. He was the 48th to receive the award of the Swords on 21 February 1944 as General der Panzertruppe and commanding general of the III. Panzer-Korps. Only 58 were awarded to Army personnel with 49 award winners surviving the war.

Major WWII Commands:
1938 - 1940 Commanding Officer 36th Panzer Regiment
1940 - 1941 Commanding Officer 5th Panzer Brigade
1941 - General of Motorized Troops General Staff
1941 - 1942 General Commanding 3rd Panzer Division
1943 - 1945 General Officer Commanding III Panzer Corps

Note: The 3rd Pz Div (Bear Div) Fought in the Battle of Moscow, acted as a 'fire Brigade' during the Russian winter offensive of 41-42 captured Kharkov and Rostov, and later held Kharkov against massive attacks in March 1942. In 1944 to Rumania, the Ukraine and in 1945 defended Hungary, to the West, surrendered to US troops in Steyr.

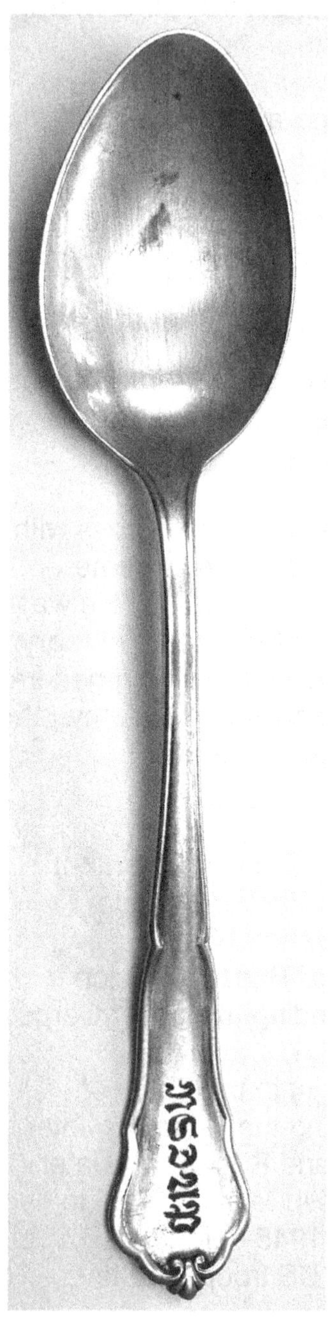

OG-35
L = 133 mm / 5 1/4"

OTHER GOVERNMENT

OG-35 'NSDAP'.
Nationalsozialistische Deutsche Arbeiterpartei

Teaspoon. Spoon carries NSDAP in Fraktur print on the obverse. Maker marked on reverse: RM, '800' and 'HTB' for Hanseatishe Silberwarenfabrik, Bremen.

National Socialist German Workers Party: Founded in 1919 as the German Workers Party (DAP), the name was changed to NSDAP in 1920 to broaden its appeal.

> Fraktur Trivia: The first FRAKTUR typeface was designed when Holy Roman Emperor Maximilian (1493-1519) had the new type (German Script) created. It remained popular in Germany into the early 20th Century. On 3 January 1941, Martin Bormann issued a circular letter to all public offices which declared FRAKTUR (and its corollary, the Sutterlin based hand writing) to be Judenlettern (Jewish letters) and prohibited its further use and replacing it with 'antiqua'. ie the spoon predates 3Jan41.
>
> A second explanation from Maik Kopleck's *BERLIN 1933-1945*, "its use was forbidden by a decree issued by Bormann on Hitler's order because in the annexed territories it had led to confusion."
>
> Surprisingly, the letterhead of Bormann's decree was in Fraktur type!

The waste of manpower, material and paper in replacing all school books, street signs, typewriter keys etc. in war time was monumental.

OG-36
L = 141 mm / 5 9/16”

OG-36 NSDAP'

Teaspoon: High Leader's spoon, the obverse carries a Swastika surrounded by oak leaves - (Eichenlaub or EL), a symbol of strength. End is squared. Maker marked on the reverse: RM, 800 GR for Gebruder Reiner, Krumbach Bayern. Founded 1914,

Under the NSDAP, the National Colors (Reichsfarben) were Black, White and Red. The early NSDAP slogan: Deutschland Erwache - Germany Awake.

> **NSDAP Promise of Loyalty** - I promise loyalty to my Fuhrer Adolf Hitler. I promise to always meet him and the leaders he will determine for me with respect and obedience.
>
> Symbolism of: Oak Leaves = Spirited Struggle
Palm Leaves = Victory

OG-37
L = 211 mm / 8 1/4”

OG-37 NSDAP/SA

Tablespoon: This aluminum tablespoon's eagle is looking to its left shoulder which symbolizes the Nazi party and was called the Parteiadler. In the absence of any specific organizational emblem, it is appropriate to assign it to either the NSDAP or the SA. Maker mark "C&C.W. 40" for Colsman & Co., Westfalen, 1940.

In 1929, Hitler described the SA man as, "The SA attracts the militant natures among the Germanic breed, the men who think democratically, unified by a common allegiance."

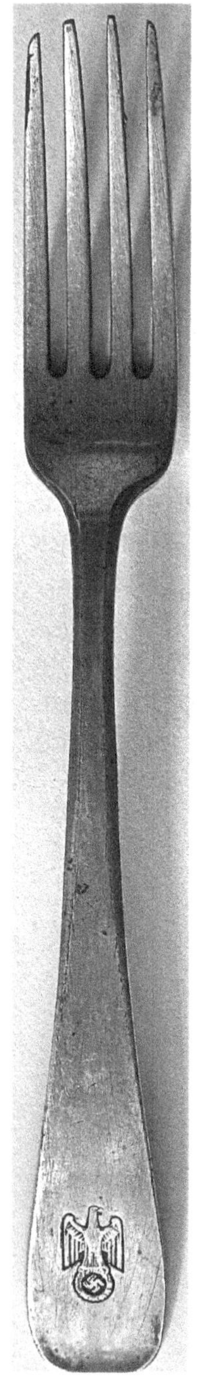

OG-38
L = 210 mm / 8 1/4"

OG-38 NSDAP/SA

Dinner Fork: The Obverse carries a very early eagle with down swept wings. A representation typical of an early service used by a political leader. The reverse is maker marked 'GEBR.HEPP' and '90'. This fork has the eagle looking to his left shoulder symbolizing the Nazi party. Again, in the absence of any specific organizational logo, it is appropriate to assign it to either the NSDAP or the SA.

Gebruder Hepp located in Pforzheim, Germany since 1863 was acquired by WMF (Wuerttemberg Metalware Factory) in 1988 and is noted for making many of the silver service items for the larger German hotels.

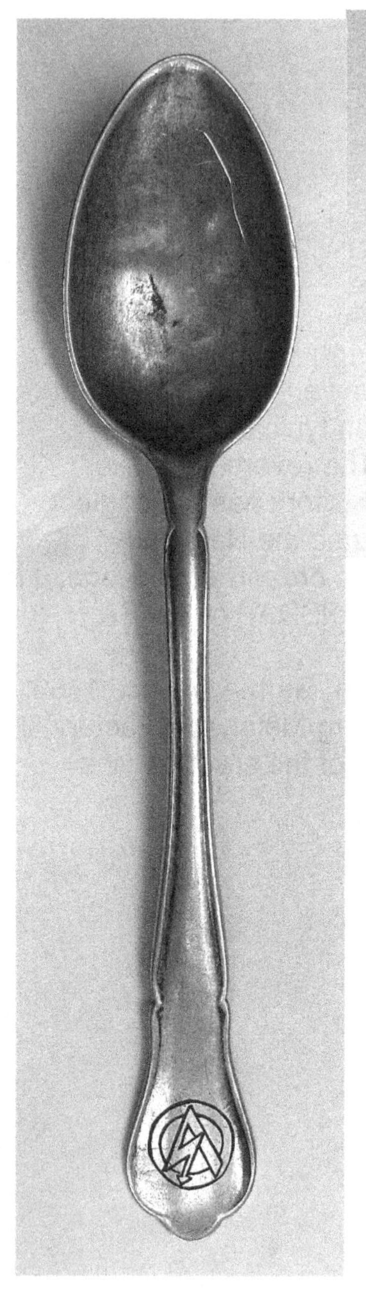

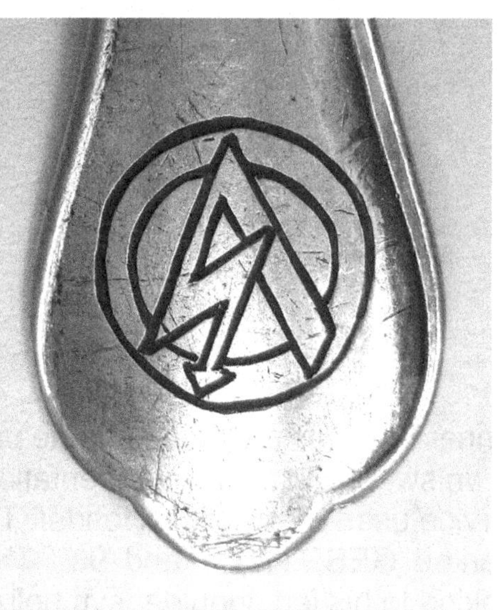

OG-39
L = 145 mm / 5/3/4”

OG-39 ‘SA’

Teaspoon: The spoon carries the stylized pseudo-runic “SA” monogram on the obverse. Maker mark: reversed ‘R’ facing ‘R’ of Rossdeutscher & Reisig of Breslau, with RM, 800.

The Sturmabteilung abbreviated SA, (German for "Assault Detachment" or "Assault Section", usually translated as "stormtroop(er)s"), It played a key role in Adolf Hitler's rise to power in the 1930s.

SA men were often called "brown shirts", for the color of their uniforms, and to distinguish them from the Schutzstaffel (SS), who wore black and brown uniforms (compare the Italian black shirts). Brown colored shirts were chosen as the SA uniform because a large batch of them were cheaply available after World War I, having originally been ordered for German troops serving in Africa.

In 1930, to ensure the loyalty of the SA to himself, Adolf Hitler assumed command of the entire organization and remained Oberster SA-Führer for the remainder of the group's existence to 1945. The day to day running of the SA was conducted by the Stabschef SA (SA Chief of Staff). After 1931, it was the Stabschef who was generally accepted as the Commander of the SA, acting in Hitler's name.

Favorite sayings: "Terror must be broken by terror", and "All opposition must be stamped into the ground."

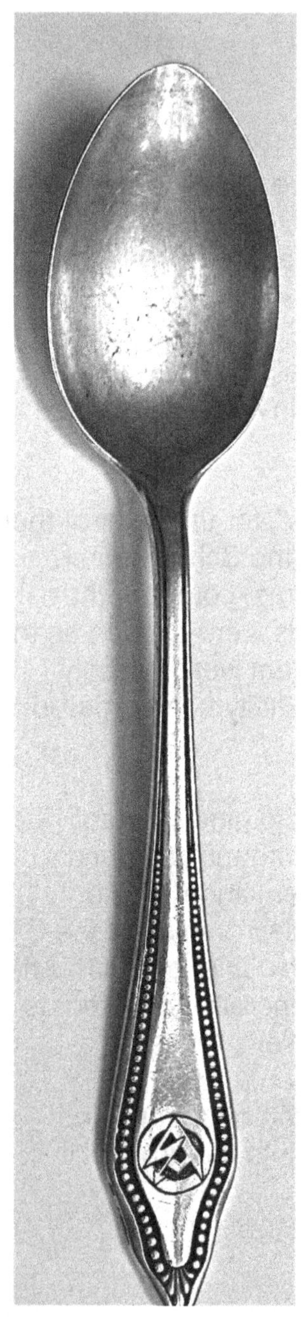

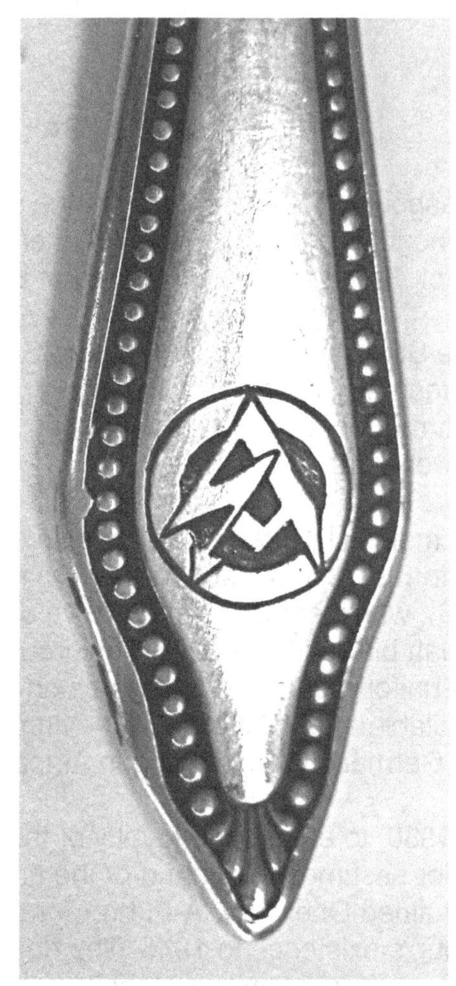

OG-40
L = 143 mm / 5 5/8"

OG-40 'SA'

Teaspoon: The spoon carries the stylized "SA" monogram on the obverse. Reverse marked with RM, '800'. maker mark 'JBN' for J. Bruschke, Niederschlesien.

Sturmabteilung (German for "Storm Department", usually translated as "stormtroop(er)s)" The SA was the first paramilitary organization of the NSDAP - the German Nazi party. These were the "brown shirts". From its inception in 1921 till its demise in 1945, there were less than 200 men that occupied the top three positions in the SA. At its height in August 1934 there were some 2.9 million members. The SA was also the first Nazi paramilitary group to develop pseudo-military titles for bestowal upon its members. The SA ranks would be adopted by several other Nazi Party groups, chief among them the SS. The SA was very important to Hitler's rise to power until they were superseded by the SS after the 'Night of the Long Knives' of 30 June 1934 when the leadership of the SA were purged.

The SA motto: Alles Fur Deutschland - Everything for Germany, was also the motto of the NSKK.

Trivia: UPS in Germany is not allowed to dress in their brown color. In Germany, UPS is dressed in green.

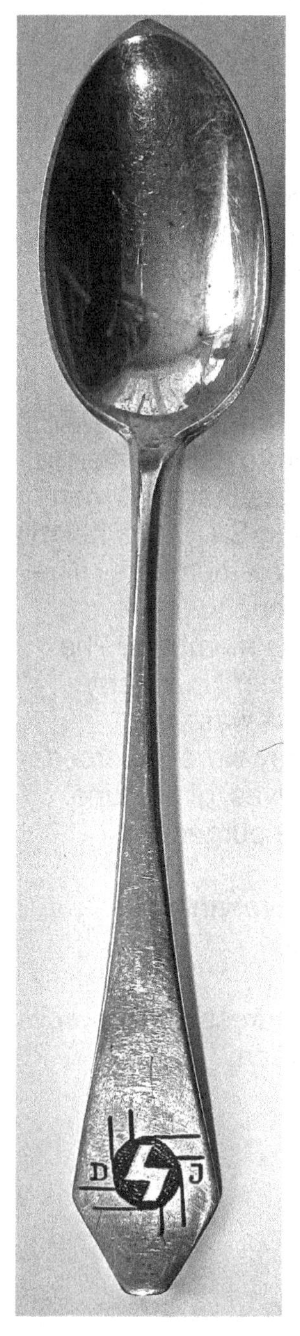

OG-41
L = 135 mm / 5 5/16"

OG-41 DJV Deutsche Jungvolk (German Youth)

Teaspoon: The obverse carries the sigrune in the center straddled by the 'D' and the 'J' over a stylized swastika. On the reverse: 'D.R.G.M' for Deutsches Reich Gebrauchsmuster (German Reich Registered Design) RM 800 'F' in a circle for Friedrich Feuerstein, Hanau.

In July 1926, the Hitler-Jugend, Bund Deutscher Arbeiterjugend (Hitler Youth, League of German Worker Youth) became an integral part of the Sturmabteilung. By 1929, the Hitler-Jugend had enlisted over 25,000 boys aged 14 and upwards. It also set up a junior branch, the Deutsches Jungvolk (DJV) for boys aged 10 to 14.

The sigrune emblem first became associated with the DJV on 9 November 1929 on the 6th anniversary of the failed Beer Hall Putsch when their first official flag consisting of a black field with a central silver sigrune was presented. The sigrune was adopted as the official emblem of the DJV and was used on assorted insignia but the design was unusual as even the early youth memorabilia usually only featured the more conventional Nazi swastika.

> Jungvolk Oath (taken by ten-year-old boys on first entering the DJV)
>
> "In the presence of this blood banner which represents our Führer, I swear to devote all my energies and my strength to the savior of our country, Adolf Hitler. I am willing and ready to give up my life for him, so help me God."

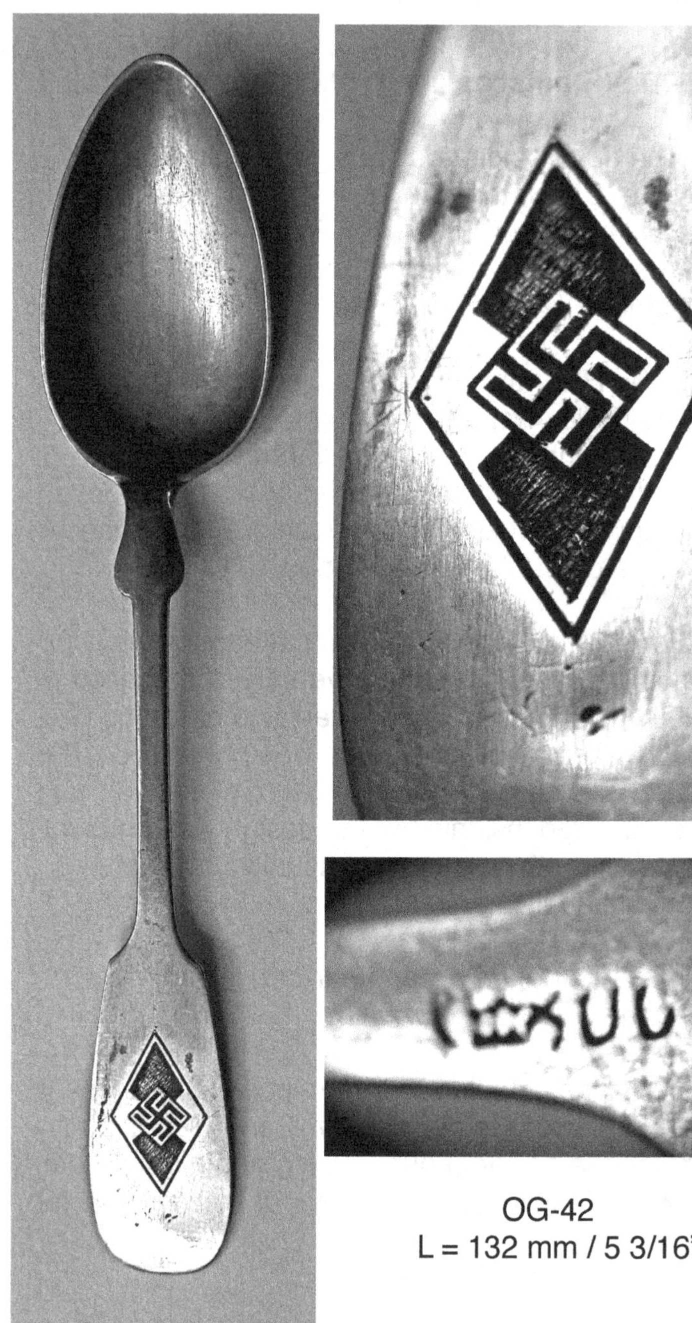

OG-42
L = 132 mm / 5 3/16”

OG-42 'HJ', Hitler-Jugend

Teaspoon: Obverse carries the HJ Logo. Reverse marked RM 800.

The HJ existed from 1922 to 1945, the 2nd oldest paramilitary NAZI group founded one year after the Sturmabteilung (SA) and attached to the SA. In July 1926 The Hitler-Jugend Bund der Deutschen Arbeiterjugend (Hitler Youth, League of German Worker Youth) received its final name. The HJ was banned in April 1932 by Chancellor Bruning but Chancellor von Papen lifted that ban in June 1932. The HJ diamond was adopted as the organizations emblem in 1933 along with its colors of Red and Black.. Membership became compulsory in December 1936. By 1945, the Volksturm commonly drafted 12 year old HJ members into its ranks for the defense of the fatherland. HJ motto: "Blut Und Ehre - Blood and Honor. Notable slogans: "Live Faithfully, Fight Bravely, and Die Laughing!" and "We were born to die for Germany!"

> **Hitler Youth Oath** - In the presence of this blood banner which represents our Fuhrer, I swear to devote all my energies and my strength to the savior of our country, Adolf Hitler, I am willing and ready to give up my life for him, so help me God.

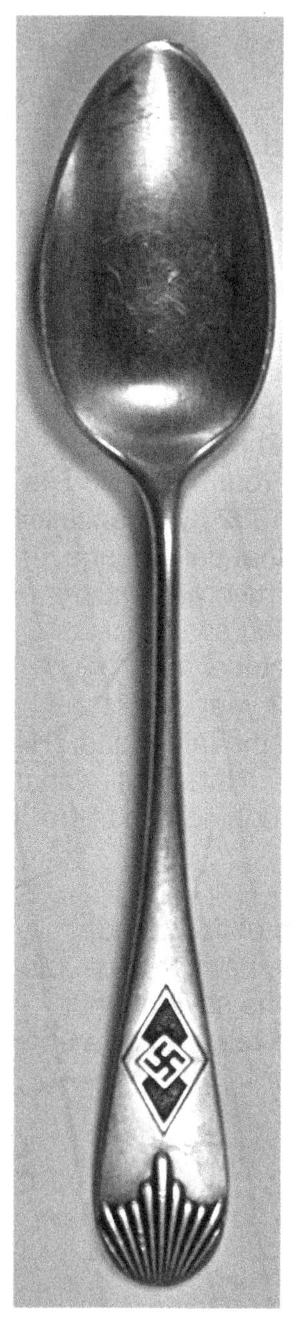

OG-43
L =148 mm / 5 13/16”

OG-43 Hitlerjugend (Hitler Youth)

Teaspoon: Obverse with the HJ symbol. Reverse marked RM, 800, unidentified maker's mark.

As early as 1922, the NAZI youth organization, Jungeturm Adolf Hitler was formed. At the 4 July 1926 Reichsparteitag (National Party day) meeting in Nurnberg, the name Hitler Jungend (Hitler Youth) was announced. In 1933 at age 26, Balder von Schrach became Reich Youth Leader (1933 - 1940) head of the HJ. In 1936 at age 29 he achieved the SA rank of Gruppenfuhrer (2 star General) and also became a State Secretary and later Governor of Vienna (1940 - 1945). Interestingly, two of Schrach's ancestors were signatories of our Declaration of Independence and his father in law, Heinrich Hoffmann, supplied the photos for his books which focused on NAZI ideas of character, discipline, obedience and leadership as described in his best selling Die Hitler-Jugend (1934).

At age 10, boys joined the Deutsches Jungvolk (German Young People), at age 13 they transferred into the Hitler Jugend until age 18. The HJ became compulsory in 1936 which drove membership to 8.8 million. This was the venue for the para-military training of a generation of soldiers. Girls from ten to eighteen were given their own parallel organization, the Bund Deutscher Mädel (BDM), League of German Girls. Hitler's goal for the HJ, "The weak must be chiseled away. I want young men and women who suffer pain. A young German must be as swift as a greyhound, as tough as leather and as hard as Krupp's steel."

Per Schrach, 'Loyalty is everything and everything is the love of Adolf Hitler."

OG-44
L = 213 mm / 8 6/16

OG-44 HJ/RFS

Hitler Youth “Reichsfuhrerschule der HJ (National-Leaders-School of the HJ)

Tablespoon: The obverse is stamped with the Hitler Youth diamond and swastika, beneath which is similarly impressed “RFS” for ‘Reichsfuhrerschule” (National-Leaders-School). The reverse is jeweler engraved “Mehlem” and maker marked with “Hanseat” the manufacturer’s name, followed by the silver plate of “90”.

Under the direct control of Reichsjugendfuhrer Balder von Schirach, the RFS were to train HJ leaders. Mehlem being the location of one of the three HJ National Leaders Schools - this one near Bonn, the others in Potsdam and for women, in Godesberg. Upon successful completion of the training, graduates were authorized to wear a special insigne over the right breast tunic pocket. This insigne consisted of a silver embroidered bar of oak leaves with the initials, "RFS" outlined in black surmounting the oak leaves.

In addition to the traditional German school system, and the HJ special training, the Nazis established elite schools for the training of the young Nazis: the exclusive Ordensburgen (Order Castles) took the top graduates from earlier schooling and at a nominal age of 18 they were trained for another three years to be ready to assume high level positions in the Nazi Party. An example would be the Ordenberg Vogelsang where the original buildings have been preserved at this new national park and although designed to appear as a medieval castle, its NS architecture is easily recognizable. Most of the original grandiose statuary remains but with the obvious NS markings removed. Construction on this hugh complex was started in 1936!

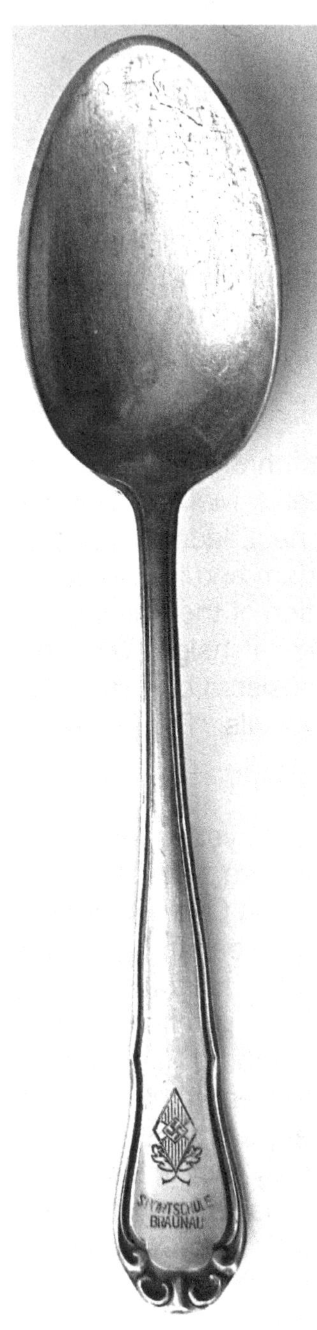

OG-45
L = 212 mm / 8 6/16"

OG-45 HJ Sportschule Braunau

Soupspoon: Obverse with enhanced HJ emblem over 'SPORTSCHULE BRAUNAU'. Reverse has maker mark 'EMD' for Erich Marx, Duesseldorf and 90 plate.

The HJ put more emphasis on physical and military training than on academic study.

In 1935, about 60 percent of Germany's young people belonged to the HJ. With the annexation of both Austria and Czechoslovakia in March of 1938, the various German created youth organizations (HJ, DJV, BDM & DJM) added over 1 million to their numbers and by 1939, about 82 percent (7.3 million) of eligible youths within the Greater Reich belonged making it the largest youth organization in the world. 1939 was declared "The Year of Physical Training" and introduced the Sports Competition. Medals were awarded to youths who performed rigorous athletic drills and met strict physical fitness standards. Every summer, a day would now be set aside as the "Day of the State Youth" for these events. School schedules were adjusted to allow for at least one hour of physical training in the morning and one hour each evening. Prior to this, only two hours per week had been set aside. Hitler also encouraged young boys to take up boxing to heighten their aggressiveness.

> Note: this training center (Sportschule / Physical Training Academy) for selected HJ athletes was located in the town of Hitler's birth, Braunau, Austria. After the 13 March 1938 annexation, Hitler made his first entry into Austria at Braunau

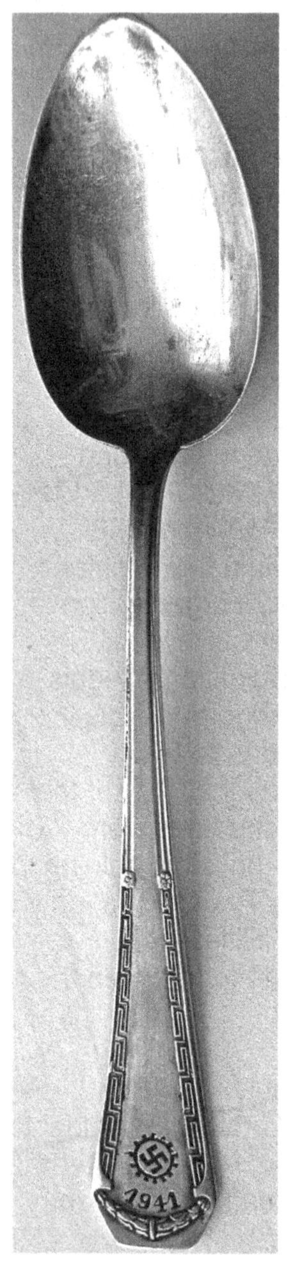

OG-46
L = 183 mm / 7 1/4"

OG-46 DAF (Deutsche Arbeitsfront)

Spoon: Obverse carries DAF emblem over '1941'. Reverse with Reichsmark, 800 and maker marked of Gebruder Koberlin, Dobeln founded 1828.

The Deutsche Arbeitsfront (abbr. DAF, often translated to German Labor Front) was founded on 10 May 1933 under the patronage of Hitler and directed by Robert Ley, Reichsorganisationsleiter der NSDAP as the Nazi's substitute organization for trade unions that were made illegal after their rise to power in 1933. It soon grew to be a giant bureaucratic machine with 25 million members and 40,000 staff with a considerable influence within the Nazi regime. Conceived as an alternative to trade unions, it was supposed to be representative of employers and employees alike. However, in reality it was a means by which workers were controlled, ensuring wage demands were not made and that the position of the employer was the 'leader' with the worker cast as 'follower'. Wages were set by the 12 DAF trustees, who followed the will of the employers. It became part of the NSDAP organization in October 1934, having its base in Berlin.

Within the DAF, several sub-organizations were set up:

Kraft durch Freude (KdF; Strength through Joy)
Schönheit der Arbeit (SdA; Beauty of Work)
Reichsarbeitsdienst (RAD; Reich Labour Service)

In 1937 Robert Ley, stated DAF's aim as "to create a true social and productive community" and on Hitler in 1938 "I believe on this earth in Adolf Hitler alone. I believe in one Lord God who made me and guides me, and I believe that this Lord God has sent Adolf Hitler to us."

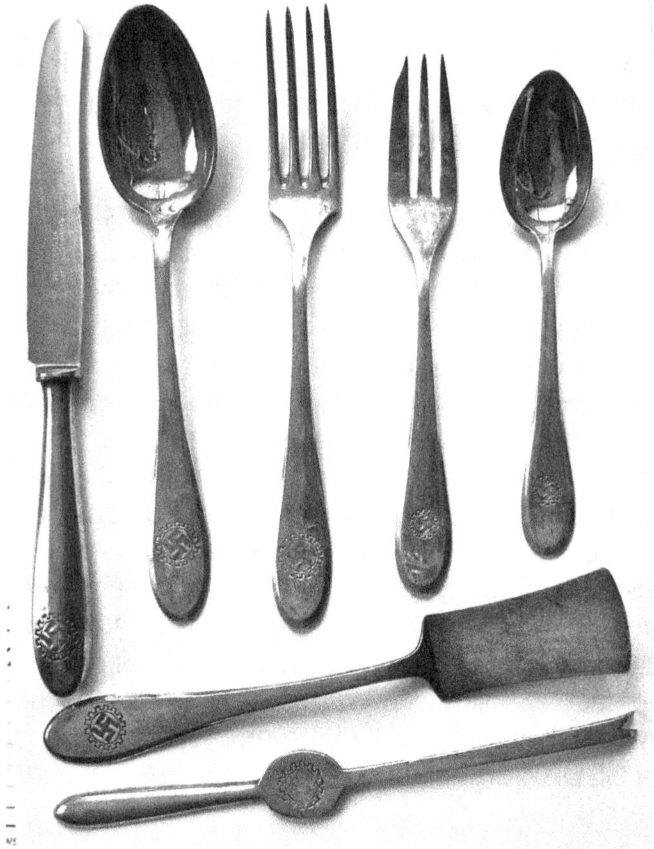

GEBR. HEPP 90

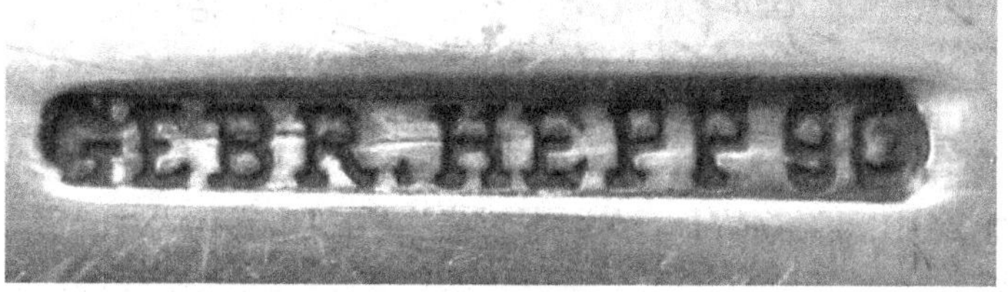

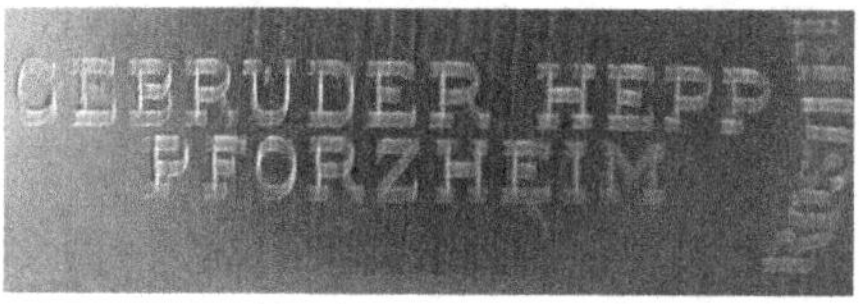
GEBRUDER HEPP
PFORZHEIM

OG-47

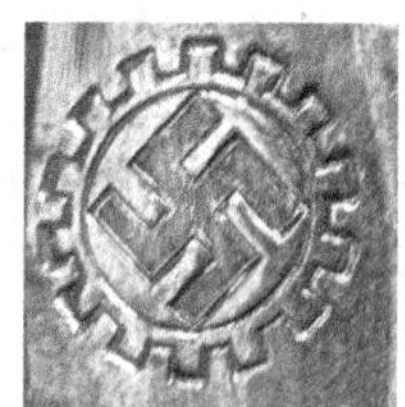

OG-47 DAF (Deutsche Arbeitsfront) (7 Piece Set)

Obverse carries the DAF logo. Reverse maker marked GEBR.HEPP and '90' plating.

This group (dinner knife, dinner spoon, dinner fork, salad fork, teaspoon, butter curler and lobster fork) is reportedly from the former headquarters building of DAF located at Berlin's Potsdamer Strasse 182. The original building is still in use today.

There were 2 main components of the DAF:

* Nationalsozialistische Betriebszellenorganisation (NSBO; National Socialist Factory Organization)
* Nationalsozialistische Handels und Gewerbeorganization (NSHABO; National Socialist Trade and Industry Organization)

Several other sub-organisations were set up:

*Kraft durch Freude (KdF; Strength through Joy) – Organization giving the workers cheap/free holidays in addition to subsidized sporting and leisure facilities.

*Schönheit der Arbeit (SdA; Beauty of Work) – Aimed to make workplaces more enticing to workers (e.g. renovations of outdated factories, new canteens for workers, smoking free rooms, cleaner working spaces.

*Reichsarbeitsdienst (RAD; Reich Labor Service) A Solution to the unemployment crisis the Nazis inherited. Provided cheap labor for big state projects. such as the Autobahns. Made compulsory for unemployed men 16-25 in 1935. Provided work security to many unemployed.

Note: This dinner knife blade style is termed 'New French'.

OG-48

OG-48 DAF Mystery Cup

This massive Gebr. HEPP cup weighs 341 grams / 12 Oz. Its base metal is alpacca with a silver plate of 90. It has a 95 mm / 3 3/4" diameter and is 60 mm / 2.3" high. Mystery - what was its use? With hot coffee, it can not be held.

DAF miscellaneous: Membership dues were in the range of 15 Pfenning to 3 RM, depending on the category a member fell into of the 20 membership groups. A substantial amount of money was raised through dues, in 1934, the total intake was 300,000,000 RM / $ 71.5 million.

Organizationally, the smallest form of the DAF was the Block (block) which consisted of 15 members, headed by a Blockwalter (block warden). Two to six blocks formed a Zellen (cell) which was led by a Zellenwalter (cell warden). Each commerce or industrial organization that had at least 10 cells was considered a Betriebsgemeinschaft (plant community) under the leadership of a Betriebsfuhrer (plant leader) and under the control of a Betriebswalter (plant warden). Several small industrial or commerce businesses that each had less than 10 workers were grouped together in street communities after the street they were located on. Plant communities and the individual members of the plant communities within the jurisdiction of a local party group of the NSDAP formed an Ortsgruppe (local group) of the DAF under a Ortsgruppenwalter (local group warden). Ortsgruppe (local groups) within a NSDAP Kries (circle) comprised a DAF Kries (circle) under the leadership of Kreiswalter (circle warden). The DAF Kries (circles) were then organized into Gau (regions) under the command of a Gauwart (region warden). The largest organizations of the DAF were the DAF Bezirke (districts) which were headed by Besirkwalter (district wardens). There were 13 DAF Bezirke in 1935.

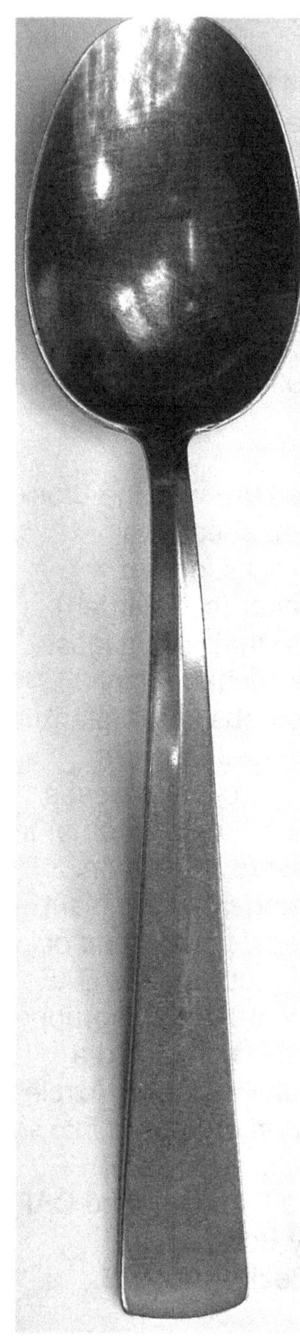

OG-49
L = 210 mm / 8 1/4"

OG-49 DAF / SdA
(Schonheit der Arbeit / Beauty of Work)

Tablespoon: The obverse has a raised central spine and is unmarked. Reverse carries the logo of the 'Modell Des Amtes/Schonheit der Arbeit' (Model of the Office / Beauty of Work) with the DAF cogwheel, the maker mark HMZ for Hessische Metallwerke, Ziegenhain and "Rustfrei.

Within the DAF, was the Kraft durch Freude - KdF (Strength through Joy) and within the KdF was Amt für Schönheit der Arbeit. The SdA, Schonheit dr Arbeit" (Beauty of Labor) organization was established as a subsection of the KdF under the control of Albert Speer (from 1933 to at least 1936) who was responsible for improving working conditions in factories, including setting up canteens and supplying the cutlery.

The SdA goal was described in Shelley Barunowski's "Strength Through Joy" as "Aestheticizing the shop floor meant eliminating class conflict and creating the plant community, as well as reconstructing the identities of workers so that they would become full-fledged members of the racial community."

The Governments focus was to create practical workplace benefits while simultaneously instilling a sense of community between the totalitarian dictatorship and the German population, an attempt to improve the status of workers and their conditions to compensate for wage freezes, longer working hours (up to 60 hour work weeks) and restrictions on private consumption.

OG-50 L = 210 mm / 8 1/4'

OG-50 DAF SdA - I.G. Farben N.W.7

Tablespoon: The obverse is marked with Farben's emblem of "I" over "G" with "Berlin N.W.7." below. Reverse carries the maker mark of Tc, ROSTFREI plus 'MDA SchdA.

I.G. Farben was a conglomerate that before WW I had a near monopoly on world dyestuffs. Per chapter two of 'The Empire of I.G. Farben': "The Berlin N.W. 7 office (Unter den Linden 82) of I.G. Farben was the key Nazi overseas intelligence, espionage and propaganda center prior to WWII. One of the more prominent of these Farben intelligence workers (verbindungsmanner / liaison men) in N.W. 7 was Prince Bernhard of the Netherlands, who joined Farben in the early 1930s after completion of an 18-month period of service in the S.S." N. W. 7 operated under Farben director Max Ilgner, nephew of I.G. Farben president Hermann Schmitz. Max Ilgner and Hermann Schmitz were on the board of American I.G., with other directors Henry Ford of Ford Motor Company, Paul Warburg of Bank of Manhattan, and Charles E. Mitchell of the Federal Reserve Bank of New York. In 1939, of 43 major I. G. products 28 were of "primary concern" to the German armed forces. Prior to the invasions of Czechoslovakia and Poland, IG identified specific chemical plants to be delivered to Farben. At the Nuremberg trials of IG in 1947/48, "Berlin N.W.7" was identified as, "the Nazi prewar intelligence office" which resulted in sentences of Schmitz 4 years, Llgner 3 years. Note: By 1944, the Farben Auschwitz factory complex had employed some 83,000 forced laborers of which 40,000 perished. The Buna facility produced 100% of Germany's synthetic rubber and 45% of its aviation gasoline from coal.

ps. Hitler, Goering and The Reich Ministry of Economics were in Berlin postal code W.8. while Himmler & Heydrich were at Berlin S.W. 11.

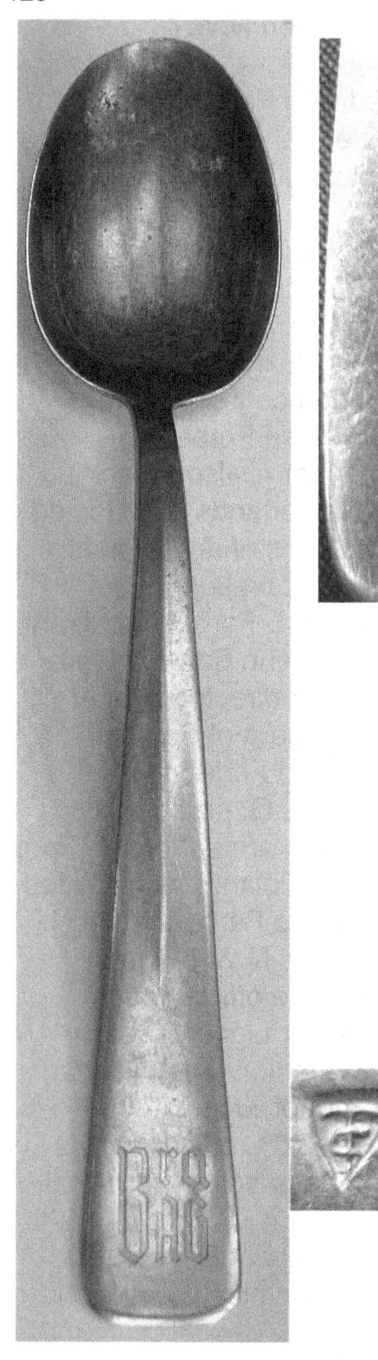

OG-51
L = 210 mm / 8 1/4”

OG-51 DAF SdA - Bra AG

Tablespoon: Obverse plain with a raised central spine and carries the logo Bra AG. Reverse has the DAF wheel with a mobile swastika and below the initials MDA (Modell Des Amtes / Model of the Office) and below that SchdA (Schonheit der Arbeit / Beauty of Labor. Maker marked Tc and RUSTFREI.

The Bra AG logo is unknown but the spoon recently came from Poland and may have been a company in the East of war time Germany.

The SdA (Speer) decided what constituted good industrial design, ie simplicity of line etc. The majority of the cutlery carried organizational logos on either the obverse or reverse such as BMW for the cutlery at their Munich factory or like the early Berlin N.W 7 - I. G. Farben, even Luftwaffe eagles. Others carried no logo.

Nazi's rejected:

Marxist "Class Conflict" as a violation of their vision of a unified racial community and

"Fordism" (consumerism) which placed little value on German "Quality" work, worshiped commodities and instant gratification of individual wants.

SdA embraced the totality of the workers "creative lives" with emphasis on the workplace as the key to regulating leisure time and disciplining consumption. SdA was less able to build popular support for the regime due to the inherent coercion of SdA's plant communities by emphasis on "pride of work" vs material rewards.

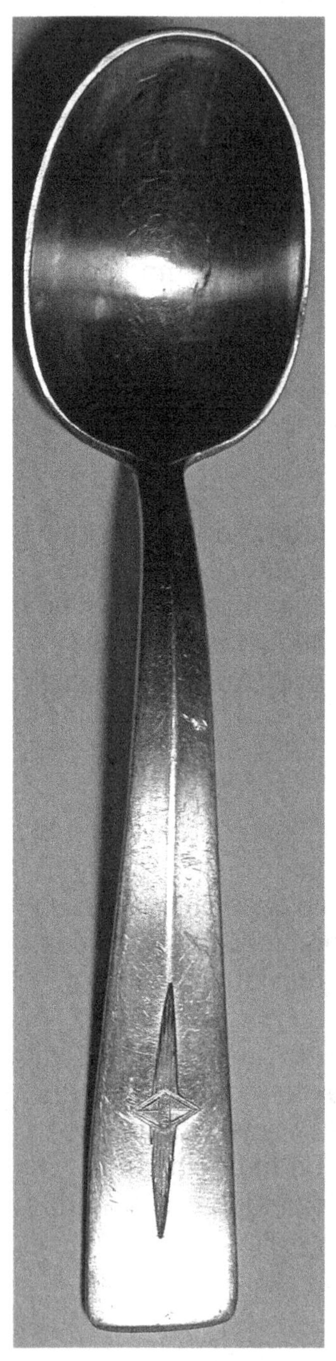

OG-52 L = 142 mm / 5 9/16”

OG-52 DAF / SdA - Borgward Auto

Teaspoon: The obverse has a raised central spine and is marked with the logo of the Carl F.W. Borgward Automobile Company (Carl F.W. Borgward GmbH Automobil und Motorenwerke) of Bremen, Germany.. Reverse carries the logo of the 'Modell Des Amtes/Schonheit der Arbeit' (Model of the Office/Beauty of Work) with the DAF cogwheel, the maker mark Tc and "Rustfrei.

Borgward founded in 1924 became the 4th largest German automobile manufacturer. During WWII, Borgward manufactured the "Goliath', a wire guided demolition vehicle as well as the Borgward IV, a large radio controlled demolition vehicle with a weight of 4 tons. Its B2000 was a staff car seating 11 with the switchable drive of either 2, 4 or 6 of its wheels.

The company was put out of business by a combination of the government and competitors in 1961 with Mercedes Benz taking over the Bremen factory complex.

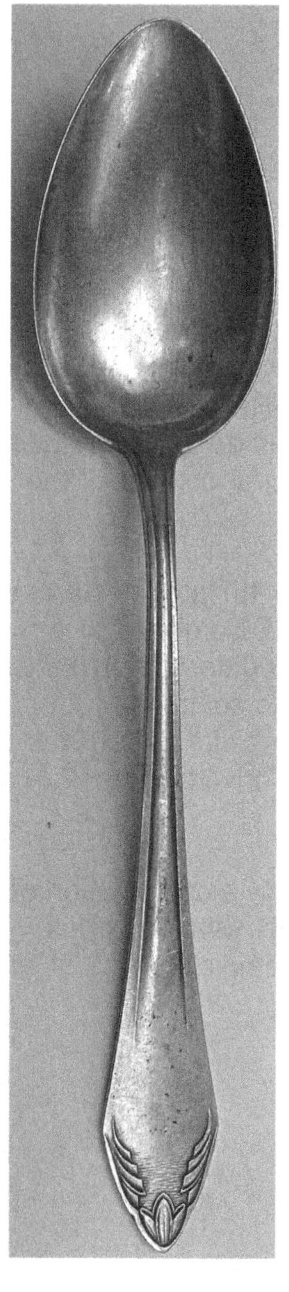

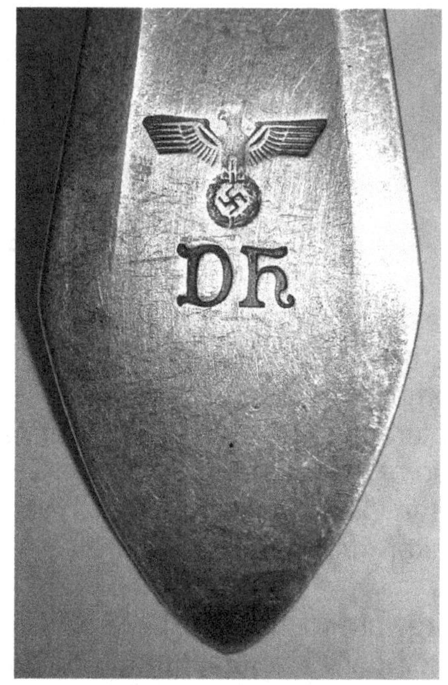

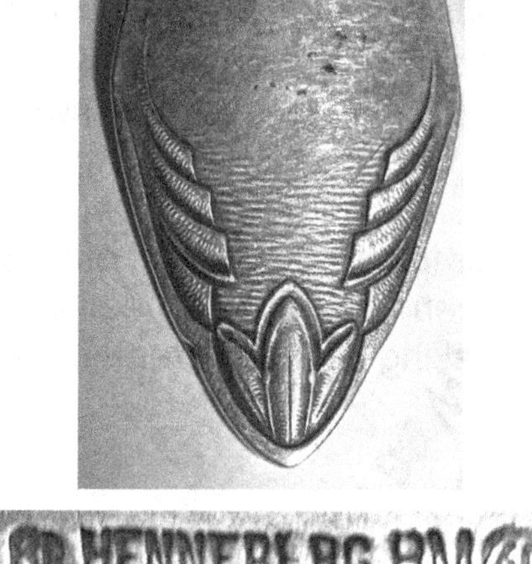

OG-53
L = 207 mm / 8 1/8”

OG-53 Dh - Dienststelle Heismeyer?

Tablespoon: Obverse with flower detail on tip. Reverse with right looking eagle over 'Dh' and maker marked Br Henneberg BM and '40' in a circle.

Reference PS-18, the 'Dh' logo is associated with Bernard Rust and education generally. Another association could be with Hauptamt **D**ienststelle SS-Obergruppenführer **H**eißmeyer. The National Political Institutes of Education (Nationalpolitische Erziehungsanstalten); officially abbreviated NPEA, were secondary boarding schools in Nazi Germany founded as "community education sites" after the National Socialist seizure of power in 1933. The goal of the schools was to raise a new generation for the political, military, and administrative leadership of the Nazi state. Only boys and girls considered to be "racially flawless" were admitted to the boarding schools. No children with poor hearing or vision were accepted. "Above-average intelligence" was also required, so those seeking admission had to complete 8-day entrance exams. The first three NPEA's were founded in 1933 by the Minister of Education Bernhard Rust in Plön, Potsdam, and Köslin. The schools reported directly to the Reich Ministry for Education, rather than to any states like regular schools. From 1936, the NPEA's were subordinated to the Inspector of the National Political Institutes of Education, SS Obergruppenführer August Heissmeyer. With the outbreak of WWII, Heissmeyer set up the "Dienststelle SS-Obergruppenführer Heissmeyer" – his own bureau – and was thereby responsible for NPEA students' military training. The schools were now under the direct influence of the SS. Boys eventually entered the SS in much higher rates (13%) than in the general German population of 1.8%. In 1941, there were a total of 30 NPEA's with 6,000 students enrolled in all of Nazi Germany. See M-201, pp 487.

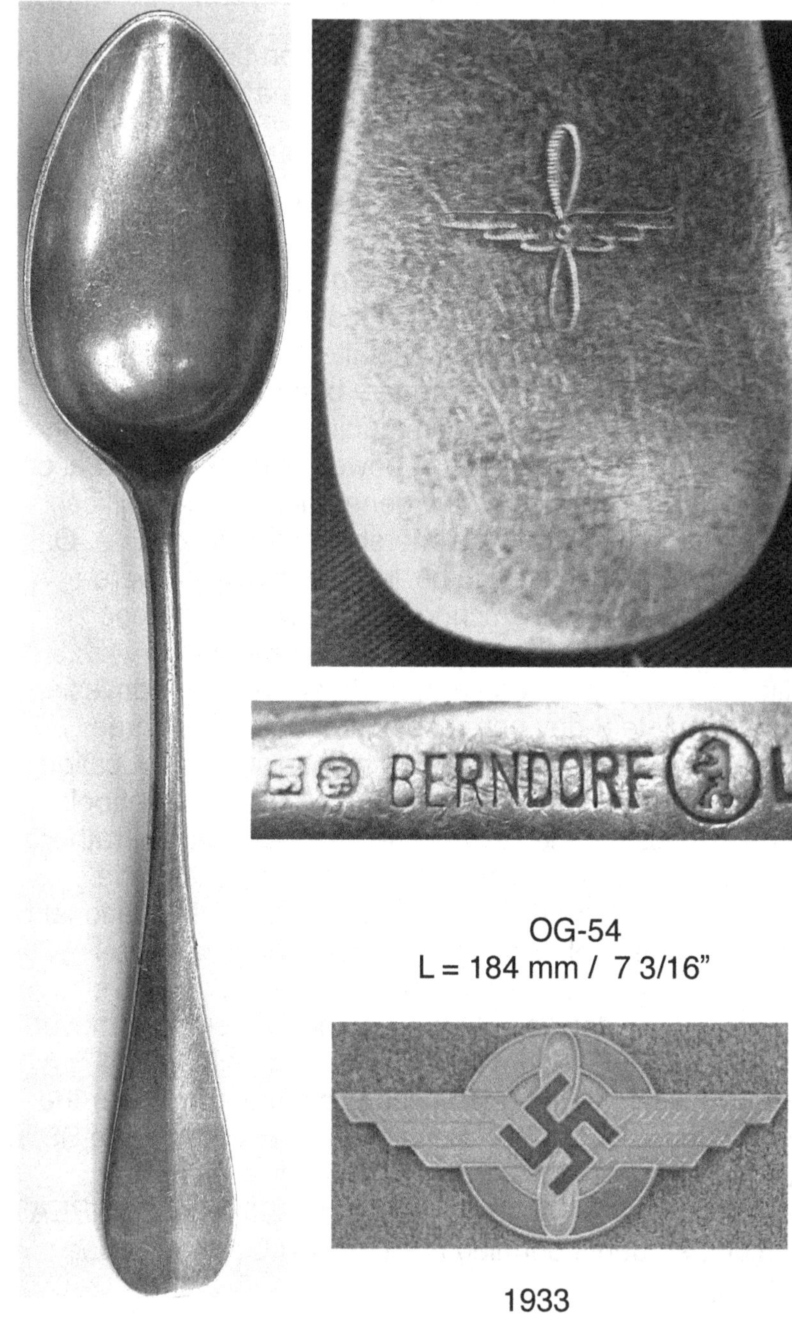

OG-54
L = 184 mm / 7 3/16"

1933

OG-54 DLV - Deutscher Luftfahrt Verband
(German Aviation League)

Dessert spoon (10 ml): Obverse is unmarked with a raised spine. Reverse carries the early emblem (1922-33) of the DLV and has a style mark of "30" in a square, the silver plating indicator of '90' in a circle, "Berndorf", a standing bear in a circle and the letter 'L' for their Swiss plant in Luzern.

The Deutscher Luftfahrt Verband (DLV) was founded in 1922. It was a civilian aviation club promoting both sport and commercial aviation. In 1933, under the Nazi's, it became the Deutscher Luftsport Verband or German Air-Sport League and added a mobile swastika on the propeller hub . The DLV was very closely associated with the Hitler Youth. Events involved model building with flying competitions of the completed projects, aeronautical educational classes followed by building and flying actual glider aircraft. The DLV was divided into three sections - powered flight, gliders and ballooning. The DLV owned sixteen gliding aviation schools and three larger State Soaring Schools. Under the Nazi's this was a covert organization for the training of both pilots and support personnel for the, then secret, Luftwaffe. In April 1933 Hitler's pilot Captain Hans Bauer, usually described as 'bibulous', sported the DLV uniform which had been personally approved by Hermann Goering and was later adopted with slight modification by the Luftwaffe. By the time Hitler officially called for volunteers for the Luftwaffe in March 1935, there were actually some 1,888 aircraft of all types and some 20,000 officers and men who quickly changed from the DLV uniform to the Luftwaffe uniform, On 17 April 1937, the DLV was disbanded and was superseded by the NSFK Nationalsozialistisches Fliegerkorps (National Socialist Flying Corps).

OG-55 L = 141 mm / 5 9/16”

OG-55 DR - Deutsche Reichsbahn
(German National Railways)

Teaspoon: On the obverse is the modified DR emblem where the original flanged wheel has been replaced by a mobile swastika which became mandatory in 1933, Reverse carries RM, 800 and maker's mark GR (Gebruder Reiner, Krumbach Bayern 1910 - present).

Hitler became Reich Chancellor 30Jan33, Reichstag fire 27Feb33, the Enabling Laws 23Mar33, The Law for the Reconstruction of the Professional Civil Service 7Apr 33. By 15Jul33 the DR had ordered the Nazi swastika to rolling stock and for employees to use the 'Heil Hitler' greeting. In addition, the elimination of women, elderly men, Jews and communists from the DR is underway as well as their replacement by young, male members of the Nazi party.

Operationally, the DR abandons the U.S. cost accounting standards used during the Weimar era (that had significantly increased efficiency) on the grounds that they were capitalistic, profit seeking, and focused on commercial values. They restored the Voelkish ideal of 'serving the community'. No more paying employees on a capitalist incentive basis but according to social standards.

During World War II, the Reichsbahn was an essential component of German military logistics, providing transportation services for the Reich throughout the occupied lands of Europe and employed 1,600,000.

The DR was not included in Armament planning until 1941. In 1942 it was assigned "Highest Priority" along with 69,500 tons of steel monthly to produce 500 locomotives monthly. In 1943 its priority was superseded by the "Adolf Hitler Tank Program", a commitment Hitler made to the Heer.

OG-56 & 57
Tablespoon = 211 mm / 8 5/16", Tea 140 mm / 5 1/2"

OG-56 DR - Deutsche Reichsbahn

(Hitler's Private Dining Car)

Tablespoon and matching teaspoon from Hitler's executive dining car. The spoons obverse carries the "DR" logo, on the reverse the spoon is maker marked: RM, 800, eagle of Bruckmann & Sohne followed by a large '205' indicating it is from Sonderzug / Fuhrerwagon car #10205 / #205.

Prior to 1939, Hitler's private train was labeled Fuhrerzug - Leader's Train. In 1939, Hitler's 1st Wartime Headquarters was placed on the 17 car Fuhrersonderzug or Leader's Special Train. All the coaches were specially constructed of welded steel and therefore weighing in at over 60 tons each. Hitler's 'saloon coach' #10206 was fitted out to Hitler's own specifications. The Fuhrerwagen was mahogany-paneled with a large rectangular table, 12 red leather chairs and indirect lighting and both a gramophone (his favorites were the symphonies by Bruckner and Beethoven, the songs of Richard Strauss and the last act from Aida) and a radio. It also had a bed compartment, bathroom and small compartments for the manservant and adjutants. He may have had personalized cutlery for use in his saloon coach.

Car #10205 (the executive dining car with rose wood paneling and indirect lighting) was abbreviated as 205 on the car's china, flatware, silver serving pieces, and linens. The porcelain was maker marked: Nymphenburg. The train was code named "Fuhrersonderzug F' until 1940, then "Amerika" from a French town near Hitler's WWI location and finally "Brandenburg". Hitler used the train as his FHQ during the campaigns in Poland and the Balkans, and traveled across France several times including to the Spanish boarder for talks with Franco in 1940. During the Russian campaign it was stationed at Gorlitz within FHQ Wolfsschanze".

OG-57 DR - Deutsche Reichsbahn
(Details)

Details of Hitler's private dining car's silverware.

In 1924, the Deutsche Reichbahn was created as a state enterprise under the Reich Ministry of Transportation. On 10 Feb 1937, the Nazi government took total control of the rail network. To emphasize this, swastikas were added to the Hoheitsadler (sovereignty eagle) - the traditional symbol of Germany on all railcars, and the initials "DR" were held to stand for "Deutsches Reich" but were construed to be for "Deutsches Reichbahn. Maker marks identical to OG-56.

Trivia: There were two full time silver polishers assigned to the Fuhrersonderzug! His 206 coach was blown up by German Army engineers in April 1945 on Hitler's orders. One of the Fuhrersonderzug sleeping carriages, #10222 survived the war and was used by the President's of the Federal Republic of Germany into the 1980's.

Special DR Note: The DR's participation was crucial to the implementation of the "Final Solution of the Jewish Question". The Reichsbahn was paid to transport victims of the Holocaust from towns and cities throughout Europe to the Nazi concentration camp system and were paid by the track kilometer, so many pfennigs per Km. The rate was the same throughout the war. With children under ten going at half-fare and children under four going free. Payment had to be made for only one way. The guards of course had to have return fare paid for them because they were going back to their place of origin. Slovakia paid the SS 500 RM / $ 200 for the transportation of each of the 60,000 deported Slovakian Jews that were sent to the concentration camps.

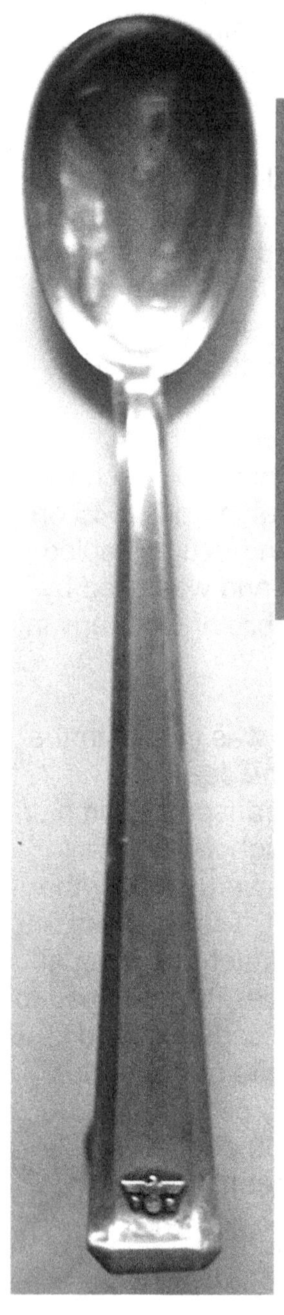

OG-58
L = 122 mm / 4 13/16”

OG-58 Deutsche Reichsbahn

(Staff Dining Car #213)

Demitasse sugar spoon: Obverse carries the "DR" eagle with the swastika straddled by the 'D' and 'R'. The reverse carries the Fuhrersonderzug's number 213 identifying it as from the Staff dining car 10213 with RM, 800 and a Bruckmann & Sohne eagle maker's mark.

Additional details on the Fuhrersonderzug: The sequence of cars (subject to minor modifications) was: Cars 1 & 2 were two BR86 tank locomotives in tandem. Car 3 a flakwagon (armored railroad car), each end open with a 4 barreled M-1938 20 mm cannon manned by 26 Luftwaffe personnel. Car 4 was a combination baggage and auxiliary power car. Car 5 was the Fuhrer's Pullman No 10206. Car 6 the Befehlswagen (command car) which included a conference room with map tables and a separate communications compartment. Car 7 the Begleitkommandowagen (escort) car for Hitler's 22 man FuhrerBegleit-Kommando and the RSD personnel. Car 8 the Executive dining car No 10205. Cars 9 & 10 sleeping cars for staff, guests and entourage. Car 11 Badewagon (bathing car). Car 12 staff dining car No. 10213. Cars 13 & 14 sleeping cars for enlisted men. Car 15 Presswagen (Press chief Otto Dietrich's car No 10251). Car 16 another baggage and power generator car. Last Car 17 a second flakwagon. Note: From 1928-43, 775 Baureihe BR86 2-8-2T locomotives were built.

First used for the Polish campaign with the thought that it could be rapidly deployed West in case France were to attack. On board were Hitler's military adjutants, liaison officers, party officials, Generals Keital (IQ 129) and Jodl. (IQ 127). (The Generals would have their own trains shortly.) Hitler's last train ride was from FHQ Adlerhorst to Berlin on 15 January 1945.

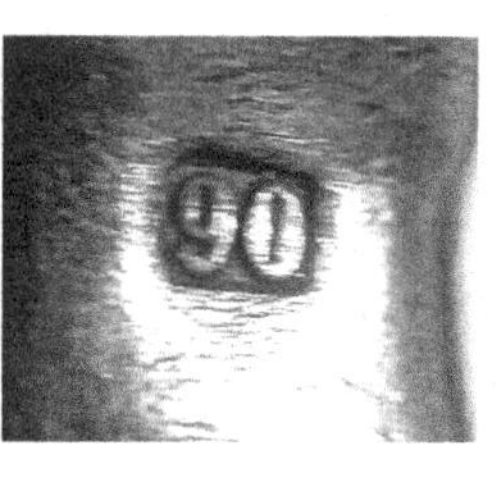

No problem
with the handle marking

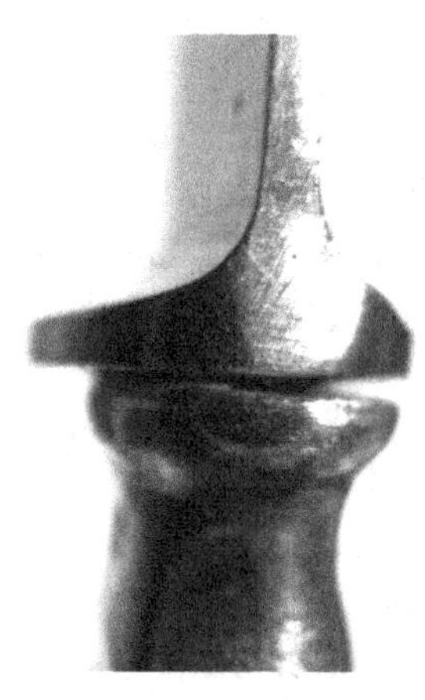

OG-59
L = 165 mm / 6 1/2"

Trouble: the blade not fitting the handle!. Looks like someone had a handle and to make a sale able knife, added a blade that unfortunately - does not mate properly. You do not have this problem with spoons!

OG-59 DR - Deutsche Reichsbahn

(Otto Dietrick's 'Press Wagon' #251)

Relish Knife: Obverse carries the DR logo. On the neck of the knife is the Railcar ID number 251 (short-form for car # 10251) which was Otto Dietrich's "Press Wagon' attached to Hitler's Fuhrersonderzug and on the opposite side '90'. Replaced blade carries Gustav Wirth of Solingen-Graefrath's maker mark over Nicht Rostend.

Otto Dietrich, Phd (1897-1952) was a Reichsleiter, the Reich Press Chief of the NSDAP from 1933 to 1945, a State Secretary in the Propaganda Ministry, the President of the Reich Press Chamber and an SS Lt. General. He was a key propaganda creator for Hitler. In this role he was at Hitler's side at all times. Creating 'news' for the government controlled press to fulfilled Hitler's desires To this end, he directed the news, daily. By 1934 Dietrich and his German Press Division controlled 3,097 newspapers and 4,000 periodicals having a total circulation of more than 30 million in a country of 17.7 million households. His skills at lying and creating news were very much appreciated by Hitler. The murder of the SA leadership during the Night of the Long Knives in 1934, personally directed by Hitler, was reported in the press via Dietrich's creativity as coming as a "shock" to Hitler and focused on the 'moral degeneracy' of the victims. On 22 February 1942, Hitler expressed his admiration for Dietrich's resourcefulness "he is exceptionally gifted at his job... I am proud of the fact that with his handful of men I can at once throw the rudder of the press through 180 degrees as happened on 22 June 1941 [the day Germany invaded Russia]. There is no other country which can copy us in that." In 1949 he was sentenced to seven years in Landsberg prison, released early and died in 1952 at age fifty-five.

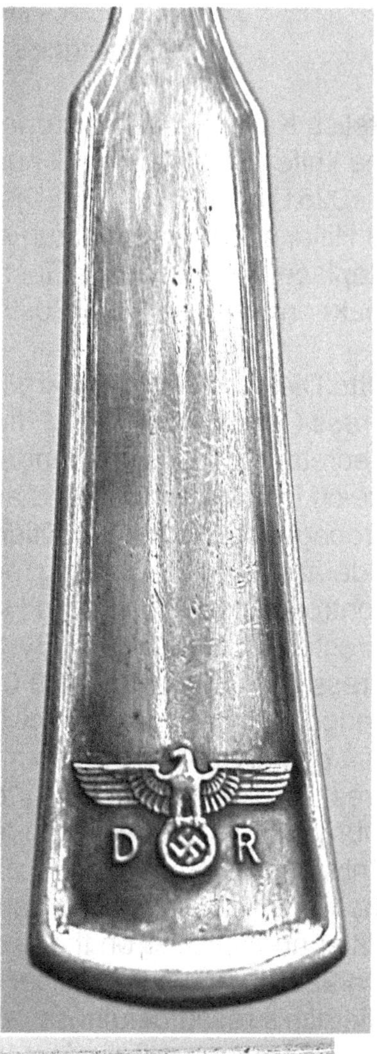

OG-60 L = 216 mm / 8 1/2"

OG-60 DR - Deutsche Reichsbahn

(Table spoon from Goering's private dining car)

As with Hitler but on a grander scale, Herman Goering's two personal trains were in Obersalzburg in April 1945. His primary private dining car was number 10243 '243'. Other cars were '233', '234' and '244'. This tablespoon carries the Goring dining car number '243' and is maker marked: Capital 'B' (Bruckmann) with a locomotive symbol followed by a '90'. There have recently surfaced a number of the raised edge 243 spoons which are now the most prevalently available. The demonstrably different shape of this Goering spoon is evident when set side by side with the A. H. DR spoon and is generally described as with 'raised edge'.

> Trivia: Goering's Sonderzuge were first named *Asien I* and *Asien II* and later renamed *Pommern I* and *Pommern II.*

> Note: I have recently seen DR cutlery marked 244 and identical in form to the Hitler 205 above.

In the East: By 1 Sep 1939 - The DR had moved 86 non motorized divisions to the Polish border. During the Polish campaign, both sides participated in the destruction of the Polish rail system. The program to double the existing capacity for the invasion of Russia started In Oct 1940. By June 1941, east traffic was raised from 84 to 220 trains a day and 141 German divisions moved to the Soviet border.

From the Invasion of Russia on 22 June 1941 to 1 Jan 1943, the DR converted 22,000 miles of Soviet wide gauge rail to German standard gauge. East bound trains from Germany, daily: Dec41 = 122, 1Jan42 = 140 and 1Mar42 = 180 or a train to the East front every 8 minutes!

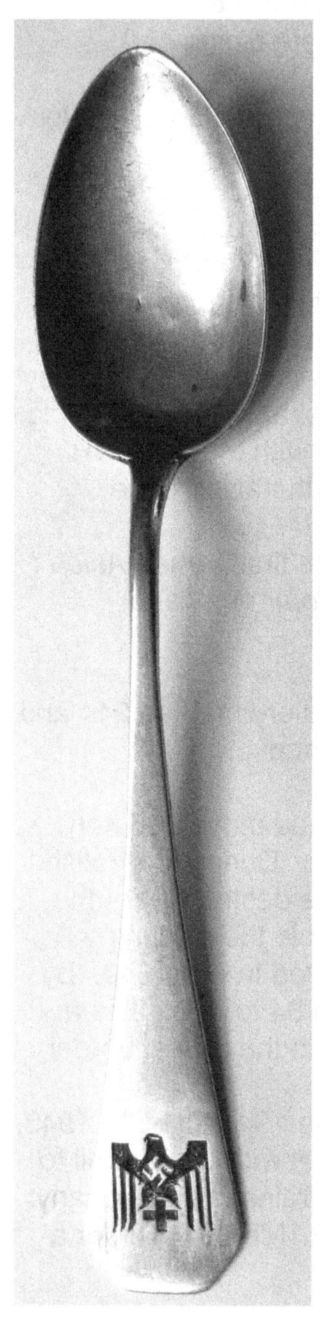

OG-61
L = 136 mm / 5 6/16”

OG-61 DRK - Deutsches Rotes Kreuz
(German Red Cross)

Teaspoon: The spoon carries the DRK logo on the obverse and maker marked on the reverse: CB for C. Backhausen, Tangermuede, 800 and RM.

Originally a voluntary civil assistance organization started in 1864. The NSDAP recognized the DRK in December 1937 and took control in 1938. During the Third Reich, the DRK emblem had a black eagle with elongated down swept wings and a white, mobile swastika superimposed on its breast, clutching a red Balkan cross (known in English as a Greek cross - a cross with straight lines) in its talons while the standard international red cross flag was also still utilized to denote first aid and medical locations.

DRK Trivia - typical of Nazi protocol, daggers were a standard item of dress. Due to its noncombatant status, the DRK had to conform to the international Geneva convention which directed that members not carry any weapons, including edged weapons. As a result, the DRK 'Subordinates Hewer', introduced in 1938, was designed with a squared blunt tip and blunt scabbard to preclude its classification as a weapon and allowed its wear in the field. The DRK Leaders dagger, with a pointed tip and pointed scabbard, was classified as a weapon and could only be worn as a dress dagger, when not in the field.

Note: The DRK was headed by **SS**-Obergruppenfuhrer Prof. Dr. Ernst-Robert Grawitz.

OG-62
L = 149 mm / 5 14/16”

OG-62 National-Socialistische Deutsche Studenten Bund - NSDStB

(National Socialist Student Federation)

Teaspoon: This teaspoon carries the Studentenbund Ehrenzeichen (Student Federation Decoration) on the obverse The reverse carries distributor 'GARTEN', unknown maker mark, 800, RM. This decoration has no eagle . The NSDStB emblem has the eagle clasping their elongated swastika as per the Sport Shirt Patch photo below. There is also a stylized initial H on the reverse as per below.

All German students at the universities were required to belong to the Studentenschaft (Student Corps). The Student Corps was responsible for making the students conscious of their duties to the Nazis State and was obliged to promote enrollment in the SA and labor service. Physical training of students was the responsibility of the SA. Political education was the responsibility of the National-Socialistische Deutsche Studentenbund (NSDStB), (National Socialist German Student Bund) and was the Nazi "elite" of the student body and responsible for the leadership of the university students, and all leaders of the Student Corps were appointed from its membership. The Nazi Student Bund was solely responsible for the entire ideological and political education of the students.

OG-63
L = 142 mm / 5 5/8”

OG-63 National Socialist Student Federation
(National-Socialistische Deutsche Studenten Bund) - NSDStB

Teaspoon: This teaspoon's obverse carries a hand engraved simplest / minimalist Studentenbund logo (Student Federation logo). Reverse Maker marked: Vereinigte Silberwarenfabriken, Dusseldorf, founded 1899, '800', RM.

The NSDStB was originally formed as a semiautonomous National Socialist organization in 1926 at Munich University, infiltrating the majority of institutions including Universities, Technical Colleges, Trade Schools and Business Colleges by 1930 and was under full control of the Nazi party by 1934.

In 1933 there were only 6,300 male and 750 female members. With the Nazi power take over, membership was restricted to 5 percent of the student body, accepting only the cream of the crop of pupils. All had to be members of the NSDAP, SA, SS, NSKK or HJ. This select group was viewed as 'the intellectual SS'.

After 1939, most male members joined either the Wehmacht or the SS. By 1943 women accounted for 35% of the student population.

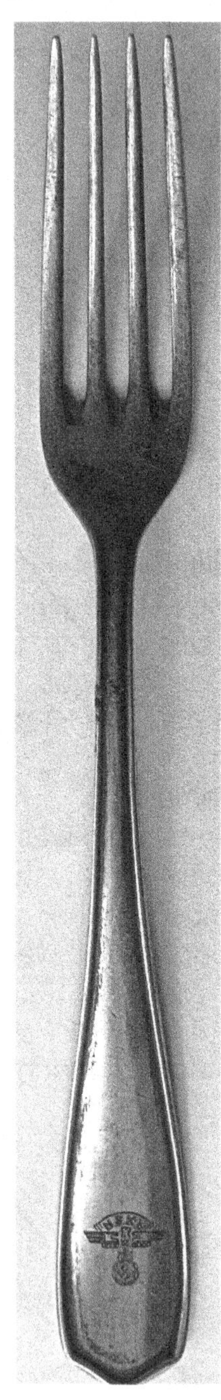

OG-64
L = 178 mm / 7”

OG-64 NSKK - Nationasozialistisches Kraftfahrkorps
(National Socialist Motor Corps)

Table fork: Obverse carries the NSKK logo. Reverse with maker mark of a stylized 'A' over 'H', followed by HANS for Albert Hans, Zurich, Switzerland and 90-30'.
The National Socialist Motor Corps, (NSKK), began on 1 Apr 1930 when the Nationalsozialistisches Automobil Korps (NSAK) was founded on the order of Martin Bormann as a paramilitary organization of the Nazi Party. It was to organize all NSDAP members who owned a car or motorcycle into a single nation-wide unit. SA-Gruppenführer Adolf Hühnlein was made commander of the NSAK and suggested renaming it NSKK and this was accepted by SA-leader Ernst Röhm who was in the process of reorganizing the SA. When Adolf Hitler became chancellor in 1933 the NSKK expanded rapidly to 30,000 members. After Röhm and the SA-leadership were murdered during the Night of Long Knives (30 June 1934) the Motor-SA became a part of the NSKK and it was made an independent organization. The NSKK took over all German motor clubs Sep 1933 and expanded to 350,000 members. After Austria was made a part of Germany (Mar 1938) the NSKK expanded to over 500,000 members. With the outbreak of World War II in 1939, the National Socialist Motor Corps became a target of the Wehrmacht for recruitment, since NSKK members possessed knowledge of motorized transport, whereas the bulk of the Wehrmacht relied on horses. Most NSKK members thereafter joined the regular military, serving in the transport corps of the various service branches. In 1945, the NSKK was disbanded and declared a "condemned organization" (although not a criminal one) at the Nuremberg Trials . This was due in part to the NSKK's origins in the SA and its doctrine of racial superiority required from its members.

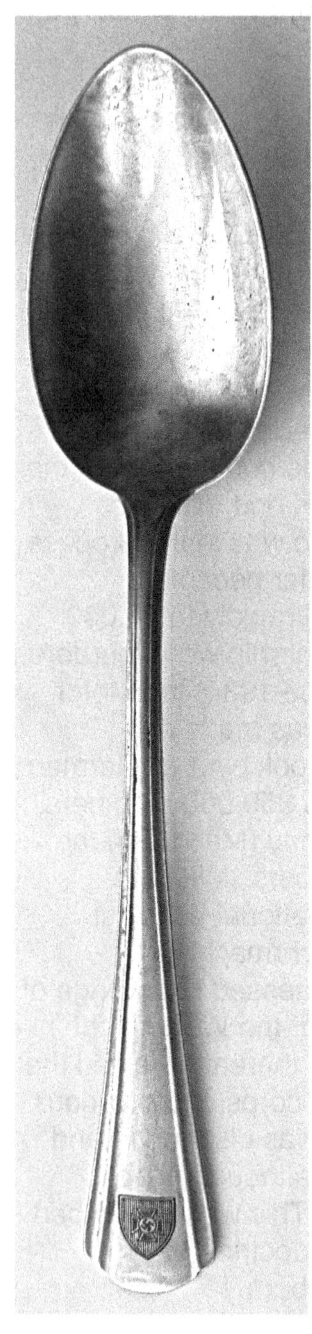

OG-65
L = 217 mm / 8 9/16”

OG-65 NS-Kriegsopferversorgung

NSKOV

(National Socialist War Victim's Welfare Service)

Soupspoon: The obverse carries the NSKOV shield decoration composed of a black mobile swastika within a circle and the circle set against a black iron cross all within a shield. The reverse carries the maker mark of Koch & Bergfeld, Bremen, founded 1829, 800, RM.

The NSKOV (National Socialist War Victim's Welfare Service or War Disabled Support Organization) was established in 1930 and institutionalized in 1934 as a social welfare organization to assist NSDAP party members who had become disabled as a result of First World War injuries.

Although an NSDAP affiliated charity, it maintained a degree of independence in assets and organizational issues. Together with the National Peoples Welfare (NSV) it was a charitable organization and supported health programs from its establishment till 1945.

By Law No. 5 (The Denazification Decree) of the American Military Government dated 31 May 1945, the NAZI Party with all its institutions and organizations were disbanded.

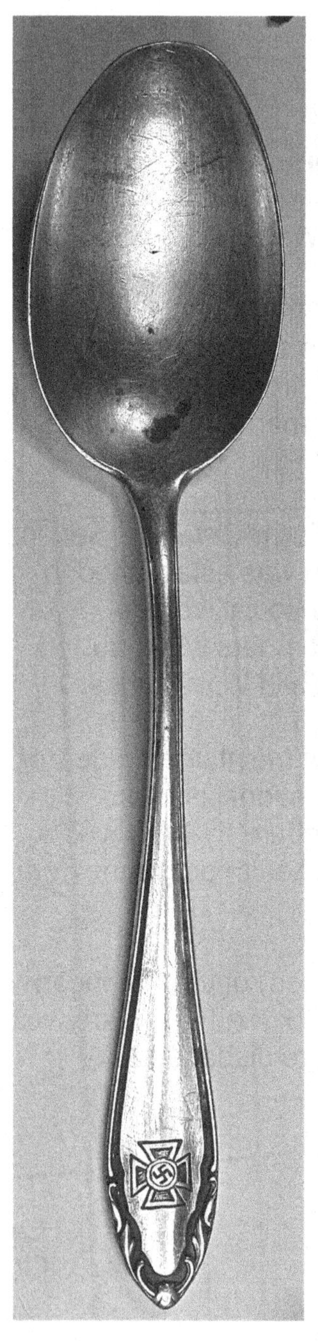

OG-66
L = 139 mm / 5 1/2"

OG-66 NS-Kriegsopferversorgung
NSKOV
(National Socialist War Victim's Welfare Service)

Teaspoon: The obverse carries the basic NSKOV decoration composed of a black mobile swastika within a circle and the circle set against a black iron cross. Reverse carries the maker's mark of capital 'E" in a lozenge for Julius Eispert, Breslau, 800 and RM.

The Nationalsozialistische Kriegsopferversorgung (NSKOV), meaning "National Socialist War Victim's Care" was a social welfare organization for seriously wounded veterans as well as frontline fighters of World War I. The NSKOV was established in 1934 and was affiliated to the NSDAP.

After Nazi Germany's defeat in World War II, the American Military Government issued a special law outlawing the Nazi party and all of its branches. Known as "Law number five", this Denazification decree disbanded the NSKOV, like all organizations linked to the Nazi Party. The organizations taking care of the welfare for World War I veterans had to be established anew during the postwar reconstruction of both West Germany and the DDR.

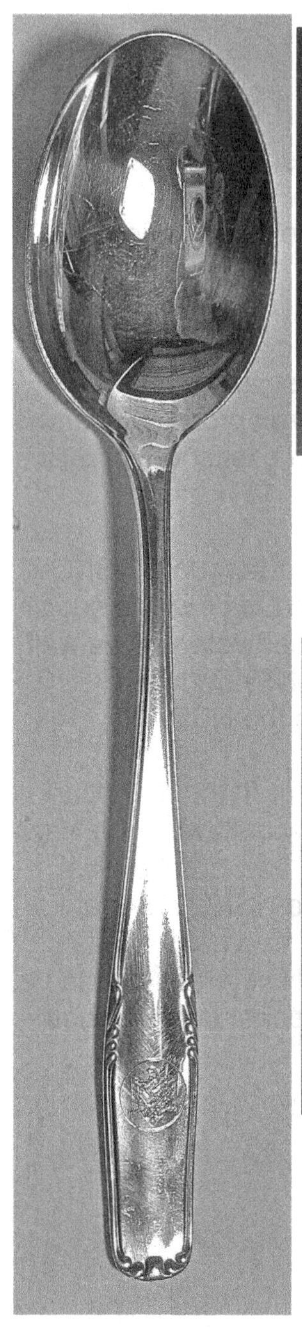

OG-67
L = 192 mm / 7 9/16”

OG-67 **NSRL - NS Reichsbund für Leibesübungen**
(National-Socialist State-league for Physical-fitness)

Spoon: Obverse carries the NSRL logo, Reverse with Wellner, Patent, 90 plate, silver gram weight 4.

Known as Deutscher Reichsbund für Leibesübungen (DRL) until 1938, the NSRL was the umbrella organization for sports during the 3rd Reich. In March 1933, after the Enabling Act, which legally gave Hitler dictatorial control of Germany, all sports organizations connected to the Social Democratic Party, the Communist Party, as well as all churches, were banned. In April 1933, the NSRL was led by Reichssportführer, Hans von Tschammer und Osten (1933–1943) who after 1934 also presided over the German National Olympic Committee. The German Eagle with the swastika on the chest, worn as a badge by the athletes of the 3rd Reich Olympic Team became the official symbol of the Nazi Sports Body; "the swastika on the eagle's chest displays ... the ideology of the DRL" On March 17, 1937, all German athletes were called by Hans von Tschammer und Osten to join the Hitler Youth, his goal to use sports "to improve the morale and productivity of German workers." Sporting skills were made a criterion for school graduation as well as a necessary qualification for certain jobs and admission to universities. The aims of the promotion of sports in the Third Reich included hardening the spirit of every German as well as making German citizens feel that they were part of a wider national purpose. This was in line with the ideals of Friedrich Ludwig Jahn the "Father of Physical Exercises", who connected the steeling of one's own body to a healthy spirit and promoted the idea of a unified, strong Germany. A more controversial aim was the demonstration of Aryan Physical Superiority. Later leaders were, Arno Breitmeyer(1943–1944) and Karl Ritter von Halt (1944–1945).

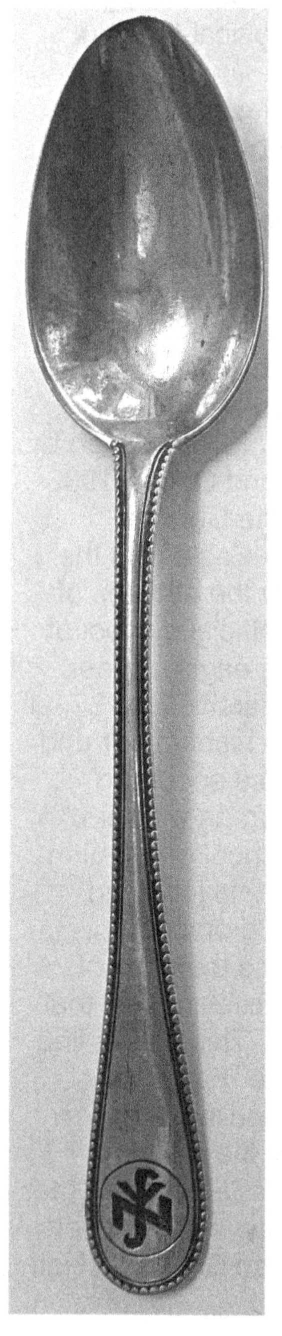

OG-68
L = 144 mm / 5 11/16”

OG-68 National Sozialistische Volkswohlfahrt (NSV)
(National Socialist People's Welfare)

Teaspoon: Obverse carries the NSV Logo. Reverse with distributor C.A. Krall, makers mark M.H.Wilkens, Bremen-Hemelingen, founded 1810, still active, 800 RM.

The NSV was established on 3 May 1933, shortly after the NSDAP took power and was the umbrella organization for a range of social and welfare programs, at first helping poor families with food and fuel, gradually shifting to performing services such as organizing and managing day care centers, caring for children, assistance to youth and pregnant women, and various family health and nutrition programs. The NSV was financed through voluntary contributions such as the Nazi Winter Support Program (Winterhilfswerk). With the advent of the War, the program was massively expanded, so that the régime deemed it worthy to be called the "greatest social institution in the world." One method of expansion was to absorb, or in NSDAP parlance 'coordinate' already existing but non-Nazi charity organizations such as church run day care centers. The NSV became the principal national effort devoted to children and youth welfare efforts which increased membership from 1 million in 1938 to 11 million making it the second largest Nazi group organization by 1939, second only to the German Labor Front.

Notes: 1. A major slogan at NSV day care centers was "Hände falten, Köpfchen senken - immer an Adolf Hitler denken "-- Hands folded, head lowered - always of Adolf Hitler thinking"
2. Winter Support Program slogan: "None shall starve nor freeze".

Trivia: The head of NSV was **SS**-Gruppenfuhrer Erich Hildgenfeldt who was also in-charge of the Winterhilswerk.

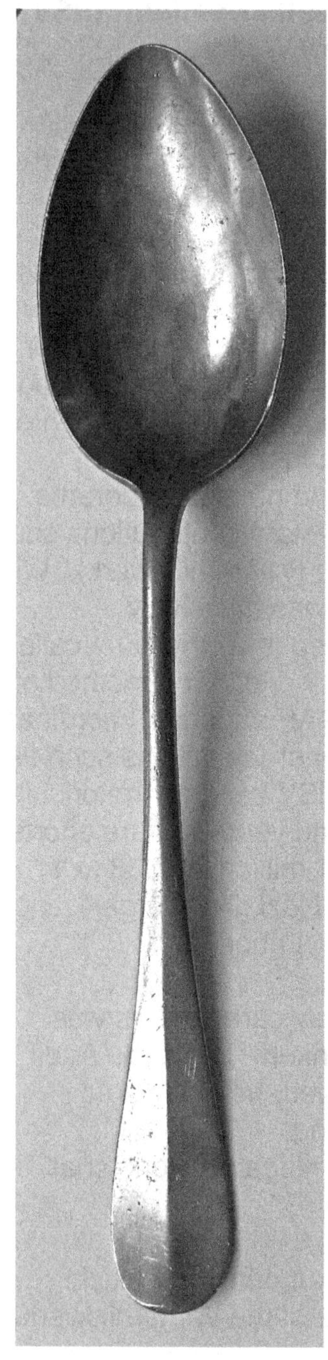

OG-69
L = 217 mm / 8 9/16"

OG-69 RAD - Reichs Arbeitsdienst
(National Labor-Service)

Tablespoon: This Mess Hall tablespoon (Essloeffel). Marked on the reverse side with "REICHSARBEITSDIENST" "1936". Manufactured by Duralit and of stainless steel (Rostfrei).

RAD basis dates back to 1929's formation of AAD "Anhalt Arbeitsdienst" (Anhalt Labor-Service) and the FAD-B, "Freiwillingen Arbeitsdienst-Bayern" (Volunteer Labor-Service [of] Bavaria). In 1933, the NSDAP consolidated labor organizations into the NSAD, "Nationalsozialist Arbietsdienst" (National-Socialist Labor-Service); a national labor service. In June 1935, NSAD was re-designated RAD, in July RAD service became compulsory for both young men (prior to military service) and women, with all German citizens between 19 and 25 required to enlist for a 6 month term and military conscripts to serve 9 months. Typical work projects were road construction and farm labor.

The RAD motto: ArbeitAdelt - Work Ennobles.

OG-70
L = 215 mm / 8 1/2”

OG-70 RAD - Reichs Arbeitsdienst
(National Labor-Service)

Fork, Mess Hall (Kantine Gabel): Obverse is clear with a raised central spine. Reverse carries the RAD symbol of a shovel and 'Art Krupp"NICAD' 'Berndorf' '1941'. Note: "Art" was supposedly dropped in 1938 do to his death.

Reichsarbeitsdienst 'RAD' (National Labor Service) was under the Deutsche Arbeitsfront, 'DAF' (German Labor Service). In 1931, to combat German unemployment, a voluntary work service was formed. When Hitler was made Chancellor 1933 he soon appointed Konstantin Hierl as Secretary of State for the Labor Service, the control of which at this time was transferred from the states to the central government. The RAD was formally founded on 26 June 1935 making service in the RAD compulsory. RAD's mission was to provide labor for public projects for both civil and military projects mainly for reclaiming land for farming, helping with the harvests and construction of roads, but also for various emergency relief projects. In 1939, the RAD lost over half of its men to the armed forces. During the war, RAD was classified as a reserve troop, an auxiliary to the Wehrmacht, not actually in the armed forces but close enough to be protected by the Geneva convention. Major activities were focused on the supply to the front lines of food and ammunitions, repairing roads, construction and repair of Luftwaffe airfields. Eventually, RAD personnel were drawn into active military service, especially on the East front where by the wars end, there were eight major RAD front line units in service.

Motto: Working men are healthy, happy, self-conscious work soldiers.

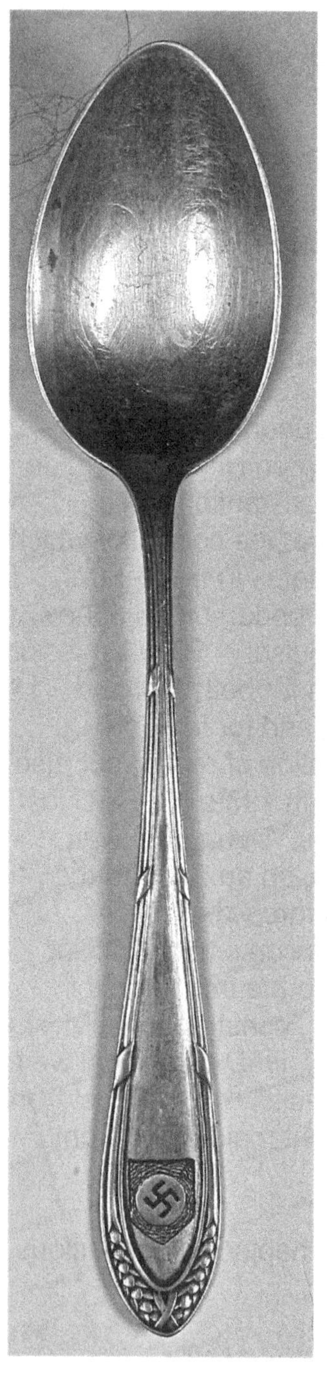

OG-71
L = 138 mm / 5 7/16”

OG-71 RAD Reichsarbeitsdienst (German Labor Service)

Teaspoon: Thanks to *Treasures of the Third Reich*'s Dan Kelley for the following analysis of the obverse: "Note on your spoon handle the shape of a shovel and the wheat stalks wrapping around the edge of the spoon, this has all of the imagery of the RAD or Reichs Arbeitsdienst; the German Workers Service." The reverse marked 800, Reichsmark and maker mark of Gebruder Koberlin, Dobeln, founded 1828.

With the war, the RAD was classed as Wehrmachtgefolge (lit. Armed Forces Auxiliaries). Auxiliary forces with this status, while not a part of the Armed Forces themselves, provided such vital support that they were given protection by the Geneva Convention. Some, including the RAD, were militarized.

During the early war's Norwegian and Western campaigns, hundreds of RAD units were engaged in supplying frontline troops with food and ammunition, repairing damaged roads and constructing and repairing airstrips. Throughout the course of the war, the RAD was involved in many projects. The RAD units constructed coastal fortifications (many RAD men worked on the Atlantic Wall), laid minefields, staffed fortifications, and even helped guard vital locations and prisoners.

The role of the RAD was not limited to combat support functions. Hundreds of RAD units received training as anti-aircraft units and were deployed as RAD Flak Batteries. Several RAD units also performed combat on the eastern front as infantry. As the German defenses were devastated, more and more RAD men were committed to combat. During the final months of the war RAD men formed 6 major frontline units, which were involved with serious fighting.<w>

OG-72
L = 238 mm / 9 5/16"

OG-72 RAD Reichsarbeitsdienst
(German Labor Service)

Knife: Obverse clear. Reverse marked 'RAD'. maker marked H.M.Z. for Hessische Mettallwerke, Ziegenhain 37 and blade marked HMZ Rustfrei.

The Nazi's viewed manual labor as a way to break down social and class barriers and to mold the character of young people, "the dignity of manual labor". A 1935 law required all Aryan Germans (ages 17-25) to serve in the RAD for 6 months. Thus, prior to the war it was a program to create jobs for unemployed youth.

The RAD was divided into two major sections:
Reichsarbeitsdienst Männer (RAD/M) for men
Reichsarbeitdienst der weiblichen Jugend (RAD/wJ) for women.

The RAD was composed of 40 districts each called an Arbeitsgau (lit. Work District). Each of these districts was headed by an officer with headquarters staff and a Wachkompanie (Guard Company). Under each district were between six and eight Arbeitsgruppen (Workers Groups), battalion-sized formations of 1200-1800 men. These groups were divided into six company-sized RAD-Abteilung units. Each rank and file RAD man was supplied with a spade and a bicycle. The RAD symbol, an arm badge in the shape of an upward pointing shovel blade, was displayed on the upper left shoulder of all uniforms and great-coats worn by all personnel. The pre war RAD undertook the construction of the Autobahn as well as other roads, land reclamation as well as the construction of military installations. <w>

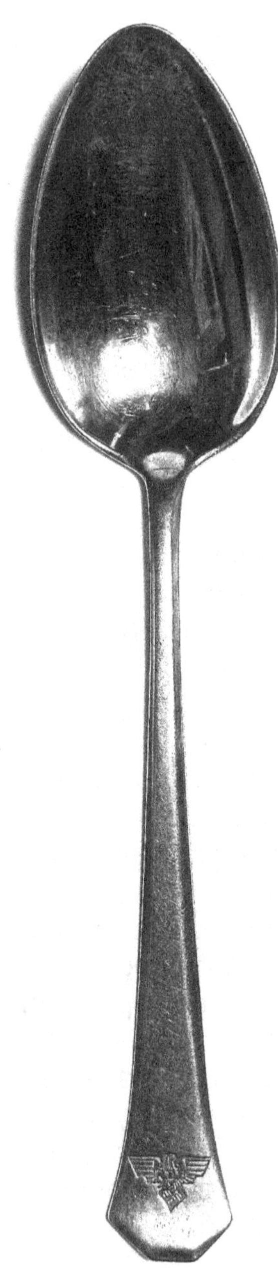

OG-73
L = 208 mm / 8 3/16"

OG-73 RDB Civil Servants Federation

Soupspoon: Obverse with RDB logo, reverse with maker mark of W over MF (Wurttembergische Metallwarenfabrik, Geislingen 1853 to the present), Patent, 90 (in a square), 30.

The Reichsbund Deutscher Beamter (RDB), meaning "Reich Federation of German Civil Servants", also known as NS-Beamterbund (National Socialist Civil Servants Federation), was the trade union for German State Officials during the Third Reich. The RDB was established as an organization affiliated to the Nazi Party in October 1933. Their eagle looks left (a Parteiadler) to symbolize its affiliation with the Nazi party. Its leader was Hermann Neef. Neef had been previously leading the RDB's predecessor organization, Deutscher Beamterbund, the German Civil Service Federation which had been founded in December 1918.

Although it was not compulsory for RDB members to be Nazi party members, most of them chose to be. In addition to the training and development of its members, the RDB ensured that German Civil Servants toed the line of the Nazi Party. Information on either this organization or its leader is virtually nonexistent.

Following Nazi Germany's defeat in World War II the American Military Government issued a special law outlawing the Nazi party and all of its branches. Known as "Law number five", this denatzification decree disbanded the National Socialist Civil Servants Federation. Like all other organizations linked to the Nazi Party. In the postwar years, it was reestablished as the German Civil Service Federation in the Federal Republic of Germany.

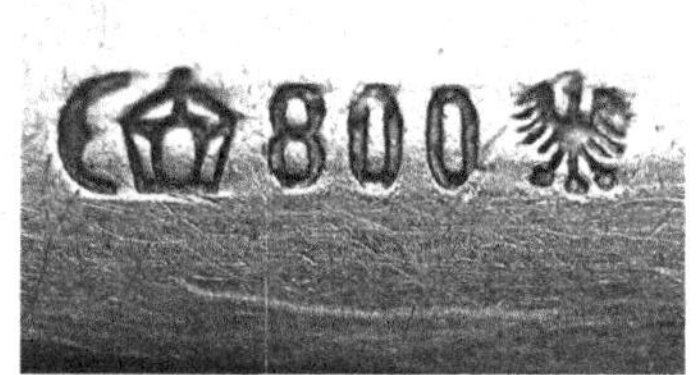

OG-74
L = 210 mm / 8 5/16”

OG-74 'R.K' - Reichs-Kanzlei
(The New Reich Chancellery)

Tablespoon: The obverse has the eagle facing to his right, legs apart on a static swastika in the double wreath with an 'R' on the left and on the right a 'K'. There is no Greek key design. The reverse carries the RM, 800 and Bruckmann eagle. This is official, silver Besteck, from the **'New' Reich Chancellery** / Neureichskanzlei. Interestingly, the Bruckmann's "RK" had both this "Straight Wing" and a "Swept Wing" (spread) eagle on serving pieces.

This was Hitler's Berlin chancellery and one of his official residences where all the most important state affairs were conducted. When present, Hitler used his formal 'AH' pattern, (see PS-1) otherwise, only the likes of Mussolini, Ciano, Chamberlain, Goring, Goebbels and Himmler used this flatware when the Fuhrer himself was not seated. Probably 100 times more rare than the 'AH' formal pattern. Considered a museum piece as the Chancellery was destroyed by fire in 1945 and afterwards occupied by the Russians so that very little survived. Shown here with a companion fork.

> RK trivia: The cost of construction was estimated to be $ 100 million equivalent to $ 1 billion today. Hitler was very impressed when Speer managed both the design and had it constructed in a few days shy of one year by coordinating multiple construction teams working in parallel. The classic of "Nazi Architecture".

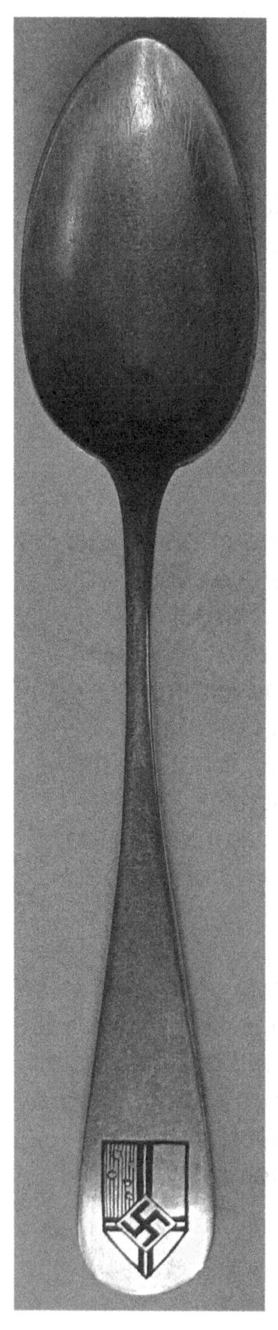

OG-75
L = 138 mm / 5 7/16"

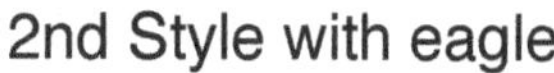
2nd Style with eagle

OG-75 RKB - Reichskolonialbund
(German Colonial League)

Teaspoon: Obverse carries the 1st style emblem of the RKB - Reichskolonialbund. On the reverse, 800, RM, and the maker mark of Gebruder Koberlin, Dobeln, Founded 1828.

The RKB was established on 13 June 1936 to "keep the population informed about the loss of the German Imperial colonies, to maintain contact with former colonial territories and to create conditions in opinion favorable to a new German African Empire." The aim was to claim back the overseas colonies that Germany had lost as a result of the Treaty of Versailles.

Since Germany had no colonies, the Reichskolonialbund was mainly engaged in mostly virulent political agitation, primarily in Germany. This in an effort to keep open the "Koloniale Frage" (Colonial Question).

The League had its own youth organization, the Kolonialjugend which was incorporated as a wing of the Hitler Youth. With WWII, the League began to decline as the Nazi State was focused on other higher priorities. In the early 1940's, the 2nd style emblem was adopted with an eagle (looking left) perched in the top of the shield.

In 1943, Reichsleiter Martin Bormann pressed for the dissolution of the League on the grounds of "kriegsunwichtiger Tatigkeit" (activity irrelevant to the war). The Reichskolonialbund was swiftly disbanded by virtue of a decree of the Fuhrer in 1943.

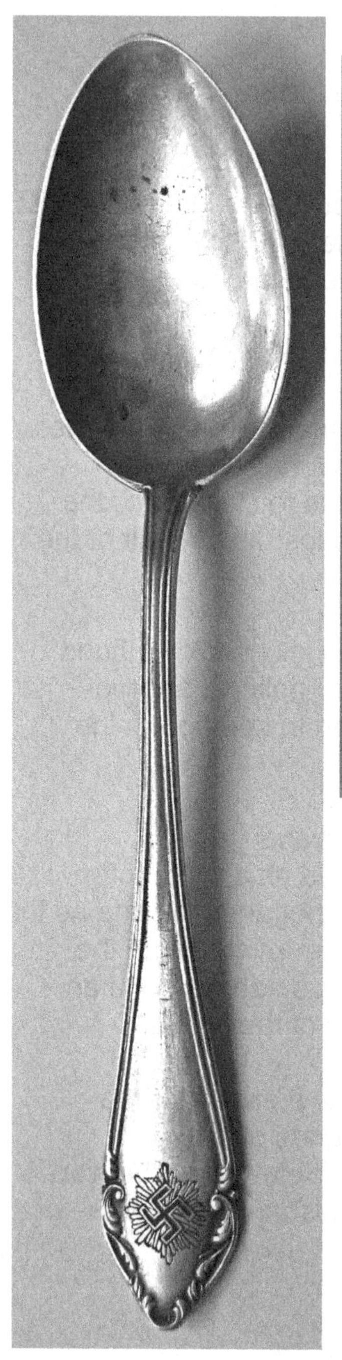

OG-76
L = 142 mm / 5 10/16

OG-76 Reichs Luftschutzbund
(National Air Protection League)

Teaspoon: The obverse carries the decoration of a mobile swastika in an ornate 48 point white star burst background as illustrated in Brian Davis's *'Badges & Insignia of the Third Reich',* plate 34, item #16 and is identified as the second pattern used by the RLB from 1938. Maker marked: Vereinigte Silberwarenfabriken, Dusseldorf, founded 1899, '800', RM.

Reichs Luftschutzbund (National Air Protection League / State Air protection Federation) was originally formed in late 1932, The Deutscher Luftschutzverband (German Air Protection League) was a voluntary organization designed to provide civil air raid protection in large civilian centers. In 1933 it was placed under the supervision of Hermann Goering's Reichsluftfahrt Ministerium (National Air Ministry). On 29 April 1933 the DLB was re-designated the Reichs Luftschutz Bund (National Air Raid Protection League) or RLB, now responsible for all aspects of civil air raid defense. Voluntary up to June 1935 - when obligatory service was established. By 1939, more than 15 million men had joined.

Note: The 1st pattern RLB emblem (circa 1933-38) was a 48 point white star burst pattern with stylized "RLB" initials to the center positioned above a small mobile swastika. In October 1938 the RLB emblem was redesigned and replaced the RLB letters with a large swastika and was used till the end of the war.

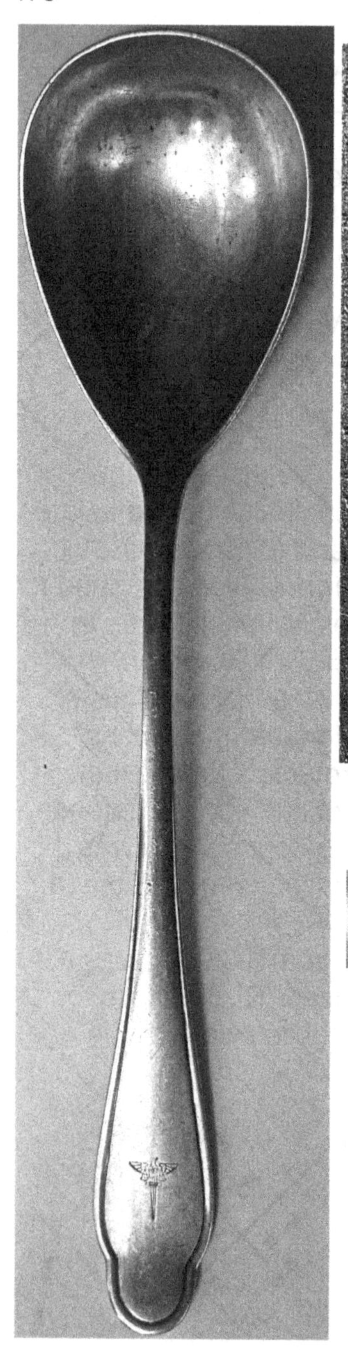

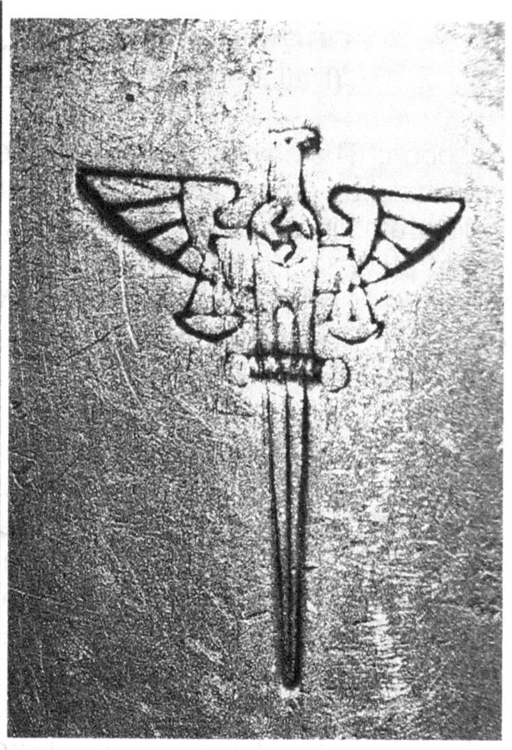

OG-77
L = 238 mm / 9 6/16”

OG-77 RMJ - Reichministerium der Justiz
(German Ministry of Justice)

Serving Spoon: Obverse carries the “Ministry of Justice” logo while the reverse is maker marked Wellner Patent 90 3.

The four Nazis who bore much of the responsibility for allowing the legal system of Germany to be taken over by Nazi ideology were Franz Schlegelburger (RMJ 1941-42), Roland Freisler. Otto Thierack (RMJ 1943-45) and Curt Rothenberger.

At the 1946 Nuremberg ‘Judges' Trial, Schlegelberger was one of the main accused, He helped create the “Enabling Act” of 21Mar1933 to strengthen the executive. Helped pass the 13July1934 retroactive law justifying the “Night of the Long Knives” murders of 30 June which effectively established Hitler above the law. In August 1934, all judges and public prosecutors were bound to Hitler by an oath of loyalty. During his time in office he authored bills such as the (Polenstrafrechtsverordnung) so called Poland Penal Law Provision under which Poles were executed for tearing down German posters. He sharply increased German death sentences and by 1943 there were 46 Capital Offense Crimes with the death penalty including: listening to foreign broadcasts, engaging in rumors, having or aiding an abortion and scavenging rubble. He was sentenced to life in prison for conspiracy to perpetrate war crimes and crimes against humanity.

Hitler’s earliest direction to the judiciary was to protect the interests of the Volk (nation) above those of the individual.

Note: Serving spoons are always the rarest of any assemblage since there is usually only one or two to a set.

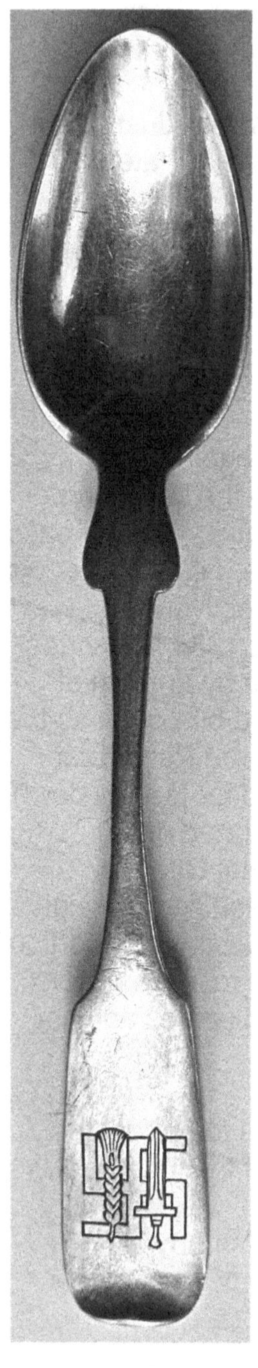

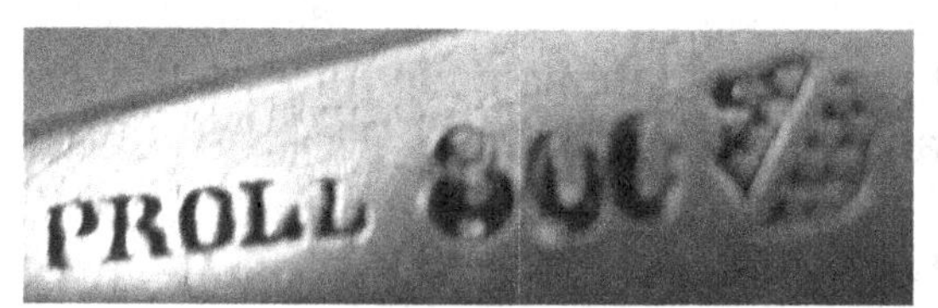

OG-78
L = 147 mm / 5 13/16”

OG-78 RNS - Reichs Nahrstand
(German Food Corporation)

Teaspoon: Obverse carries the Reichs Nahrstand logo while the reverse “Proll’ 800 & unknown maker mark.

The German Food Corporation was created on 13Sep1933 when all previous agricultural associations and organizations were disbanded. Walter Darre, (SS-Obergruppenfuhrer) the leading ideologist of Blut und Boden (Blood / Descent and Soil / Homeland) was the Reichminister of Food from 1933 to 1942. He had come to Hitler’s attention via his 1929 book: *The Peasantry as a Life Source of the Nordic Race.* Focused on the peasantry as the life source of the Nordic race, the goal was to preserve a healthy peasant stock via the compulsory organization of agriculture which took total control of the markets and prices as well as stabilized ownership of land. The farmers were organized into this grandiose sounding, nationally directed agrarian estate - the Nahrstand.

It eventually was perceived by the farmers as a bureaucratic encroachment on their autonomy and due to restrictions on land sales, forced the farmers to remain farmers. As unemployment decreased: Oct 1933 - 6.0 Million, Oct 1934 - 4.1 Million and Feb 1935 - 2.8 Million, available farm labor became a problem leading to higher labor costs and reduced production which made autarky or independence of food imports from other nations unattainable. In spite of all efforts, prior to the outbreak of WWII, agricultural self sufficiency never exceeded 80%.

Note: In 1937, although farmers were 22% of the German population they made up only 9% of the SS which was noted by the responsible authorities.

Wehrmacht Introduction
(Armed Services)

Per Wikipedia: Wehrmacht ("Defense Forces" or more literally "Defense Power") was the name of the unified armed forces of Germany from 1935 to 1945. It consisted of the Heer (Army), the Kriegsmarine (Navy) and the Luftwaffe (Air Force).

The Waffen-SS, an initially-small paramilitary section of Heinrich Himmler's Allgemeine SS that grew to nearly a million strong during World War II, was not part of the Wehrmacht, but under operational command of the OKW (Oberkommando der Wehrmacht / German Armed Forces Supreme Command ie Hitler (as of 4Feb1938) and OKH (Heer).

Albert Kesselring, (Smiling Albert) Luftwaffe Field Marshal summed up the philosophical differences between the 3rd Reich's Defense services as: "the 'republican' Army, the 'imperialist' Navy and the 'national socialist' Luftwaffe." These adjectives reveal the patent disunity of the Service's political attitudes.

These 'disparate attitudes' can be seen in their tableware via the presentation of the Nazi swastika to the traditional national eagle via the Army's middle of the road, the Navy's minimal and the Luftwaffe's excessive presentation of the swastika.

Note: The obverse of Army and Navy cutlery is typically clear whereas the Luftwaffe typically decorated the obverse.

German Military Philosophy

German military success was to be based on superior leadership, organization, supply and morale. This was believed to overcome material / manpower limitations. In *War and Peace*, Leo Tolstoy observed that the effectiveness of an army is "the product of a mass multiplied by something else; by an unknown X...the spirit of the army." A more realistic assessment made when Germany invaded Russia: "the German's came to play tennis, the game was actually rugby".

German WWII Military Service and Casualties

The numbers below were reliably acquired up till November 1944. From that date on, the reporting systems tended to break down. In general terms, it is known that 80 percent of German military deaths took place in the last 2 years of the war. That three quarters occurred on the East front where, as an example, 180,310 died in January 1943 at Stalingrad in that one month alone. In an effort to soften the blow of deaths reported from the East front, emphasis was placed on reporting 'MIA' (missing in action) when possible.

	Served	KIA & MIA	%
Heer / Army	13.6 M	4.2 M	31
Luftwaffe	2.5 M	.433M	17.3
Kriegsmarine	1.2 M	.138M	11.5
W-SS	.9 M	.314M	34.9

Note: Nearly 2 million foreigners served in the German fighting forces.

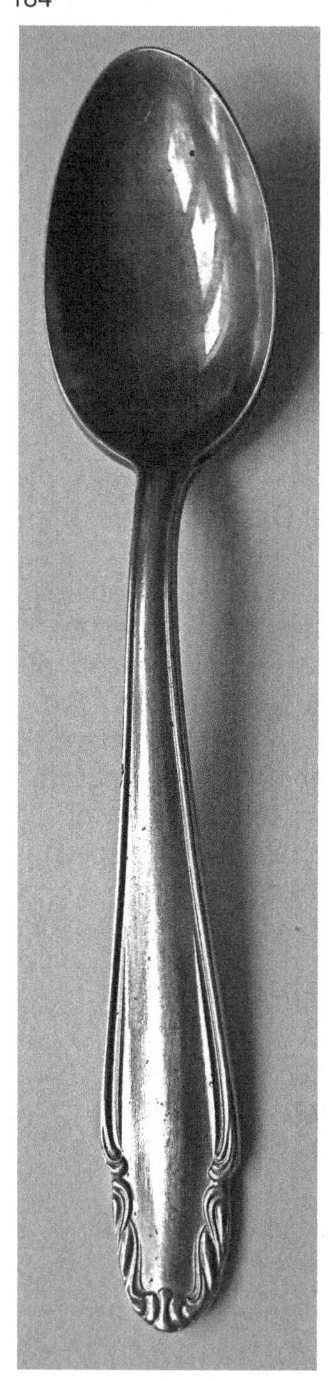

W-79
L = 141 mm / 5 9/16"

W-79 Wehrmacht Adler (Eagle)

Teaspoon: The eagle (Reichsadler) on this teaspoon's reverse faces to its right (a State organization) over '1942'. The Manufacturer's figure is for Wilhelm Pfeiffer & Co., Solingen. 'Mangasil', a proprietary stainless steel material?

The National Emblem - (Hoheitsabzeichen) was the eagle and swastika of the NSDAP and later Nazi Germany.

Regarding the German Eagle: Per Wikipedia, "The Nazi party used the traditional German eagle, standing atop a swastika inside a wreath of oak leaves, When the eagle is looking to its left shoulder, it symbolizes the Nazi party and was called the Parteiadler. In contrast, when the eagle is looking to its right shoulder, it symbolizes the country / state / military (Reich) and was called the Reichsadler." After the Nazi party came to power in Germany, they forced the replacement of the traditional version of the German eagle with their modified party symbol highlighting the swastika throughout the country and all its institutions.

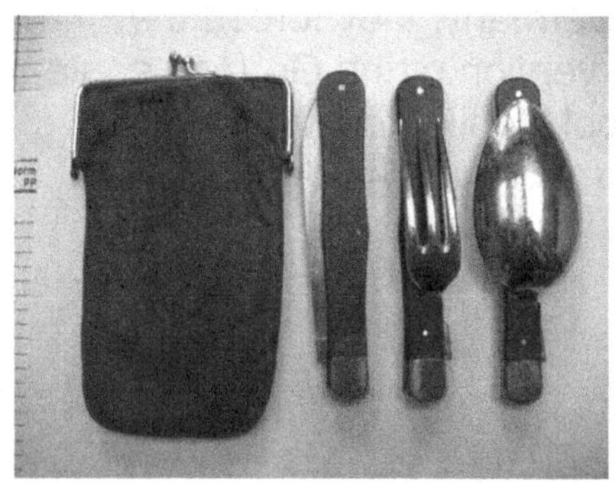

W-80

W-80 OFFICER'S FIELD BESTECK

This matched set of a foldable knife, fork and spoon is from J. A. Henckels and is typical of those used by German Army officers when in the field. The knife is maker marked with the Henckels trademarked 'two stick figures' for the Zwillingswerk facility and impressed with "J.A.Henckels" over "SOLINGEN". When folded, the three pieces fit into a companion buckskin lined leather pouch that snaps shut.

Spoon folded: 112 mm / 4 3/8"
Spoon open: 198 mm / 7 3/4"

Note: Officers Field Besteck: German officers in the field have traditionally shared the enlisted men's food and eaten with the troops. There are many photos of Hitler in the field with the troops and eating with them whereas the British and US have traditionally separated officers from the enlisted men with officers eating their own subsidized, superior rations in private.

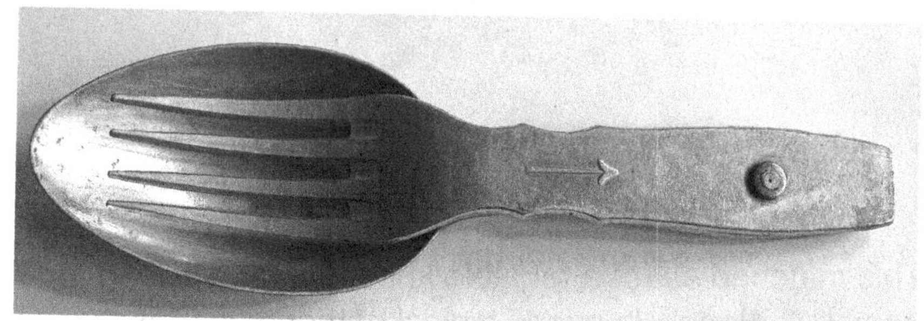

W-81

W-81 Army Field Issue Folding Spoon / Fork Combination Cutlery Set (Essbesteck)

This is the standard issue, aluminum construction, slip-joint, folding tablespoon and four tine fork combination (spork) and in German a (goffel) gabel und loeffel. On the reverse of the spoon handle maker unknown, initials (WSuCL) in a rectangular border. Owners initials, “LB” scratched on the front of the fork between the arrow and the pivotal rivet.

Folded length is 6 inches while opened length is 9 1/2 inches.

Major Early Campaigns

Poland: Invaded 1 Sep 39, ends 6 Oct 39 German losses: 13,111 KIA / MIA and 27,278 WIA vs 800,000 Poles KIA or captured.

Western Campaign begins 10 May 1940, ends 22 June 40 German losses: 27,074 KIA, MIA 18,383 and WIA 111,034. Allies lost 90,000 KIA, 200,000 WIA, 1.9 M captured or MIA.

W-82

W-82 Field Issue Cutlery Set (essbesteck)

The set is composed of a knife (195 mm / 7 3/4"), a four tined fork (193 mm / 7 5/8")and a tablespoon(195 mm / 7 3/4"), each of which slide into the slotted handle of a can opener (155 mm / 6 1/8"). The opener is stamped on its solid side with a spread-winged eagle clutching a wreathed mobile swastika in its talons, below which is stamped "FBCM43" all other components are similarly marked with the exception of the unmarked knife. An indentation is along the side of the knife handle which mates with a right angled hook to the top of the can opener. Made in 1943, the basic material is steel with a coating, possibly zinc. The coating has broken down in places and corrosion has occurred. The 1942 models were still made of stainless steel.

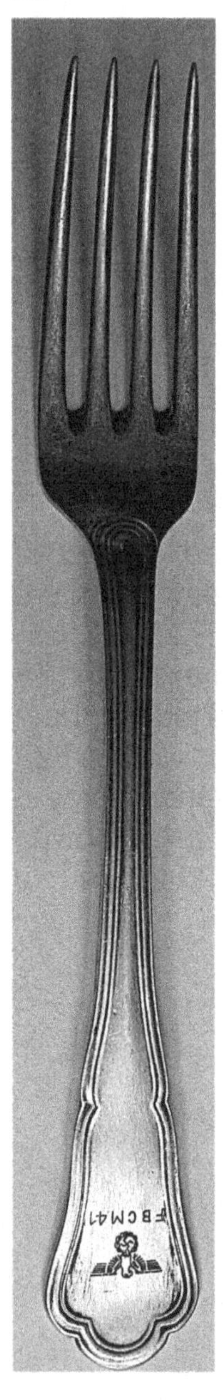

W-83
L = 208 mm / 8 3/16 “

W-83 Heer 'FBCM' MYSTERY Solved

Table Fork: Obverse carries the German eagle looking to his right symbolizing the country / state / military and as such was called the Reichsadler. FBCM is the most often found maker's mark on Army cutlery. The pieces can be marked on either the obverse and the reverse with 'FBCM' and typically the year '41'.

In my earlier book, *A Guide to 3rd Reich Cutlery,* the maker identification was one of the 3 mystery items.

I recently saw the following add:

"ARMY FIELD FOUR PIECES SET CUTLERY
Four pieces stainless steel set.
Fork, spoon and can opener have same handle marked manufacturer's initials and date, FBCM 43 and stamped national eagle.
Knife blade marked: F R BURBERG & CO.A-G.
METTMANN - SOLINGEN ROSTFREI"

Solingen is located within the district of Mettmann in North Rhine-Westphalia and the Solingen area still produces some 70% of German knives.

Reference W-82's FBCM 43 knife that does not carry the full manufacturers information and I missed buying the one that does.

FBCM = F. Burberg & Co. Mettmann

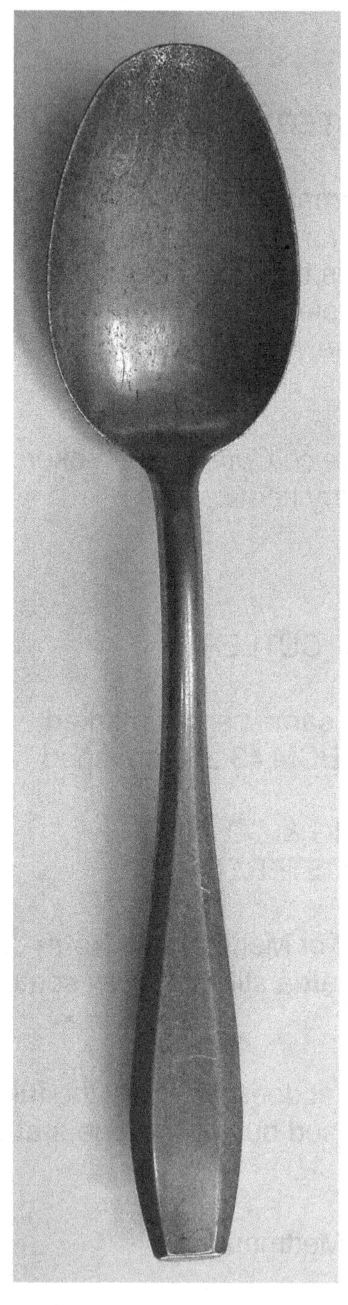

W-84
L = 212 mm / 8 6/16”

W-84 HEER (Army)

Mess Hall Tablespoon: (Kantine Essloeffel) Roughly 8 3/8" long, natural aluminum alloy. Handle obverse is flat. The reverse of the handle is well marked with an impressed national eagle with outstretched wings and the manufacturers initials "W.S.M." and dated "42".

Fact: Of the 13,600,000+ that served in the German army from 1939 to 1945, some 4,200,000+ were killed or missing in action. Total German losses in the Eastern Campaign from 1941 to 1944 alone were 1,400,000+ killed in action with an additional 1 million missing in action.

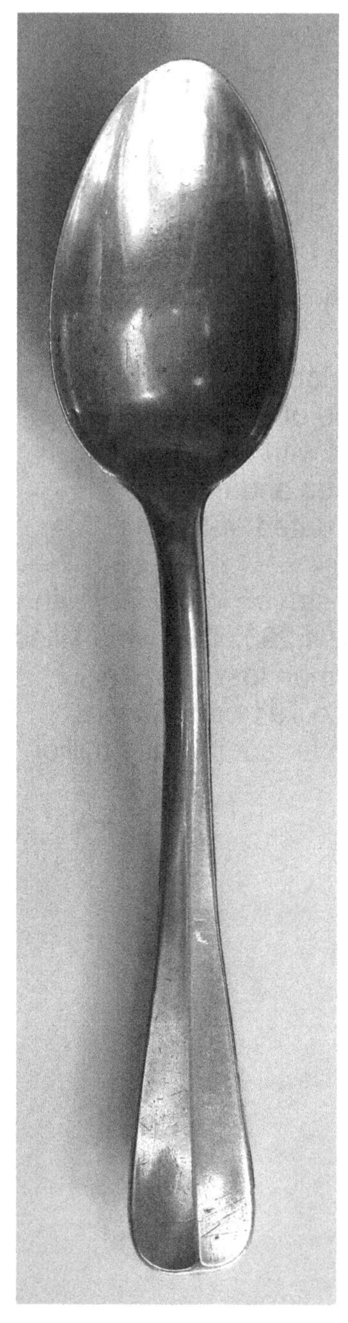

W-85
L = 210 mm / 8 1/4”

W-85 HEER

Mess Hall Tablespoon: Aluminum with raised central rib on obverse. Reverse handle maker marked “E100” and “WH” indicating Wehrmacht (Armed Forces), Heer, (Army). Plus an owner's? initial “W” scratched on reverse.

> Trivia: To appreciate the pre 1943 logistics of a German Infantry Division, per “*The German Infantry Handbook*” by Alex Bucher - the 12th Infantry Division in the Eastern campaign from 22 June to 31 Dec 1941, a strengthened division of 20,000 men and 5,500 horses consumed 8,110 tons of food and fodder plus 15,100,000 cigarettes, 98,000 liters of alcohol, 6,516 kilo of chocolate etc. The eastern campaign started with 99 Infantry Divisions and quickly built up to 119!

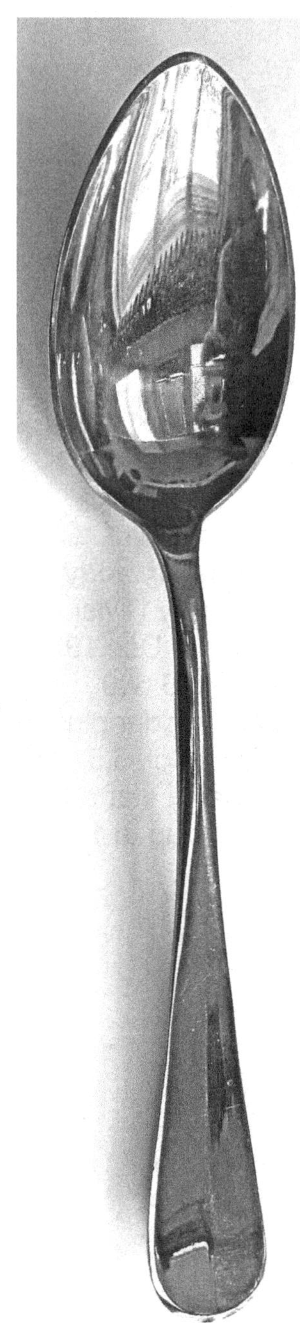

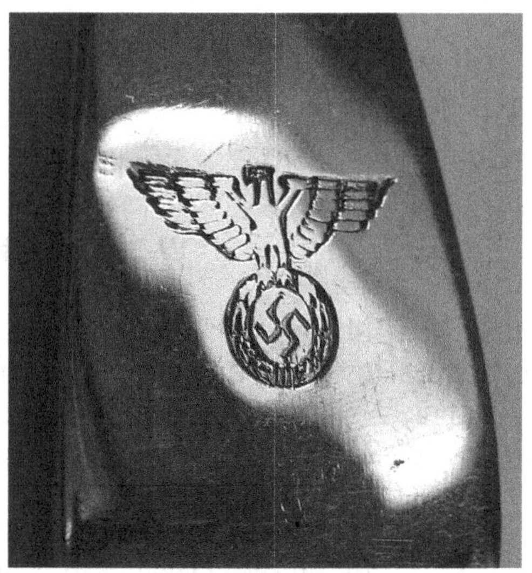

W-86
L = 209 mm / 8 1/4”

W-86 HEER

Tablespoon: Mil Issue, aluminum 8 1/4" long. The obverse of the handle has a raised central rib while the reverse carries a manufacturers mark "LGK&F" over 39 and the eagle.

Trivia: Due to manpower shortages and a scarcity of reserves, by the Spring of 1942, German forces in the East had 'absorbed' some 800,000 former Red Army soldiers, including an estimated 6,000 officers and former commissars. Ultimately, more than one million former Red Army soldiers would serve with the Germans. These Soviet citizens that volunteered to be unofficially employed as manual laborers and/or as German Army combat reinforcements were called HiWis for Hilfswillige "volunteer auxiliary" and within the operational military totaled some 250,000 in 1943 and were officially permitted to the level of 15% of divisional strength. In the East: as of Oct 1943 the German Infantry Division of 16,860 was reduced to 11,317 Germans and 1,455 HiWi's, a reduction of 28%. In Dec 1944 a further reduction was made to 11,211 Germans and 698 HiWi's. The HIWI's suffered some 215,000 killed for a death rate of over 25%.

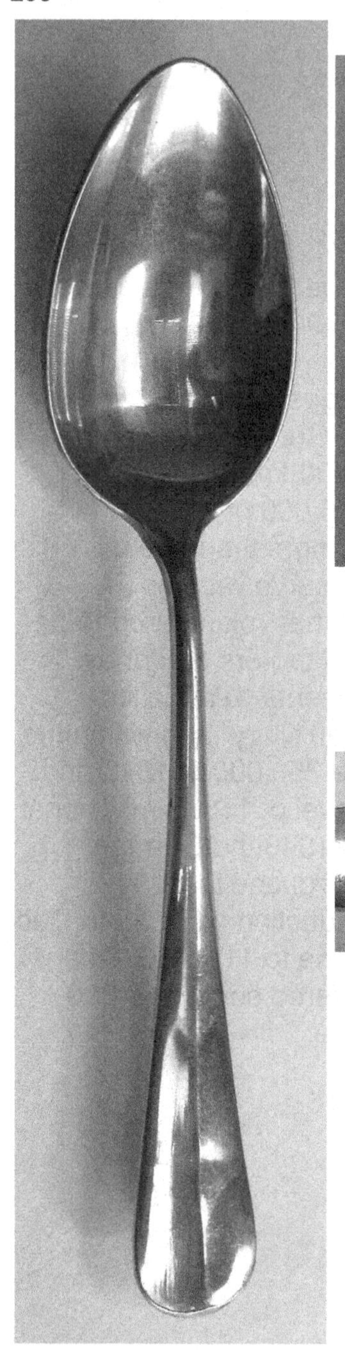

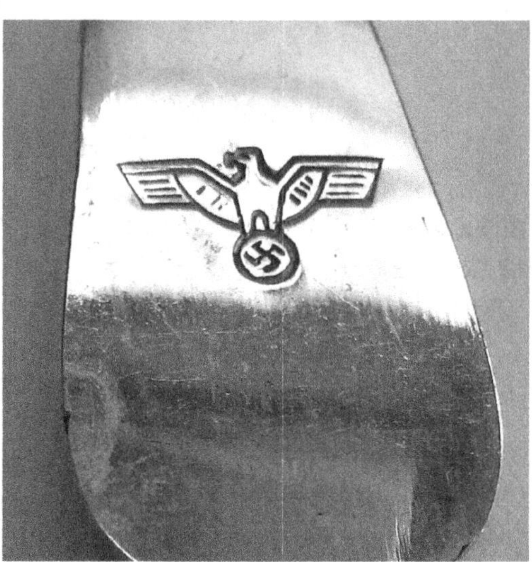

W-87
L = 139 mm / 5 1/2”

W-87 HEER

Demitasse spoon: Alloy with a central raised spine on the obverse. Reverse maker marked "B.A.F. N. for Bayerische Alpaccawarenfabrik AG, Neu-Ulm a. Donau, 39" with eagle facing right on a mobile swastika..

Fact: WWII Campaigns length: Poland 27 Days, Denmark 1 Day, Norway 23 Days, Holland 5 Days, Belgium 18 Day, France 39 Days, Yugoslavia 12 Days, Greece 21 Days.

Blitzkrieg? German Infantry Divisions typically relied on their 5,000+ horses to supply 80% of their motive power. Each horse required 30,000 calories a day and consumed 22 pounds of fodder, or 55 tons of fodder daily per division. For the Polish campaign, the 197,000 horses required 135 railway trucks of fodder daily. On the East front, some 1,000 horses were lost daily during the last 2 years of the war. Of the 3 million horses and mules enlisted by the German Army between 1939 and 1945, more than 1.75 million perished. These numbers do not include the smaller Panje horses of the East which were used in large numbers but were not officially recognized by the military command system.

In Leon Degrelle's book, '*Campaign in Russia*' he describes an incident in 1942 in the Poltava area where two Cossack cavalry divisions surrendered but only after killing their 12,000 horses so as not to let them fall into German hands.

W-88
L = 142 mm / 5 10/16”

W-88 HEER?

Teaspoon: ‘1944’ over ‘Eagle’ looking to his left over **D.H.** (Deutsches Heer - German Army). Marked with RM, 800, ‘N’ for Bayer, Silberbestedkfabrik, Krumbach i, Bayern.

Although marked with the D.H., the eagle is a Partei eagle (looking left), that, with the 1944 date would indicate some type of award or commemorative, possibly to an Army veteran working in the Partei organization. Dated cutlery tends to disappear by 1943 when "Advancing on All Fronts" was a bitter memory as Germany had suffered some 1,686,000 casualties the year before.

Also in 1943, with the fall of Italy, the Germans appropriated large stockpiles of Italian clothing materials including field grey Italian material. As a result, the 1943 winter German army overcoats were mostly made from that Italian field grey material.

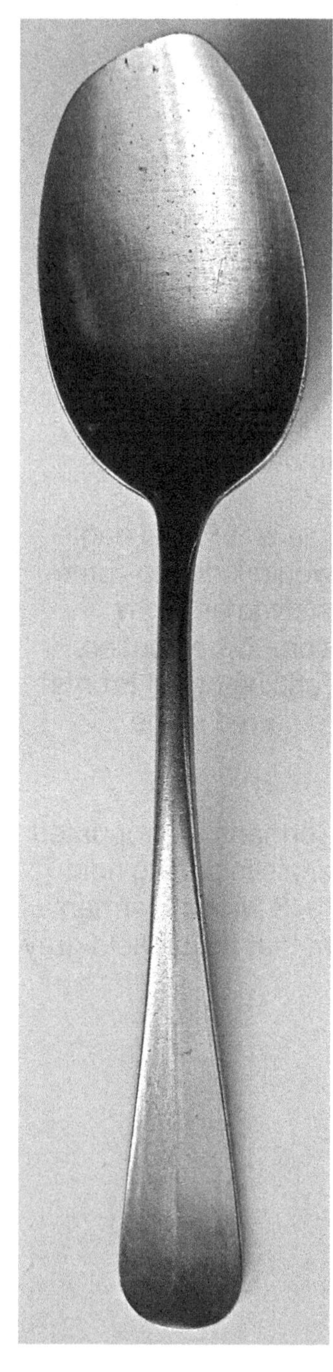

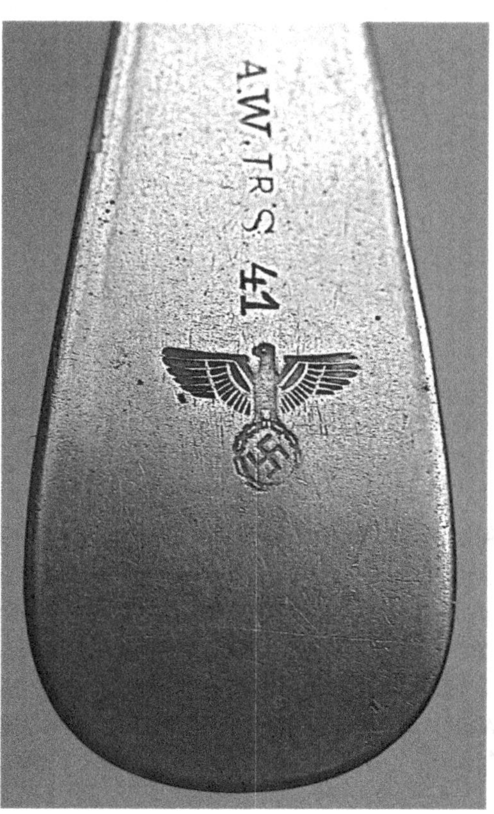

W-89
L = 202 mm / 8"

W-89 Heer

Tablespoon: Obverse unmarked with raised spine, reverse carries A.W.JRS 41.

War in the East!

Germany invaded Poland 1 Sep 1939 with 53 divisions (6 armored and 4 motorized). The Western Front had 33 divisions behind the Siegfried Line (West Wall) short of manpower, heavy equipment, artillery and not fully trained. Only 11 divisions were considered fully efficient. France had some 70 divisions facing the Germans. Hitler was surprised when England and France declared war but was confident they would do nothing. In the event, France killed some 200 german soldiers and retired to the Maginot Line. England's philosophy was they could starve Germany into submission by sea control as they had done in WWI.

Germany's surprise attack on The Soviet Union started on 22 June 1941 (Napoleon invaded on 24 June) with 3.2 M soldiers, 2,000 aircraft, 3,350 tanks, 7,184 pieces of artillery 750,000 horses and 20,000 vehicles of some 2,000 types scoured from all over the occupied countries as well as Germany. Advanced 350 miles in 10 days, Started the Leningrad siege on 8 Sept 41, took Minsk in August and Kiev in Sept, Reached Moscow suburbs in December. By the end of 1941, almost 1M Soviet jews had been murdered, all before the Wannsee Conference of Jan 42. The East front exceeded 1000 miles in depth with a length of 2,500 miles! It was here that the major strategic weaknesses of the German military became obvious as contributing factors in its failure. The three failed areas were intelligence, personnel and logistics.

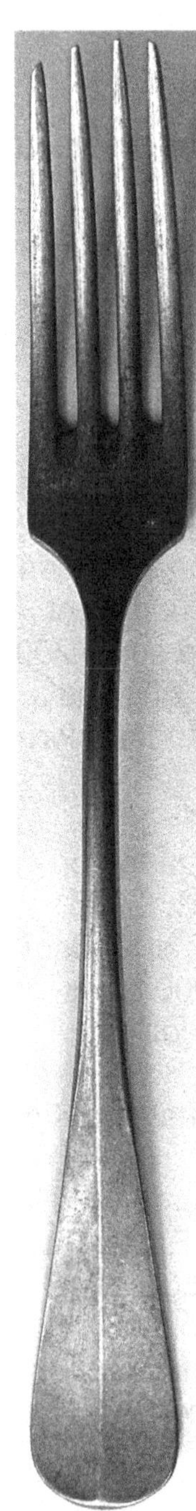

W-90
L = 207 mm / 8 2/16"

W-90 Heer

Table fork: Obverse clear with a raised center spine. Reverse still carries the Weimar Republic Eagle (as this fork was undoubtedly contracted for in 1933) over 'H.U.' and over '1934'. The H.U. is short form for Heeres Unterkunft (Army Quarters / Billets). Maker marked with a shield with an 'A' above, a 'B' to the left and an 'F' to the right (the N below is not struck) for Bayerische Alpaccawarenfabrik AG., Neu-Ulm a. Donau followed by 'ALPACCA'.

n 1933 Germany had a 100,000 man Military as prescribed by the Treaty of Versailles in 1920. The Wehrmacht (Armed Forces) was founded on 15Mar35 and the German military was expanded to 3,180,000 in 5 years under Hitler.

The Wehrmacht on 1Sep39 had 3,180,000, (with 2.7 Million heer/army). Maximum strength achieved was 9.5 Million under arms with 5.5 Million in the Heer and at 9 May 1945 some 7.8 Million were still under arms with 5.3 Million Heer. Heer typically accounted for 75% of the Wehrmacht and within the Heer, 82% were Infantry Divisions.

In 1934, Government regulations forbade the export of nickel-silver (alpacca) products to preserve strategic nickel stocks.

W-91
L = 240 mm / 9 7/16"

W-91 Heer

Mess Hall Knife: Marked with "H. U. 38 " on the reverse. H.U. is the short form for Heeres Unterkunft (Army Quarters / Billets) 1938, UNIAL.

By 1937, preparations for the German economy for the forthcoming war had been worked out in amazing detail. Recognizing that wartime controls, to be effective, must be based on adequate information, comprehensive surveys of 180,000 industrial plants in Germany had compiled statistics concerning the composition of the labor force as to sex, age, and training, the consumption of raw and auxiliary material, fuels, power, the productive capacity, the domestic and foreign trade as well as the supply of material and products in the beginning and at the end of the year.

In parallel, 80 million ration cards had already been printed and deposited with the Landrats, Chief Mayors, and corresponding authorities. The further distribution of the ration cards to the individual households was to be prepared by these authorities to take place within 24 hours after mobilization has been ordered.

The needs of the Armed Forces and the civilian minimum needs in wartime were compared with the covering thereof by supplies and production.

Note: This knife blade style is termed 'New French'.and is identified by the indentation that appears on the lower side where the blade connects to the handle.

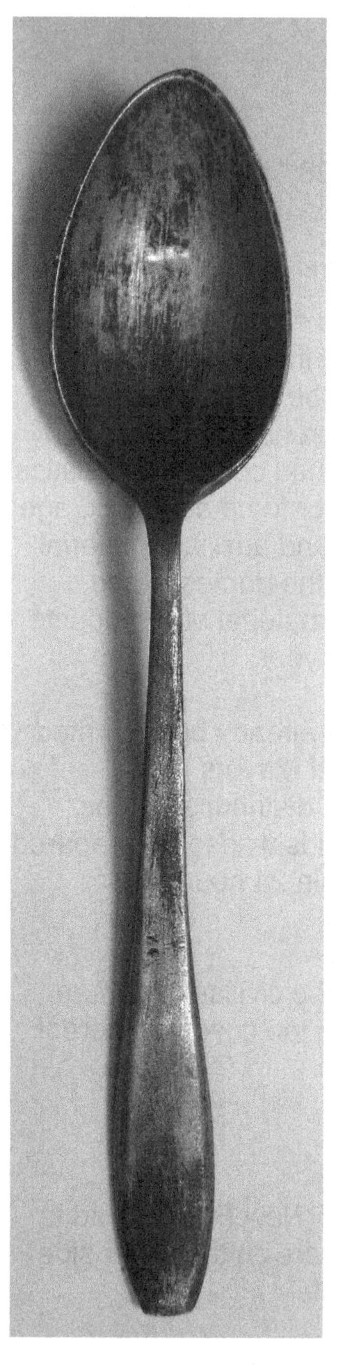

W–92
L = 153 mm / 6”

W-92 Heer

Mess Hall Spoon: Marked with "H. U." on the obverse. H.U. is the short form for Heeres Unterkunft (Army Quarters / Billets). This spoon appears to be a 'dug' item with heavy corrosion but carries the Heer eagle looking right with no makers mark. The material is undetermined but indicates a late war product as does the workmanship.

Now we have H.U. utensils from 1934, 1938 and most probably 1944/45.

It is interesting to see how fast Germany was able to prepare the military for the anticipated aggressive war aims of Hitler. "Defense" spending in the 3rd Reich in billions of Reichsmarks (1934 rate: 2.5 RM = $1) leading up the the War and increasing the National debt by 300% was:

1Jul/-30Jun	RM-B	% of GDP	Wehrmacht
1932			100,000
33/34	1.9	4	
34/35	1.9	4	240,000
35/36	4.0	7	300,000
36/37	5.8	9	
37/38	8.2	11	
38/39	18.4	22	
1Sept1939			3,180,000 Heer = 2.7M

Compare this spoon with the tableware of the elite Fuhrer Begleit Brigade W-94.

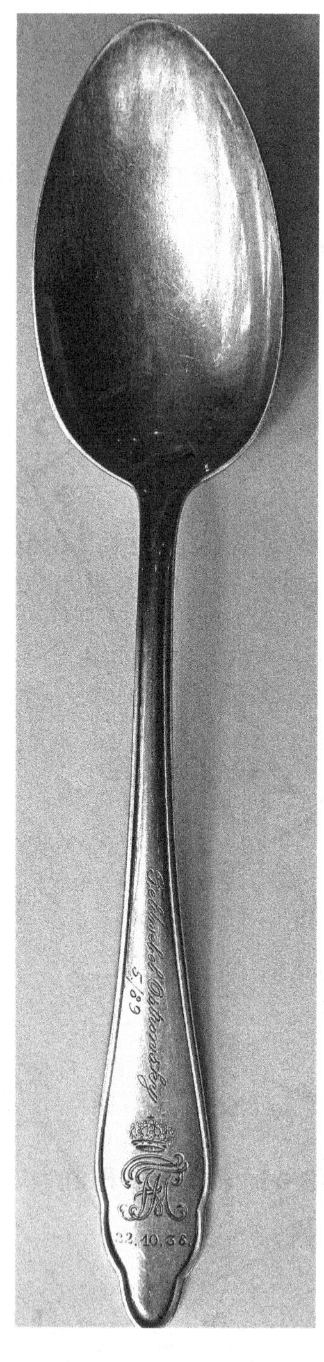

W–93
L = 212 mm / 8 5/16”

W-93 89th Infantry Regiment's, 5th Company
(Prize for extraordinary shooting skill)

Tablespoon: This award to "Feldwebel Ostrowsky 5./89" dated 22/10/38 is on a spoon from the original officer's club of the 89th Mecklenburg Infantry Regiment which fought in both the Franco-Prussian War and WWI and was disbanded in 1919. Reverse Maker Marked with Wellner's "GOWE", 800, RM.

A new 12th division was secretly formed in 1934 and recognized with the creation of Wehrmacht in 1935. Initially, the division included Infantry Regiments 27 & 48. In 1937, Infantry Regiment 89, raised in Schwerin (Mecklenburg's capital) was added. An Infantry Regiment was composed of 3 Battalions, each with 4 companies, (3 rifle and 1 machine gun). In 1939 it fought in Poland and in 1940 it participated in the invasion of France. It was on occupation duties until May 1941, in the Netherlands. In June 1941 the division joined Operation Barbarossa under Army Group North, and remained under that command until the end of 1943. In 1942 it was one of the divisions encircled in the Demyansk Pocket. In December 1942, it was renamed Grenadier Regiment 89. At the beginning of 1944 the division was transferred to Fourth Army, under Army Group Center; in June, it was one of those facing the Soviet offensive in the Belorussian SSR, It was ordered to hold Mogilevat at all costs, and was destroyed there. Very few troops escaped back to German lines from the encirclement. Thus disappeared the 89th Regiment and its 5th Company.

W-94
L = 138 mm / 5 7/16”

W-94 Fuhrer Begleit Brigade, Heer

Teaspoon: Fuhrer Begleit Brigade (FBB: Fuhrer Escort Brigade) Obverse bears the mark of the “Fuhrerstandarte” the Reichskanzlers personal flag with the four corner eagles and a wreathed swastika in its center. The reverse marked: BSF (Bremer Silberwarenfabrick, Bremen) 90. The spoon is from the mess hall dining sets most likely from their garrison H.Q. in Fallsingbostel next to Hitler’s (Wolf’s lair) at Rastenberg, East Prussia where they were responsible for guarding the outer perimeter of the headquarters, The SS being responsible for protection inside the perimeter.

After the 1 September 1939 attack on Poland, Hitler put Rommel in charge of a new Army battalion being organized to function as his personal escort to the front in the absence of the Leibstandarte. This led to the Führer Begleit Battalion (FBB). The FBB started accompanying Hitler on his train (OG-58) and on his battlefield tours following the Battle of France, and later was upgraded to Division.

Note: Otto Remer commanding this elite unit was the man who almost single handed as an “Oberst” (Major) with his loyal troops were ultimately responsible of completely foiling the July 20th 1944 assassination plot against Hitler. If you see the film Valkyrie (Walkurie) he was the officer who upon orders from the Wehrmacht High Command was sent to arrest Doctor Goebbels, but after the Doctor handed him the phone, he heard on the other end, “Hello Oberst Remer- Do you know who I am? Do you recognize my voice?” It was then that Remer knew that Hitler was alive and he now knew who needed to be apprehended. In the movie, it is he who walks up to all the assembled big wigs including General Beck and announces, “You are all under arrest for high treason!”. Remer ultimately rose to the rank of Major General.

W-95

W-95 "107th" Infantry Regiment Cutlery Set.

A three piece set of cutlery consisting of a butter knife, tea spoon and fork. Each piece is engraved with "IR 107" (Infantry Regiment 107). Likely from the 107th Regiment officers mess. Reverse carries GEBR.HEPP for Brothers Hepp founded in 1863 by brothers Carl and Otto and '90'.

The regiment was one of three comprising the newly formed 34th Infantry division in Heidelburg during 1936. It is interesting to see its operational areas to better understand German deployments: 1939 - Saarpfalz, Jan 40 to the Eifel on Germany's western border, May 40 Luxembourg then France, July 40 Belgium, Jun 41 Minsk, Smolensk, Gomel Sep 41 to Feb 42 Wiasma, Moscow, Mar 42 Juchnow, Feb 43 Orel, Sep 43 Poltawa, Nov 43 Tscherkassy, Mar 44 Uman and was burned out after three straight years of combat in Russia. From Apr 44 to Jun 44 carried as 'Remnants Not Operational" Those remnants ended the war in Northern Italy intact and unchanged but as a secondary fighting unit moving into Genoa in Jul 44 and spending the period Aug 44 to Apr 45 in Liguria (Nice).

The German Heer, or army, was formed in May of 1935 with the passing of the "Law for the Reconstruction of the National Defense Forces". This law brought back into existence a free standing German army, navy and air force, something that had been essentially banned after the end of World War I. The Heer was defeated with the German capitulation on May 8th 1945, The Allied Control Council passed a law formally dissolving the Wehrmach on the 20th of August 1946, the official "death" date of the German Heer.

Note: Coincidentally, on 2 Nov 1812 during Napoleon's retreat from Moscow, his army lost a battle at Wiasma.

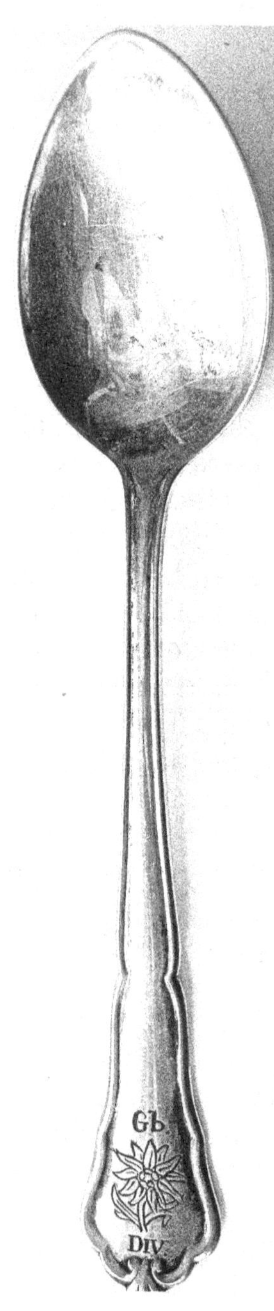

W-96
L = 144 mm / 5 11/16"

W-96 First Mountain Division, Heer

Teaspoon: Obverse with edelweiss and reverse RM, 800, HTB for Hanseatishe Silberwarenfabrik, Bremen

The 1.Gebirgsjäger-Division was formed on April 9th, 1938 in Garmisch Partenkirchen from the original Gebirgs-Brigade, the sole mountain unit of the German military since 1935 when the Wehrmacht was formed. After WWI ended, because of their record in battle, the Weimar Republic kept a small cadre of mountain troops to use as the nucleus for a future mountain force. In 1935 this cadre of men helped form the basis of the Gebirgs-Brigade, and by April of 1938, it was raised to a Divisional unit, the 1.Gebrigs-Division.

Campaigns: Poland 1939. Western 1940: After the Campaign in France, the Division was posted to take part in the planned invasion of Great Britain, and then for the planned invasion of Gibraltar, but in both cases, the planned operations were canceled. Balkans 1941: After training for the above two invasions, the Division was transferred to Austria to take part in operations in Yugoslavia. On April 9th, 1941, two years after the Division was formed, it crossed the Yugoslav frontier and fought through central Yugoslavia with the bulk of the German forces. Eastern Front: 1941-1943 After the Campaigns in Yugoslavia, the Division took part in the Invasion of the Soviet Union and fought in the highest positions held by any unit in all of German military history when the 4300 meter (14,100 ft) heights of Mt. Elbrus in the deep Caucasus region was held by the Gebirgsjäger against repeated Soviet attacks and the harsh high alpine elements. Balkan/Italian Fronts: 1943-1945 In December, 1944 the Division was again moved to Hungary where it took part in offensives against the Red Army, and was then moved to the Austrian Region in 1945 where it surrendered to the Americans in May of 1945.

W-97
L = 128 mm / 8 3/16”

W-97 Fork: GTPp - MYSTERY Solved

Table Fork: Obverse clear. Reverse carries a detailed eagle looking left - symbolizing the Nazi party and thus called the Parteiadler. Below is a detailed tower with an overlay of GTPp. The maker mark is WMF (Wurttembergische Metallwarenfabrik of Geislingen, 1853 to the present), 'Patent', '90' in a square for plating and '45' in a lozenge for silver gram weight. An 'S' is also impressed on the throat.

You may know that the identification of this fork was one of the MYSTERY items in my *Guide to 3rd Reich Cutlery*. With great thanks to Shawn Bernhardt, this case is closed. Shawn, who actually visited the site, was able to place the building in Grafenwoehr, Bavaria, near Nuremberg and was kind enough to send the photo left. Grafenwoehr is the site of the Bavarian Army's Training center opened in 1907 and in 1936 expanded to 90 sq. miles and now the largest US training area in Europe. The building shown is the post's water tower, circa 1910. The impression has been deciphered as: Grafenwoehr Truppenuebungsplatz (Grafenwoehr Training Area) The little p remains a little mystery but could be partei?

Hitler's visit of 24 June 1938

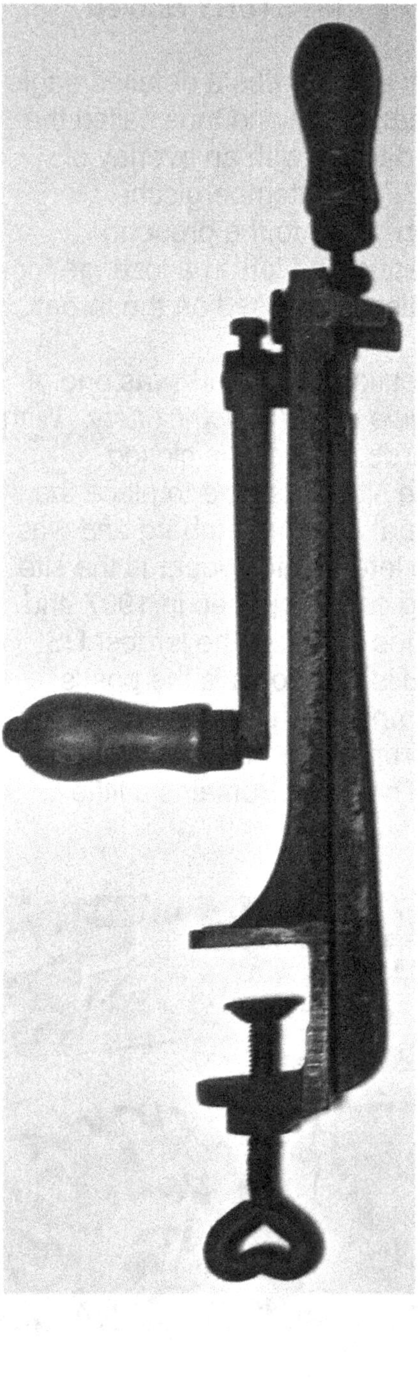

W-98
L = 415 mm / 16 1/4”

W-98 Army Field Kitchen Can Opener. (Dosenöffner)

Can Opener: Well marked "Reichsheer - 1943 - PeDe".

This is a vintage military can opener from the Pe De Dienes Company and is of cast steel construction weighing 1250 grams / 2 3/4#. Peter Dienes founded the Pe De Dienes Company in Reimscheid, Germany in 1869. The area was a center for mechanical engineering. PeDe's fame is based on their various grinders and mills as Peter Dienes had 11 patents on grinders and mills and invented what most now consider the best German coffee grinder mechanism which was also used by Robert Zassenhaus. The coffee mills remain highly collectible. The German Pe De Dienes Company lasted until 1960.

Source states "All complete, functions well. Scarce."

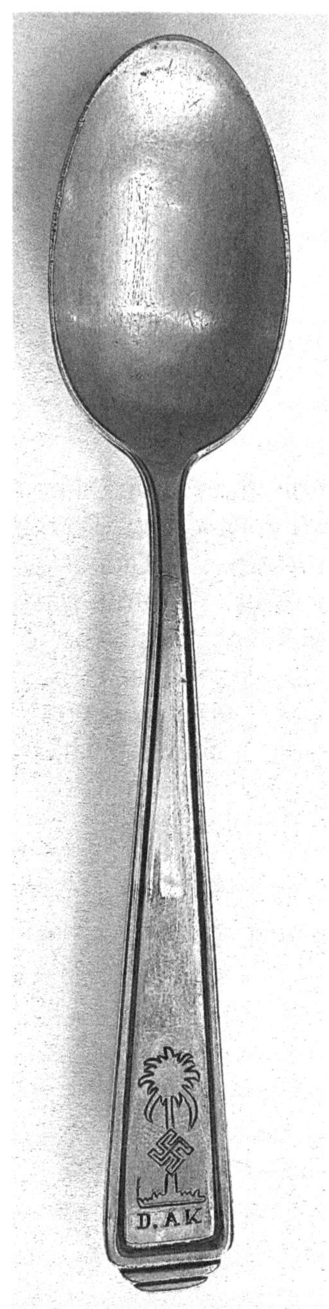

W-99
L =145 mm / 5 11/16"

W-99 D.AK,
das Deutsches Afrikakorps
(The German Africa Corps)

Teaspoon: Marked with DAK logo with maker mark 'AWS' in a squared box (August Wellner & Sohne), The AWS maker mark was used by Wellner from 1928 to 1941, 800, RM.

The D.AK was formed on 12 Feb 1941 as the original German expeditionary force in Libya, Tunisia and Egypt during the North African Campaign of World War II. Its original mission was to act as a blocking force in Libya and Tunisia to support the routed Italian army group which was under great pressure by the British forces.

The force was kept as a distinct formation and became the main German contribution to Panzer Army Africa which evolved into the German-Italian Panzer Army (Deutsch-Italienische Panzerarmee) and Army Group Africa.

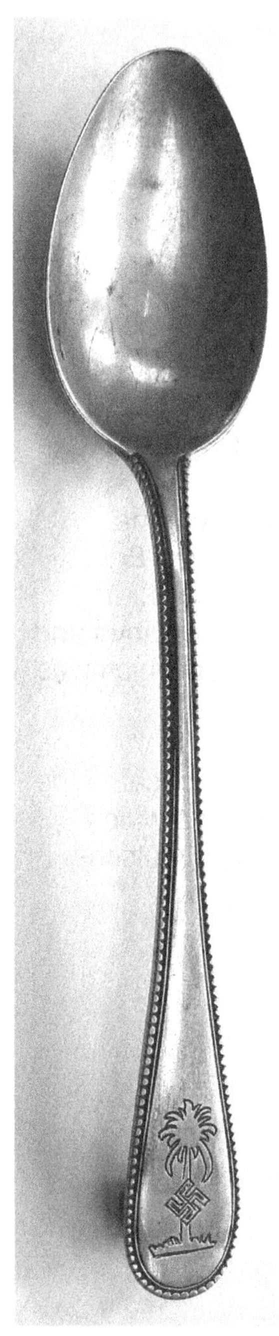

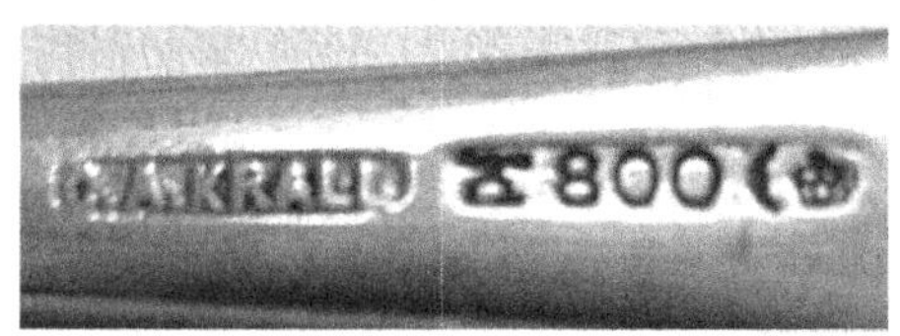

W-100
L = 144 mm / 5 11/16”

W-100 D.AK,

Teaspoon: das Deutsches Afrikakorps Obverse marked with D.AK logo. Small dots surround the top handle of the spoon. Reverse carries retailer C.A. Krall, and maker mark of M.H.Wilkens, Bremen-Hemelingen, founded 1810, 800, RM.

Rommel's AfrikaKorps required 70,000 tons of material monthly to operate but typically received much less as the Allies had broken the German codes and thus were able to intercept many of the resupply ships. On 13 May 1943 the remnants of the Afrikakorps surrendered in Tunisia having suffered some 12,808 killed in action. By this time, due to the absence of German supplies, the D.AK transport vehicles were predominately made up of captured British trucks.

W-101
L = 118 mm / 4 5/8"

W-101 German Africa Corps

After Dinner Teaspoon: Obverse DAK logo, Reverse: 800, no RM, the Danish “Three Tower Mark” with year ’53’ (1853) and Assay Master mark of Peter R. Hinnerup served from 1840 to 1863. The Danish cutlery was undoubtedly confiscated after occupation and both DAK and the German ‘800’ over stamped later.

The Afrika Korps was derived and formed upon Adolf Hitler's personal choice of Erwin Rommel to its command on February 12, 1941 (Rommel himself landed on African soil in Libya on February 14, 1941 to begin leading his forces that would be brought into action). The German Armed Forces High Command or Oberkommando der Wehrmacht (OKW) and Army High Command or Oberkommando des Heeres (OKH) had decided to send a "blocking force" or Sperrverband to Libya to support the Italian army. On August 15, 1941, the German 5th Light Division5./ leichte "AFRIKA" Division was re designated 21st Panzer Division (commonly written as 21./PD), On February 23, 1943 Panzer Army Africa, (now called the German-Italian Panzer Army,) was re designated as the Italian 1st Army and put under the command of Italian general Giovanni Messe, while Rommel was placed in command of a new Army Group Africa (Heeresgruppe Afrika), created to control both the Italian 1st Army and the 5th Panzer Army. The remnants of the Afrikakorps and other surviving units of the 1st Italian Army retreated into Tunisia. Command of the Army Group was turned over to von Arnim in March. On May 13, remnants of the Afrikakorps surrendered, along with all other remaining Axis forces in North Africa.

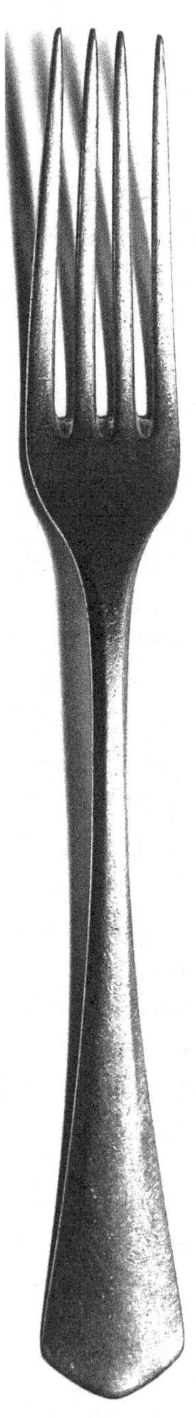

W-102 L = 215 mm / 8 7/16”

W-102 Weimar Republic's Navy Mess Fork.
(Kantine/Schiffsküche Gabel)

As described by the consignee:

"PHYSICAL DESCRIPTION: The single piece, german silver plated construction mess hall/galley four tine fork is roughly, 21cm long. The reverse is well marked with an impressed Imperial Eagle over "M", indicating Kaiserliche Marine issue, and the impressed manufacturer's initials, "V.S.F. 90" (1890). Typical silver tarnish, would clean up perfect."

Referring to W-114, this Luftwaffe piece carries the identical V.S.F.90 where V.S.F. is Vereinigte Silberwaren-Fabrilen AG.. Duesseldorf and the 90 indicates the weight of silver plate and not 1890. Regarding the "Kaiser" reference, this is a pre-Hitler, post Imperial era piece from the early 1920s. There are no signs of imperial or NSDAP national insignia incorporated in the design of the logo. The eagle is a Weimar Republic eagle as the Kaiser military eagles typically had a crown as per W-93.

This Weimar Republic eagle can be compared to W-90's.

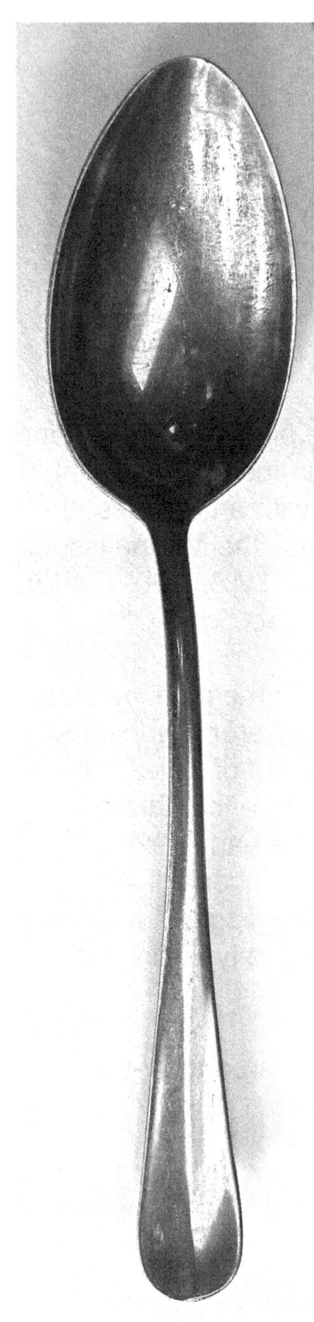

W-103
L = 212 mm / 8 3/8”

W-103 KRIEGSMARINE

Tablespoon: Mil Issue, stainless steel with raised spine on a clear obverse. On the reverse the manufacturers initials, 'HHL' for (Heinrich Haupt Luedenscheid, Westfalen) in an octagonal border, "ROSTFREI' with KM logo of a minimal / rudimentary eagle over a mobile swastika in a circle over the 'M'.

Fact: From the Versailles Treaty strength limitation of 15,000 personnel, over 1,500,000 served in the KM, with some 65,000 killed in action.

Note: The Navy appears to be the least interested in the incorporation of the Nazi symbols and their renderings show it.

W-104
L = 144 mm / 5 11/16”

W-104 KRIEGSMARINE

Teaspoon: Mil Issue with raised spine on obverse. On the reverse the makers mark is a circle divided diagonally by crossed swords with a letter 'V' at the top, letter 'D' on the left and a letter 'N' on the right with a letter 'S' at the bottom, the maker mark for (Vereinigte Deutsche Nickelwerke AG Schwerte) followed by 'BLANCADUR'* and at the bottom of the spoon the Kriegsmarine symbol with the 'M' in bold double outline.

*Blancadur identifies the Blancadur Process of the electrolytic deposition of pure rhodium to achieve a brilliant extremely bright and glossy surface layer.

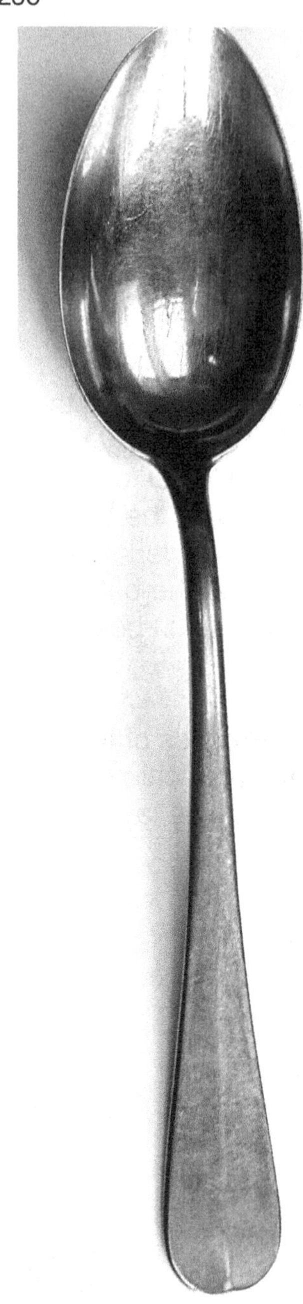

W-105
L = 211 mm / 8 5/16”

W-105 Kriegsmarine

Tablespoon: Obverse of the handle is unmarked with a low, central ridge. Reverse maker marked F.W.W. 41. Impressed Kriegsmarine eagle with 3 feathers but no 'M', Rustfrei.

The U-Boat Commander's Handbook, New Edition 1943 was translated by the US Navy and published by Thomas Publications in 1989. This handbook was the bible for the 1,244 German naval officers that served as U-Boat commanders.

The U-Boat pens at Lorient, France used 250,000 tons of cement and 17,000 tons of steel and are still in use by the French navy.

On 4 May 1945 - Messages were sent to all U-Boats to cease action. On 5 May, the U-835 sank a collier four miles off Point Judith, Rhode Island and in turn was the last German U-boat sunk with the loss of all hands.

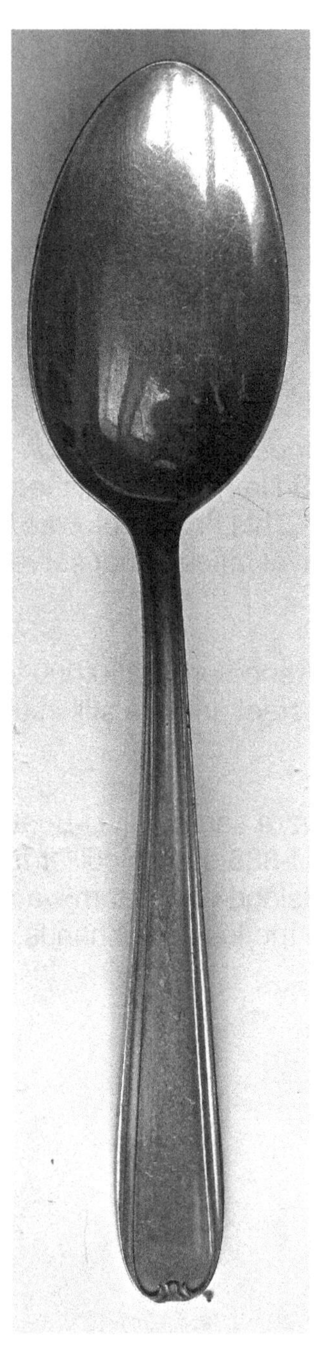

W-106
L = 202 mm / 7 15/16"

W-106 TORPEDOVERSUCHSANSTALT
(Torpedo Testing Facility, Kiel)

Tablespoon: Obverse clear. Reverse marked TORPEDOVERSUCHSANSTALT and ROSTFREI.

Source stated that this tablespoon was from the torpedo training/testing facility in Kiel. The spoon is of tooled stainless steel construction mess hall/galley tablespoon roughly, 21cm long with a roughly, 4.5cm wide "bowl". Well marked "TORPEDOVERSSUCHSANSTALT".

The submarine programs commenced with a regular course for future commanders which started on 3 January 1933 at the Navel Academy at Kiel.

The submarine school was established on 1 October 1933 in Kiel-Wik. The first crew at this school comprised eight officers and 75 NCO's and seamen, all of whom assembled in Kiel in the summer of 1933. The torpedo activity was spread around between the Torpedo Trial Institution (TVA) Eckernfourde, The Torpedo Trial Station (Marine-Torpedo-Versuchsstation), the torpedo school at Muerwik, Torpedo courses at the Torpedo and Radio School in Flensburg-Muerwik, the Eckernfoerde Torpedo Testing Station as well as the Torpedo Testing Facility in Kiel. See the U-47 write up M-177 regarding early torpedo performance.

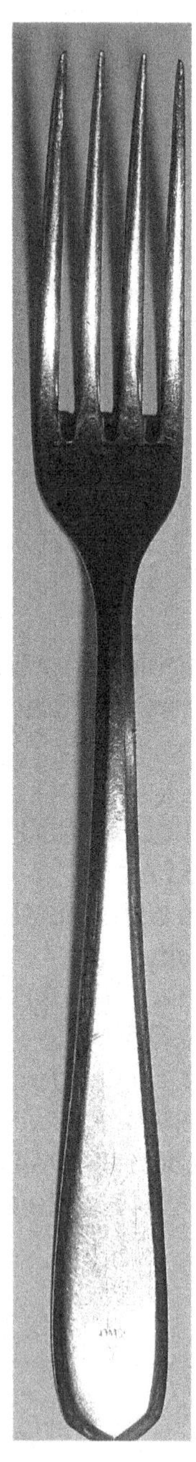

W-107
L = 208 mm / 8 3/16"

W-107 Companion fork with W-89

Fork accompanied the torpedo testing facility spoon above. The obverse has a Kreigsmarine eagle & swastika over what appears to be MSTVep.. The reverse carries an unidentified makers mark and ROSTFREI.

Source stated that both W-106 and W-107 were from the same location, reportedly Kiel.

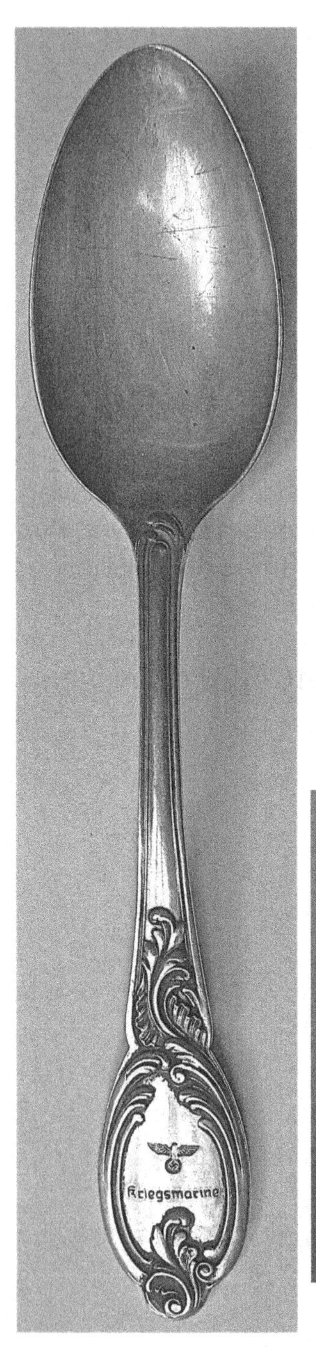

W-108

L = 215 mm /
8 7/16”.

W-108 KM/Partei Retirement Gift?

Tablespoon: Very ornate with obverse carrying a Parteiadler looking left (symbolizing the Nazi Party) over "Kriegsmarine". The reverse carries retailer: 'Gebr. Friedlander', unidentified maker mark: '800', 'RM' with engraved initials: JJS.

This spoons conflicted markings on the obverse make it difficult to place or understand. We can hypothesize that it is not official KM ware due to the Partiadler but as it is expensive, it could be a Partei award?

Navy officer careers consisted of four varying grades: High, Elevated, Medium and Low. Upon promotion or the retirement of High ranking Kriegsmarine officers, it was traditional to be presented with a commemorative set of table ware. This spoon is not typical of that naval tradition as it is Nazi Party generated and is an obvious departure from the official minimal approach to marking tableware by the Kriegsmarine.

Note: The Kriegsmarine can be said to have had three main components between 1935 and 1945, individual naval vessels, naval formations consisting of specific types of ships and a wide variety of ground based units. From these three main components the Kriegsmarine fielded thousands of ships and hundreds of naval formations and ground units. Between 1939 and 1945 over 1.5 million served in the Kriegsmarine. Over 65,000 were killed, over 105,000 went missing and over 210,000 were wounded. Of the 7,361 men awarded the initial grade of the highest German combat honor of WWII, the Knights Cross, 318 were from the Kriegsmarine making up 4% of the total awarded

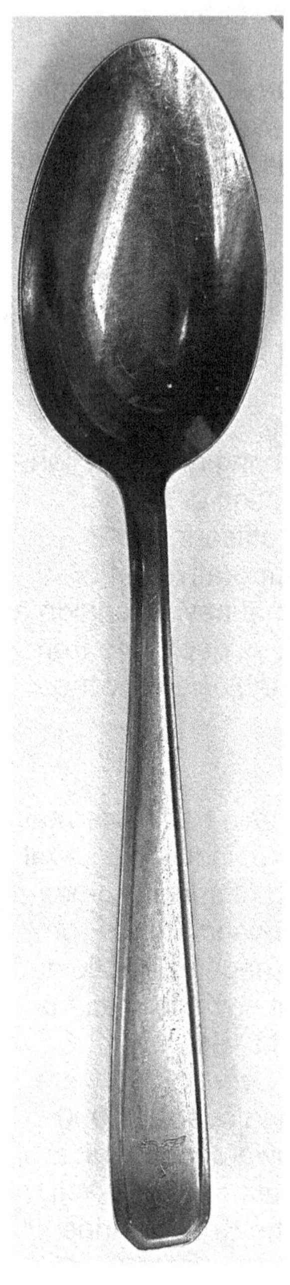

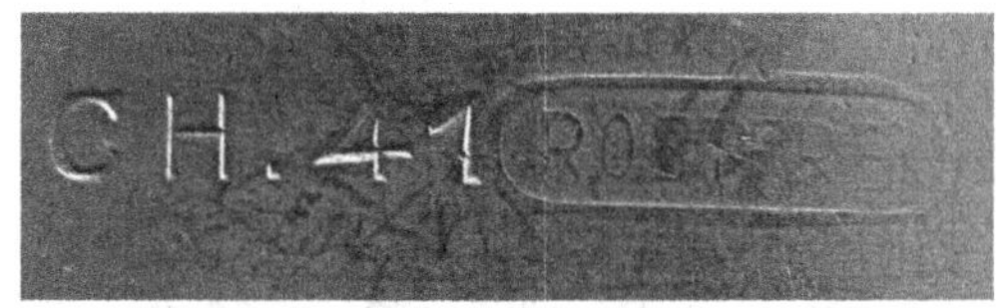

W-109
L = 206 mm / 8 1/16"

W-109 Luftwaffe

Tablespoon (Essloeffel): Air Force mess hall, one piece stainless steel. The obverse of the handle is marked with a faint, impressed early style "droop tailed" Luftwaffe eagle. This 2nd Pattern eagle (1937 - 45) "Droop Tailed" has a pronounced downward pitch to the tail feathers and the eagles free leg lifts upward in a pronounced curve. The reverse of the handle is well marked with impressed manufacturers initials "CH" for (Chromolit) and date "41", followed by "Rostfrei" (Rust Free). At the end of the handle, stamped crosswise are the initials, "Fl.U.V." indicating, Flieger Unterkunft Verwaltung (Flight Barracks Administration).

The Luftwaffe is considered to be a child of the Nazi party. Under the Versailles Treaty of 1919, Part V, Germany was forbidden from having any military air organizations. It is not a coincidence that the Luftwaffe Eagles look left as does the Parteiadler whereas the Army and Navy Eagles look right, Reichsadler.

The Luftwaffe was officially recognized by Hitler on 9 March 1935 when he called for volunteers to serve in the German Air Force.

Fact: Of the 3,400,000 that served in the Luftwaffe during the period 1935 to 1945, some 165,014 were killed in action including 70,000 aircrew.

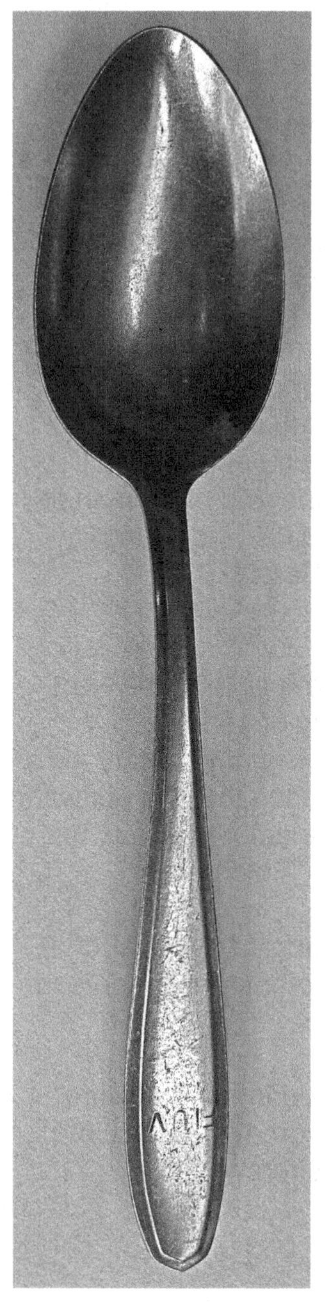

W-110
L = 210 mm / 8 1/4"

W-110 Luftwaffe

Tablespoon: mess hall stainless steel. Obverse of the handle is well marked with impressed initials "Fl. U.V." indicating, Flieger Unterkunft Verwaltung, (Flight Barracks Administration). Manufacturer's name "Oxydex", logo of a 4 leaf clover in a square and "rustfrei" is impressed on the reverse. The FIUV is impressed upside down.

Luftwaffe Trivia: In 1942, an army study showed that army strength had peaked and from then on, it would be unable to make up manpower losses. To make up Heer losses, Luftwaffe Field Divisions were rapidly mobilized from Luftwaffe ground personnel. From Oct 42 to early 1943 some 200,000 Luftwaffe personnel were organized into 21 Field Divisions - as 7,000+ strong M1942 Rifle (Jager) Divisions to replace the massive loss of men on the Eastern front. Due to the lack of training and poor leadership (the officers were Luftwaffe) results in the field were poor. Of the 21 divisions formed, 17 were either destroyed or disbanded before the end of the war.

Note: The Army had intended for the 200,000 to be used to make up Army losses by their integration into existing army units but Goring successfully opposed that idea as he did not want his National Socialist airmen going into the 'reactionary' army. To compound the army's problem, it had to equip those divisions.

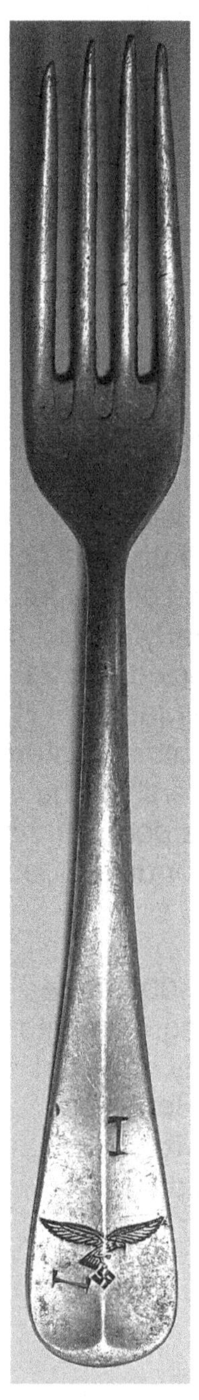

W-111
L = 208 mm / 8 3/16”

W-111 Luftwaffe

Fork: One piece, natural aluminum construction four tine mess hall fork. The obverse of the handle has a central, raised, ridge and a well impressed, second pattern, (Circa 1936/1937-1945), Luftwaffe style eagle with out-stretched wings, clutching a mobile swastika in one talon. There are also two "I"'s stamped to the front which are probably a unit marking of some sort. The reverse of the handle is well marked with impressed manufacturer's initials and date, "H.M.Z" for Hessische Mettallwerke, Ziegenhain 40. The reverse of the handle also has the impressed designation, "Fl. U.V." indicating, Flieger Unterkunft Verwaltung, (Flight Barracks Administration). Shows period wear and use.

Some Luftwaffe Unit Types:

Kommandobehörden	Higher Headquarters
Kampfverbände	Bomber Units
Jagdverbände	Single-engined Fighter Unit
Zerstörerverbände	Twin-engined Fighter Unit
Nachtjagdgverbände	Night-Fighter Units
Sturzkampfverbände	Ground-Attack Units
Aufklärungsverbände	Reconnaissance Units
Kampfverbände z.b.V.	Transport Units
Küsten/Seefliegverbände	Maritime Units
Lehrverbande	Demonstration Units
Sonstige fliegendeverbände	Miscellaneous Units
Schulen	Schools

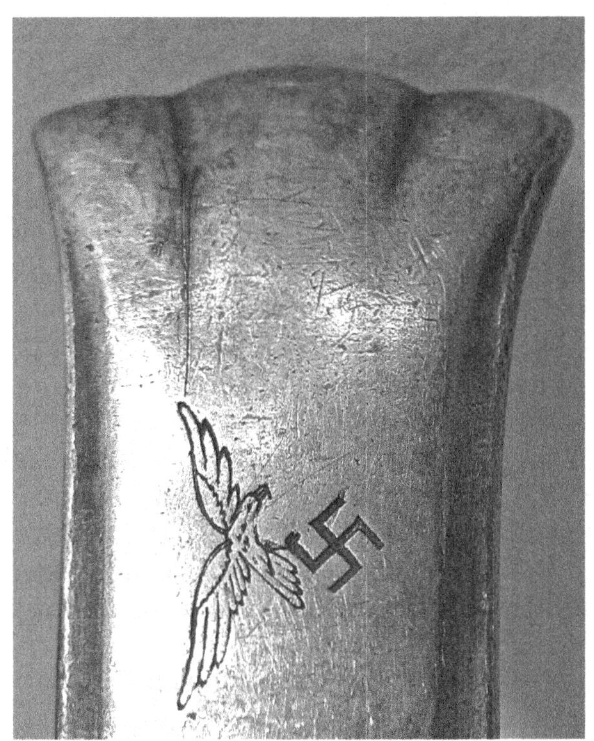

W-112
L = 205 mm / 8 1/16"

W-112 Luftwaffe, crosswise marking

Fork: One piece, four tine mess hall fork. Obverse is clear but fluted in 3 sections. The reverse of the handle has a second pattern, (Circa 1936/1937-1945), Luftwaffe style eagle with out-stretched wings, clutching a mobile, swastika in one talon. The reverse also carries markings: "Wellner" "Patent" "90" within a circle and "45" within a square. The Luftwaffe style eagle is stamped crosswise which is unique. Neither my source nor I have ever seen this placement and was the reason for its acquisition. Shows period wear and use.

Although officially announced in 1935, the Luftwaffe had existed in one form or another practically since the day the treaty banning it had been signed. Initially there were Freikorps air units, then later glider and sail plane formations tasked with finding ways around the rigid restrictions of Versailles, a secret training base in the Soviet Union, and various cover organizations for the initial forming of the new German air force. The Luftwaffe was officially disbanded in August of 1946 by the Allied Control Commission.

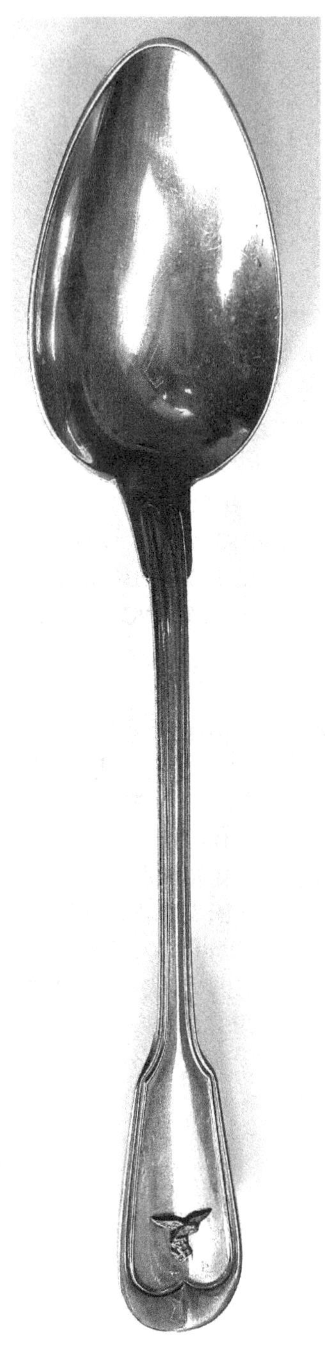

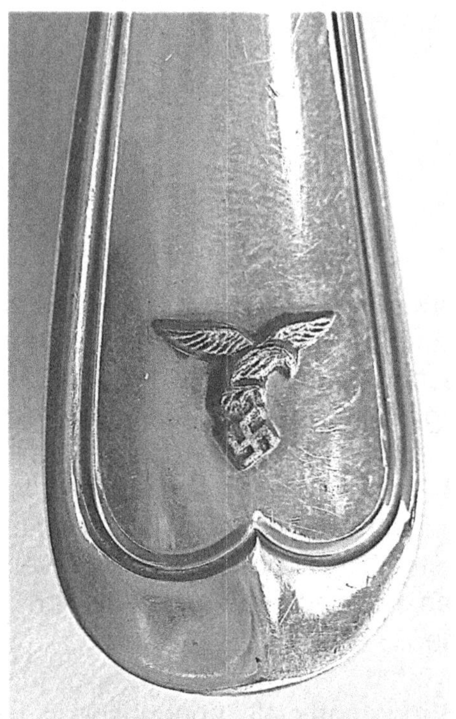

W-113
L = 209 mm / 8 1/4"

W-113 Luftwaffe

Tablespoon: With raised, early Droop-Tailed Eagle (1935/6) and swastika on obverse. Maker marked reverse: Roman numeral 'II' which could be an indication that the piece has a double layer of silver plate and a diamond enclosing crossed swords and the letters ''V' at the top of the cross, 'D' on the left, 'N' on the right and 'S' below the cross, the maker mark for Vereinigte Deutsche Nickelwerke AG Schwerte.

Germany's front line fighter plane was the Messerschmitt Bf 109 with direct fuel injection as opposed to the Spitfire's carburetor engine which gave the Messerschmitt significant advantages in certain maneuvers. The kill ratio (almost 9:1) made this plane far superior to any of the other German fighters during the war and over 33,000 were produced. The closest rival was the Focke-Wulf Fw 190 with a kill ratio of 4:1, but introduced later in the war when things were more difficult. Some 20,000 Fw 190's were built. These two aircraft were half the total aircraft manufactured by Germany in WWII.

Note: Regarding the Bf 109: Erhard Milch disliked Willy Messerschmitt and as State Secretary of the Luftwaffe he forbid Messerschmitt from competing for the Luftwaffe's Modern Fighter Aircraft program. Messerschmitt responded by secretly submitting their proposal through the Bayerische Flugzeugwerke (BFW), winning the competition. Immediately Messerschmitt acquired BFW, Milch's response was to require that the aircraft carry the Bf-109 designation on all official documentation and not the universally used ME-109.

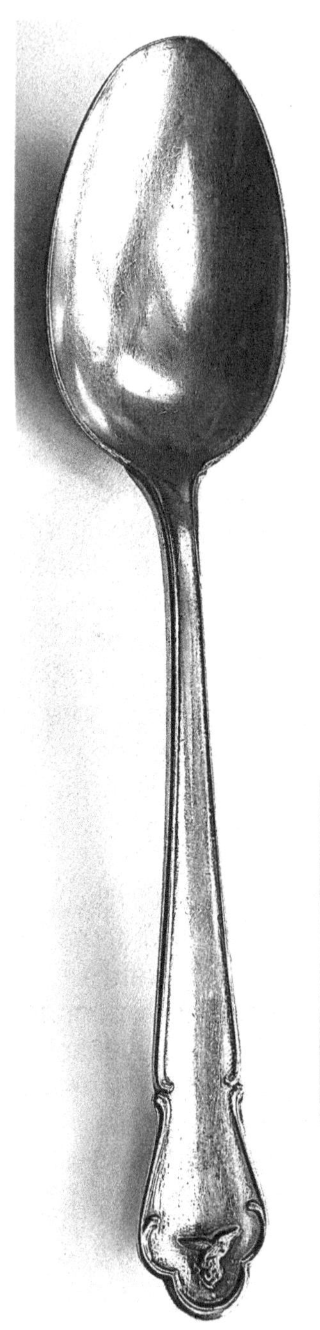

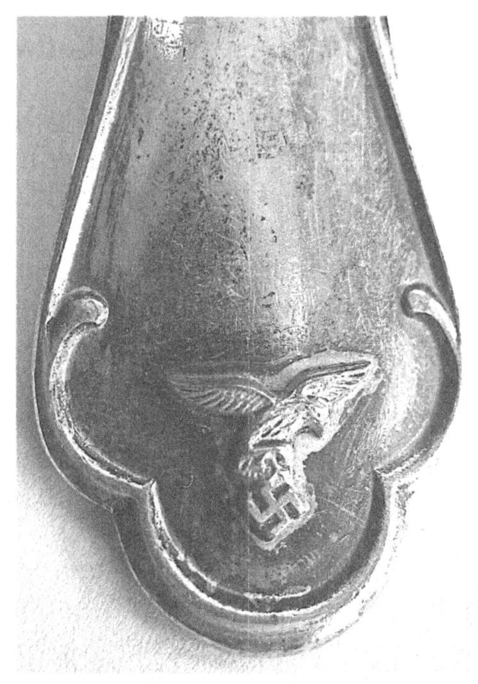

W-114
L = 207 mm / 8 1/8"

W-114 Luftwaffe

Tablespoon: Officers Service, in silver plate with raised, early Droop Tailed Eagle and gold plated swastika on obverse. Maker marked on reverse: V.S.F. for Vereinigte Silberwaren-Fabriken AG., Duesseldorf. 90.

1st Pattern Luftwaffe eagle (1935 & 1936) has the leg positioned horizontally across the eagles body compared to the upward curving leg of the 2nd pattern. Other items of note: 1st pattern's short, stubby wings, and very large swastika.

From as early as 1936, the Luftwaffe had their own dishes and plates. In fact in 1941, Luftwaffe bottled beer came in bottles with raised 'Luftwaffe' on the exterior and on the porcelain 'corks'. Favored dish and plate suppliers were Bohemia, Thun and in 1942 Tielsch-Altwasser.

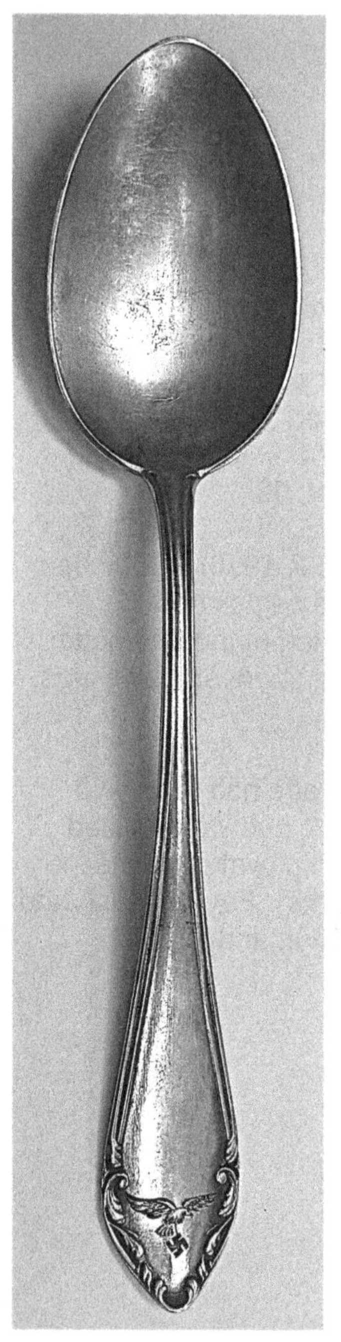

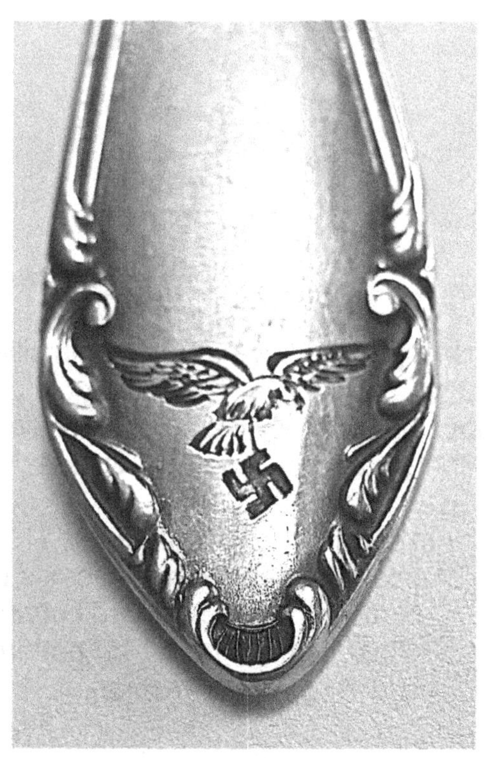

W-115
L = 142 mm / 5 10/16 "

W-115 Luftwaffe

Teaspoon: General Officer's service piece. Marked on obverse with Luftwaffe emblem. Reverse maker mark of Vereinigte Silberwarenfabriken, Dusseldorf, founded 1899 followed by 800, RM.

Maximum air strength in Europe during WWII: Germany 5,000 combat aircraft, America 21,000, England 8,500 and Russia 17,000.

German WWII FIGHTER aircraft production rates:

1939	37/ month.
1940	126/ month
1942	250/ month under Udet
1943	1,000/ month under Milch
Fall 1944	4,000/ month under Speer

Notes: 1. At 5'3", Ernst Udet was Nazi Germany's shortest General. Albert Speer was 6'3".

2 See OG-55, in 1942 the BR-52 Kriegslok (War Locomotive / freight) empty weight 75.9 tons were being built at a rate of 500 per month! Total built 6,500+.

3. In 1940, the Luftwaffe was producing more pilots than aircraft.

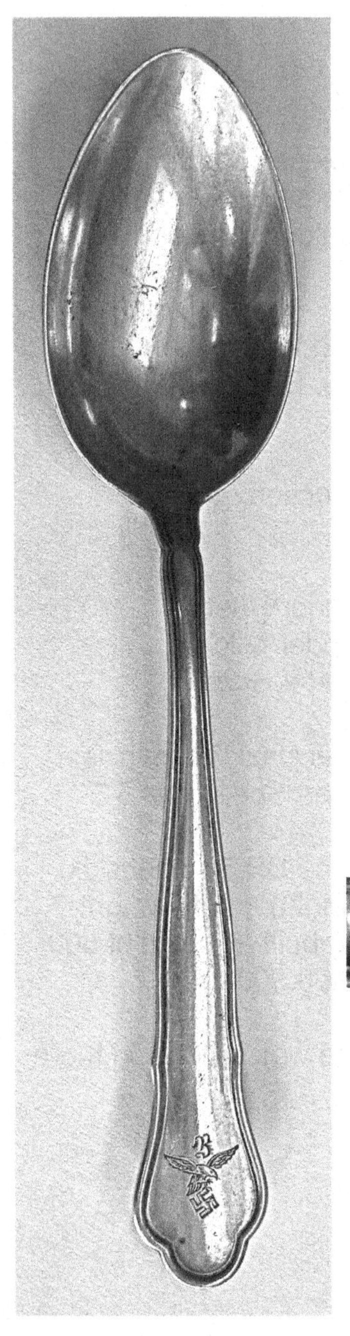

W-116
L = 174 mm / 6 13/16"

W-116 Luftwaffe

Dessert spoon: General Officers Service in silver with a fraktur personalized? letter "B" over the Luftwaffe Eagle on the obverse. The reverse is well marked with the manufacturer's name 'LAMEYER' followed by the RM of a crescent moon & crown (Halbmond und Krone) and 800 (the decimal silver standard mark) followed by a maker's mark of a small 'W' left of a capital 'L' followed by a '&' and a capital 'S' with a crown on the top. The "W" for the first name of Wilhelm, the 'L' for family name Lameyer, the '& S' most probably for 'and son' of Hanover.

Total German WWII Aircraft production: 113,515 aircraft with 100,000 destroyed and 70,000 aircrew killed.

(The US produced over 100,000 aircraft in 1944 alone of a total 300,000).

For comparison, the most produced military aircraft in history was the Russian Il-2 Sturmovik ground attack aircraft at 42,330. In 1942 alone, Russia produced 40,000 aircraft vs Germany's 5,000.

Note: The English teaspoon holds 5 ml, a dessert spoon 10 ml and the tablespoon 15 ml.

W-117
L = 152 mm / 6”

W-117 Luftwaffe. Fliegerhorst "Julich" 1936
(Air Base Julich)

Nut Cracker: One arm: Fl. H.Kdtr.Jü. 1936 (Fliegerhorst Kommandantur Jülich 1936), or Air Base Headquarters Julich 1936. Other arm: first pattern (1935 & 6) eagle with swastika and reverse maker marked WELLNER, 10 and 3.

Jülich is a good size German city strategically located near the German border with Holland, Luxembourg and Belgium, and played an important role in the invasion of those countries by Wehrmacht forces in 1940. This is a rare and beautiful example of the standard 6 inch heavy (230Gr / 8.1Oz), silver plated nutcracker manufactured during the Third Reich in Aue, Germany by the firm of August Wellner & Sohne and is one of the rarest pieces of Wellner Luftwaffe table service. Founded in 1935, during this early period of the Luftwaffe, German base specific cutlery made its appearance which by itself is rare. The engraving style and time frame is harmonious with W-93 & M-168's Maker Mark. Hermann Göering personally chose an insignia for the Luftwaffe that differed from that of the other armed branches. The eagle, an old symbol of the German Empire, was used, but in a different posture. Since 1933, when Hitler's National Socialist Party came to power, the eagle held between his claws the symbol of the party—the swastika (an old symbol of sunrise)—which usually was enveloped by an oak wreath. Göering rejected the old heraldic eagle because he felt it was too stylized, too static, and too massive; instead he chose a younger, more natural and lighter eagle with wings spread as if in flight, as he considered this a more suitable symbol for an air force. While the Wehrmacht eagle held the symbol of the National Socialist Party firmly in its talons, the Luftwaffe eagle held the swastika with only one talon while the other was bent in a threatening gesture.

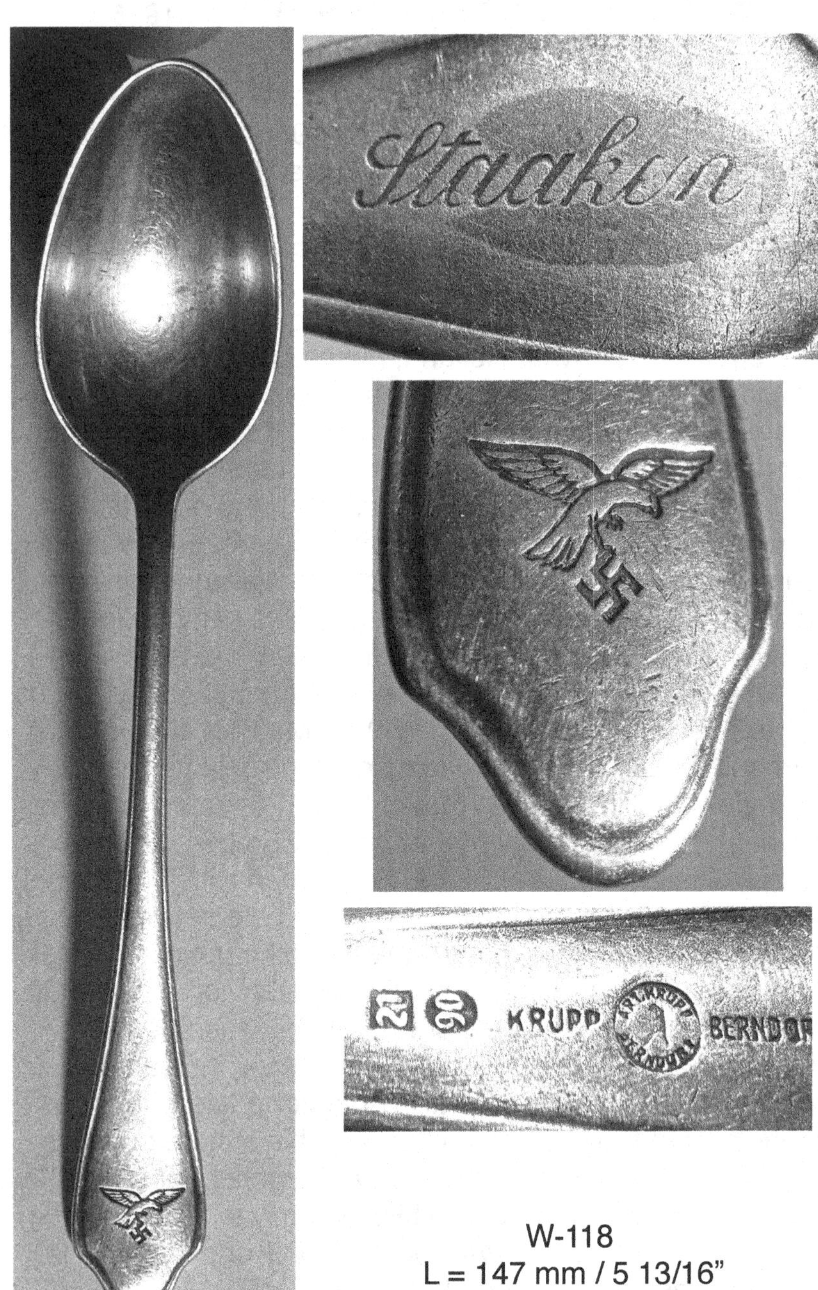

W-118
L = 147 mm / 5 13/16”

W-118 Luftwaffe Fliegerhorst "Staaken"
(Air Base Staaken)

Coffee Spoon: Obverse marked with a well-detailed, incised, 2nd pattern (1937 - 1945) Luftwaffe eagle and swastika. Reverse: Silver weight "21", Silver "90" and maker mark "Krupp Berndorf" and air base ID "Staaken" in jeweler script.

Staaken is located approximately 17 km west of central Berlin. Here during WWI the Luftschiffbau Zeppelin company manufactured zeppelin airships and R.VI biplane strategic bombers. In 1919 the regulations of the Treaty of Versailles ended zeppelin production and the area was transformed into an airfield. In 1927, the former zeppelin manufacturing halls were locations for various film productions including parts of Fritz Lang's Metropolis (a favorite of Hitler and the most expensive silent film ever produced!). In 1929 the estate was sold to the City of Berlin, while parts of the airport were still used by the Lufthansa airline for flight training and maintenance purposes.

From the founding of the Luftwaffe in 1935 till 1945, this field was the home of Luftwaffe Air Base Staaken (Fliegerhorst Staaken) although it shared the property with the Demag (Deutsche Maschinenfabrik AG) that built Panther tanks during World War II using forced labor of over 2,500 prisoners held in the nearby Falkenhagen labor camp, a sub camp of Sacksenhausen concentration camp.

Source comment: Spoon shows light surface wear/age with some loss of silver plating to underside of the spoon bowl and adjacent to the Staaken personalization.

Note: This style/length spoon is called a 'Five O'Clock Spoon' by English/American collectors and is my favorite!

Wehrmacht's Military Justice

Oath: From "*The Hitler Salute*" by Tilmer Allert: "Oaths are by their nature unconditional: they are made to ward off the possibility that the intensity of the relationship they govern will slacken and fall prey to moral weakness or negligence."

> Until 1933, members of the German military swore their oath of allegiance in the following words: "I swear by God this sacred vow that I will faithfully and truly serve my people and my country at all times, and that I will be prepared as a brave and obedient soldier to be ever willing to risk my life to uphold this vow."
>
> In 1934, the wording was changed to: "I swear by God this sacred vow that I will offer my unqualified obedience to the leader of the German Empire and the German people, Adolf Hitler, the commander-in-chief of the military, and that I will be prepared as a brave soldier to be ever willing to risk my life to uphold this vow."

For comparison

> US Military enlistment oath: "I, (NAME), do solemnly swear (or affirm) that I will support and defend the Constitution of the United States against all enemies, foreign and domestic; that I will bear true faith and allegiance to the same; and that I will obey the orders of the President of the United States and the orders of the officers appointed over me, according to regulations and the Uniform Code of Military Justice. So help me God."

Initial problems were created with the basic requirement to take the oath. The Jehovah's Witnesses were the only group of people in German society which refused as a unified body to serve in the armed forces. In addition, after their occupation, the citizens of Luxembourg as well as the French citizens of Alsace and Lorraine were made ethnic German citizens and therefore subject to being drafted by the Wehrmacht. Polish citizens that were classified as ethnic Germans were also subject to the draft. In all these cases, to refuse to take the oath of allegiance to Hitler automatically triggered the death penalty which was administered by the military courts.

The next level of legal enforcement of military discipline occurred after joining the Wehrmacht and having taken the oath. Now the focus is the maintenance of discipline.

Obedience to orders is fundamental to military organization. The individual abandons the right to self determined decisions by joining the armed forces. Unconditional obedience, subordination and military unity is the goal.

Some one million Wehrmacht soldiers were subjected to military courts for failing (wehrkraftzersetzer) "subverting the power of defense". Of these some 20,000 were executed for this offense. (Numbers executed for criminal crimes is not included). For comparison, the US actually executed one soldier in WWII and Germany had executed 48 during WWI.

Example: An enlisted soldier in Poland was ordered to shoot an old woman who refused to surrender her 2 pigs to his forage unit. After refusing 3 direct orders, he was arrested, tried and shot.

SS

An explanation as to the plethora of SS Besteck comes from an item in a Germania International write-up: "Traditionally, in Germany, tableware was the gift of choice. This involved sets of spoons, knives and forks sometimes in special cases. There was born a tradition in the Waffen-SS of presenting tableware to couples who were about to be married. This went back to the 1930's with the Allgemeine-SS. From 1939 on, thousands of war wounded of the Waffen-SS had nothing to do other than lie around in hospital beds or languish about with no actual mental therapy. The SS command decided that various artistic projects should be offered to them that would fill the bill. The question was what therapy would give the recuperating soldier something to occupy his hours, and at the same time be something that would add to the cultural expression and acumen that was always the professed agenda of the SS. Then someone came up with the idea of supplying the men with simple tools for constructing various items such as presentation dinnerware and also engraving tools and applique kits were supplied for acid etching and hand engraving. The men were allowed to sell these hand tooled gifts. One of the most popular of the art projects was making up sets of dinnerware--knives, forks, spoons--with the SS symbols applied. The actual flatware was not produced by these wounded men, rather it was a matter of certain companies who produced these utensils to donate them to the soldiers who, with their newly acquired tools, applied carefully the SS runic symbols to the various pieces. Firms such as Krupp, Sy and Wagner, Tiger, Eickhorn, Wellner etc., donated sets from vendor stocks to be decorated and sold with the benefits going to the soldiers families.

These were often called wedding sets because SS men of various Waffen-SS units would often give them as presents to a comrade and his wife as a marriage present. It became a respected tradition among the ranks of the Waffen-SS and continued on to the end of the war." With over 900,000 serving in the Waffen-SS, and over 400,000 wounded in action, this was a large number to find distractions via the Verwundete (wounded) Program!

Legal Problems for the SS

Due to its creation by Hitler personally and its subsequent involvement with the NSDAP as a Party-affiliated organization, the SS was listed as a criminal organization at Nuremberg in 1945. The Waffen-SS (the militarized formations of the SS were named Waffen-SS in the winter of 1939-40 having originally been formed as the SS-VT or SS (Special Troops) was thus denied the rights of the other military service veterans. Only conscripts sworn in after 1943 were exempted from criminal charges on the basis of involuntary servitude. All Allgemeine-SS members were listed as criminals.

The SS mottos: Meine Ehre Heisst Treue -
My Honor is Loyalty
&
Believe! Obey! Fight!

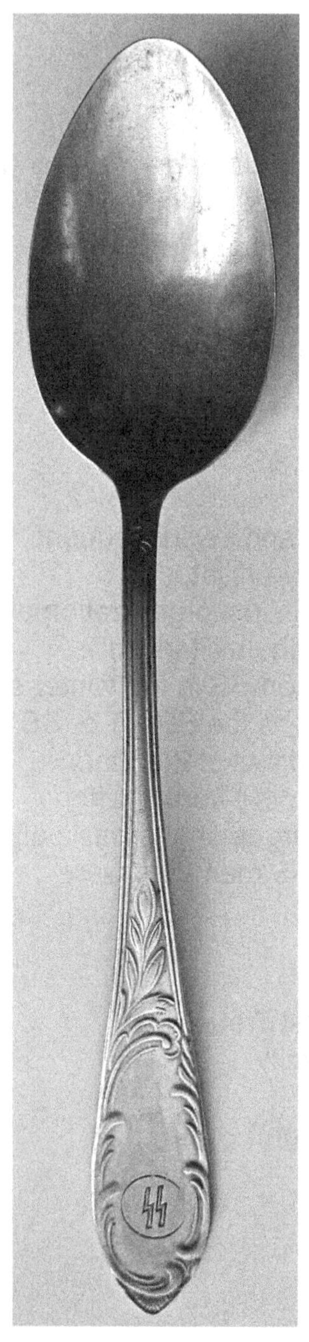

SS-119
L = 211 mm / 8 5/16”

SS-119

Tablespoon: Obverse carries the SS Runes in a circle while the reverse is marked 'NEUSILBER'. Neusilber was created by the Gebrueder Henninger (Henninger Bros.) as a substitute for silver and was composed of 5-30% nickel, 45-70% copper and 8-45% zinc with trace amounts of lead, tin and iron. It later used the trade name Alpacca.

SS Regalia: Adopted as a link to the past, the Totenkopf (Death's Head) was the only common badge of all SS formations such as the Allgemeine-SS and Waffen-SS.

From a 15th Century poem by Garnier von Susteren:

Behold the Knight
in solemn black manner.
With a skull on his crest
and blood on his banner

The Stosstrupp Adolf Hitler adopted the Totenkopf in 1923 whose regimental song included:

In black we are dressed,
In blood we are drenched,
Death's Head on our helmets.
Hurrah! Hurrah!
We stand unshaken!

The SS Runes was designed by Walter Heck in 1931 by combining two Sig-Runes side by side. The Sig-Rune was a symbol of victory.

An SS motto: "To accept death and to hand out death".

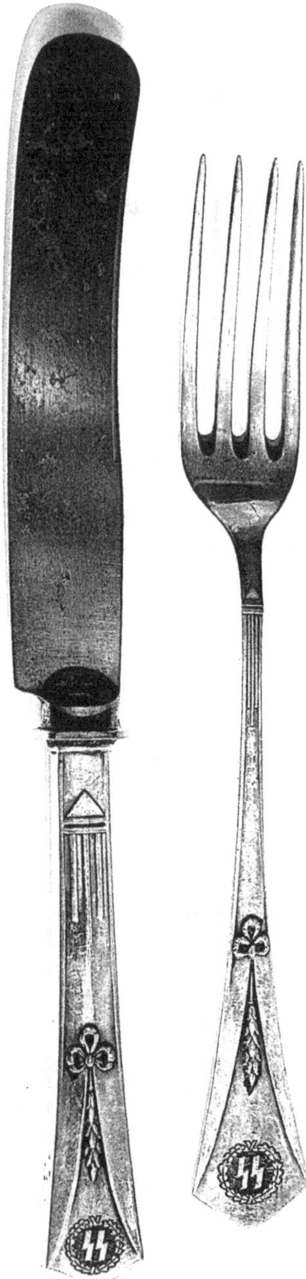

SS-120

SS-120

Fork: Obverse carries SS in a wreath. Reverse RM, 800, 'A' in a 6 pointed star, the maker mark of Robert Altermann, Gorlitz (with companion knife)

Short SS History: 9Nov1925 Schutzstaffel named. 6Jan 1929, Himmler becomes leader of its 280 members. Nov1933 - 'Adolf Hitler' Life Guards. 20Jul34 SS becomes an independent organization with 200,000 members. . 24Sep34, the SS-VT (Verfugungstruppe) or Political/Order Troops. In Dec35, a third branch of the SS was formed to run the new concentration camps, SS-TV (Totenkopfverbande) the Deaths Head Units and in 1939 Waffen-SS formalized.

The SS was a state within a state holding such positions as Hitler's secretary, personal adjutant, chief medical officer, his personal pilot, his chauffeur, the majority of his young valets and aides. Within the NSDAP, Party treasurer, Supreme Party Judge, Chief of the Party Press Office, Head of the Party Chancellery, Chief of the NSDAP Racial Department and Deputy Gauleiter of the Foreign Section of the NSDAP. State cabinet posts: Head of the Reich Chancellery, Foreign Ministry, Red Cross etc. etc.

The permanent SS group at each concentration camp was small. For example, at Dachau there were only 300 SS, all over 40 years of age, to oversee some 17,000 inmates. The camps were essentially run by the inmates with the Greens (police preventive detention = criminals) mostly in charge. In January 1945, some 715,000 including 200,000 women were still interned in concentration camps.

Note: This knife blade style is termed "Old French".

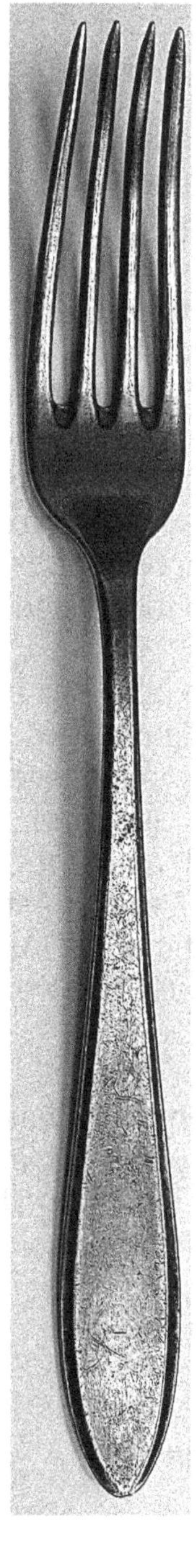

SS-121
L = 202 mm / 7 15/16”

SS-121 Allgemeine SS-F.S. Braunschweig

Fork: Obverse clear, Reverse Marked SS-F.S. where F = (Fuss / Foot / Infantry) S. = (Standarte / Standard unit) over 'Braunschweig'. Maker mark 'WMF' (Wurttembergische Metallwarenfabrik of Geislingen, 1853 to present. 'Cromargan' is a registered trademark of WMF composed of 18% Chrome, 10% Nickel and 72% steel.

This is an Allgemeine-SS fork. Allgemeine translates to General or Universal.. Hitler assisted Himmler in his first great victory over the SA by decreeing on November 7, 1930: "The task of the SS is first the practice of the police service within the party. No SA leader is entitled to give instructions to the SS!" Its original role was to protect Hitler then to support the police in maintaining order which later developed into a force to combat internal uprisings. By the start of the war, the Allgemeine-SS had 485,000 members in Germany. With the war, only 100,000 were exempted from military service and by 1945 that number had been reduced to 48,500.

Braunschweig (Brunswick, Brunswiek) is a city in central Germany's Lower Saxony. It is the city in which Adolf Hitler sought and found employment with the Braunschweig State Government in February 1932 to qualify for German citizenship (Hitler being Austrian) which was required to become a candidate for the German Reichstag. This was his first step to becoming the leader of the state (Reichskanzler).

Note: The Standarte was originally composed of 2,000, reduced to 1,000 in 1941 and finally to 400 in 1945. There were 127 Standarte in November 1944 each associated with a particular metropolitan area. Braunschweig's Standarte was designated number 49.

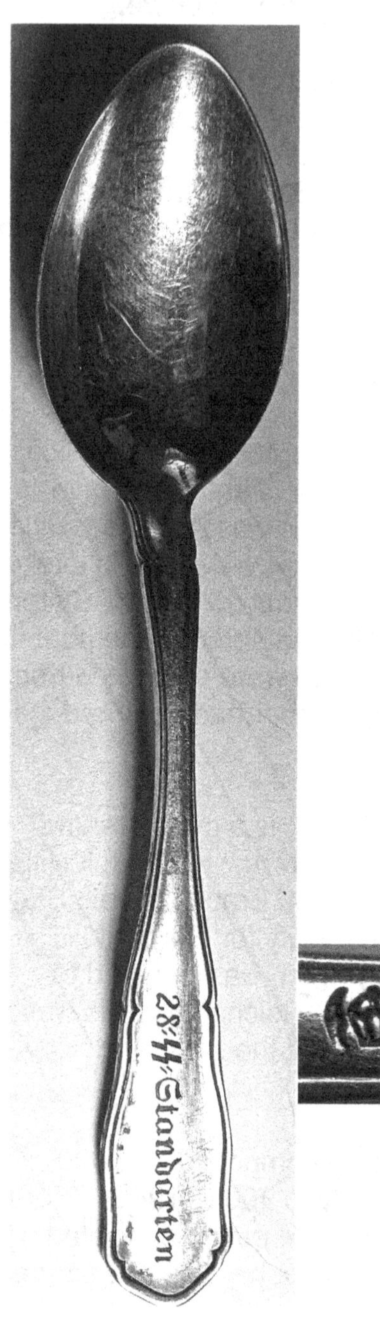

SS-122
L = 145 mm / 5 11/16”

SS-122 Allgemeine-SS Standardt 28, Hamburg

Teaspoon: Obverse marked '28=SS=Standarten'. Reverse Reichsmark, 800 unknown Maker Mark of a bird in a circle looking left and 'ARON'.

The Standarten was the standard unit of the Allgemeine-SS / General SS as set up in 1930 with a nominal goal of 2,000 men. Each SS Stardarte was composed of three active Sturmbanne or battalions one reserve Sturmbann and a marching band. The Sturmbann strength was nominally between 500 and 800 men. Within the Sturmbannn were four Sturme or companies, a medical squad and a fife and drum corps. A Sturm nominally had between 120 and 180 men. The Sturm was further divided into 3 or 4 Truppen (platoons) each composed of 3 Scharen (sections). The Schar composed of between 10 and 15 men. Standarten were numbered consecutively from 1 to 127. Number 28 being located in Hamburg.

On 26 July 1934, Adolf Hitler announced that "in consideration of the very meritorious service of the SS, especially in connection with the events of 30th June 1934, (night of the Long Knives when the SA leadership was killed by the SS) I elevate it to the status of an independent organization within the National Socialist Worker's Party."

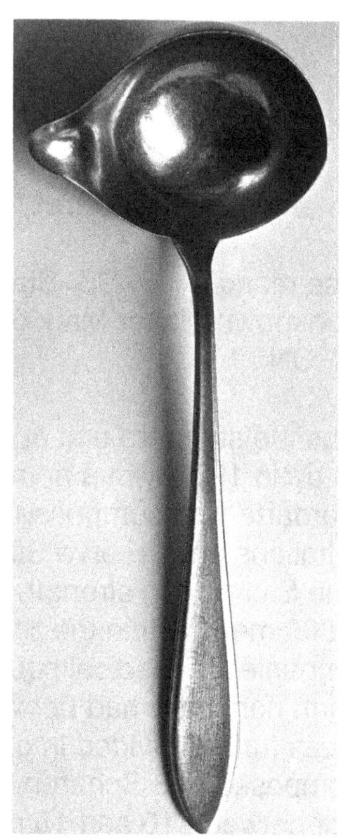

SS-123
L = 180 mm / 7 3/16”

SS-123 SS-VT Reich

Gravy Ladle: Obverse clear, reverse SS-VT Reich, WMF & Cromargan.

Führer Order on the armed units of the SS of 17 Aug 1938 established the SS-VT as political / order troops at the special disposal of the Nazi regime. Under the Reichsfuhrer-SS for internal security duties, except in time of war when it would be at the disposal of the army.

Fuhrer Order II. The armed units of the SS

“The SS Verfügungstruppe is neither a part of the Wehrmacht nor a part of the police. It is a standing armed unit, exclusively at my disposal. As such, and as a unit of the NSDAP its members are to be selected by the Reichsführer SS according to the ideological and political standards which I have ordered for the NSDAP and for the Schutzstaffeln.”

This ladle was made for one of the most well known and researched Panzer Divisions of the Waffen-SS. "Das Reich", as it was ultimately named, was composed of some of the most intensely trained and battle hardened troops in the world at the time. They took part in their first campaign in the West against the low lying countries in France as the SS-VT Division Reich, composed of 3 of the original 4 SS-Standarten (Regiments): Deutschland, Germania, and Der Fuhrer. The 4th was the SS LAH which was developed on it's own. After the Western campaign the SS-VT was reorganized and saw many name changes including “Reich” until it ultimately became the SS-Panzer-Grenadier-Division "Das Reich".

SS-124
L = 208 mm / 8 3/16

SS-124 Waffen-SS

Tablespoon: Obverse baroque with engraved owner initials of 'DJC'. Reverse with impressed 'Waffen-SS', RM, 800 and a Bruckmann & Sohne trade mark 'eagle'.

In September 1934, the SS-VT (Verfugungstruppe) or Political Troops (after the 'Night of the Long Knives') took over many of the guard functions at important Government locations. In October 1934 they were motorized. Their cadet school was opened in October 1934 at Bad Tolz.

> Note: In early 1935, Bad Tolz passed out the first 54 cadets. Nearly all of whom were killed in battle between 1939 and 1942.
>
> SS- VT: SS- Verfiigungstruppe - SS Special Purpose Troops; the militarized formations of the SS renamed Waffen-SS in the winter of 1939-40.
>
> Originally, Waffen-SS personnel requirements called for a minimum height of 5'11" for all volunteers except for the LAH which required a minimum height of 6'1".

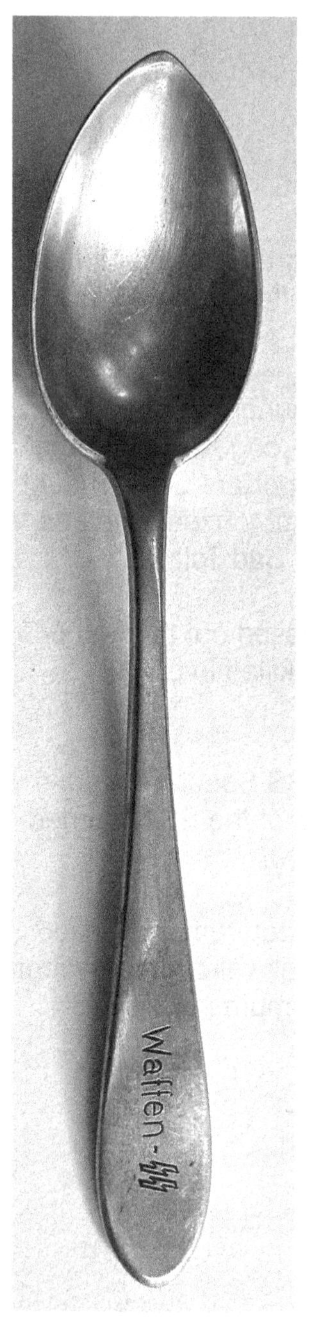

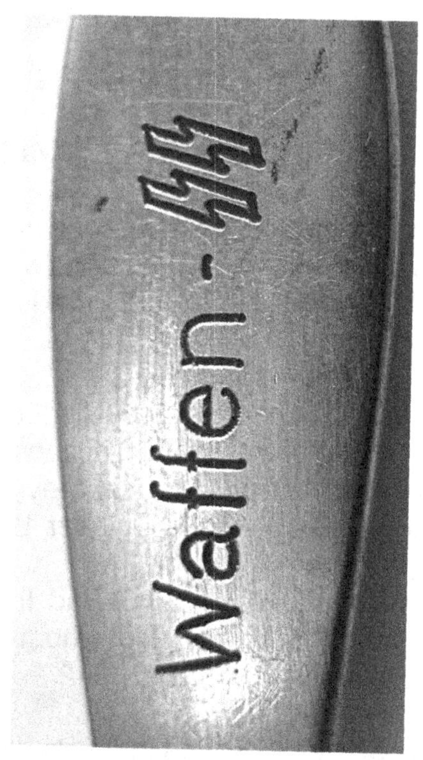

SS-125
L = 149 mm / 5 14/16”

SS-125 WAFFEN-SS

Teaspoon: Obverse plain with no decoration marked 'Waffen-SS'. Reverse hallmarked with a Wellner's 'elephant' over 'Alpacca' enclosed in an oval.

Waffen-SS or Armed-SS, literally Weapons-SS was the combat arm of the Schutzstaffel and founded in 1939.

Waffen-SS consisted of 38 combat divisions, each with numerical designations followed by such names as "SS Panzer Division", "SS Panzergrenadier Division" and "Waffen Grenadier Division Der SS". The 3rd SS Panzer Division = "Soldiers of Destruction" and the 12th SS Panzer Division = 'Fighters not Soldiers". Waffen-SS KIA estimated at 180,000, WIA 400,000 and MIA 70,000.

> Waffen SS Trivia: Although some 922,000 served in the Waffen-SS, ultimately 57 percent were non-German nationals! Breakdown: Reich Germans 400,000, West Europeans 137,000, East Europeans 200,000 and Volksdeutsche (ethnic Germans) 185,000. Initially the W-SS was 'German'. In 1940, with the founding of the Wiking Divison it became 'Germanic' The so called 'Germanic' divisions being the 1st LSSAH, 2nd Das Reich, 3rd Totenkopf and the 5th Wiking. From 1941 on, it became, per Leon Degrelle, the first truly European Army, ultimately composed of volunteers from 30 countries such as the 54,000 from Rumania and the 50,000 Islamic volunteers.

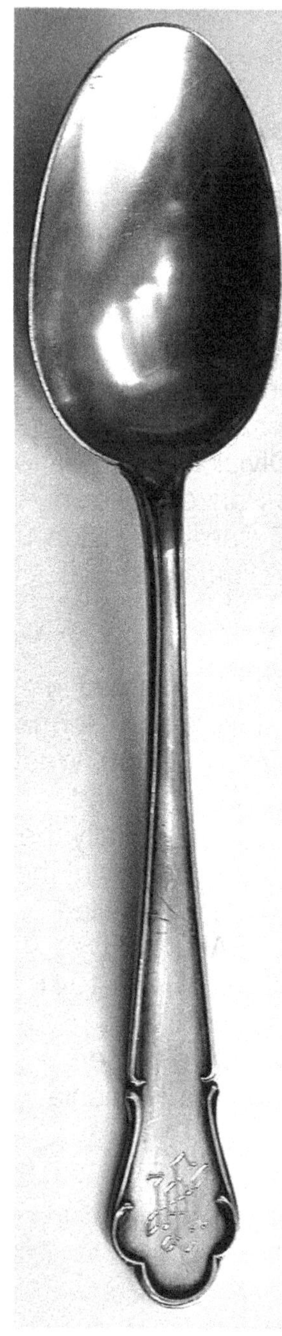

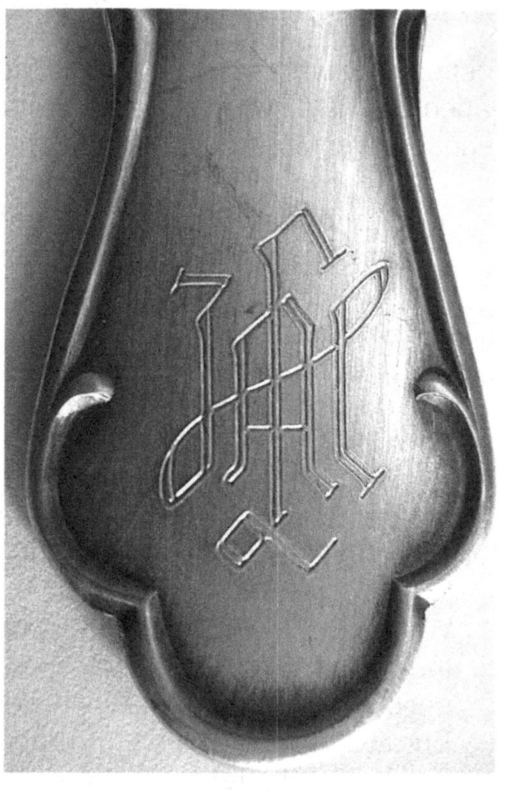

SS-126
L = 208 mm / 8 3/16"

SS-126 1st SS Panzer Division 'Leibstandarte Adolf Hitler'

Tablespoon: Obverse carries the formal pattern (also referred to as 'twisted wire' pattern) of intertwined LAH letters as used in the barracks of the SS-Leibstandarte Adolf Hitler, the elite soldiers of the Schutzstaffel, or Black Corps. Reverse maker marked 'V.S.F.' for Vereinigte Silberwaren-Fabriken AG., Duesseldorf. 90.

9 November 1933 (the 10th anniversary of the Beer Hall Putsch) the Leibstandarte-SS 'Adolf Hitler' = 'Adolf Hitler' Life Guards (in the fashion of the famous Imperial Royal Lifeguard Regiments) was created. It was funded from the national budget rather than the NSDAP's and thus became in Himmler's own words, "a complete law unto itself". They served Hitler as guards, adjutants, drivers, servants and waiters. The original LSSAH compound was located in South West Berlin at the Lichterfelde Kaserne (Berlin-Lichterfelde) which was an old Prussian cadet training school and became the headquarters for the Leibstndarte-SS "Adolf Hitler". This was also the location of some forty or more SS executions during the 'Night of the Long Knives". Later became the headquarters for the SS-Panzer-Division Leibstandarte under 'Sepp' Dietrich .

The spoon is in the Beidermeier pattern which evolved in such cities a Vienna, Munich and Berlin during the 'Beidermeier' period of 1815 - 1848 in Germany and Austria.

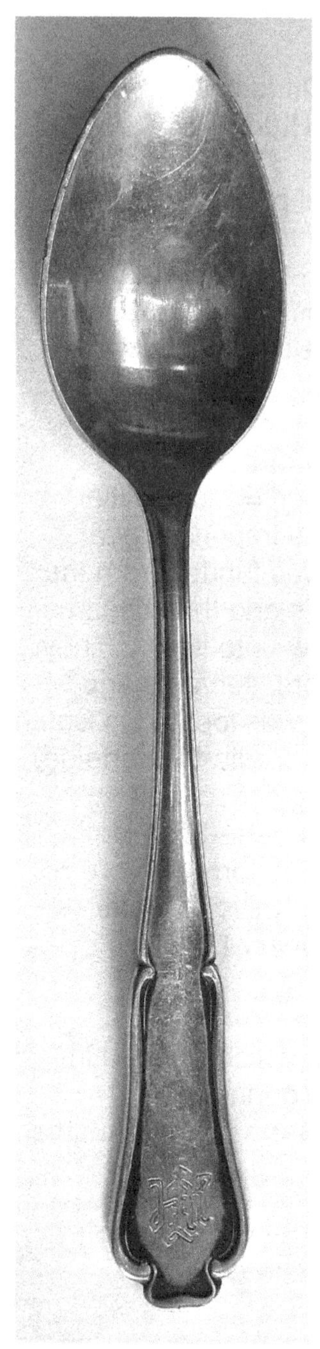

SS-127
L = 144 mm / 5 11/16"

SS-127 LSSAH

Teaspoon: Intertwined script letters L-A-H. Sometimes referred to as twisted wire design. Maker marked "Becker 90".

Commanded by SS-Gruppenfuhrer Josef 'Sepp' Dietrich it fought in Poland, Czechoslovakia, Holland, France, Yugoslavia, Greece, Russia, Belgium, and Hungary. Of the June 1944 strength of 19,700 troops, the remaining 1,500 survivors with 16 tanks surrendered to US troops in Austria in 1945.

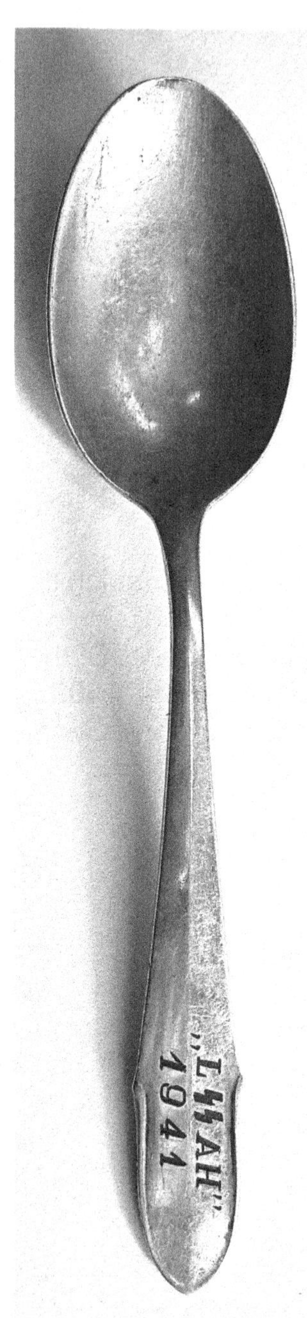

SS-128
L = 138 mm / 5 7/16”

SS-128 LSSAH 1941

Teaspoon: Obverse marked "LSSAH" 1941. Reverse maker marked: WMF, (Wurttembergische Metallwarenfabrik of Geislingen, Germany 1853 to the present), RM, 800.

SS Oath - Nov 33 - "I swear to you, Adolf Hitler, as Fuehrer and Reich Chancellor, loyalty and bravery. I vow to you, and those you have appointed to command me, obedience unto death. So help me God."

In 1929, Hitler described the SS man as, "Those who throng to the SS are men inclined to the authoritarian state, who wish to serve and obey, who respond less to an idea than to a man."

Half of all the W-SS Division commanders died in combat!

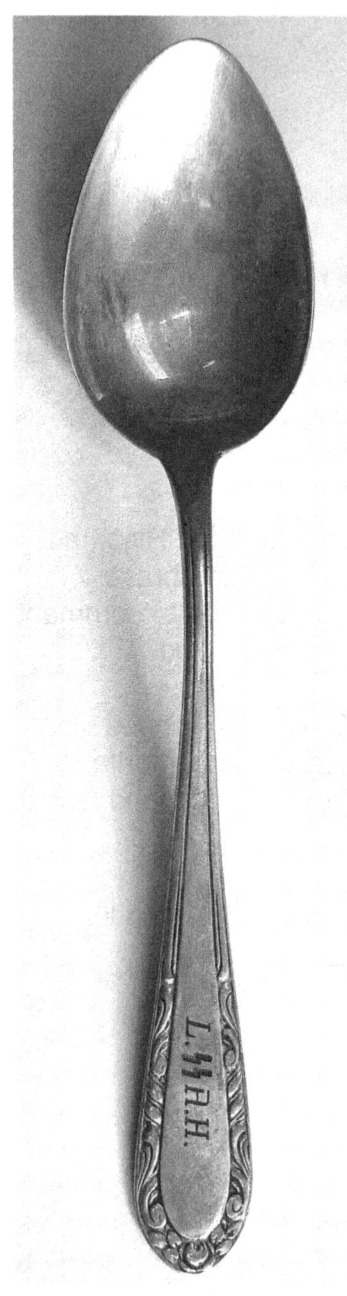

SS-129
L = 136 mm / 5 6/16"

SS-129 LSSAH.

Teaspoon: Obverse monogram: Capital 'L', 'SS' runes, Capital 'A' and Capital 'H'. Maker marked on the reverse: RM, 800, LW in a crest (Lutz & Weiss, Pforzheim founded 1882). Pattern: High relief, floral pattern, both sides, asymmetrical with roses at base.

In the early years prior to and of WWII, the Army resented the SS for taking the best candidates (volunteers) and as the Army controlled procurement for both, they took the best weapons first, supplying the W-SS with weapons from acquired / captured stocks.

Weapons fielded to each organization during those early years:

	Army	W-SS
Pistol	P.08 & P.38	Belgian High Power
Rifle	K98k Mauser	Hungarian 98/40 re-chambered
LMG	MG34 & MG42	Czech ZBvz26

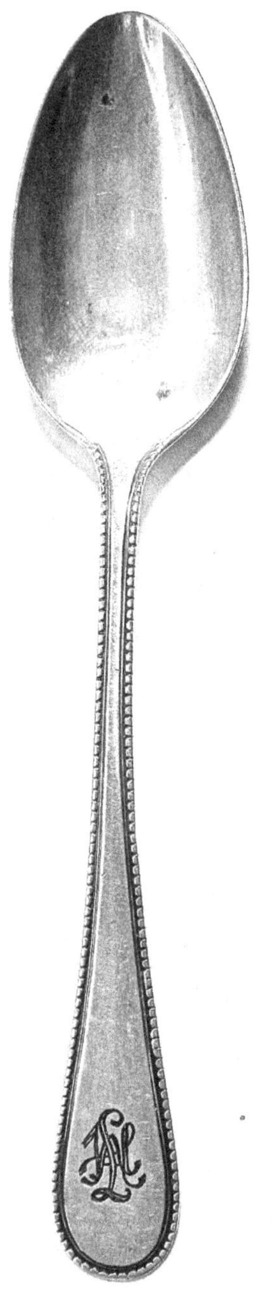

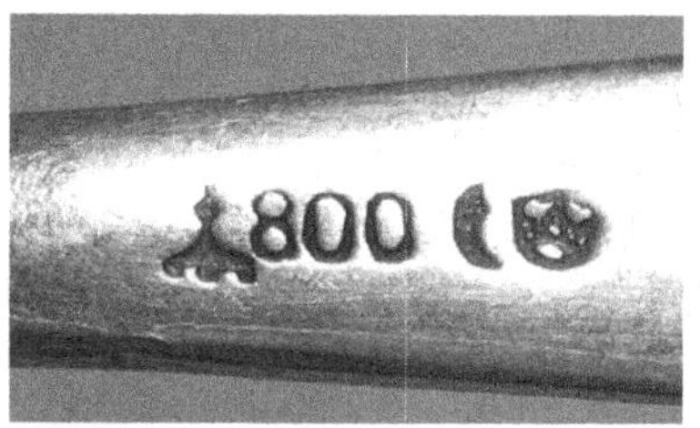

SS-130

L = 133mm / 5 1/4 "

SS-130 LSSAH

Teaspoon: Obverse carries the L-A-H intertwined initials. The obverse maker marked by Koch & Bergfeld, Bremen founded 1929, 800 and RM. Also has a hand engraved "G" over "M".

As a result of the occupation of Czechoslovakia in 1938 - 1939, Hitler was able to detail weapons acquired as: 1,582 airplanes, 2,175 pieces of field artillery, 469 tanks, 500 antiaircraft guns, 43,000 machine guns, 1,090,000 rifles, 114,000 revolvers, a billion rounds of ammunition and 3 million artillery shells in his 28 April 1939 Reichstag speech. Those MG's ended up in the W-SS. See the 3rd SS Panzer Division description SS-138.

Note: Track 16 of the 2005 digitally re-mastered "Triumph of the Will" DVD of the 1934 Nazi Party Rally in Nuremburg filmed by Leni Riefenstahl has some 5 minutes of the LSSAH review accompanied by their band playing Hitler's favorite, the Badenweiler March with appearances by both Himmler and Sepp Dietrich.

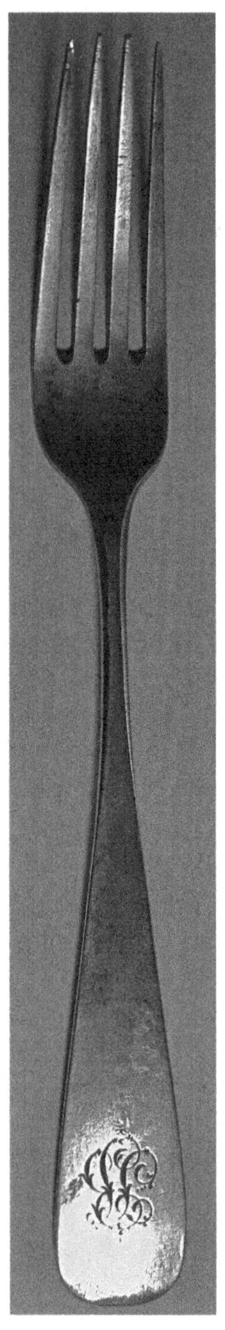

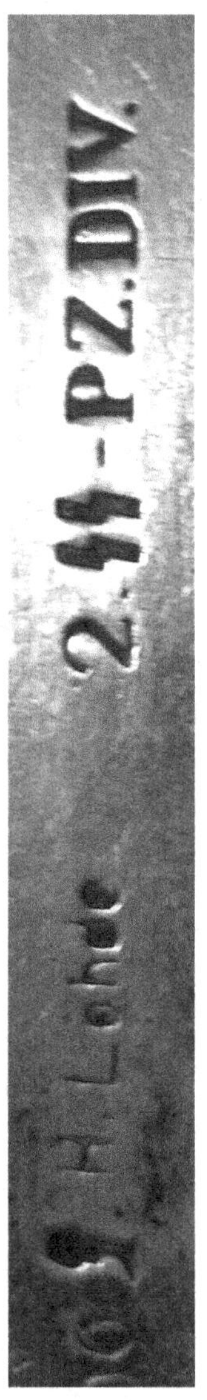

SS-131
L = 175 mm / 6 7/8"

SS-131 2nd SS-PZ. DIV. (Reich)

Fork: Obverse with undecipherable entwined engraved initials. Reverse with RM, 800, unknown maker mark, retailer 'H. Leher", 2 SS Panzer Division.

Originally established as the SS-VT Div in October 1939 with later name changes from the April 1940 designation as SS-Division Deutschland to October 1940's 2nd SS-Panzer Division "Reich" and in May 1942, after refitting with more tanks, assault guns and armored personnel carriers it was renamed SS-Panzer Division 'Das Reich'. The 2nd SS having acquired superior motorized units was able to accomplish wonders in what became to be known as the 'lightening' campaign in the Balkans in the spring of 1941.

In the SS, a German citizen (Reichsdeutsche) could immediately wear the SS collar runes upon entering the Waffen-SS. Racial Germans (Volksdeutsche) those definitely of German stock but resident outside of the Reich. typically wore a division collar patch and the SS rune on the breast..

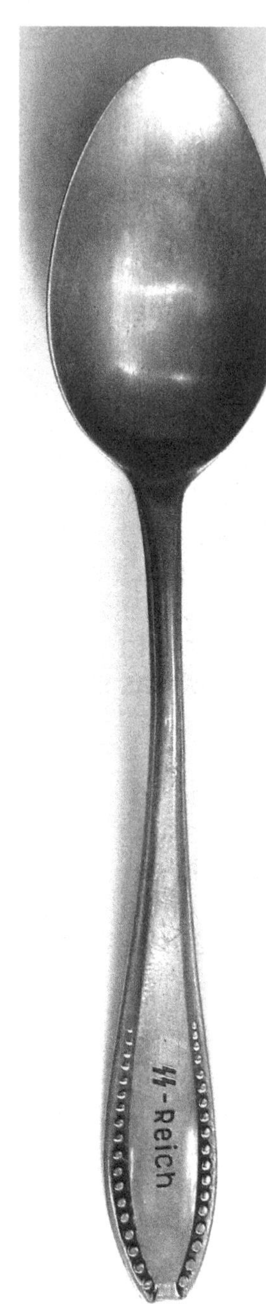

SS-132
L = 139 mm / 5 1/2"

SS-132 SS-Reich

Teaspoon: Obverse SS-Reich. Reverse hallmark: RM, "800", followed by "LSF" in an oblong enclosure for Liegnitzer Silberwarenfabrik, Liegnitz. Pattern: bottom 1/ 3rd of obverse has 18 symmetrical dots of increasing size on each side with largest at bottom.

During 1939 and 1940, German forces occupied western European countries which allowed the W-SS to recruit pro-Nazi's, anti communists, Volksdeutsche etc. while the Wehrmacht was not authorized to do so. By the end of 1942, the W-SS fielded some 200,000 troops.

Das Reich received more high bravery / valor awards than any other W-SS Division i.e., 69 Knight's Crosses.

The designation of Das Reich was changed eleven times from September 1939 till February 1945 due to status changes as well as later in the war to camouflage the units true identity and confuse enemy intelligence.

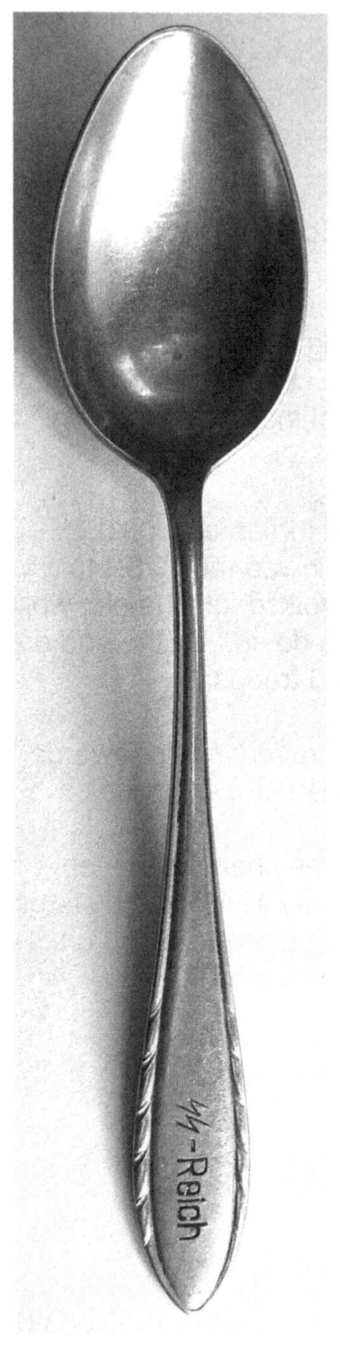

SS-133 L = 146 mm / 5 3/4 “

SS-133 SS-Reich

Teaspoon: Obverse 'SS-Reich' with the SS in what is termed 'lightning bolt' style. Highlights on edges of lower 1/3. Reverse maker marked; Berndorf over their trade mark 'walking bear' and Alpacca below in an overall oval shape.

SS enlistment requirements were 25 years for officers, 12 years for NCO's and 4 years for enlisted men. The Officer and NCO enlistment durations date from those specified by the Treaty of Versailles for the German Army in an effort to discourage enlistments.

Note: Responsible for issuing personal equipment items, control of SS mess hall supplies and rations was under SS-WVHA, SS-Wirtschafts und Verwaltungs Hauptamt (SS-Economic and Administration Department).

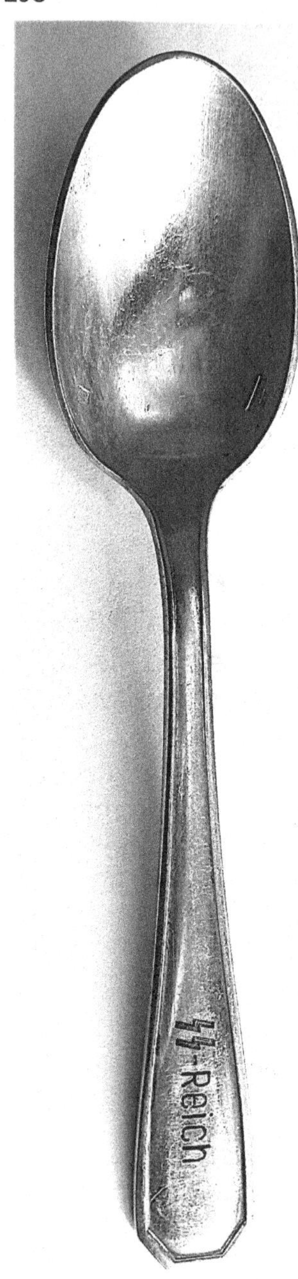

SS-134
L = 138 mm / 5 7/16”

SS-134 SS-Reich

Teaspoon: Obverse carries a textured SS - Reich. Reverse is unmarked.

On 5 Dec 1941, SS-Obergruppenfuhrer (4 Star) Paul Hausser, commanding SS Division 'Reich' came within 16 kilometers / 10 miles of the outskirts of Moscow, Temperature was -36C / -33F. They actually captured a beginning station of a tram line to Moscow.

SS-Oberstgruppenfuhrer Hauser, whose nickname was "Papa Hauser", lost an eye in combat and became famous as 'the SS general with the eye-patch'.

In 1946, Hauser stated. "The guards of the concentration camps and the personnel in the command did not belong to the Waffen-SS." See the 3rd SS-Panzer Div description SS-138.

Regarding uniform colors: Within the NSDAP, the three "teeth" organizations were the Sicherheitsdienst (SD) security police with grey uniforms, the Gestapo secret police in plain street clothes and the Waffen-SS in grey uniforms. The black uniformed SS were the Allgemeine-SS.

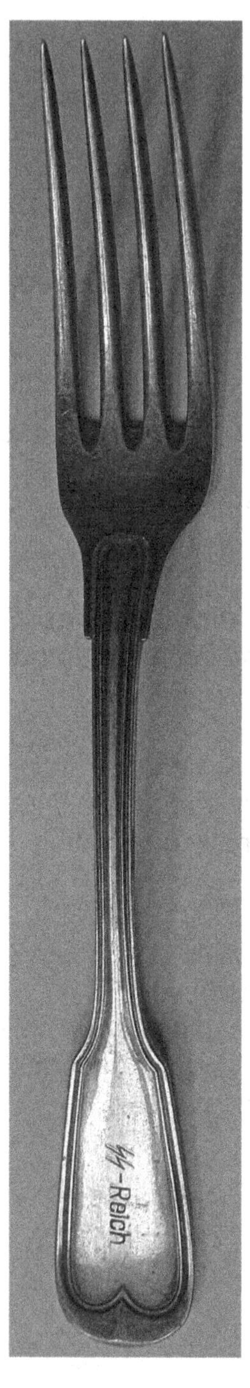

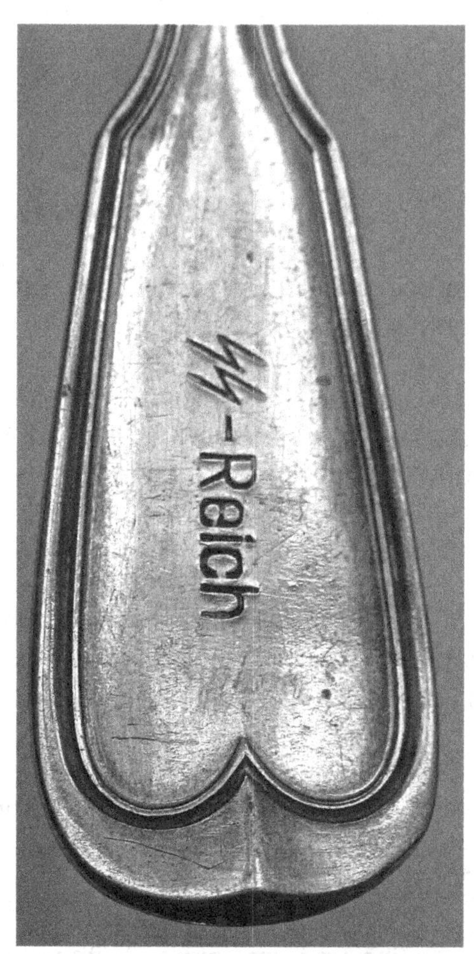

SS-135
L = 103mm / 8 1/16"

SS-135 SS-Reich
(Austria)

Table fork: Obverse carries the 'lightening' SS and Reich. Reverse has an Austrian crowned double headed eagle followed by 'maker mark 'BMF' (Berndorf Metallwaaren Fabrik / Berndorf Metalware Factory) with the M and F sharing the vertical line indicating the plant location as Vienna.

The 2nd SS was initially sent to the Balkans in 1941. Then participated in the invasion of Russia along the track from the Dneiper crossing, Smolensk, Kiev and on to Moscow. In 1942 to France for R&R. As a Panzer Grenadier Division participated in the occupation of Vichy France. March 1943 returned to Russia where Paul Hausser recaptured Kharkov presenting Hitler with a long sought victory, then on to Kursk and Kiev. Back to France in February 1944 and into Normandy in June. By the end of August, the Division had been reduced to some 450 men and 15 tanks. By September the tank count was down to three. Back to Paderborn area for R&R then participated in the failed Ardennes attack, followed by the final transfer to Hungary. By the end of the war they were able to maneuver into the area near Pilsen and surrender to the U.S. Army on 8 May 1945.

Special note; Although Austria had only 8 percent of the population of Germany, it supplied 14 percent of the SS manpower.

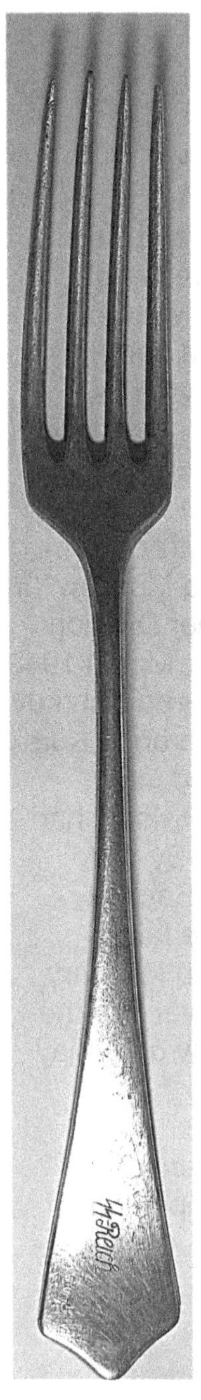

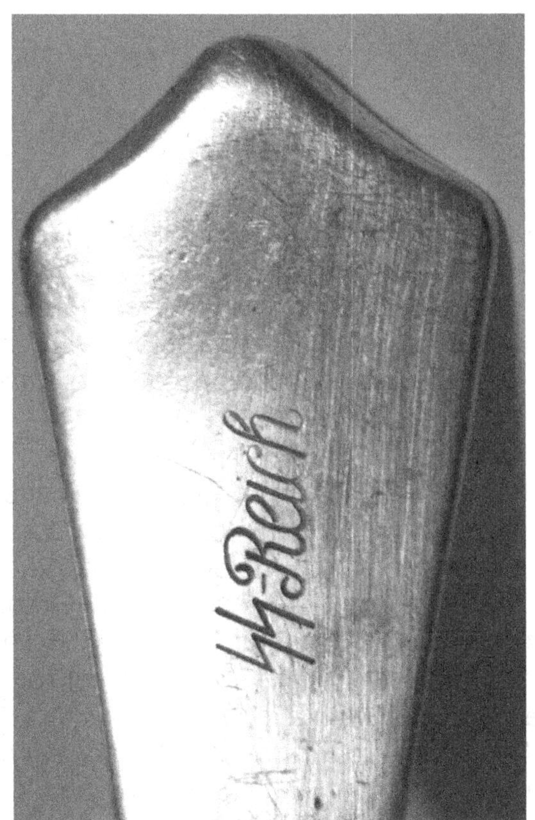

SS-135
L = 213 mm / 8 3/8"

SS-135 SS-Reich (China Silber)

Fork: Obverse with SS-Reich. Reverse with China Silber. Between the China and Silber is a bear. Above it is 'PFG' and below 'CHS'. Berndorfer Metallwarenfabrik, A. Krupp AG, Berndorf / Osterreich used the maker mark: bear and PFG.

In the early 17th Century, Imperial China had exported the first metal alloy called Packfong to Europe. It was not until 1770 that the constituents of Packfong (copper, zinc and nickel) were identified and the alloy reproduced in the independent city of Suhl in the South of the Free State of Thuringia, Germany gave it the name of 'White Copper Suhler'. In 1823 the Prussian Society for the Promotion of Commercial Diligence started a competition to produce a white alloy with the appearance of .750 silver that could be used for cooking utensils. In 1823 Dr. Ernst August Geitner of Aue developed Argentan and in 1824 the Brothers Henniger in Berlin created German Silver a replacement for white copper which had used arsenic. The first use of the term China Silver was in 1844 in Austria and referred to heavily silver plated brass. Later the name China Silver was used to describe a nickel silver / German silver base upon which silver has been electroplated. To better identify the actual amount of silver electroplated, the marking of the amount in grams applied to 24 pieces was standardized, overwhelmingly at 90 grams per 24 pieces and the pieces so marked.

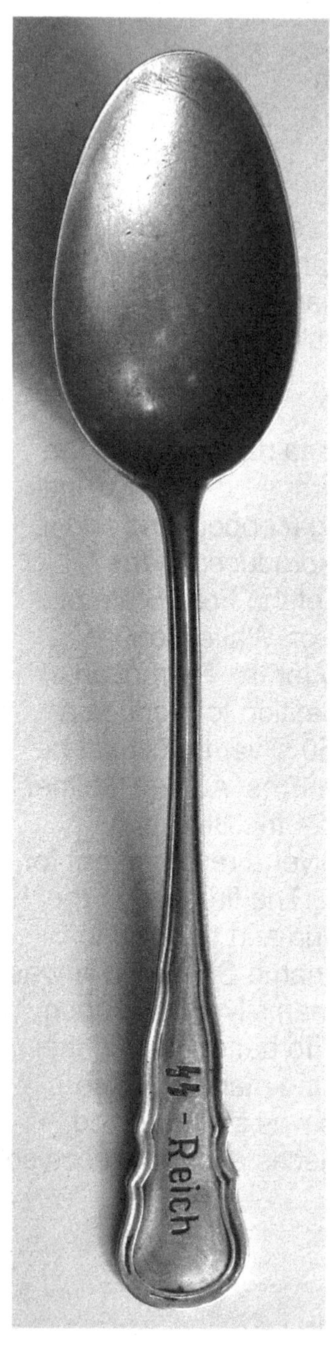

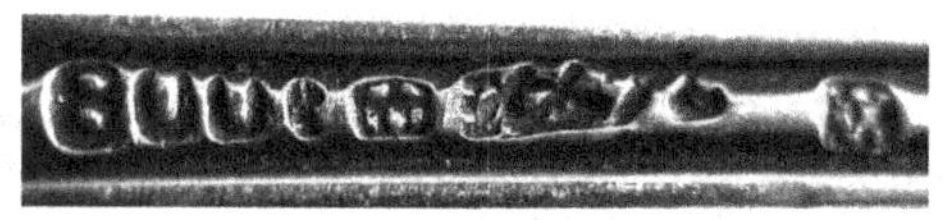

SS-137
L = 140 mm / 5 9/16”

SS-137 SS-Reich

Teaspoon: Obverse monogram SS-Reich, Maker marked: 800, RM, unreadable entry, XX, for Wilhelm Muller of Berlin. Scalloped handle, double outline.

Führer order on the armed units of the SS of 17 Aug 1938 established the SS-VT as political troops at the special disposal of the Nazi regime. Under the Reichsfuhrer-SS for internal security duties, except in time of war when it would be at the disposal of the army.

This translation is from Document 647-PS [translation], in Nazi Conspiracy and Aggression. Volume III: US Government Printing Office, District of Columbia: 1947. pp. 459-466 from the above referenced Fuhrer order:

II. The armed units of the SS
A. The SS-Verfügungstruppe
1. The SS Verfügungstruppe is neither a part of the Wehrmacht nor a part of the police. It is a standing armed unit, exclusively at my disposal. As such, and as a unit of the NSDAP its members are to be selected by the Reichsführer SS according to the ideological and political standards which I have ordered for the NSDAP and for the Schutzstaffeln.

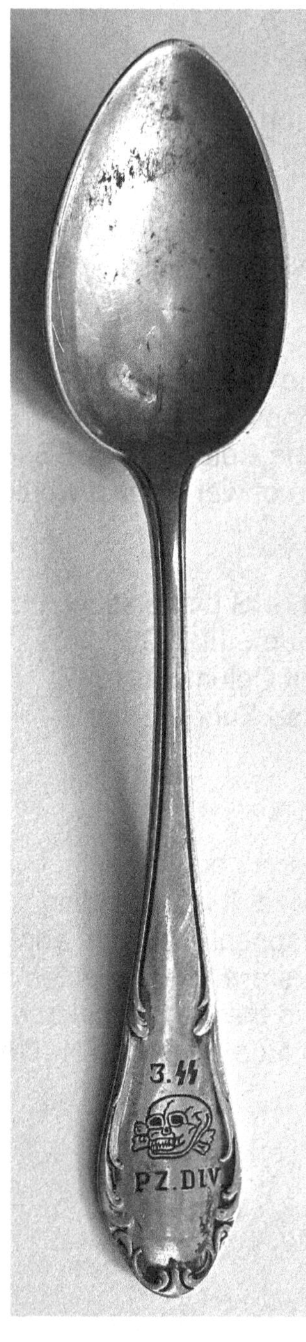

SS-138
L = 141 mm / 5 9/16"

SS-138 3rd SS Panzer Division 'Totenkopf' (Death's Head)

Teaspoon: Obverse carries the 3rd's Coat-of-Arms, reverse distributor: E. Kludas, MM: Koch & Bergfeldhas 800, RM.

Raised Nov 1939 with most of the initial enlisted men coming from the SS-Totenkopfverbande, (SS Concentration Camp Guards). Through the Battle of France the division was generally equipped with ex-Czech weapons. In November 1942, 'Das Reich', 'Totenkoph' and 'Wiking' were officially re-designated as SS-Panzergrenadier Divisions, and finally acquired the same type and quantity of equipment to that of army panzer divisions. Surrendered to US troops in Austria 9 May 1945 with less than 1,000 men and 6 tanks from an original strength of 19,000. Handed over to the Russians.

Note: Commanded by Theodor Eicke from 14Nov1939 till his KIA on 16Feb1943, shot down behind Russian lines on a recognizance. The 3rd Panzer acquired the identity as "that lost lot" or the Bones Companies. Under Eicke, 'Totenkopf' Div had 60,000 KIA/WIA/MIA vs 'Wiking' Div's 19,000, (the divisions mostly served side by side), the difference is attributed to the commanders. Eicke's favorite guidance: "There is only one thing that is valid, orders!"" and "Tolerance is a sign of weakness". Totenkopf had the most requests for "transfers out" of any W-SS Division and supplied most of the volunteers for the SS paratroop battalion, generally recognized as a suicide squad.

Note: Eicke, a "dangerous lunatic" imprisoned as a violent hardened criminal was released from a mental hospital in 1933. He personally shot Ernst Rohm on 2July1934, In 1936 he styled himself, Commander of Death's Head Units or "Fuhrer der Totenkopfverbande" after they were allowed to wear the death's head collar patches.

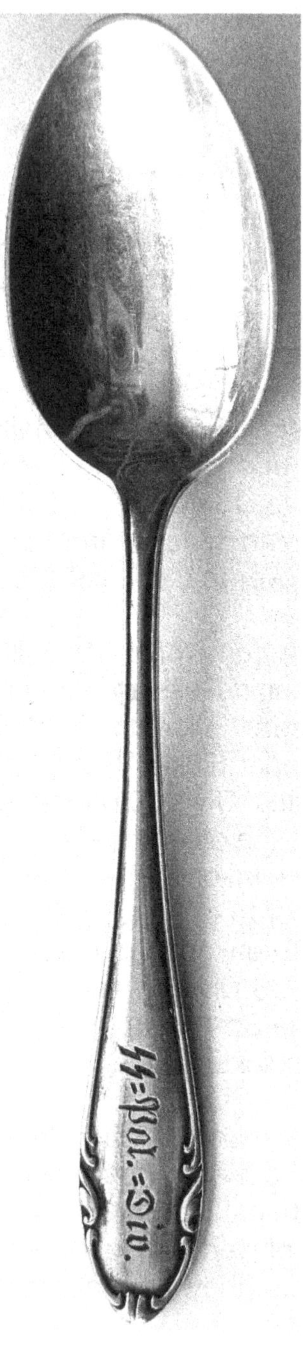

SS-139
L = 141 mm / 5 9/16”

SS-139 4th SS-Panzer Grenadier Division “Polizei”

Spoon: Obverse ‘SS=Pol.=Div.” and reverse 800, RM and maker marked ‘Siberce’.

This Division was formed and composed of members of the Ordnungpolizei (OrPo / Order Police), the uniformed police on 1 October, 1939 and was not considered to be an elite SS Division because of the manner in which the members of the unit were allowed to join, resulting in the wearing of the Ordnungpolizei uniform with a Heer Eagle on the arm. At the time, SS uniforms were not provided for the unit.

The Division’s first action was during the Campaign in France. In 1941, the Division was transferred to the Eastern Front and during heavy fighting for the Luga bridgehead, held by a number of Soviet Divisions, the 4th SS Division lost over 2000 soldiers in bloody frontal assaults but managed to fight into the Northern edge of Luga and encircle and destroy the Soviet defenders.

It was not transferred to the Waffen-SS until 10 February 1942, when the Division was given "official" Waffen SS status, and in June 1943 its title was changed to 4th SS Panzer Grenadier Division “Polizei” and was sent to the Balkans area. Elements of the Division saw action in Greece on anti-partisan duties and also fought near Belgrade. In January 1945, the Division was pushed into Slovakia, soon after, the 4th SS was moved to Danzig where it was trapped by Soviet forces. After dire battle the Division was shipped across the Hela Peninsula and over sea to Swinemude. There, the Division rested and on 8 May 1945, surrendered to the Russians although some members, attached to Army Group Steiner, surrendered to the Americans.

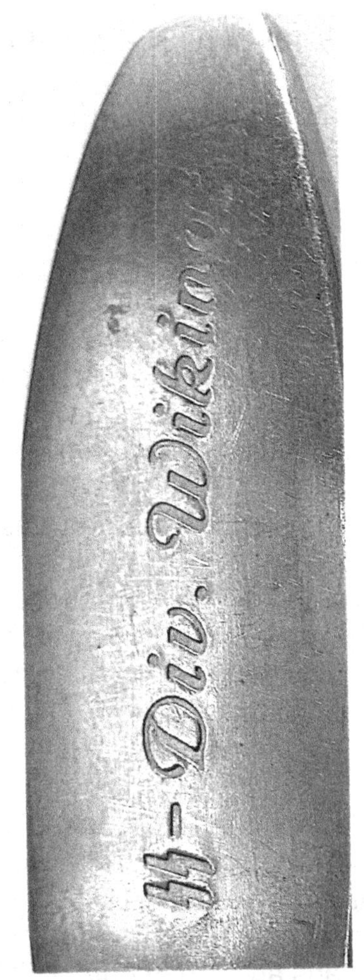

SS-140
L = 215 mm / 8 7/16"

SS-140 5th SS Panzer Division 'Wiking'

Tablespoon: Obverse is flat and unmarked. Reverse carries 'SS-Div. Wiking' & 'ROSTFREI'.

The 5th SS-Panzer-Division (Viking) was originally formed in November 1940 as the SS-Division (mot.) Germania by consolidating the regiments Germania, Nordland (Scandinavians), Westland (Dutch, Flemings) and the 5th SS-Artillerie Regiment into a new divisional unit. On January 1st 1941 the division was renamed, SS-Division "Wiking" and on November 9th 1942 the division was upgraded and renamed SS-Panzer-Grenadier-Division "Wiking". The division was upgraded again and received its final designation on October 22nd 1943 as 5th SS-Panzer-Division "Wiking" and surrendered in Furstenfeld, Czechoslovakia in May 1945. Although the enlisted men were predominantly Nordic volunteers, it was officered by Germans.

SS-141
L = 133 mm / 5 1/4"

SS-141 9th SS Panzer Division 'Hohenstaufen'

Teaspoon: Obverse carries the 9th's Coat-of-Arms. Reverse carries the RM, 800 and maker's mark HTB for Hanseatishe Silberwarenfabrik, Bremen.

The Hohenstaufen, named after the family of the first German Emperors and specifically for family member Frederick Barbarossa whom the Fuehrer considered a great hero. Activated in early 1943 and faced with manpower shortages, 70 percent of the division's manpower were conscripts with 60% to 70% from the years 1925/26 or about 18 years of age. Included were a number of ethnic Germans from Hungary. In June 1944 engaged in Normandy fighting with a strength of 15,849. By 21 August only 460 men, 20 guns and 23 tanks remained as a result of losses particularly around Caen and Avranches. Transferred to Western Germany in late September to be brought up to strength, their numbers were made up with Luftwaffe personal and other remnants. Participated in the failed Ardennes offensive, moved to Hungary and suffered severe losses against the Russians in March 1945 west of Budapest. Hitler was so enraged by their failure to defeat the Russians that he ordered the men of the 1st, 2nd, 9th and 12th Divisions of the Waffen-SS to be deprived of their decorations and cuff bands. The 9th reportedly returned their decorations in a chamber pot. They fought their way back to Austria and on 5 May 1945 surrendered to US troops near Steyr.

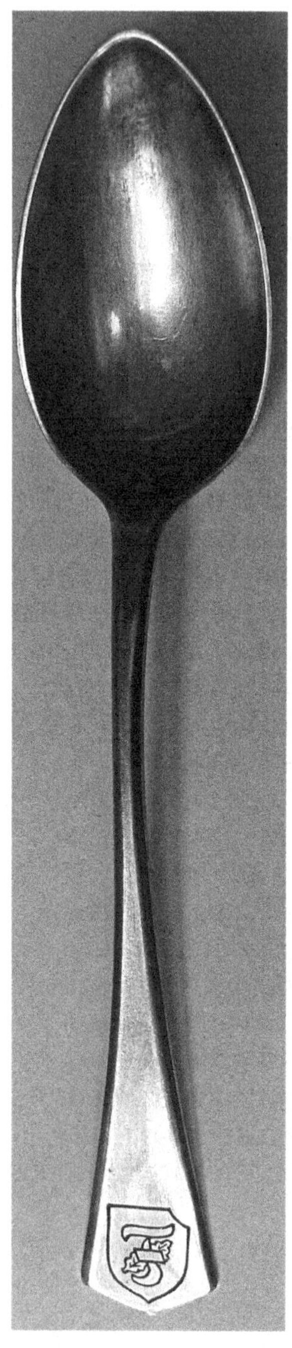

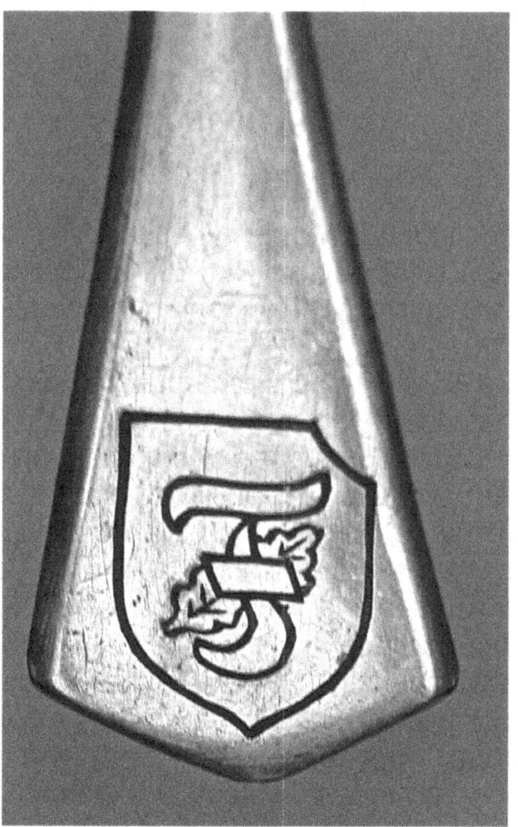

SS-142
L = 138 mm / 5 7/16"

SS-142 10th SS Panzer Division 'Frundsberg'

Teaspoon: The obverse carries the 10th's Coat-of-Arms while the reverse carries designer 'A. Finster', 800, RM, and the maker's mark of Herman Walter, Halle.

This unit was named after Georg von Frundsberg who lived from 1473 to 1528. Frundsberg was a well known soldier and hero who fought in the services of the Hapsburg Monarchy during several wars.

Recruiting of German conscripts started on 8 January 1943. Reichsführer Heinrich Himmler, when questioned by Adolf Hitler concerning the average age of the soldiers and officers of the division, stated "Achtzehn Jahre" (18 years). Division raised in Charente, France and originally named 'Karl der Grosse'.

To the Russian front in March 1944, returned to France June 1944 involved in heavy fighting at Caen, Avranches and Falaise. Moved through Belgium to Arnhem area fighting the British. Moved into Pomeranian on 2 March 1945 and fought heavily in areas Stettin, (Poland) Stargard, Furstenwalde. On 7 May, 1945 remnants of the division destroy 5 Soviet T-34 tanks en-route to Sudetenland.
From 10 to 12 May, 1945 the division's remnants attempt unsuccessful reassembly, and disband on their own in an effort to make their way west individually. A number of survivors, who are not captured by either Soviet or Czech forces en-route, surrender to the US 102nd Infantry Division at Tangermünde, on the Elbe River.

SS-143
L = 145 mm / 5 3/4”

SS-143 11th SS Freiwilligen Panzer Grenadier Division "Nordland'.

Teaspoon: Obverse carries the 11th's Coat-of-Arms. Reverse carries retailer G H DANZIGER, maker mark of Koch & Bergfeld, Bremen (founded 1829)'800' no RM.

Formed in the summer of 1943 of various existing foreign volunteer units. It was the first SS Division to be officered by foreign volunteers. Most of the volunteers were from Scandinavia but the division had the widest range of nationalities found in a single German division including Danish, Hungarian, Dutch, Norwegian, Estonian, Finnish, French, Romanian, Spanish, Swedish, Swiss and British volunteers that had either served in the division or been attached to it. Its emblem is the "Sun Wheel" Swastika (Sonnerrad Hackenkreuz) - a circular swastika - the symbol of eternity. On 25 April 1945, the primary defender of the Reich Chancellery in Berlin was the SS Division Nordland with virtually no Germans. They had never taken a prisoner and did not expect to be made prisoners.

Motto: When all were unfaithful, we remained faithful.

Note: Along with Nordland, the other W-SS defenders of Berlin were the 33rd W-SS Div Charlemagne (French) and the 15th W-SS Div (Latvian).

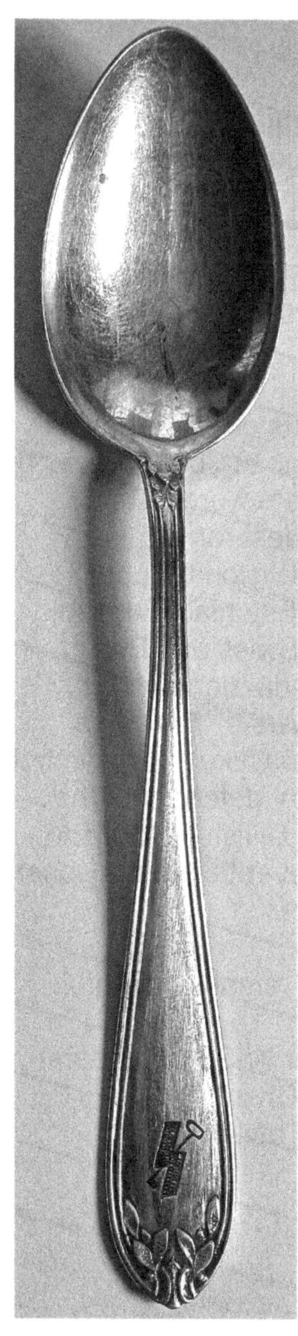

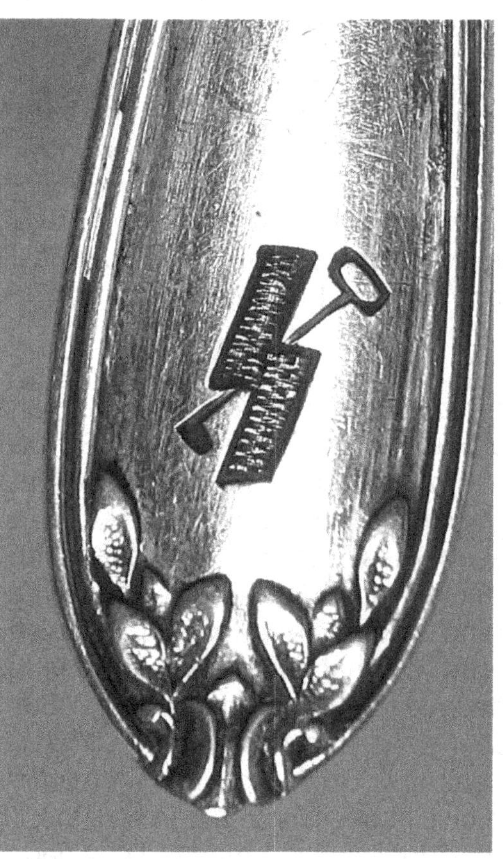

SS-144
L = 133 mm / 5 1/4”

SS-144 12th SS Panzer Division 'Hitlerjugend'

Teaspoon: Obverse with 12th's Coat-of-Arms, reverse 800 RM, maker mark 'FUCHS' for Gebrueder Fuchs, Solingen.

Described as a "crack" division, the Hitlerjugend was unique because the majority of its junior enlisted men were drawn from members of the Hitler Youth born in 1926, (age 17) while the senior NCOs and officers were generally supplied by the 1st SS Panzer Division. They were referred to as the "candy soldiers" as they were too young for normal military rations of spirits and tobacco. The Division insignia depicts the Hitlerjugend sigrune crossing the key of the 1st SS Panzer Division LSSAH's insignia.

The idea of a Waffen-SS division composed of Hitlerjugend (HJ) members was proposed in January 1943. Himmler soon became an enthusiastic advocate as did Hitler, and on 13 February 1943, the official order for the creation was issued.

The division, with 20,540 personnel, first saw action on 7 June 1944 as part of the German defense of the Caen area during the Normandy campaign and it came out of the Falaise pocket with a divisional strength of 12,500 men. In 1944, its commander Kurt "Panzer" Meyer became the youngest general ever to serve in the German military at age 34. On 16 December 1944, the division was committed against the US Army in the Battle of the Bulge, suffering 60% casualties in the 4 week period. After the failure of the Ardennes offensive the division was sent east to fight the Red Army near Budapest. The Division eventually withdrew into Austria and on 8 May 1945, the surviving 7,500 men surrendered to the US Army at Enns.

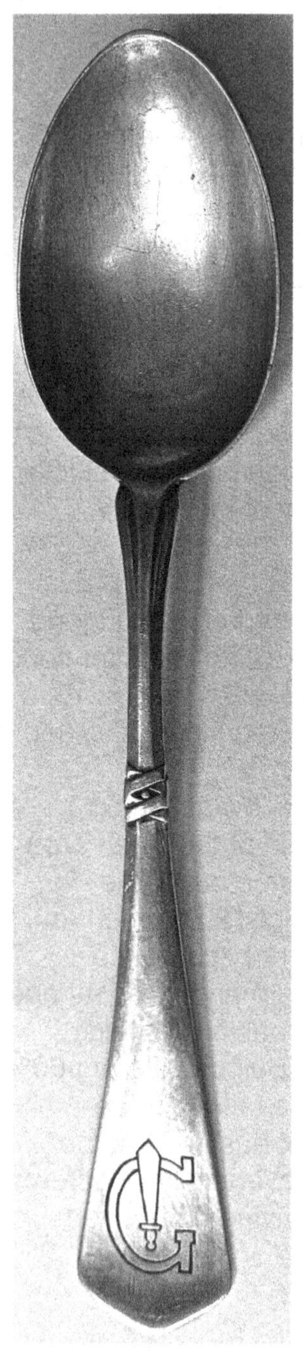

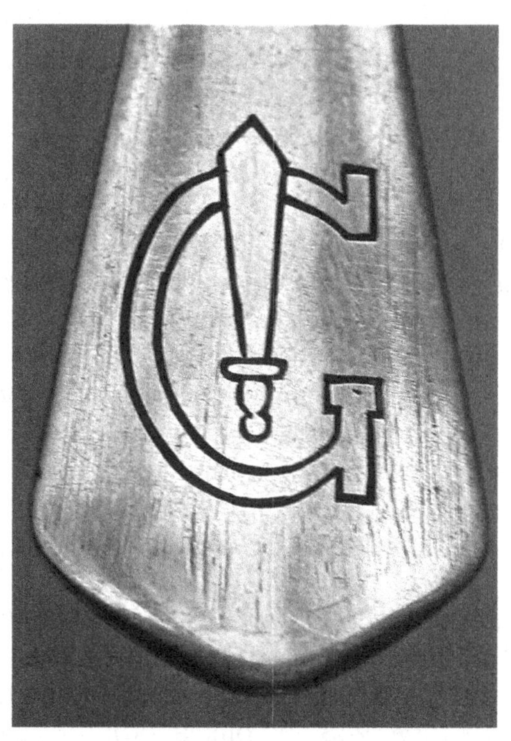

SS-145
L = 125 mm / 4 15/16”

SS-145 Regt. Gruppe 13. SS Gebirgs 'Handschar'.

Teaspoon: The obverse carries the Regt. Gruppe 13's Coat-of-Arms while the reverse: 800, RM and maker mark of Vereinigte Silberwarenfabriken, Dusseldorf,

In the Fall of 1942, SS Reichsfuhrer Heinrich Himmler and SS-General Gottlob Berger approach Hitler with the proposal to raise a Bosnian Muslim SS division. Himmler thought that Muslim men would make perfect SS soldiers, as Islam "promises them Heaven if they fight and are killed in action." Hitler formally approved the project on 10 February 1943 and SS-Obergruppenführer Arthur Phleps, a Romanian ethnic German commander, was charged with raising the division. The 13th Waffen Mountain Division of the SS Handschar (1st Croatian) was commanded by German officers, and composed of native Germans from Croatia (Volksdeutsche), and Bosniaks, who are Muslims from Bosnia and Herzegovina. It was the largest of both the Muslim-oriented divisions and the SS Divisions with 21,065 men, of whom 10% were Croatians. The division had a Muslim Imam for each battalion and a Mullah per regiment. Handschar (Bosnian/Croatian: Handžar) was the local word for the Turkish scimitar, a historical symbol of Bosnia and Islam. The Handschar division was a mountain infantry formation, known by the Germans as "Gebirgsjäger". It was used to conduct operations against Yugoslav's primarily Christian Serb Partisans in the Independent State of Croatia from February to September 1944. Recruitment for the division fell as the war progressed and when rumors spread that the division was going to fight the Soviets, the Muslims deserted in droves and was disbanded in October 1944.

The German Volksdeutsche cadre then formed the SS-Gebirgs 'Handschar' (a regimental Group) fought in Hungary and ultimately surrendered to the British in Austria 5/45.

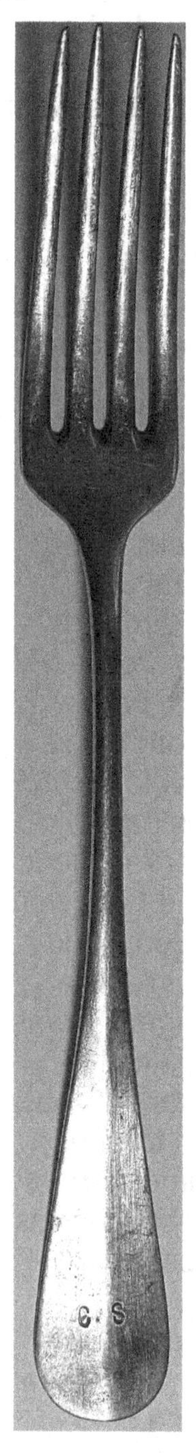

SS-146
L = 204 mm / 8"

SS-146 34th Grenadier Regiment of the 15th SS Waffen Grenadier Division - 'Latvian No. 1'

Fork: Obverse carries 'CS' for Cesis-Schule. Reverse with 'SS' in a circle, '90' and an unidentified Maker Mark of three die (cubes) showing the Four sides, Wellner?

The Latvian city of Cesis was the location of the 34th Gren Regiment's headquarters. The school building and its cutlery were used by the 34th during its formation and this fork had the 'SS' added at that time.

The SS had success in 1942 in recruiting in the Baltic States forming 'Legions' of 'volunteer' units promising German citizenship, free land and restriction to the war on Communism. The 15th Waffen-Gren Div der SS was formed when manpower shortages became obvious after the invasion of Russia. Latvian (Lettland) conscripts formed the 15th Waffen-Gren-Div and the "Voluntary" title was dropped when to increase the unit strength, Himmler enforced compulsory military service in the Ostland in age groups 1915 to 24 in 1943 and 1904 to 14 & 1925 & 26 in 1944.

The 15th fought on the Eastern Front but lost enthusiasm when their homeland was occupied by the Soviets. The 15th was decimated in the defense of Pomerania in early 1945. The survivors participated in the defense of Berlin (see SS-143). Other remnants surrendered to the Americans at Gutergluck near the Elbe River.

Note: Some 15,000 Latvians served in the two Latvian SS Divisions: The 15th SS Grenadier Div. 'Latvian No 1 and the19th SS Grenadier Div 'Latvian No 2'. All officers were German.

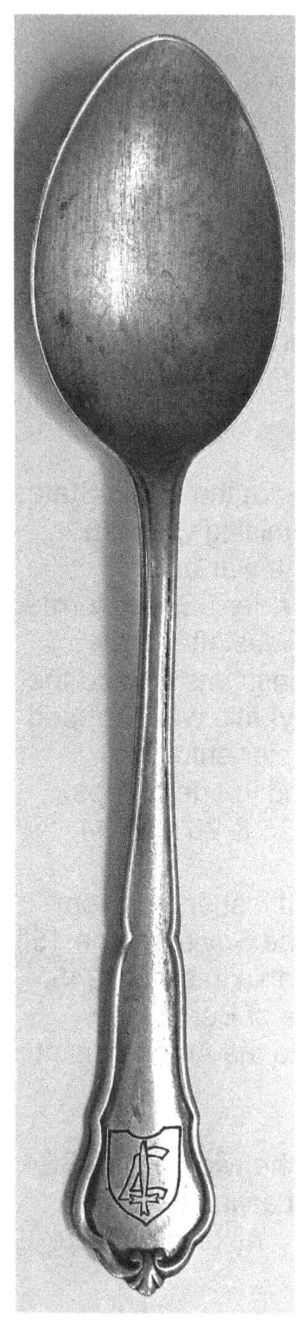

SS-147
L = 142 mm / 5 10/16"

SS-147 37th SS Freiwilligen Kavallerie Division 'Lützow'

Teaspoon: Obverse carries the 37th SS Cavalry Division's Coat-of-Arms. Reverse marked RM, 800, HTB for Hanseatishe Silberwarenfabrik, Bremen.

The 37th SS Volunteer Cavalry Division - Lutzow was listed for the first time on 1March1945. It had been officially established 19Feb1945 following the near-complete annihilation of the 8th and 22nd SS Cavalry Divisions during the Budapest breakout attempt on 11/12 Feb 1945. It consisted of remnants of 8th SS Cavalry Division Florian Geyer and 22nd SS Volunteer Cavalry Division Maria Theresia, including former's SS Pioneer Battalion 8, in addition to mostly 16- or 17-year old German, Hungarian Volkdeutsche, and ethnic Hungarian recruits. The 37th SS also inherited the horses of the two annihilated divisions as both the 8th and 22nd were fighting dismounted when Budapest was surrounded. The new division never exceeded regimental strength. The 37th was the 3rd and last cavalry division of the W-SS. The Division emblem sword was the emblem of the original SS Cavalry Brigade. The division saw action against Soviets as a part of 6th. SS-Panzerarmee during the final weeks of war, before surrendering to Americans in Austria in May.

The Division's namesake, Ludwig Adolf Wilhelm Freiherr von Luetzow (1782-1834) led the swashbuckling German volunteer cavalry unit known as the "Black Troop" in the war against Napoleon in 1813.

Note:
1. The Division motto: "You came very late, still you came".
2. In its last month of existence its strength was reduced from 2,000 to 180.

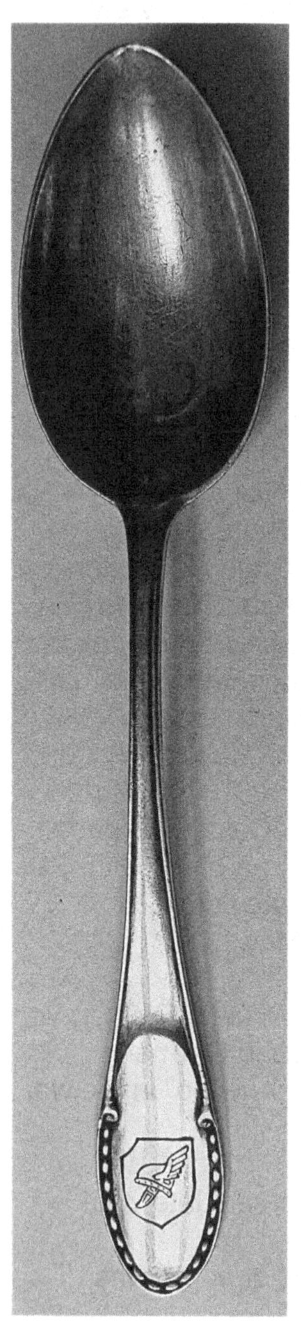

SS-148
L = 142 mm / 5 5/8"

SS-148 39th SS Grenadier Division 'Nibelungen'

Teaspoon: Obverse carries the 39th's Coat-of-Arms. Reverse has the RM, 800 and maker mark of Gebuder Reiner, Krumbach Bayern 1910 - present.

The SS-Junkerschule Bad Tölz was the officers training school for the Waffen-SS. It was the equivalent of the United States Military Academy. The school was established in 1937, in the town of Bad Tölz which is about 30 miles south of Munich. The location selected was primarily due to the beauty of the surrounding area. A sub camp of the Dachau concentration camp was located in the town of Bad Tölz to provide labour for the SS-Junkerschule. The 38th SS was formed on 27 March 1945 from four infantry battalions mainly composed the staff and students from the school combined with Himmler's bodyguard battalion and stragglers from the 30th SS-W Gren Div. It never exceeded a strength of 6,000 men. The Division was at first named Junkerschule because of its formation from the members of the SS-Junkerschule. It was then renamed to Nibelungen from the medieval poem of the name Nibelungenlied made famous by Richard Wagner in his opera Ring des Nibelungen. The original medieval poem and Wagner's opera both revolve around themes of epic German mythology. The Division never achieved anywhere near full division status but did see some combat with its first action in the Landshut area of Upper Bavaria. The engagement was against American troops where the 38th over ran a few American positions. The 38th then saw brief action in the Alpen and Donau areas before surrendering to the Americans on 8 May 1945 in the area of the Bavarian Alps.

From 1945 to 1991, the former SS-Junkerschule was the base of the U.S. Army's 1st Battalion, 10th Special Forces Group.

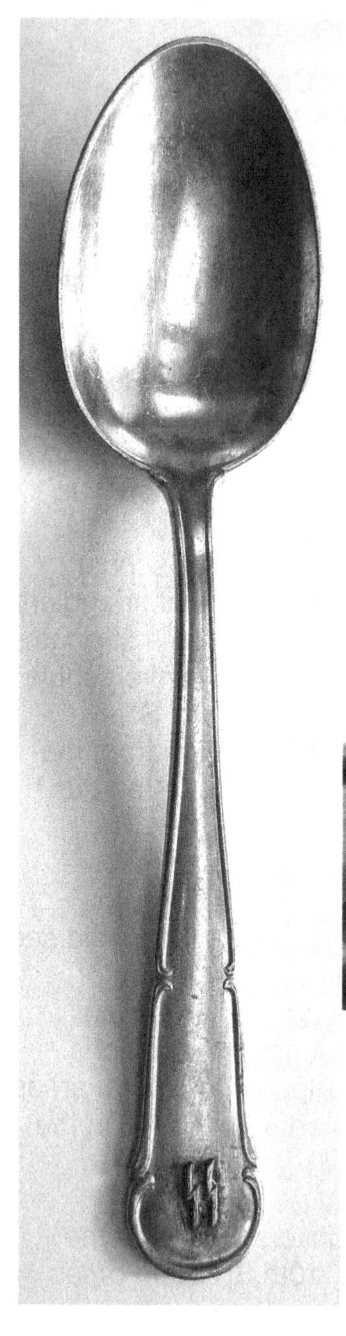

SS-149
L = 133 mm / 5 1/4"

SS-149 SS

Teaspoon: A formal pattern in art nouveau style. It is heavily silver plated approximating the look of real silver. Reverse stamped: “P” “100”. The SS runes may have been soldered in place and originally had 14K gold applied which has worn off in this case. This service has been identified with the 3rd SS-Totenkopf Division’s Headquarters in the Bavarian Mountains (SS-Oberbayern).

> Trivia: Initially, W-SS Divisions had no Division chaplain and in 1941 Heinrich Himmler was quoted, “I have six divisions composed of men absolutely indifferent in matters of religion. It doesn’t prevent them from going to their deaths with serenity in their souls.” As the composition of the W-SS broadened to that of a European Army, so did religious tolerance with such examples as the 28th W-SS Division, Wallonia (French speaking Belgians) having catholic chaplains and the 13th W-SS Division, Handshar (an Islamic Division) with both Imams and Mullahs.
>
> Leon Degrelle, CG ‘Wallonia’ observed that had it not been for the W-SS and its heroic sacrifices in the East, the Russians would have arrived in Normandy before the Allies and all of Europe would have been communist.

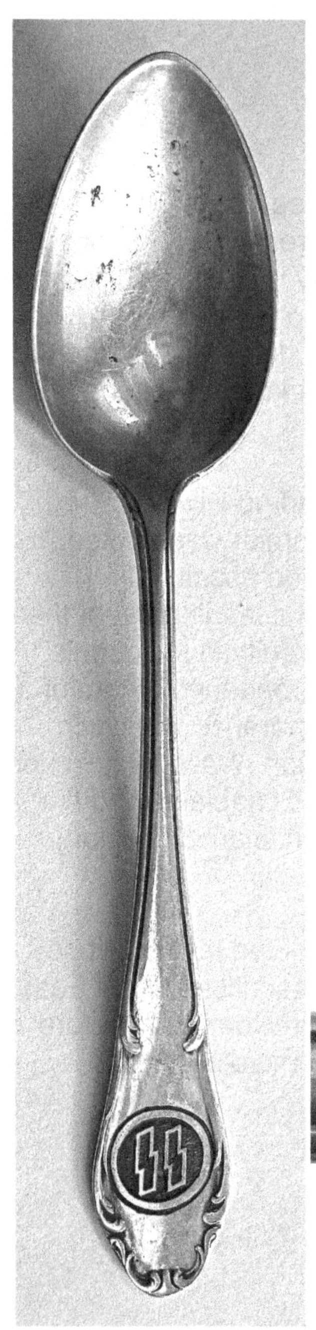

SS-150
L = 142 mm / 5 9/16"

SS-150 SS

Teaspoon: Obverse has the SS in a double circle with scolloped edges Reverse distributor: "E. Kludas", maker mark: Koch & Bergfeld, Bremen founded 1829, 800, RM. The double circle was also seen on the saddle blankets of the SS equestrians as well as their athletic sport shirts (sporthemd).

Note: When Germany took over the northern part of Italy on 8 September 1943 as the Italian Social Republic, the SS could then accept Italian volunteers. Himmler forbid them the SS Sigrunen and the SS sleeve eagle. He required them to use Italian specific emblems such as a sleeve eagle clasping a fasces in its talons but they did wear the universal death's head cap emblems.

Also, with the fall of Italy, the Germans appropriated large stockpiles of Italian clothing materials including camouflage material and the Waffen SS as a result, took a large percentage of that camouflage material for later Waffen SS uniforms and headgear. The 12th SS tank crews got German U-boat leather jackets and trousers (originally sold to Italy's navy) protecting them from serious burns.

Trivia: The SS colors were black and white, the same as worn by the Teutonic Knights.

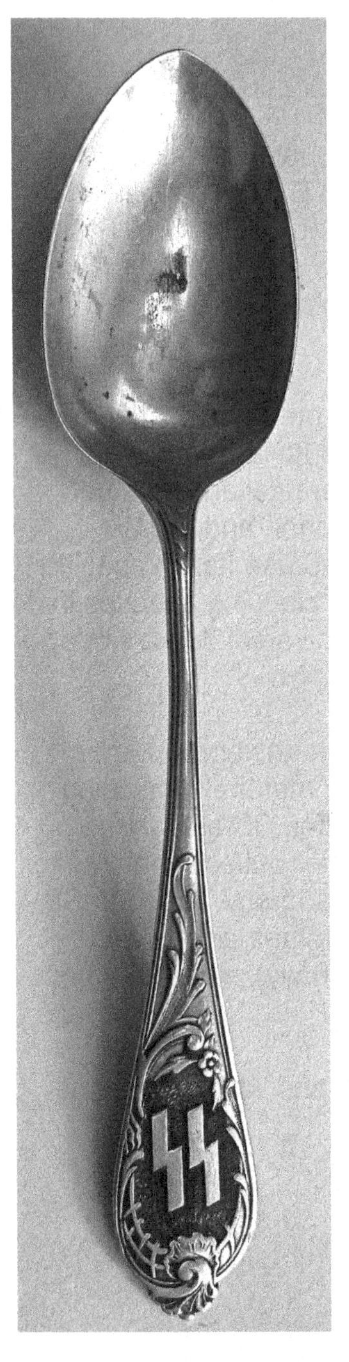

SS-151
L = 127mm / 5”

SS-151 SS

Mocha spoon: Obverse carries a very bold SS with high ornamentation. Reverse maker marked RM, 800, crossed hammers of Gebruder Petersfeldt of Berlin, founded 1848.

The Algemeine-SS or General-SS was order formed by Hitler in March 1923 as the Strosstrupp Adolf Hitler (Shock Troops Adolf Hitler) composed of 30 men. The NSDAP was banned after the 9 November Putsch. Released from prison in December 1924, in April 1925 Hitler formed a new bodyguard called the Schutzkommando which on 9 November 1925 became the Schutzstaffel (Protective Squad). Himmler was appointed the Reichsfuhrer-SS on 6 January 1929 and was granted, by Hitler, the status of an independent organization under direct control of the NSDAP, Nationalsozialistische Deutsche Arbeiterpartei, (National Socialist German Worker's Party) in July 1934.

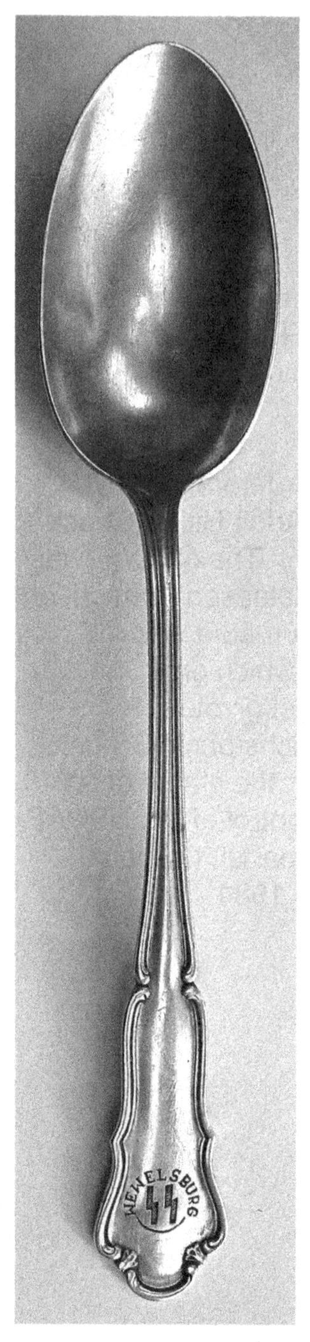

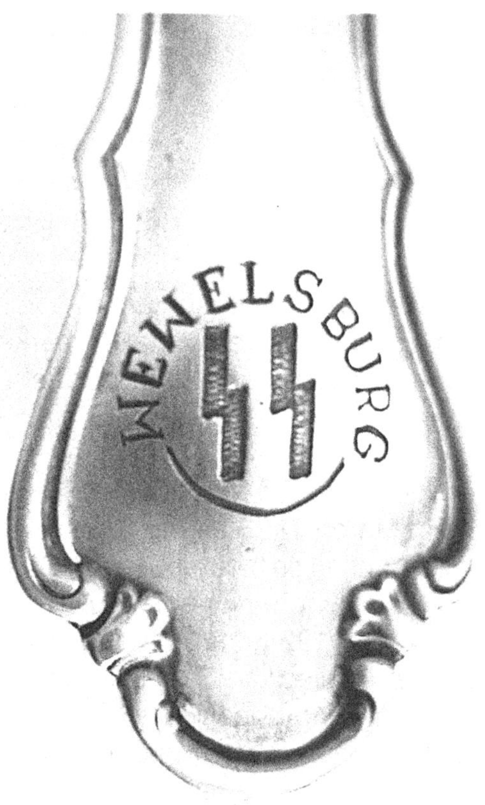

SS-152
L = 216 mm / 8 9/16"

SS-152 SS Wewelsburg,

Tablespoon: Obverse carries the SS with Wewelsburg wrapped around the top and raised ribs, both sides, interrupted at 1/3 above bottom, two lobes. Reverse carries the maker mark of M. H. Wilkens, Bremen-Hemelingen, founded 1810 and still active + 800 + RM.

On 27 July 1934 Himmler leased Wewelsburg castle for 100 years. The castle, one of only 3 triangular castles in the world, was to become the ritual headquarters of the SS Ordensburg und Reichsfuhrerschule (Cultural Relics and Leadership School) under the command of SS General Siegfried Taubert with a library of 12,000 volumes. SS honor rings of deceased SS elite members were to be returned. Himmler was to have been buried in the crypt. The spoon has been hand engraved, not stamped, leading to the possibility that this was done on site by "Niederhagen Labor Camp" ie concentration camp detainees as the smallest KZ or konzentracion camp collocated with the castle as a labor source. These silver pieces were only used in the North Tower by VIPs at this "Camelot of the SS". The castle was the venue of various Ahnenerbe-Forschungsund Lehrgemeinschaft - (Society for the Research and Teaching of Ancestral Heritage) ceremonies, the body for the research of ancestral heritage.

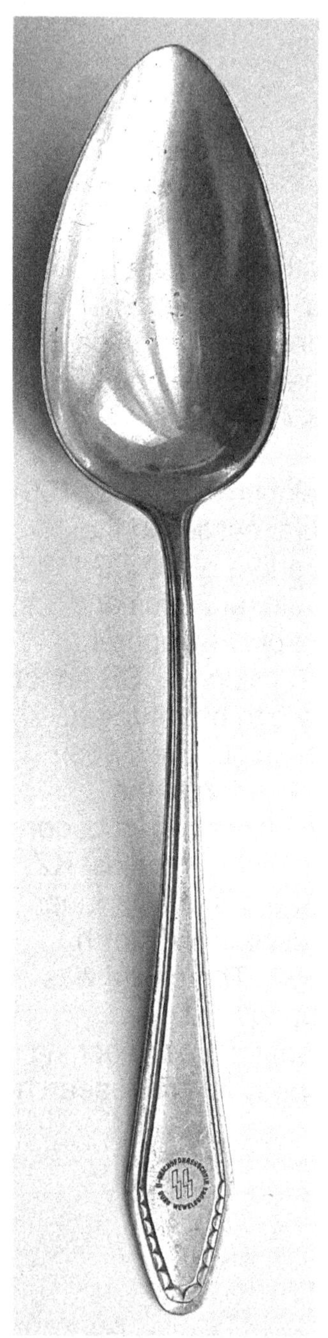

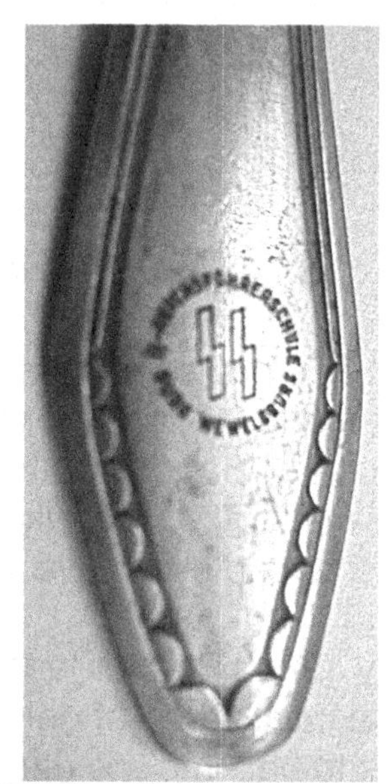

SS-153
L = 211 mm / 8 5/16”

SS-153 Wewelsburg
SS/RFS

Tablespoon: Obverse carries the circular emblem of the SS-Reichsfuhrerschule (SS-National Leaders School) at Wewelsburg. encompassing the SS runes. Reverse maker marked: A Centaur for H. A. Erbe AG.,Schmalkalden with a “20” in a square.

Himmler intended that Wewelsburg should ultimately be used as a Reichshaus der SS-Gruppenfuhrer or SS Generals' Residence, but with the outbreak of the war, it was converted into a staff college for senior SS officers and was where they would complete their education. The commandant, SS-Obergruppenfuhrer Siegfried Taubert was formerly Heydrich's chief of staff and the father-in-law of Ernst Robert Grawitz, the SS medical chief.

The Centaur is a symbol of the dark and unruly forces of nature.

Note: SS Amtsgruppe W's Amt VII Section 2 of Bauer & Co. was the SS picture restoration company employed by major European art galleries which also confiscated valuable paintings for display at Wewelsburg and the House of German Art, Munich.

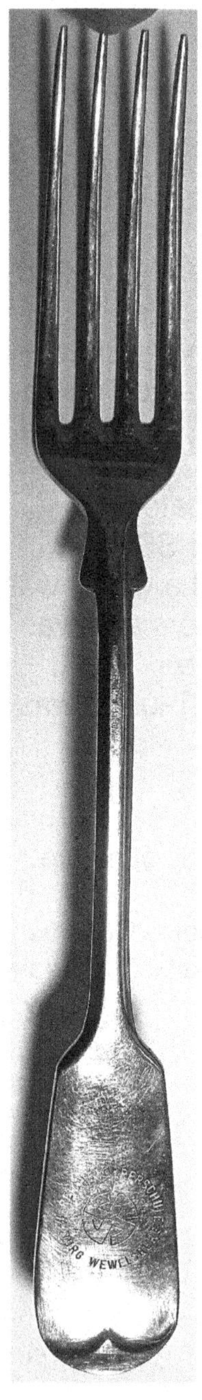

SS-154
L = 198 mm = 7 13/16”

SS-154 Wewelsburg
SS/RFS

Fork: Obverse carries the SS-Reichsfuhrerschule (SS-National Leaders School) at Burg Wewelsburg encircling the Sun Wheel Swastika. Reverse carries maker mark of Friedrich Wilke, Westig i, Westfalen and 'ALPACCA'.

From its 1934 acquisition, the SS spent some 12 million Reichsmarks refurbishing the castle to reopen in 1937 with a grand staircase, forged iron hardware threw-out, huge tapestries depicting Germanic scenes, oak woodwork, and statues of German heroes. The dining room was 100 X 145 ft. with a massive circular Arthurian table in solid oak.

The redesign referred to certain characters in the legends of the Holly Grail for example, one of the arranged study rooms was named Gral ("Grail"), and others, König Artus ("King Arthur"), König Heinrich ("King Henry"), Heinrich der Löwe ("Henry the Lion"), Arier ("Aryan"), Runen ("Runes"), Deutscher Orden ("Teutonic Order"), Reichsführerzimmer ("Room of the Empires Leader(s)"; "Reichsführer-SS", or "the Empire's Leader of the SS" was Himmler's title). In addition to these study rooms, the SS created guest rooms, a dining room, auditorium, a canteen, kitchen and a photographic laboratory with an archive.

There was also a magnificent guest room set aside for Adolf Hitler, who never visited the castle.

Note: The 11th SS-Freiwilligen Panzer Grenadier Division "Nordland" also used the "Sun" swastika as its coat-of-arms.

SS-155

SS-155 Wewelsburg's Village Assembly Hall (VAH)

Five piece set of a knife, fork and spoon, dessert spoon and sugar tongs. Obverse inscribed "Gemeinschaftshaus Wewelsburg". Reverse 'WMF' (Wurttembergische Metallwarenfabrik, Geislingen founded in 1853 as the result of the merger of Schweizer and A. Ritter & Co. and still in operation), 'Patent', '90' and '45' in a losenge. The knife's steel blade with "WMF Nirosta". as well as manufacturer's marks "WMF - 90" on the handle neck.

This (village) assembly hall had previously been an old half-timbered farm that was purchased by the SS, rebuilt and enlarged, starting in 1935/36, under the direction of SS-Hauptsturmführer Walter Franzius and with the help of the SS and the SA, the RAD as well as the HJ and the BDM. It was supposed to function as a meeting point for the villagers and the members of the SS from the nearby SS school at Wewelsburg and as such the SS runes were down played. The house still exists today, now hosting a restaurant. Cf. Karl Hüser, "Wewelsburg 1933 bis 1945 - Kult- und Terrorstätte der SS", pp. 216/217, and Russell/Schneider, "Heinrich Himmlers Burg - Bildchronik der SS-Schule Haus Wewelsburg 1934 - 1945", p. 86 - 94.

Note: The acquisition of this set was stimulated by the fact that my wife and I had a pleasant K&K (Koffee and Kucken) at the restaurant. Unfortunately I was unaware of the assessment of a 23% commission on the successful? bidder. So ignorance has a heavy price but it is a very nice addition with both pleasant and unpleasant memories.

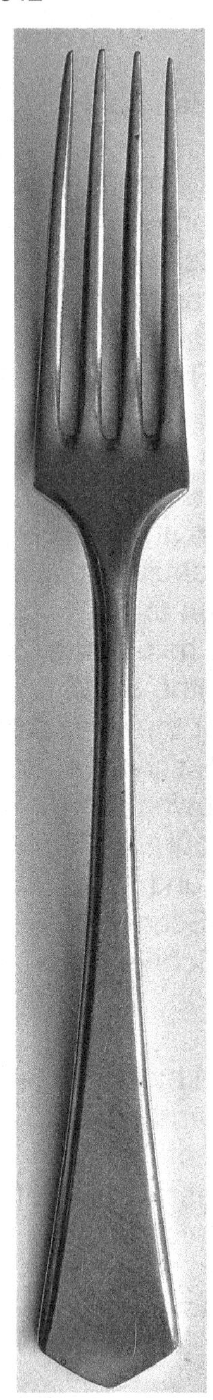

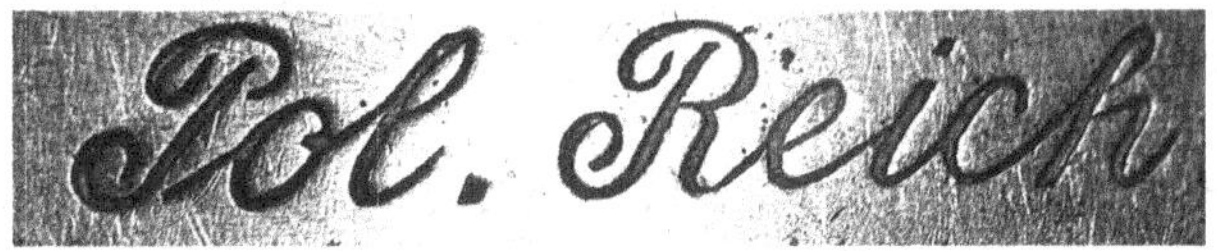

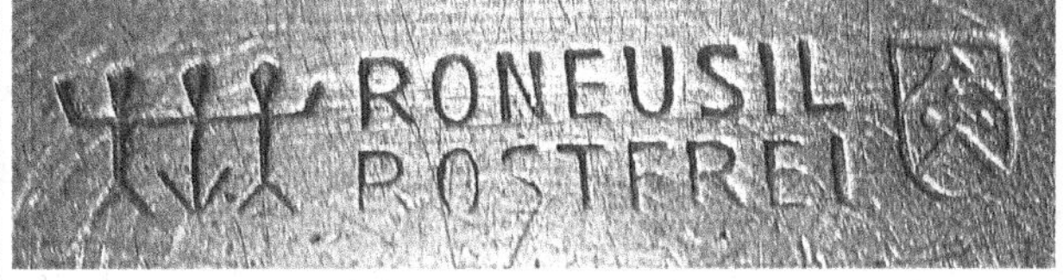

SS-156
L = 211 mm = 8 5/16”

SS-156 Police

Fork: Obverse clear. Reverse carries "Pol. Reich" in stamped scroll plus maker mark of RONEUSIL over ROSTFREI and shield.
On June 17th 1936, Reichsführer-SS, (National Leader of the SS), Heinrich Himmler was appointed to the newly created position of Chef der Deutschen Polizei im Reichsministerium des Innern, (Chief of the German Police in the National Ministry of the Interior), effectively giving him full control of all police agencies within Germany. The Police were divided into eight, assorted, branches of service consisting of the, Schutzpolizei des Reiches, (National Protection Police), the Gendarmerie, (Rural Police), the Wasserschutzpolizei, (Water Police), the Feuerschutzpolizei, (Fire Protection Police), the Polizei Medizinal Beamte, (Police Medical Officials), the Polizei Verwaltungs Beamte, (Police Administration Officials), the Polizei Veterinar Beamte, (Police Veterinarian Officials) and the Schutzpolizei des Gemeinden (Municipal Protection Police), with each branch having a distinguishing truppenfarbe, (Branch of service color), and distinct insignia for specialized personnel. On acceptance into full-time or auxiliary police service individuals were issued a Dienstausweis, (Service Identification Card), and a Dienstpass (Service Pass), for internal administration to record the individuals police service record. Service with the police did not exempt individuals from auxiliary military service and when called for service with the Wehrmachtgefolge, (Armed Forces Retinue), the civil police were issued a specific police Soldbuch (Pay Book), which remained in the recipients possession as his official military identification document. Quite often when called for service with the Wehrmachtgefolge the civil police personnel would be issued an SS Soldbuch. Note: Civil police serving as military auxiliaries were not considered military police.

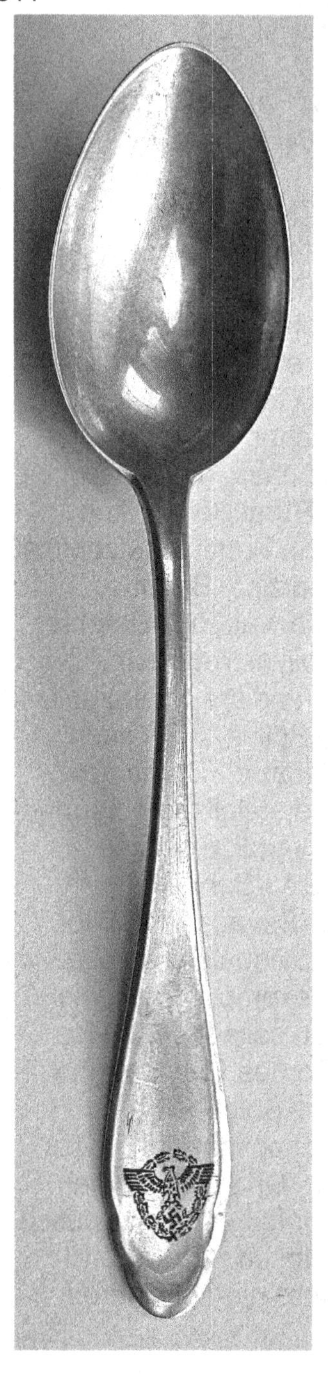

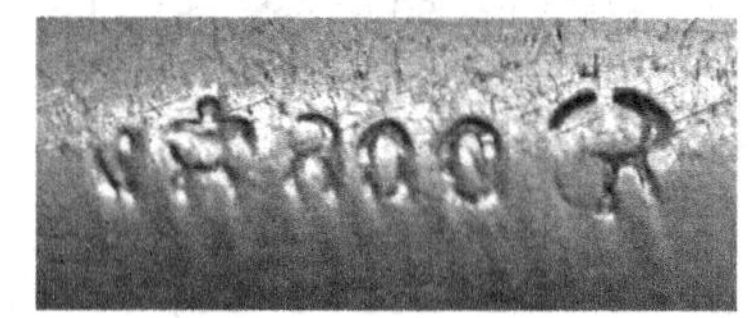

SS/P-157
L = 142 mm / 5 9/16"

SS/P-157 Police

Teaspoon: Obverse carries the Police eagle looking right (indicating a 'state' organization with the swastika which was added in 1933 while the reverse is maker marked: RM, '800' 'G' facing 'R'. for - Gebruder Reiner, Krumbach Bayern, founded 1914.

From Hitler's assumption of power in 1933 to 1936, his focus was to take unrestricted control of the police. In June 1936, Himmler was appointed as Chief of German Police - Chef der Deutsche Polizei. Himmler then merged the SS and the Police into a single 'State Protection Corps' or Staatsschutzkorps under Himmler as the Reichsfuhrer SS und Chef der Deutsche Polizei (RFSSuChdDP). To do this, he absorbed the police into the SS. The German Police now fell into two distinct groups: The Ordnungspolizei or Orpo, the uniformed police and the Sicherheitspolizei or Sipo, the security police. These two were folded into the RSHA - Reichssicherheitshauptamt (Reich Security Main Office) under Heydrich on 22 September 1939, just prior to the start of WWII.

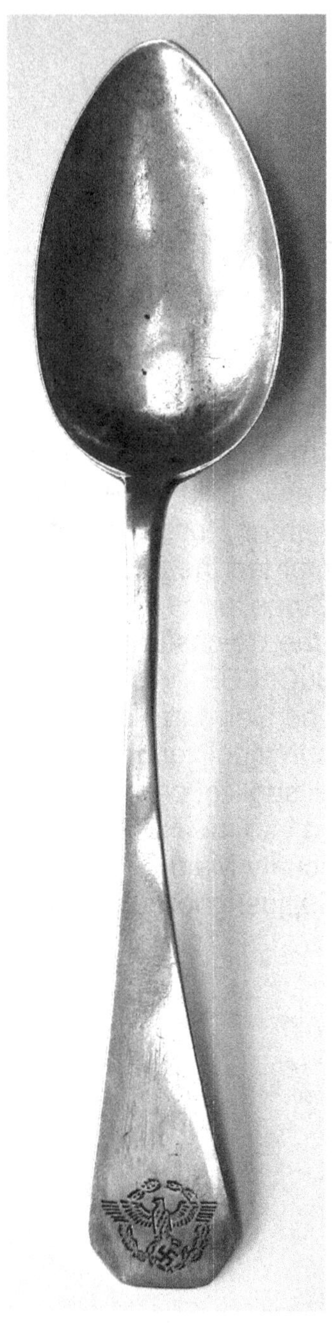

SS/P-158
L = 137 mm / 5 6/16”

SS/P-158 Police

Teaspoon: Obverse carries the police eagle looking right with swastika. Reverse carries marker mark CB for C. Backhausen, Tangermuende, 800 RM.

The police emblem is typically a six feathered eagle. The exception was sleeve eagles which were six feathered for NCO's and enlisted men whereas the Officers and Generals sleeve eagles were 3 feathered.

OrPo Ordnungspolizei although separate from the SS their commander was Oberst-Gruppenfuhrer Kurt Daluge. They maintained a system of insignia and ranks unique to OrPo. They were the uniformed, regular police force and as a result of their green uniform, they were called the Grune Polizei (Green Police).

SiPo Sicherheitspolizei or secret police included the Gestapo (secret state police) and Kripo (criminal police) both directly under the SS.

It was Himmler's intent to wipe out the OrPo and have everyone under direct SS control.

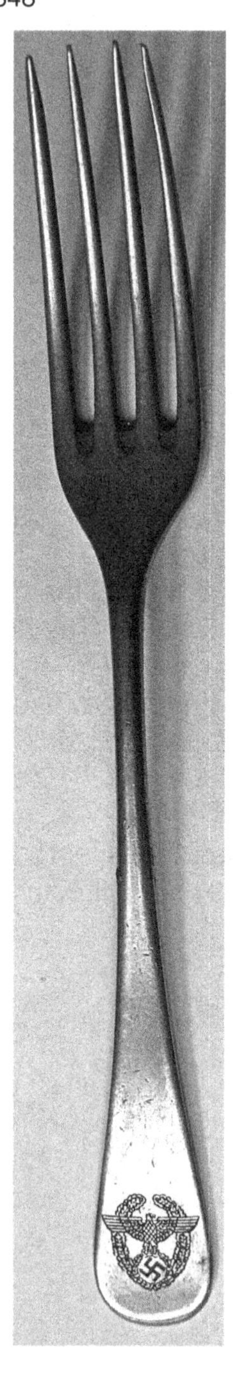

Kasino
Polizei-Praesidium
Breslau

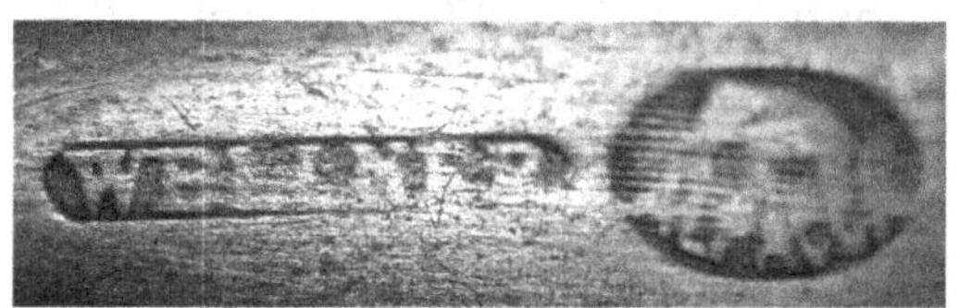

SS/P-159
L = 214 mm / 8 7/16”

SS/P-159 Police Headquarters - Breslau

(Kasino Polizer Praesidium)

Dinner Fork: Obverse carries the police logo, the six feathered eagle looking to its left holding a mobile swastika in its talons. The left looking eagle symbolizing the Parti may be due to the items creation after being included in the SS. Reverse maker marked 'Wellner' with the elephant over 'Alpacca' followed by a 3 line impression: "Kasino' over 'Polizei Praesidium' over Breslau".

After WWI, Breslau, located on the Oder River, was in the German 'Province of Lower Selesia'. Breslau was one of the focal points for transport of victims to Auschwitz and in particular the Inspector of the Security Police and the security service's local representative of the RSHA (Reich Security Head Office) in Breslau. were very active in this respect. On July 25, 1944 Adolf Hitler declared the city a Festung (fortress) that was to be defended at all cost. Battle of 1945: The Wehrmacht, aided by the Volkssturm and slave laborers started to convert the city into a military fortress, capable of lengthy defense against a possible Soviet assault. Much of the city centre was demolished and turned into an airfield. On February 13 the Soviet forces laid siege to the city and the battle started. On February 15 the Luftwaffe started an airlift to aid the besieged garrison. For 76 days, until May 1, the German air force made more than 2000 sorties with supplies and food, more than 1638 tons of supplies were delivered. During the battle in the heavily-bombarded city, both sides resorted to setting entire districts on fire. Finally, on May 6, only two days before the unconditional surrender of Germany, General Hermann Niehoff, the German commander of the Festung Breslau surrendered the city to the Soviets. After WWII, the Potsdam Conference assigned Breslau to Poland and it was renamed Wroclaw.

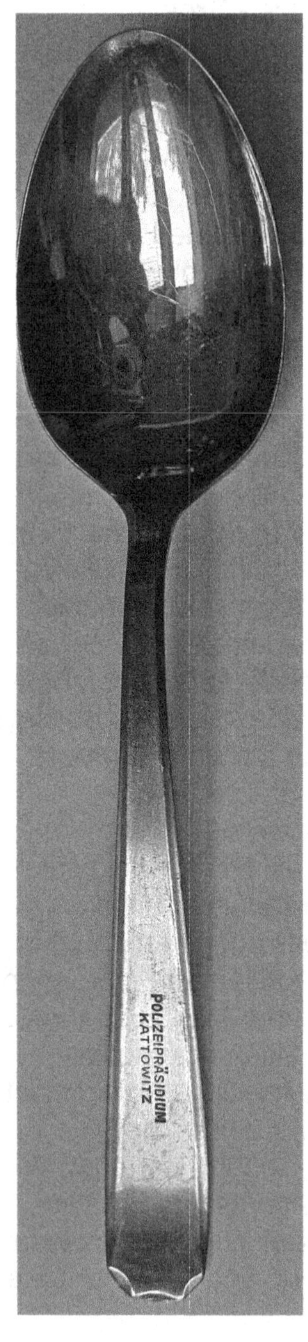

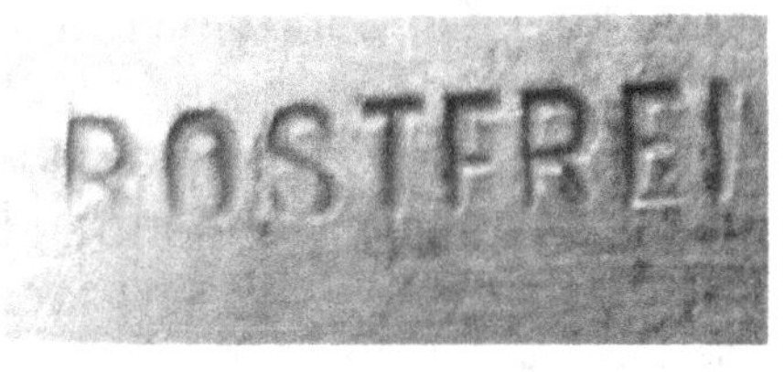

SS/P-160
L = 202 mm / 8”

SS/P-160 Police Headquarters - Kattowitz
(PolizeiPrasidium - Kattowitz)

Tablespoon: Obverse carries 'POLIZEIPRASIDIUM over Kattowitz. Reverse marked 'Rustfrei.

Prior to W.W.I, the city of Kattowitz, being located in Prussia's upper Silesia, was German. After W.W.I, upper Silesia was granted to Poland by a League of Nations plebiscite and the cities name was changed to Katowice although the city residents had overwhelmingly voted to remain German, the rural vote carried the day for Poland. With German occupation in 1939, the city again became Kattowitz. It was during this period that the German Polizei Prasidium existed. The first Jews to be exterminated at Auschwitz (located in the Kattowitz district) were arrested by the Kattowitz police in September 1941. From Kattowitz, a police court-martial tribunal visited Auschwitz concentration camp every four to six weeks and passed judgement both on prisoner misconduct and hostage liquidation cases. In most cases a death sentence was pronounced. With the arrival of Red Army troops in 1945, the city reverted to Katowice.

Note: In 1953 the city was renamed Stalinogrod (Stalin's City). This was so unpopular with the residents that in 1956 it again became Katowice.

Misc: During the dismemberment of Czechoslovakia, Poland seized the area of Olsa.

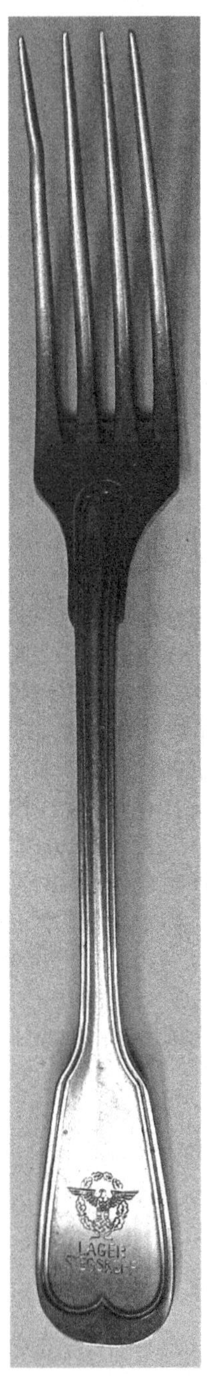

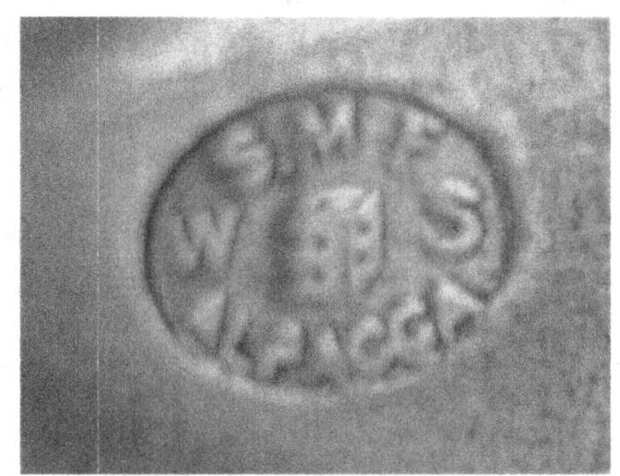

SS/P-161
L = 210 mm / 8 4/16"

SS/P-161 LAGER STEGSKOPF
(Camp Stegskopf)

Table Fork: Obverse carries a Police logo, but here with a three feathered wing and the eagle looking to its right holding a mobile swastika in its talons. Reverse maker marked with an Wellner device composed of 'S.M.F.' in an arch over the Wellner trademark 'die' with the 4 side showing, straddled by the 'W' and 'S' for Wellner & Son over 'Alpacca' all encompassed in an oblong oval.

Stegskopf is located in the north Rheinland-Pfalz near Koblenz and was the site of both a WWII POW camp and a training center for young German radar technicians.

The 3 feathers indicative of a service for higher officer?

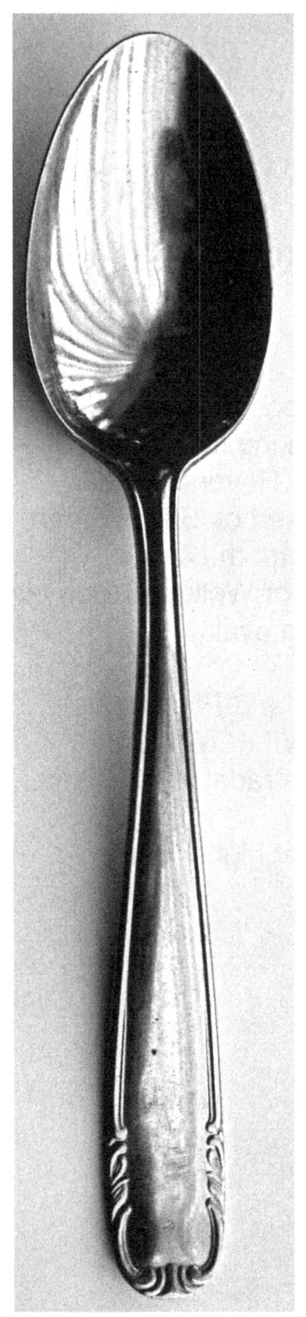

SS-162
L = 139 mm / 5 7/16"

SS-162 K.L.Buchenwald

Teaspoon: Obverse clear, reverse carries DAW over K.L.BUCHENWALD, Rostfrei-Inox for Buchenwald Concentration Camp (Konzentrationslager Buchenwald)

The KLs were founded to isolate people viewed as "subversive dangers to the German race" and operated by the SS, completely outside normal German law. Buchenwald was established on Ettersberghill near Weimar, in 1937 and eventually grew to include 140 satellite camps or sub camps. The main gate's wrought iron inscription read, "Jedem das Seine" or "To Each His Own". As KL Buchenwald was on property of the German Reich, the SS actually purchased the camp's plants in the autumn of 1940 and founded a branch of the SS arms factory, Deutsche Ausrustungs Werke GmbH (DAW) employing from 500 to 1,400 inmates manufacturing wood and light metal products. The KL system was transferred to the SS Economic Administration Main Office in March 1942 due to a decision to engage concentration camp labor to support the war effort oriented primarily towards the wartime requirements of the Waffen-SS. Although not an extermination camp, the estimated camp death rate was 18% (43,000 of the 238,380 passing through from 1937 to 1945, with an additional 13,500 sent on to extermination camps bringing the total to 24%) Prisoners were marked with triangular camp badges of 7 colors: Red = Political, Green = Police preventive detention, Black = Work Shy, Purple = Bible / religious, Blue = Emigrant, Pink = Homosexual and Yellow = Race Defiler. On 26Jan38, Himmler issued an open arrest order for all able-bodied men "who have ascertainably refused 2 offers of employment without justification or have begun employment but quit it again after a brief time for no valid reason." - these were the "Work Shy"!

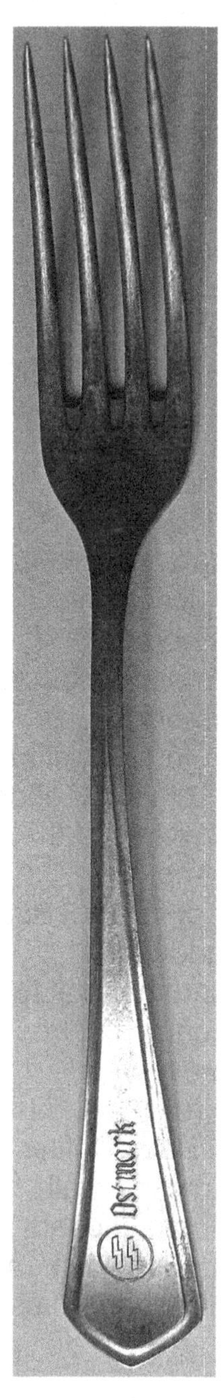

SS-163
L = 184 mm / 7 4/16”

SS-163 Totenkopfstandarte 4 Ostmark

Fork: Obverse carries “SS OSTMARK”. Reverse ‘Wellner’ and ‘Alpacca’.

The SS started staffing concentration camps in 1934. In 1936, Gruppenfuhrer Theo Eicke’s Death’s Head Units were combined into the SS-Totenkopfverbande. His recruiting focused on ‘big sixteen year olds” directly from the Hitler Youth. Most Totenkopf (Death’s Head) men were under 20, 95 percent were unmarried with few or no personal ties. They were ideally suited to Eicke’s moulding to hate the prisoners. Their job being to isolate the “dangerous enemies of the state” and to “treat them rough”. Any member allowing a prisoner to escape would be handed to the Gestapo. The initial SS-Totenkopfstandarte units were: #1 ‘Oberbayern’ at Dachau, #2 ‘Brandenburg’ at Sachesenhausen and #3 ‘Thuringen’ at Buchenwald. After the invasion of Austria on 13 March 1938, the SS formed the fourth regiment of the Death’s Head units the SS-Totenkopfstandarte 4 "Ostmark", in Linz, Austria on 1 Sept 1938. The SS-Ostmark’s mission was to staff the new concentration camp at Mauthausen.

With the war, SS-Ostmark was transferred to Prague in Oct 1939 where it relieved SS-Standarte Der Führer. Then transferred to Holland June 1940 for use in the costal defense. In 1941 It was re-designated SS-Infanterie-Regiment 4 Ostmark and attached to 2. SS-Infanterie Brigade and afterward disappeared from the records on 25 Feb 1941.

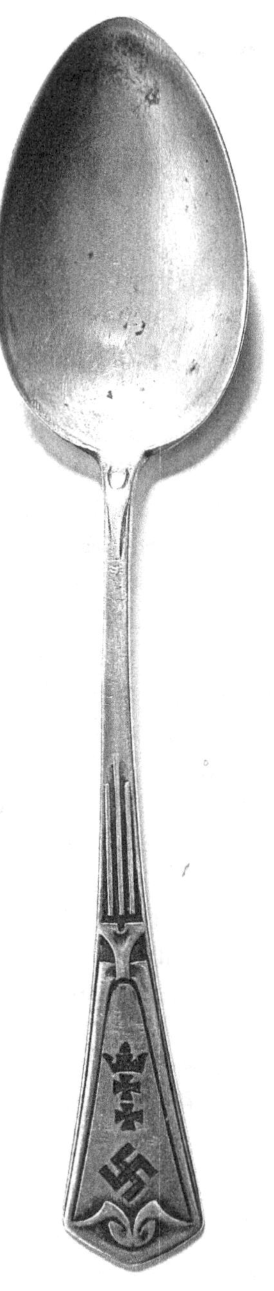

SS-164
L = 140 mm / 5 1/2"

SS-164 SS Heimwehr "Danzig"

Teaspoon: Obverse carries the Danzig crest over a mobile Swastika. Reverse marked: distributor 'F.TAEGENER' RM, 800, unreadable maker mark.

SS Heimwehr "Danzig" was an SS unit established in the Free City of Danzig (today Gdańsk, Poland) before the Second World War. Originally known as Heimwehr Danzig (Danzig Home Defense), it was officially established on 20 June 1939, when the Danzig senate under Albert Forster decided to set up its own powerful, armed force. Reichsführer-SS Heinrich Himmler supported this project and sent SS Obersturmbannführer Hans Friedemann Goetze to Danzig. Goetze was the commander of the III. Sturmbann (Regiment) of the 4th SS-Totenkopfstandarte "Ostmark," established in October 1938 in Berlin-Adlersheim. On 18 August 1939, the Polish government militarily mobilized against the German Reich. The Volksdeutsche (ethnic Germans) in Danzig "completely spontaneously" founded the 1,550-man strong Heimwehr Danzig (Danzig Militia).

On 1 September 1939, German troops attacked Poland. The SS Heimwehr Danzig fought on the German side, in the process capturing Danzig's Polish post office, an event to which Günter Grass dedicated a chapter entitled, *The Polish Post Office* in his novel *The Tin Drum*. Later, the SS-Heimwehr Danzig participated in the attack on the Danzig Westerplatte, and already was considered a part of the SS-Totenkopf Division then forming under Theodor Eicke. Later, it provided coast guard service in Danzig. On 30 September 1939, SS Heimwehr "Danzig" was dissolved, becoming a part of the 3rd SS Division Totenkopf and ceased to exist as an independent unit.

MISCELLANEOUS

M-165
L = 134 mm / 5 1/4"

M-165 Berghof 'House' Service Cream Server Spoon

Cream Server (whipped cream) Spoon: Obverse with Parteiadler, reverse RM, 800, Bruckmann.

The spoon came with Spencer Cunningham's certification in part reading: "On or about May 8, 1945, while I was on duty with the 402nd Field Artillery Battalion of the 42d Infantry Division, I was at Berchtesgaden. Since we were aware of the fact that Adolph Hitler had a "retreat" at Berchtesgaden, we went to his "house" to look for souvenirs. The house had been almost demolished by bombing. We dug in this area and found approximately 375 pieces of sterling silver with the Nazi Eagle and Swastika on them."
Obersalzberg area cutlery: as the location of Hitler's Berghof (Mountain Home) and after he took power, the entire area (Fuhrergebiet / Hitler Compound) was commandeered for security reasons. Within the area were the Teehaus Mooslahnerkopf; the Gusthof (Manor Farm) of Martin Borman; Albert Speer's House and Studios; Kehlsteinhaus, the Eagles Nest; Klaushoehe where the families of SS guards or staff lived in 4 rows of 8 houses each with 2 or 3 families per house; the Guard House Berghof; the Buchenhoehe, a 40 apartment complex with school, swimming pool, gymnasium, hotel etc. for staff members and their relatives; Goering's House; the SS Kaserne; Hochlenzer Gasthof, where Hitler stayed when he visited the area prior to taking power; Villa Bechstein, formerly owned by the wife of a rich piano builder from Berlin who sometimes invited Hitler.
We know Hitler used his AH service for dinner at the Berghof and when entertaining. We surmise that this is the "house" service used by AH when desired, staff and possibly even Eva Braun during her residence when she was not entertaining with her personal services.

M-166
L = 278 mm / 10 15/16”

M-166 Italienischer Abendessensatz

(Fuhrerbau Italian Dinner Service)

Dinner Knife: Per source, "This is a grand piece of Bruckmann table service—a dinner knife in the traditional German style with the fasces of Rome raised in high relief on the handle. RM, '800' Bruckmann eagle stamped at the top of the grip and on the blade (Nicht Rostend), "stainless." (The fasces was the emblem of authority in Fascist Italy.)

"This is a very historic piece made by the same silversmiths that made the silverware for Adolf Hitler. The purpose of this was to honor the guests among the high dignitaries who visited Germany and the NS leaders. The set of Italian service was kept in the Führerbau on the Königsplatz in Munich. This is where the most important guests to the Führer and party had their diplomatic meetings. Here is where Hitler met with Britain's Neville Chamberlain and Italy's Benito Mussolini for the famous Munich conference of September 29, 1938. This was actually a four-power conference with Edouard Daladie of France having little to say, Many Italian dignitaries, including Count Ciano, Mussolini's son-in-law and chief of the Italian press corps and Undersecretary of State for Press and Propaganda (1934) also met there. He was also a highly placed member of the Fascist Grand Council. Many other Italian leaders of military and political fame visited the Führerbau and it was for this reason that the Italienischer Abendessensatz was created. This set of Besteck, or dinnerware, was brought out only when some of these honored guests and allies were present for dinner, and this is the one and only piece of this exceedingly rare set that we have ever seen or been able to acquire. It is much rarer by far than the Hitler silverware, again, this set was to be found in only one place and that was in Munich's Führerbau and there only."

M-167
L = 245 mm / 9 11/16”

M-167 Reichswerke Hermann Goering

Dinner knife: Obverse handle with REICHSWERKE over HERMANN GOERING and blade with Wellner logo. Reverse has at top of handle WELLO with a gold washed elephant above - a Wellner trademark.

In 1936, Goering became Plenipotentiary of the Four Year Plan for German rearmament, where he effectively took control of the economy — as economics minister Hjalmar Schacht became increasingly reluctant to pursue rapid rearmament and eventually resigned. The Reichswerke Hermann Göring was an industrial conglomerate established in July 1937 to extract and process domestic iron ores from Salzgitter that were deemed uneconomical by the privately held steel mills. The vast steel plant Reichswerke Hermann Goering was named after him. Göring himself supervised the Reichswerke. He gained great influence with Hitler (who placed a high value on rearmament). With Schacht gone, in November 1937, Goering obtained unchecked access to state financing and launched a chain of mergers, diversifying into military industries with the absorption of Rheinmetall. After the Anschluss the Reichswerke absorbed Austrian heavy industries, including those owned by private German investors. The steel mills and supporting companies in Linz became its most important asset. Nazi leadership regarded captured assets as the property of the state and were not willing to share the spoils with German businesses. The Reichswerke absorbed between 50 and 60 per cent of Czech heavy industries. The pattern was repeated in occupied Poland, France and the Soviet Union. By the end of 1941 the Reichswerke was the largest company in Europe. The conglomerate was dismembered by the Allies in 1944–1945, but the Salzgitter plant continued operations as Reichswerke until 1953.
Note: The conglomerate never made a profit!

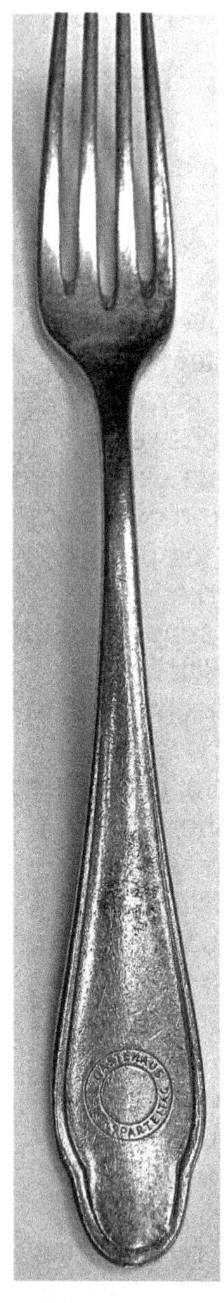

M-168
475L = 214 mm / 8 6/16”

M-168 Gastehaus Reichsparteitag

Dinner Fork: Obverse carries the logo of Nurnberg's Gastehaus Reichsparteitag; The reverse marked 'WELLNER' 'patent, '100' in an oval and '50' in a square.

This service comes from the Gastehaus der NSDAP located on Nurnberg's Bahnhofplatz. Hitler selected Nurnberg as the site for the 'Party Days' because it was the "most German of the German cities". The Reichspartitag (National Party Day) started in 1925 and were originally held in July. The creation of the Hitlerjugend was announced at the 2nd Reichsparteitag on 4 July 1926. After the 1933 take over of the German government, Reichsparteitags became the week long Nazi Party rallies that then occurred every September from 1933 to 1938. Each year had a theme: 1933 was 'Rally of Victory" to glorify Hitler's take over of the Government and 1938, 'The Rally of Greater Germany" (Annexation of Austria). The Gastehaus was for Party and guest VIP's. This Guest House was opened in 1936 near Hitler's own Nazi Party Days hotel, the Deutscher Hof. Both hotels were very near the central railway station. It was a fine, very modern, air conditioned hotel with enormous carved stone shields across the front including one featuring an eagle clutching a swastika in its talons. Foreign dignitaries and special guests of the Nazi Party stayed here during Party Days. Hermann Goring was a regular. The building remains in largely unchanged condition today.

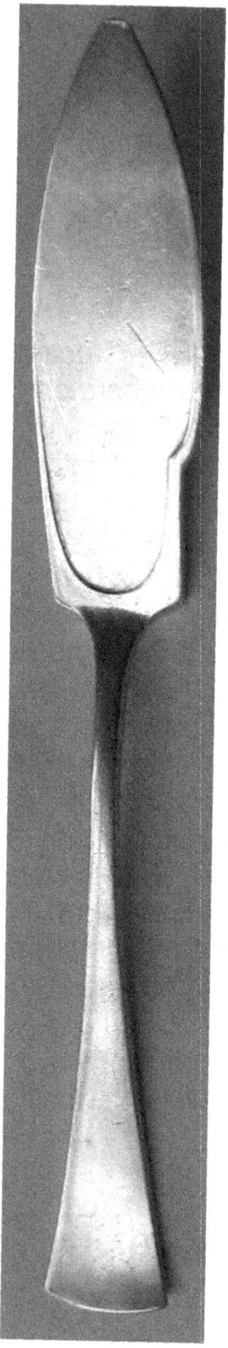

M-169
L = 208 mm / 8 3/16"

M-169 Hotel Deutscher Hof, Nurnberg

Master Butter Knife: Obverse clear. Reverse machine impressed with 'Hotel Deutscher Hof Nurnberg. Maker marked Wellner Soehne 60. Typically there is one master butter knife per table with Individual butter spreaders.

This was one of Hitler's favorites. Built in 1913 near the main train station, originally, the Hof Hotel (Court Hotel and later the Hotel Deutscher-Hof) was Hitler's Nurnberg accommodation starting in the 1920's. After 1935, his suite was on the 2nd floor looking on to Frauentorgraben Str. in the Altstadt close to the main railroad station. A special balcony was constructed for his use to review march buys and to be seen by the populace, primarily during the Party Days in September. Leni Riefenstahl's 'Triumph of the Will', track 2 has Hitler's arrival to the Hotel on 5 September 1934, a daytime appearance on the balcony and than after dark another appearance with a lit 'Heil Hitler' on the lower part of the balcony. After the war, his large suite was divided into 2 separate hotel rooms. The hotel was on the destruction list as it had the reputation as "Hitler's Hotel" / The Nazi Hotel. It was closed in 2008 and at its demise it was listed as a 3 star hotel with 60 rooms.

Note: My wife and I visited in 2009, it closed in 2008 for destruction whereas the Frankischer Hof hotel used by the Nazi Press Corps was remodeled into the present day Sheraton Hotel Carlton! As mentioned in Otto Dietrich's book, *The Hitler I Knew,* the Der Deutscher Hof Hotel was referred to as, "The Party Hotel in Nuremberg." thus ultimately dooming it.

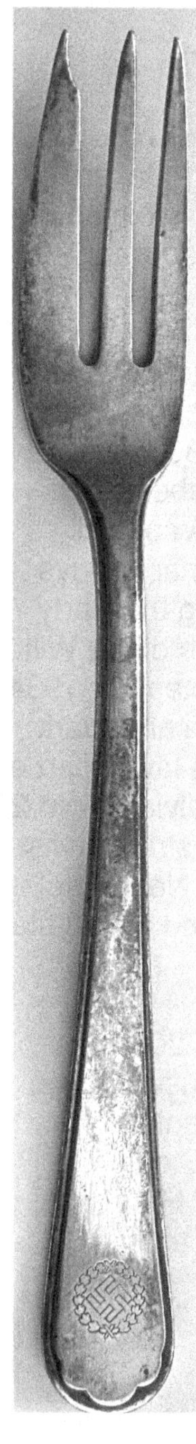

BSF 90

Der Deutsche Hof

M-170
L = 155 mm / 6 1/16”

M-170 Der Deutsche Hof - Nurnberg

Salad Fork: Obverse carries a mobile swastika inside a wreath of oak leaves. Reverse with 'Der Deutsche Hof' and makers mark "BSF90", (Bremer Silberwarenfabrik, Bremen) stamped into the stem and 90 silver plate .

In 1935 the owner of the Hotel Deutscher-Hof property was forced to sell the entire estate to the NSDAP and the hotel was renamed Der Deutsche Hof. At that time, the hotel commissary directed that all tableware forthwith would bear the swastika. Under architect Franz Ruff, the hotel was modernized and greatly extended to accommodate personal guests of the "leader" at the Party conferences which were held in early September for 8 days. Hitler always stayed in his second floor apartment with his specially constructed balcony..

Specific annual themes for Party Days were:

1933 Nazi Party Victory (Seizure of Power)
1934 Triumph of the Will
1935 Party of Freedom (Military Conscription)
1936 Rally of Honor (Rhineland Occupation)
1937 Party of Work (Unemployment Reduced)
1938 Greater Germany (Austria Annexed)
1939 Cancelled but planned as "Party of Peace"
(WWII started 1 Sep 1939!)

A 1938 City Guide Book lists the hotel at the top of the listed hotels. Quoted room rates: One bed 4.5 to 8 RM and 2 beds 8 to 15 RM (RM = $.40) (No rooms during Party Days.)

On 3 October 1944 an air raid destroyed a large part of the hotel. The hotel reopened in 1949.. Hitler's balcony (The Leader's Balcony) was removed.

M-171
This cup measures 1.5 high by a diameter of 3 inches.

M-171 Der Deutsche Hof Cook's Soup Tasting Cup

Soup Tasting Cup or a Round, Handled Coaster: Bottom outside carries the encircled mobile swastika, maker mark of GEBR.HEPP and '90'. The Gebrueder Hepp (Hepp Brothers, shortened to GEBR HEPP) Metalware Factory was founded in 1863 in Pforzheim, Baden-Wuerttemberg, German. On February 23rd 1945, the plant was destroyed, but six years later the factory was revived. In 1988 the GEBR HEPP factory was taken over by Wuerttemberg Metalware Factory (WMF).

The cup is machine stamped Hotelbetriebsges.m.b.H on the outside. Betriebs (operation) while ges is the short form for Gesellschaft (often translated as society or civil society or association). m.b.H. is the short form for Mit Beschrnkter Haftung (With Limited Liability). the German equivalent of "Ltd."

Thus "Hotelbetriebsgesellschaft m.b.H." is quite simply a hotel operation (registered as a limited liability company).

Note; In 1935 the NSDAP purchased the Grand Hotel in Berchtesgaden and the Hotel Deutscher-Hof (resulted in the name change to Der Deutsche Hof) in Nürnberg and established a corporation, the Hotelbetriebsgesellschaft (Gotthard Färber, General Manager) to operate them.

This tasting cup is in near excellent condition. The swastika with its double ring and 12 leaves on each side is identical to Hepp's Der Deutsche Hof service pieces.

Summary: Most likely from Der Deutsche Hof's kitchen

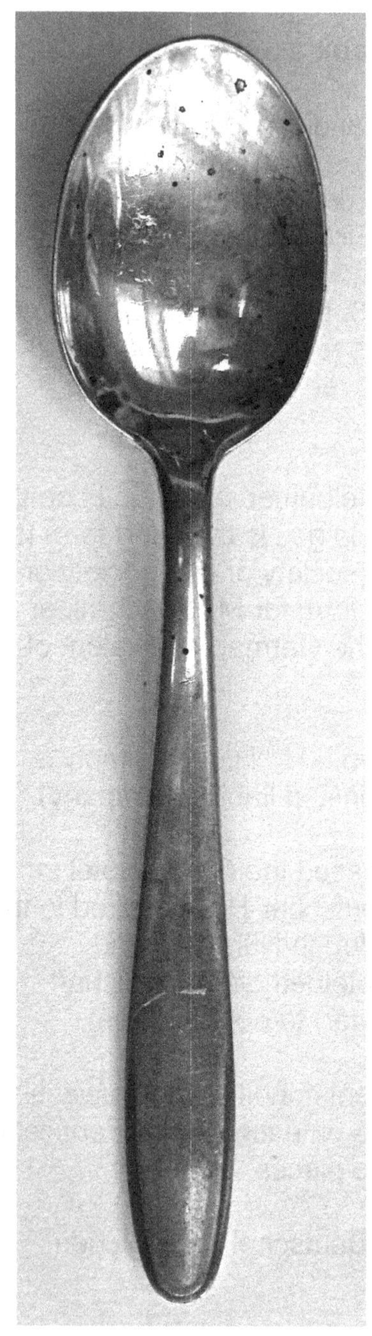

M-172
L = 128 mm / 5 1/16"

M-172 Bayerischer Hof Hotel, Munick

Sugar Spoon: Obverse clear. Reverse impressed with 'BAYER.HOF MUNCHEN' and maker marked with a stick figure of a man with a walking stick followed by BMF for Bergische Metallwarenfabrik, Deppmeyer & Co., Bayern. 30.

Luxury hotels that were favored by Hitler, from the earliest years, the years of struggle - Der Kampfzeit - the struggle for power - the period prior to 1933, when many hotels would not accept either Hitler or the Parti were the Hotel Dreesen, Bad Godesberg, Hotel Kaiserhof, was Hitler's Berlin residence from 1930 to 1933. Hotel Bayerischer Hof, Munick and for Nazi Party Days, Der Deutsche Hof, Nuremberg and after the war started, the Hotel Casino, Zoppot/Sopot, N. Poland / Baltic Sea / Danzig was used as his HQ for Polish Campaign of 19-25 September 1939. After the common use of the Nazi swastika, some of the hotels saved the expense of new service utensils by such clever solutions as attaching the swastika to the underside of the tea and coffee pots.

Hitler had a weakness for fast, luxurious automobiles too. The Benz manager in Munich was an early admirer of AH and provided autos at no charge. A 1925 Mercedes Benz advertisement showed Hitler about to board an enormous Benz with the headline, "Hitler leaves Landsberg Prison." In 1938, his preferred vehicle was the Mercedes 770K Pullman Convertible / Parade Car. Later he had the more enormous 6 wheeled, three axle, cross-country (Gelaendewagen) Mercedes G-4: The Black one was registered to the NSDAP while the Gray one license WH32288 (used for his triumphal entry into Austria via Braunau during the Anschluss on 12 March 1938, the Sudetenland October 1938 and Prague on 12 March 1939) was registered to the Liebstandarte-SS.

M-173
L = 244 mm / 9 5/8"

M-173 Hotel Post, Berchtesgaden

Table Knife (in poor condition): Obverse carries 'Hotel Post' over 'Bershtesgaden'. Reverse 90 HHL (Heinrich Haupt Ludenscheid Besteckfabrik).

The Post Hotel was popular with the Nazi Political, Military and Industrial hierarchy for both holidays and as a stop over during audiences with Hitler. Also a frequent stop for Eva Braun during the period that she was not allowed to stay at Haus Wachenfeld (that later became the Berghof), The Hotel Post was torn down in 2009 and replaced by the Hotel Edelweiss, opened in 2010.

Berchtesgaden, located 120 kilometres (75 mi) SE of Munich and 2 Km from the Obersalzberg had a new NS-Bahnhof which opened in 1940 with a special reception area for Hitler and his guests (now a travel agency). Obersalzberg was a mountainside retreat best known as the location of Adolf Hitler's beloved mountain residence, the Berghof and the Kehisteinhaus (Eagle's Nest - an official 50th birthday present for Hitler). Herman Goering and Martin Bormann also had residences there. Close by the Bahnhof is a tunnel were Goering tried to hide his art at the end of the war. There is a pizza shop on Schiesstattbrucke which was a Guardhouse and part of the security of the Obersalzberg.

Both Paula Hitler and Dietrich Eckart (see M-175) are buried in the Alter Friedhof (old cemetery).

The Berchtesgaden and Obersalzberg were liberated on 4 May 1945 by the U.S. 3rd Infantry Division.

Note: The 'Post' besteck of the 30's & 40's was from "HHL".
In the 50's the service was replaced with "WMF"

M-174

M-174 Platterhof Hotel Creamer

Creamer: Carries the Platterhof Hotel logo, an oval which contains the figure of a peasant woman standing in front of two mountains. The background sky is lined and the area beneath the woman has little flower designs. This logo was used on all hotel silverware and glassware. The creamer is 5¼ inches in length and about 2¼ inches in width. The lower rim carries the maker mark of “Gebr.Hepp and silver plate of ‘90”. On the bottom is the capacity of “0.05” liters / 2 oz and the letter “H”. This is high quality, proportional logo.

In 1937, the Nazis took over the Obersalzberg area and the Platterhof which was remodeled and a large multi-wing 200 room hotel created around the original Pension Moritz. It served high-ranking Nazi dignitaries and other important visitors waiting to see Hitler as the hotel was located a short distance from Hitler's Berghof. It had a Dietrich-Eckart-Zimmer (room) dedicated to the memory of Hitler's mentor Dietrich Eckart, who spent much of his last years in the Pension Moritz which preceded the Platterhof. Its "Bergschenke." was a popular pub for the Obersalzberg SS guard force. In 1943 it became a military hospital. The U.S. bombing of 25 April 1945 did considerable damage to the hotel and It stood derelict for several years. However, it escaped the 1952 destruction of Nazi buildings, and was rebuilt and renovated by the U.S. Army as the Hotel General Walker. The hotel was used by the US Army until about 2005, when it was torn down after being returned to the control of the Bavarian government. As was the case with many of the properties in Hitler's Obersaltzberg, the Platterhof was relentlessly looted first by American soldiers in May 1945. Later and after the US military moved many priceless items from the Eagles Nest and other Nazi buildings to the Walker hotel these were plundered by the 2005 demolition crews,

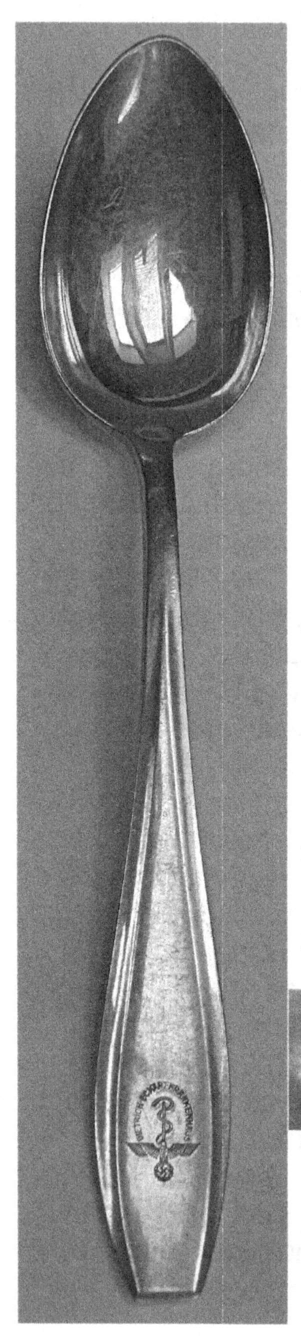

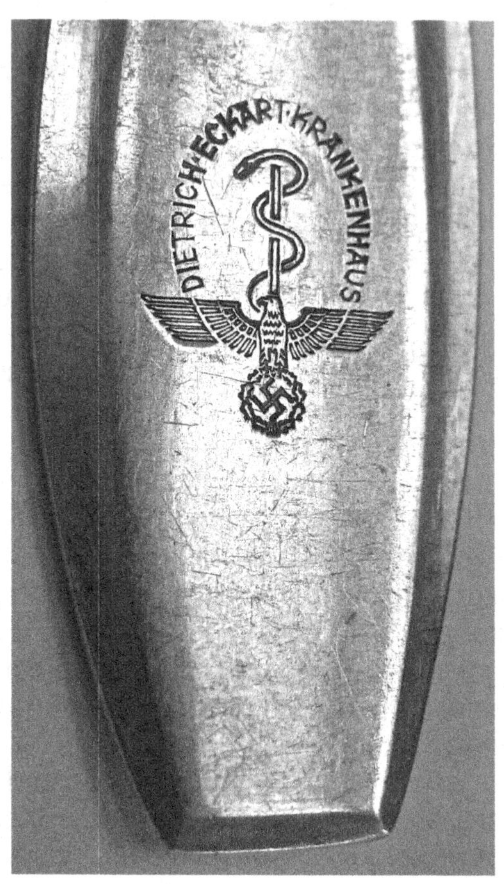

M-175
L = 213 mm / 8 6/16”

M-175 Dietrich Eckart Krankenhaus

Tablespoon: Obverse carries the logo "Dietrich Eckart Krankenhaus" which surrounds a medical staff medusa which is over an ornate eagle and swastika. The reverse: marked: “Wellner Patent 90 45”.

In 1940, the Dietrich Eckart Krankenhaus (a state-of-the-art hospital) was built in Berchtesgaden on the personal order of Adolf Hitler. This is a very scarce piece of Nazi history as it is from a location named for Dietrich Eckart (B 23 Mar 1868), Hitler’s mentor and the spiritual godfather of Nazism. Eckart was involved in founding the Deutsche Arbeiterpartei in 1919, later renamed the Nationalsozialistische Deutsche Arbeiterpartei (NSDAP); he was the original publisher of the NSDAP newspaper, the Völkischer Beobachter, and also wrote the lyrics of "Deutschland Erwache" (Germany Awake), which became an anthem of the Nazi party. Eckart met Adolf Hitler on 14 August 1919 and exerted considerable influence on him in the following years and is strongly believed to have established the theories and beliefs of the Nazi party. Hitler described his services to National Socialism as “inestimable” and called Eckart his “North Star”. Few other people had as much influence on Hitler in his lifetime. On 9 November 1923, although seriously ill, Eckart participated in the Nazi party's failed Beer Hall Putsch; he was arrested and placed in Landsberg Prison along with Hitler and other party officials, but released shortly due to illness. He died of a heart attack in Berchtesgaden on 26 December 1923.

In addition to the hospital, Hitler dedicated the second volume of Mein Kampf to Eckart, where he praised him lavishly and also named the Waldbühne in Berlin as the "Dietrich-Eckart-Bühne" when it was opened for the 1936 Summer Olympics.

M-176 L = 250 mm / 9 13/16"

M-176 Dietrich Eckhart Krankenhaus, knife

Table knife: Obverse; steel blade with Wellner's marking consisting of a shield having the name at the top of the shield and at the bottom, three gnomes carrying silverware across the surface. Beneath this is the words for stainless steel, "Nicht / Rostend". The handle is mostly plain but on the lower portion has the open-winged NSDAP eagle with swastika. The details are outstanding throughout this eagle. In an arch shape is the name, "Dietrich Eckhart Krankenhaus". In the center is a snake around a staff.

Knife observations:

I have revised my thinking regarding knives: As it turns out, knife blades are the only surface that allows makers to list their complete identity and therefore offer an opportunity to identify otherwise unknown maker marks, see W-83.

Recently I saw a Helmuth Weidling personal pattern knife handle with the maker marked 'AWS WELLNER' and the blade marked 'Henckels Zwillingwerke Solingen'. Obviously, Henckel sold knife blades to other besteck manufacturers for assembly into other manufacturers handles. Solingen being a prestige name in knives. Knives allow the mix and match of various manufacturers blades with handles.

This knife was added to my collection because it is my first Wellner marked blade. Typical of Wellner, there is no ID on the handle (see M-186) with the exception of the required plating number - usually 90.

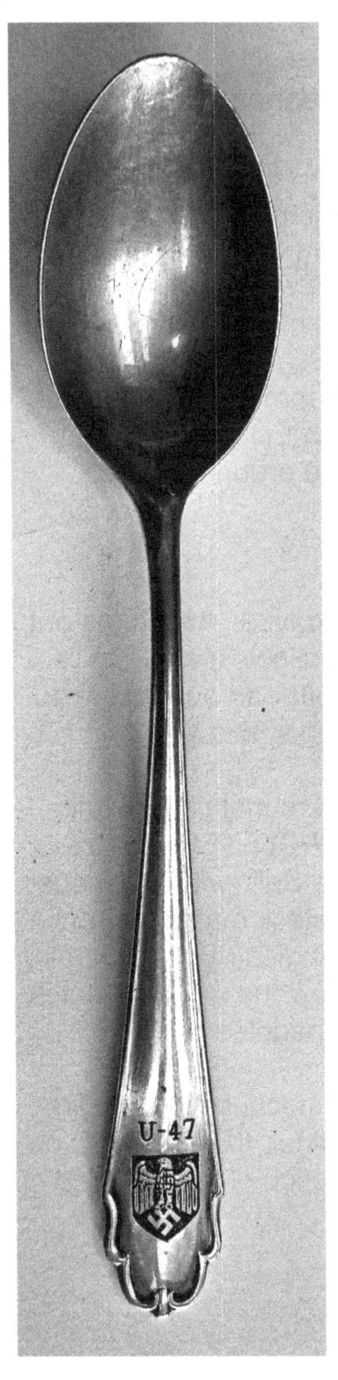

M-177
L = 160 mm / 6 5/16"

M-177 U-47

Commemorative teaspoon: Obverse carries U-47 over Eagle looking to his right. Reverse maker marked: Bruckmann, RM, 800 and Bruckman's eagle.

The U-47, a 753-ton type VIIB submarine was built at Kiel, Germany and commissioned on 17 December 1938. On 13 October 1939, Cmdr. Gunther Prien, with a crew of 53, set out in the U-47 in an attempt to attack the anchored British fleet harbored at Scapa Flow in the Orkney Islands. In a carefully planned operation, he made a daring penetration of the British anchorage and sank the battleship Royal Ark on the 14th of October 1939. Due to the poor reliability of German torpedos, he had to fire 8 torpedoes of which only 3 functioned properly. Prien became world famous, and resulted in his being the first Kriegsmariner awarded the Knight's Cross of the Iron Cross by Hitler personally on 18 October 1939. Prien and the U-47 continued their success and was the 4th highest scoring U-Boat ace credited with sinking 195,000 tons of allied shipping. Prien was the 5th recipient of the Oak-leaves to the Knight's Cross of the Iron Cross on 20 Oct 1940. On 7 March 1941, while attacking a convoy south of Iceland, the U-47 was believed to have been sunk by the British destroyer Wolverine, killing Prien and his crew.

> Trivia: The German rank of Ka-Leut (Kapitan Leutnant) was the rank assigned to U-Boat Captains. The Type VII submarine was the most produced type of war ship of all the navies in the world at 702.

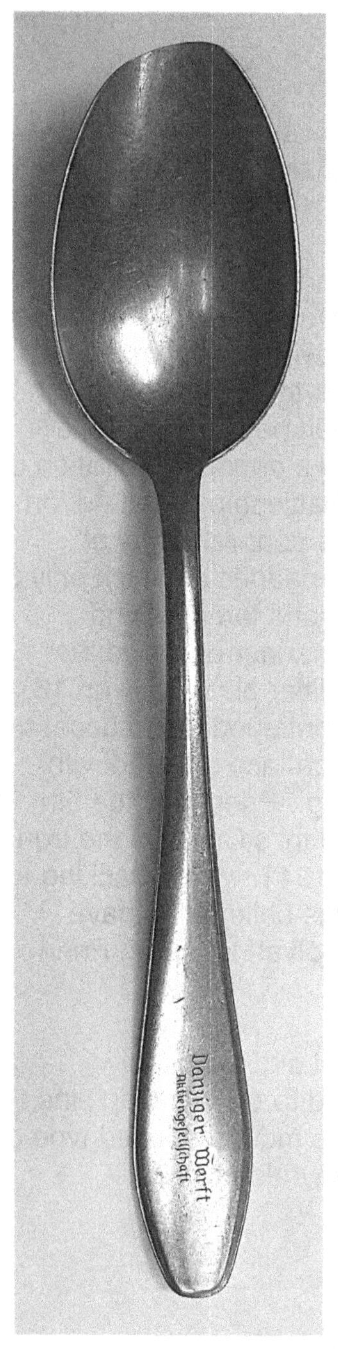

M-178
L = 210- mm / 8 1/4"

M-178 Danziger Werft

Tablespoon: Obverse marked with Danziger Werft Aktiengesellschaft (Danzig Shipbuilding Corporation) which was opened in 1921 and closed in 1945. The reverse is marked 'Hansa-Rostfrei' for Henseatische Silberwarenfabrik KG., Bremen.

At the end of WWI, this shipyard was located in the Free State of Danzig instead of Poland due to the population being 80 percent German and was subsequently taken over by Germany in 1939. Located at the escape of the Vistula River to Gdansk Gulf, the yard delivered 42 Type VII U-Boats to the Kriegsmarine between 16 December 1940 to 8 September 1943. When Danzig was taken over by the Polish government after WWII, the shipyard became the Gdansk Shipyard which gained international fame when Solidarity was founded there in 1980.

> Trivia: During WWII, Germany commissioned a total of 1,174 U-boats, with 702 Type VII's and suffered the loss of 80% of their submarine crews totaling 28,751 men lost.
>
> Rudolf Hoess, Commandant of Auschwitz wrote that the crushed to powder remains of over 3,000,000 victims cremated at Auschwitz were dumped into the Vistula.

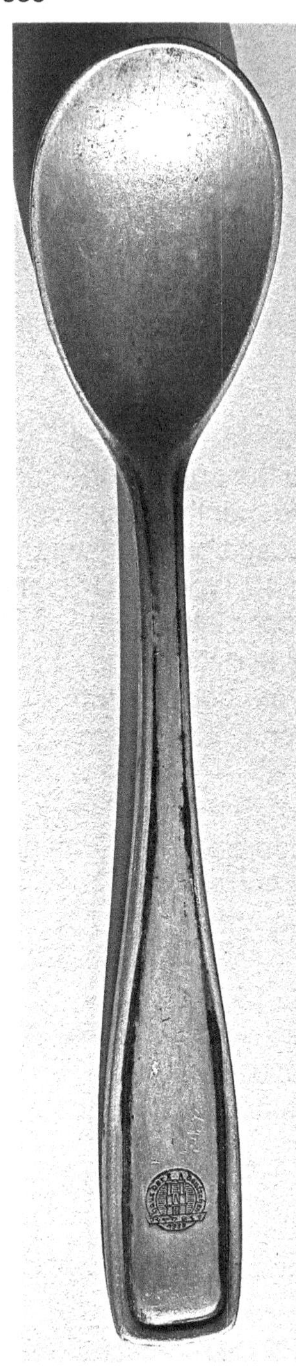

M-179
L = 139 mm / 5 7/16”

M-179 Haus der Deutschen Arbeit

Sugar spoon: This is a very rare spoon with HdD Ar. insignia impressed on the obverse and dated 1933. On the reverse, the Wellner name and maker mark (a die in a circle, showing the 4 side) and "90" in a circle, "16" in a square.

Shortly after Hitler assumed power, he banned trade unions on 2 May 1933. Per James Pool's *Hitler and His Secret Partners*, eighty-nine union leaders were arrested and total union assets of 184,000,000 marks were seized - enough money to support the Nazi party for over a year. On 10 May 1933, the Deutsche Arbeitsfront (DAF) was formed by the incorporation of all formerly free and independent trade unions. Haus der Deutschen Arbeit may have been one of those free and independent trade union houses that was disbanded by the SA and "co-ordinated" by Robert Ley into the DAF during May 1933.

A second possibility is that the HdD Ar was actually a union hall, possibly on the national level, and not itself a union per se as a literal translation is 'National Labor Hall'.

Note: Special group cutlery is extremely difficult to find, especially for the smaller more exotic groups of this period.

M-180

Knife L = 207 mm / 8 3/16"
Fork L = 177 mm / 7"

M-180 Haus der Deutschen Kunst
(House of German Art)

Salad Fork and Master Butter Knife from the formal dining area. Obverse carries the famous 1937 "Haus der Deutschen Kunst" logo by Richard Klein featuring a Trojan helmet in left profile, a flaming torch and the Parteiadler. The reverse maker marked "BRUCKMANN" and '90'.

This building was constructed in Munich from 1934 to 1937 following plans of Hitler's favorite architect Paul Ludwig Troost as the Third Reich's first representational monumental building replacing the Glaspalast, Munick's earlier art exhibition hall which burned down in June of 1931. Troost died in 1934, before the laying of the foundation stone and was declared "First master builder of the Fuehrer". The museum, then called Haus der Deutschen Kunst ("House of German Art"), was opened in March 1937 as a showcase for what the Third Reich regarded as Germany's finest art and became the venue for the greatest German art shows in history. Hitler himself opened the "Days of German Art" 16 - 18 July 1937 The inaugural exhibition was the Große Deutsche Kunstausstellung (Great German Art Exhibition), which was intended as an edifying contrast to the condemned modern art on display in the concurrent Entartete Kunst (Degenerate Art) exhibition. In the 1937 "Official Exhibition Catalogue", P. Bruckmann ran a full page ad with a photo of a place setting with text: "In der Gaststatte vom HAUS DER DEUTSCHEN KUNST speist man mit diesem BRUCKMANN-BESTECK" (In the restaurant of the House of German Art you eat with Bruckmann cutlery). The restaurant and the terrace were the formal dining areas and as such would have used the full Bruckmann version in the event a diner turned the cutlery over, they should see the complete Bruckmann name. Pieces show minor wear/age patina only.

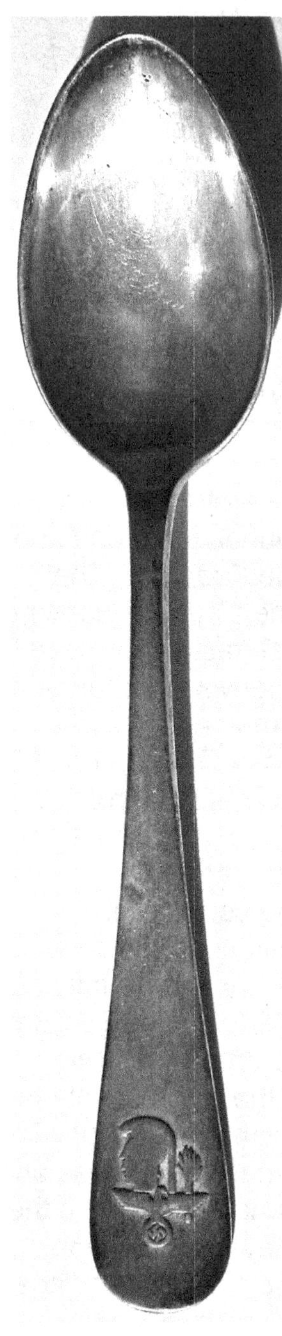

M-181
L = 110 mm / 4 5/16"

M-181 Haus der Deutschen Kunst
(House of German Art)

Mocha spoon: Obverse carries the famous 1937 “Haus der Deutschen Kunst” logo by Richard Klein featuring a Trojan helmet (helmet of Pallas Athena) in left profile, a flaming torch and the Parteiadler. The reverse maker marked ‘B’ (Bruckmann) locomotive and ’90’

This service believed to have been ordered for use in the Haus der Deutschen Kunst’s more relaxed pub-style dining area used by staff and NSDAP dignitaries seeking privacy. Today the room is the bar.

The building survived the war as the Haus der Kunst literally (House of Art) and is located at Prinzregentenstrasse 1 at the southern edge of the Englischer Garten, Munich's largest park and is included in the all day 3rd Reich Tour in Munich.

Special Note on the Degenerate Art exhibition held at the Hofgarten Arcade in Munich during the summer and fall of 1937 at the same time as the first Great German Art Exhibition in the House of German Art (Haus der Deutschen Kunst). Billed as “Communist and Jewish Garbage”, it became the last opportunity for Germans to see many works by Chagall, Van Gogh, Gauguin, Kokoschka, Modigliani, Matisse, Picasso, Klee, Levy, Feininger, Braque, Derain, Ensor, Laurencin, Pascin, Vlaminck, Marc, Nolde, Hofer, Rohlfs, Dix, Beckmann, Pechstein, Kirchner, Heckel, Grosz, Schmidt-Rottluff, Müller, Modersohn, Macke, Corinth, Liebermann, Amiet, Baraud, Lehmbruck, Mataré, Marcks, Archipenko and Barlach. After the show, these works were sold abroad.

Note: The brushed finish is unusual and is termed a ‘Florentine Finish’.

M-182
Height = 174 mm / 6 7/8"

M-182 Haus der Deutschen Kunst
(House of German Art)

Goblet: Obverse base carries the name of WELLNER over the number 6 in a circle. Reverse stamped with the letters H.D.D.K., the initials of the Haus Der Deutschen Kunst (House of German Art).

This is a rare and beautiful example of the standard 6 7/8" heavy (354 gr / 12.5 oz) alpacca Eiskaffeebecher or Eisschokoladenbecher (ice coffee goblet or cold chocolate milk goblet).

This goblet was in use in the restaurant, pub and the terrace of Hitler's spectacular art museum in Munchen, the capital of the Nazi movement.

The Becher (goblet) is listed as item 5833 on page 17 of the 1936 Sächsische Metallwarenfabrik August Wellner Söhne AG catalog. Without the personalization of the House of German Art, this heavy alpacca cup sold for 10 Reichsmark or 4 US dollars at the time the House of German Art opened in 1937. Using the AIER cost of living calculator for 1936, the conversion factor is 15.5899 yielding a today price of $62.36.

Everybody that was anybody in Third Reich Germany showed up at the House of German Art or across the street at the exhibition of the Entartete Kunst (Degenerate Art). Luminaries like Reichsführer-SS Heinrich Himmler and Adolf Hitler himself could have used this Wellner piece on some occasion! And per source, "A rarely seen Wellner piece in better than average condition".

M-183 Haus der Deutschen Kunst
(House of German Art)

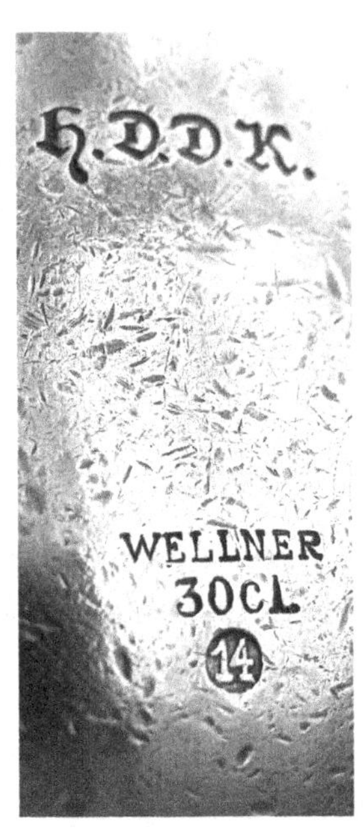

Coffee Set: This is a Wellner coffee set.

This Wellner coffee pot (individual) is 6 inches high to the top of the lid and 6 inches wide handle to spout. The bottom circumference is 9 inches. It weighs 444 grams or 15.7 oz. It is marked on the bottom Wellner 30cl. (10.1 Oz) where 100cl = 1 liter = 33.8 Oz and #14 in a circle. It also carries H.D.D.K. the short form initials of the Haus Der Deutschen Kunst (House of German Art).. The lid has a 43H on it as well as the bottom of the pot.

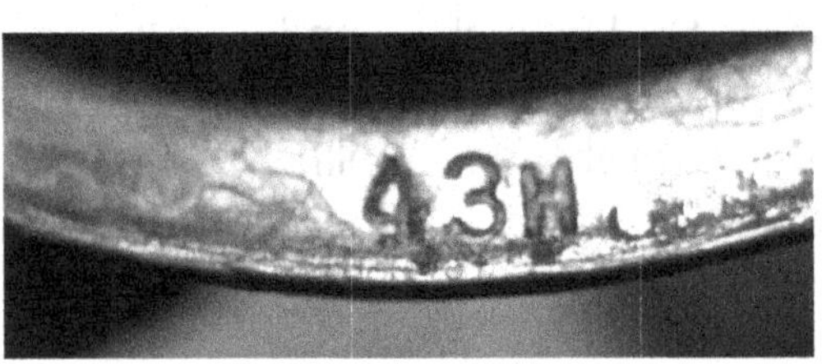

M-183 Haus der Deutschen Kunst
(House of German Art)

This Wellner milk can is 3 inches high by 4 inches wide (spout to handle). The bottom circumference is 7 inches, it weighs 168 grams or 5.9 oz. It is marked Wellner 10cl. (3.4 Oz) and a 7 in a circle. It has what appears to be a triangle on the bottom rim. These are in vintage wear condition with dings etc. common to these Alpacca items. But their condition is very good

Used in the formal dining area, the private pub-style dining area and the terrace.

	1935 RM	2010 US$
Coffee Pot	23	146
Milk Can	11.5	73

Note: The Grosse Deutsche Kunstausstellung (Greater German Art Exhibition) for 1938 opened on 10 July and ran through 16 October.

M-184 L = 189 mm / 7 7/16”

M-184 STAATSKASINO

Fork: Obverse carries 'STAATSKASINO' (Unknown which Casino). Reverse marked '30' in a square and '90' in a circle and 'Art. Krupp' the Krupp logo of a standing bear + 'BERNDORF' The short form "ART" for Arthur indicates this fork is from before Arthur Krupp's death, as from 1938 to 1945, only 'Krupp' appeared to the left of the logo.

Note: ART KRUPP BERNDORF is the name of the manufacturer (Arthur Krupp AG [joint-stock company) in Berndorf, Austria. This firm had fabrications in Austria (Berndorf), Swizerland (Luzern) and Germany (Eßlingen).

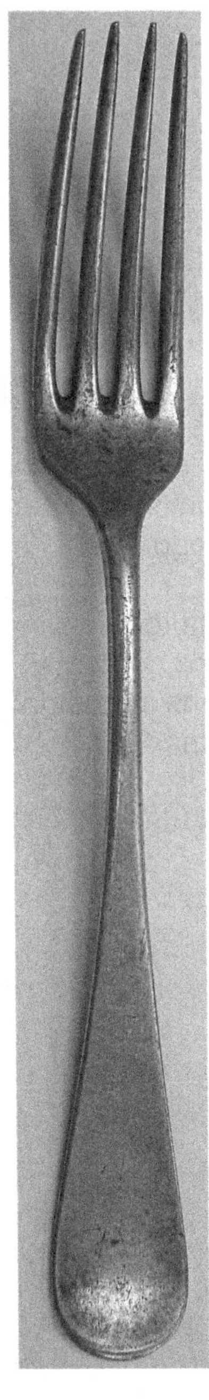

M-185
L = 213 mm / 8 6/16”

M-185 Kasino Lamsdorf (Casino Lamsdorf)

Table Fork: Obverse clear. Reverse carries 'Casino' over 'Lamsdorf' with a Prussian crown between. Maker marked Berndorf Alpacca Silber II, introduced around 1880 and used fifty (!) years until 1930. Inside the diamond there are two letterings: "BMF" (with the "M" and "F" letters being fused indicating Vienna, Austria manufacture) and "ASII" (which means Alpacca Silber II, an Alpacca base covered by a double layer of silver).

The Lamsdorf 'Offizier' Casino (mess) was located at the Bahnhofs-Hotel. Casino in the military application is 'mess' or club or smoking room. The forks' Prussian crown indicates it was carried over from WWI's Imperial German Army. Stalag VIII-B Lamsdorf was a notorious German Army prisoner of war camp, later renumbered Stalag-344. Located near the small town of Lamsdorf (now called Łambinowice) in Silesia. The camp initially built to house British and French prisoners in World War I. At this same location there had been a prisoner camp during the Franco-Prussian War 1870.

The camp was reopened in 1939 to house Polish prisoners from the German September 1939 offensive. Later approx. 100 000 prisoners from Australia, Belgium, Great Britain, Canada, France, Greece, Italy, New Zealand, Netherlands, Poland, South Africa, Soviet Union, Yugoslavia and the United States passed through this camp. In 1941 a separate camp, Stalag VIII-F was set up close by to house Soviet prisoners. In 1943, the Lamsdorf camp was split up, and many of the prisoners (and Arbeitskommandos) were transferred to two new base camps Stalag VIII-C Sagan (modern Żagań and Stalag VIII-D Teschen (modern Český Tesin). The base camp at Lamsdorf was renumbered stalag 344.

M-186
L = 248 mm = 9 11/16”

M-186 Rabbit Breeders

Dinner Knife: Obverse carries Reichsfachgruppe (Reich Specialized Group) Kaninchen Züchter's (Rabbit Breeder) logo with a raised R.D.KL. (Reichsverband Deutscher Kleintierzuchter (Reich Association of German Small Animal Breeders). The RDKL even included bees. Reverse marked "90". Comment: The handle style is typical of Wellner and typical of Wellner, the knife does not carry a maker's mark.

In the early to mid 1930s, there were between 65 and 100 registered rabbit breeders in Germany, with their state headquarters in Berlin.

With the war, Himmler had the SS establish Angora rabbit programs at some 31 concentration camps located in Germany (with all reporting to Berlin), to produce angora wool, initially, for use for the lining of Luftwaffe flying personnel jackets, socks for U-Boat crews and when production increased, for the famous W-SS winter anoraks.

SS Angora Wool Production

	Kg / #	# of Rabbits
1941	460Kg / 1,014#	6,500
1942	1,470kg / 3,241#	13,000
1943	2,800kg / 6,173#	25,000

This State special group silverware is extremely hard to find, especially for the smaller, more exotic groups.

Note: In many POW camps in Germany the prisoners were reduced to eating cats which were called, 'roof rabbits'!

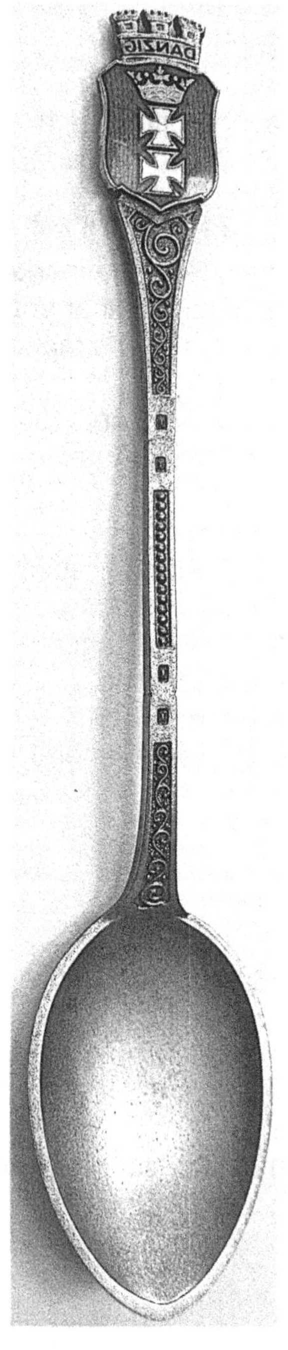

M-187
L = 117mm /
4 1/4”

M-187 Andenken (souvenir) 'DANZIG'

Small 'remembrance' spoon: Ornate obverse carries the Danzig crest with 'DANZIG' above. Reverse decorated but with no indication of material or manufacturer.

This spoon has a story! On a recent European holiday, while visiting some old friends, my earlier book, 'Collectible Spoons of the 3rd Reich' came up. Our hostess presented this spoon to me. It had been acquired by her grandfather while he served in the Heer in Danzig as a Major in charge of a sanitaeter (medical unit).

Major Walter Spiess was born on 3 June 1891 and spent the better part of WWII in Danzig. The spoon was brought home to Wesel Niederheim. The grand daugher, (photo left) Liebtraud Schwanke is the generous source of this spoon. Major Spiess passed away on 2 August 1971.

Note: (Major was a Staff Officer rank).

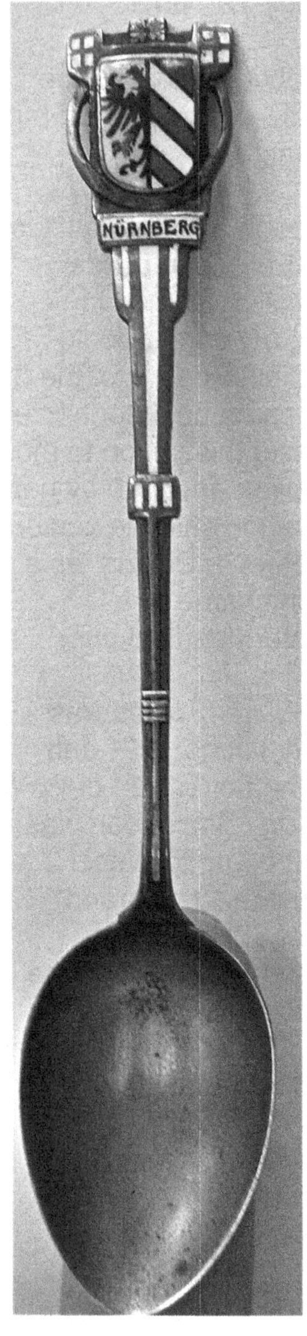

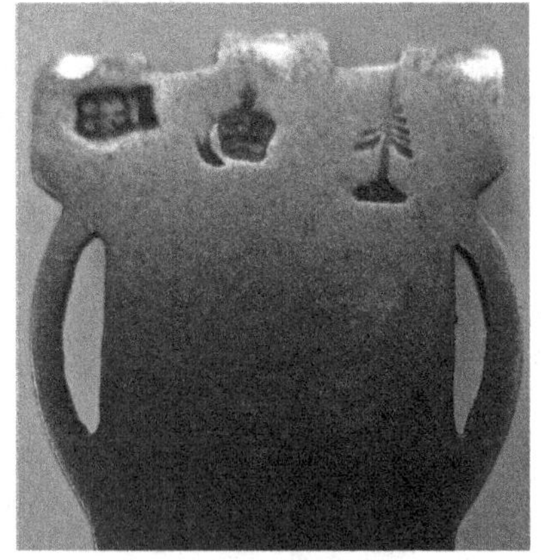

M-188 L = 120 mm / 4 3/4"

M-188 Andenken (souvenir) 'Nurnberg'

Small 'remembrance' spoon: Obverse carries the City of Nurnberg crest with 'NURNBERG' below. Reverse 800, RM, and an unidentified maker mark of a pine tree.

The collecting of souvenir spoons in Europe began about the time of the Crystal Palace Exhibition in London (1851). There developed a brisk trade in the production of souvenir spoons which travelers who visited various European cities purchased to remind them of their visit. Soon late 19th century American travelers returning from Europe brought back with them souvenir spoons from the various cities which they had visited. Two American silversmiths, both of whom had traveled extensively in Europe (M. W. Galt of Washington, DC and Seth F. Low of Salem, MA), are generally credited with being the individuals who transplanted the European "fad" (or practice) of collecting souvenir spoons to America, then these entrepreneurs proceeded to capitalize on the souvenir spoon market in the United States, see M-195.

This spoon's Crest stripes go down to the right while the stripes on PS-26 go down to the left along with the fact that there is no city or color involved. Both M-187 and M-188 are vividly colored. This indicates to me that PS-26 is NOT an andenken as stated by only one source and that PS-26 is a Bormann item as all other sources testify.

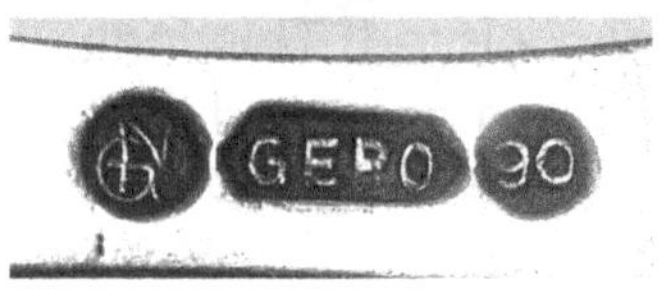

M-189
L = 123 mm / 4 13/16”

M-189 AVRO Tempelhof Andeneken

Sugar Spoon: Obverse with '1936', a representation of the AVRO facility and on the neck AVRO. Reverse maker marked NG, GERO (Gerofabriek) and 90 in a circle.

German Source represented this spoon as a souvenir spoon from the AVRO facility at Tempelhof airfield in 1936, most likely from either the opening or related to the Olympics. The '90' supports German provenance. Inquiries to AVRO have gone unanswered. Their available history does not cover the 30's. AVRO was one of the world's first aircraft builders, A.V. Roe and Company was established on 1 January 1910 and continues today as AVRO.

The site of the Tempelhof airport was originally Knights Templar land in medieval Berlin, and from this beginning came the name Tempelhof. Later, the site was used as a parade field by Prussian forces, and by unified German forces from 1720 to the start of World War I. In 1909, Orville Wright flew at Tempelhof which was first officially designated as an airport on 8 October 1923. Lufthansa was founded at Tempelhof on 6 January 1926. As part of Albert Speer's plan for the reconstruction of Berlin during the Nazi era, he ordered the replacement of the old terminal with a new terminal building in 1934 which was built between 1936 and 1941, forming a 1.2 kilometer long quadrant. The airport halls and the neighboring buildings, intended to become the gateway to Europe and a symbol of Hitler's "world capital" Germania are still known as the largest built entities worldwide, and have been described by British architect Sir Norman Foster as "the mother of all airports".
Note: The Russians flooded the lowest 3 cellar levels (where aircraft had been built) due to booby traps. They remain flooded to date.

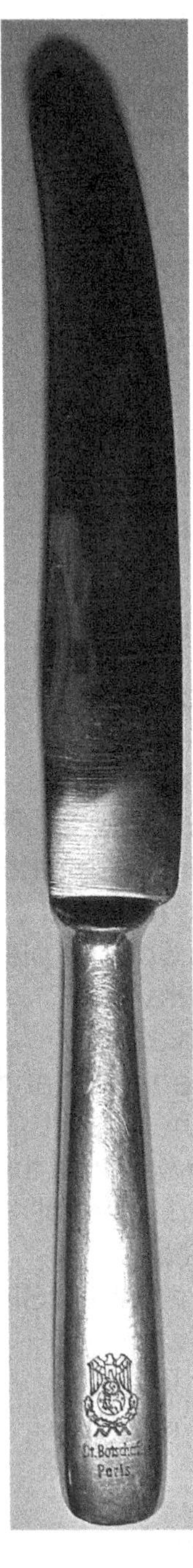

M-190
L = 225 mm / 8 7/8”

Note: This knife blade style is termed ‘New French’.

M-190 Deutsche Botschaft - Paris
(Embassy of Germany - Paris)

Knife: Reverse "Dt. Botschaft over Paris. No maker mark but in the Wellner style. Source: Shawn Bernhardt

The Deutsche Botschaft in Paris was located at 78 Rue de Lille. On 7 November 1938, seventeen-year-old Herschel Grynszpan (Gruenspan), went to the German embassy intending to assassinate the German Ambassador to France. Upon discovering that the Ambassador was not in the embassy, he settled for a lesser official, Third Secretary Ernst vom Rath. Rath was critically wounded and died two days later on November 9. A Jew, Herschel Gruenspan's action set the spark to the explosion (inflamed by Goebbels) of Kristall Nacht 9-10 November 1938. Results reported varied: "During Crystal Night over 7,500 Jewish shops were destroyed and 400 synagogues were burnt down." and " In 1938 there were approximately 1,400 synagogues in Germany, of which only about 180 were destroyed or damaged. Furthermore, Jews owned approximately 100,000 shops and department stores in Germany in 1938. Of this number, only about 7,500 had their windows broken. Ninety-one Jews were killed and an estimated 20,000 were sent to concentration camps." Up until this time these camps had been mainly for political prisoners. The damage was initially covered by insurance. Goebbels claimed that it was a spontaneous action by an infuriated German people who had had enough of Jewish crimes against our nation. The passivity with which most German civilians responded to the violence signaled to the Nazi regime that the German public was prepared for more radical measures. By 1939, approximately half the Jewish population of Germany (250,000) had left the country.

Note: Grynszpan survived the war and returned to Paris.

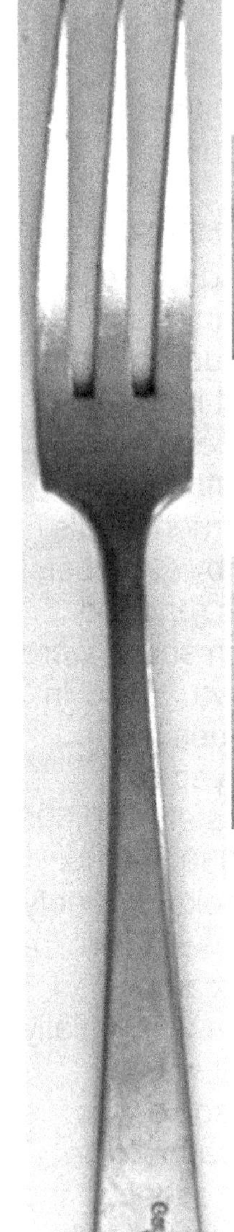

Gauhauptstadt Posen
Volkspflegeamt

M-191
L = 202 mm / 8”

M-181 Gauhaupstadt Posen Volkspflegeamt
(District Capital Posen People's Welfare Office)

Fork: Obverse marked as above, reverse unclear.

The Third Reich, was divided into 42 provinces, or Gau, administered by a Gauleiter. A Gauleiter was the highest ranking NSDAP official, responsible for political. economic and civil defense matters in his Gau. When Poland was conquered in 1939, its territory was divided into three distinct regions. The western region of Poland was annexed into the German Reich as two Gau: Gau Danzig-West Preussen and Gau Posen (later Gau Wartheland). These annexed areas also came under Wehrmacht and Waffen-SS territorial organization. The central portion of Poland came under the civilian control (Dr. Frank) of the Generalgouvernement, and the eastern portion of Poland under Soviet control from 17 September when the Soviet Union attacked Poland from the East, and was officially handed over when all German forces pulled back to the demarcation line of the Bug River. When Germany later attacked the Soviet Union in June 1941, the eastern region of Poland previously occupied by the Soviets was added to the control of the Generalgouvernement.

The capital of Gau Posen/Wartheland was Posen. The Gauleiter was SS Obergruppenfuhrer Arthur Greiser, As Gauleiter of Warthegau, including Posen and Lodz, Greiser was in charge of the mass deportation of Poles to the General Government and extermination of Jews and Poles to secure room for the 350,000 ethnic German refugees from Eastern European nations occupied by Russia and the Baltic States, Volhynia, the Balkans and the Reich proper. The result was the increase of German population from 325,000 in 1939 to 850,000 by the end of 1943. After the war, Greisler was convicted of war crimes and hanged and the Germans deported back to Germany proper.

M-192
L = 137 mm /
5 3/8”

M-192 D-LZ 129 Hindenburg

(Luftschiff Zeppelin #129; Registration: D-LZ 129)

Commemorative Spoon: Obverse with LZ over globe with air ship over 129. Reverse: personal engraved 'M.B.', 800 no RM. The Danish "Three Tower Mark" with year '33' (1933) and Assay Master Jens Sigsgaard 1932 - 1960.

This zeppelin, named after the late Field Marshal Paul von Hindenburg (1847–1934), President of Germany (1925–1934), was a large German commercial passenger-carrying rigid airship. The lead ship of the Hindenburg class it is the largest flying machine of any kind (803.8' long and 135.1' diameter) ever built. The airship construction started in 1931, was completed in early 1936 and flew from March 1936 until destroyed by fire 14 months later on May 6, 1937, at the end of the first North American transatlantic journey of its second season of service. The cost of a ticket between Germany and Lakehurst was US$400 (or US$6,050 in 2010 dollars). The airship was operated commercially by the Deutsche Zeppelin Reederei, which was established by Hermann Göring in March, 1935 to increase Nazi influence over zeppelin operations and was jointly owned by the Luftschiffbau Zeppelin, the German Air Ministry and Deutsche Lufthansa AG, and also operated the Graf Zeppelin's last two years of commercial service to South America from 1935 to 1937. The airship's first "official" function was not to be in the commercial transatlantic passenger service for which it was designed and built, but instead as a vehicle for Nazi propaganda.

Although the passenger capacity was 72, on the last flight there were only 36 passengers with a crew of 61. Landing in Lakehurst, N.J. it was engulfed in flames, destroyed in 37 seconds with 13 passengers, 22 air crew and one ground crew perishing.

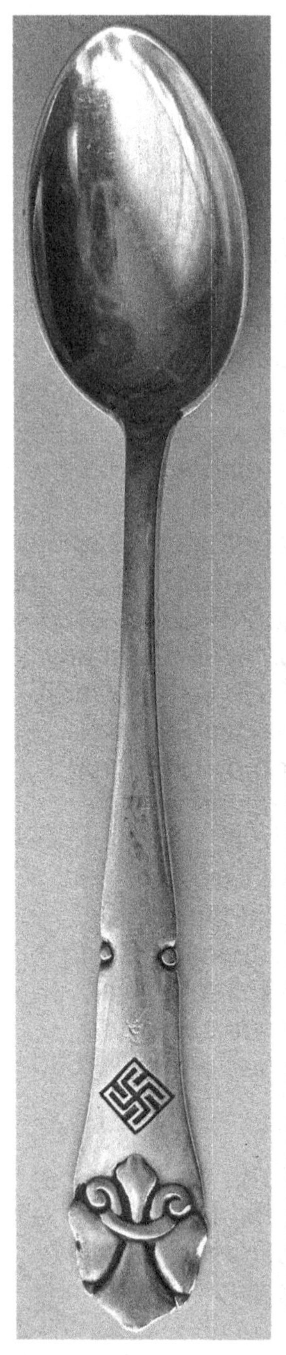

M - 193
L = 122 mm/
4 13/16"

M-193 Danish Mysteries

Mocha spoon: Obverse carries a mobile swastika. Reverse an engraved letter 'J', the Danish "Three Tower Mark" with year '23' (1923), 800, no RM, and assay master mark.

This spoon raises a number of questions. The "Three Tower Mark" was instituted in 1608 as the official mark of the city of Copenhagen. In 1893 the Copenhagen Three Towers became the national mark of Denmark. The mark guarantees a silver purity of 826/1000. The number below indicates the year (four digits used until 1771, two digits after). The three towers were always marked in conjunction with the initial mark of the Assay Master (Stadsguardein). It was he who took final responsibility of guarantee. The use of both marks was discontinued by 1977. To refresh your memory, in 1884 Germany enacted a law making 800 the minimum national standard for silver. This spoon carries both implied 826 and 800 marks! but no RM.

The engraved letter 'J' indicates a personal spoon. In addition there is a very small Assay Master mark (at the bottom of the left top photo) of a capital 'H' with a letter 'c' between the upper H legs and the letter 'f' between the lower H legs. This is the Danish Assay Master Mark (Stadsguardein Maerker) of C. F. Heise who was assay master from 1904 to 1932.

The question: How did a 1923 spoon from Denmark get a swastika??? or more interesting - why???

Note: More Danish "Three Tower Mark" items: W-101 & M-192. They are all marked German '800' but no RM indicates these are not 'official' German silver. Germany invaded neutral Denmark at 4:15 AM on 9 April 1940. Denmark surrendered 2 hours later suffering 16 KIA.

M-194
L = 210 mm / 8 1/4

M-194 VEB Wellner - Post Script

Soup Spoon: Reverse marked “VEB v. Wellner - 90 (in circle) - 45 (in a square).

Wellner survived the war and as a result of being located in eastern Germany, became VEB Wellner (Volkseigener Betrieb - People-owned Enterprise) or state owned workplace of the German Democratic Republic / Deutsche Demokratische Republik which existed from 1949 to 1990. Today the closed facility is: Wellner Silber GmbH at Wellner Str 61, Aue, Germany. having not survived the German reunification.

Per Wellner, the maker marks during the early VEB period used the earlier markings out of convenience. Another example of East German expediency or “why re-invent the wheel” was the continued use of the Heer’s ‘rain drop’ pattern poncho used in 1944/45 and manufactured in the East for the ‘Peoples Army’ into the 50’s.

The author visits the abandoned Wellner complex.

COLLECTORS
SPECIAL NOTE AND WARNING

The SA-Standart Feldherrnhalle spoon was the only besteck I paid for which I never received.

My method of purchase has been to identify an item of interest offered by a known dealer (in this case, one that had previously delivered) and to notify them of my interest and to request a confirmation as to its price and availability. In the interim I would research the items area of representation and develop a one page descriptive summary as appears on the face page. When comfortable with the item as a good addition to my collection and when receiving the assurance that the item was indeed available, I would notify the vender and submit payment. This was all done for this spoon - regrettably, I was subsequently informed some months after payment that the spoon was not to be mine, nor indeed a refund.

I have left the writeup opposite as the spoon is from a very transitional time in the SA vis-a-vis the SS and as a precautionary tale for new fellow collectors to make sure the goods are actually in the hand of the dealer selling. ps - I'm still awaiting restitution of my payment! Buyer beware!!!

Particularly with Florida's Mr. G!!!!!

OG-?? SA-Standarte Feldherrnhalle

Teaspoon: Obverse carries the SA-Feldherrnhalle (Field Marshals' Hall) emblem with the pseudo-runic SA while the reverse has the maker mark 'WMF' for Wurttembergische Metallwarenfabrik, Geislingen 1853 to the present and '90'.

The initial unit, the SA-Standarte Feldherrnhalle (a Standarte was an organization of regimental size) was formed in 1935 after the death of Ernst Röhm (Night of the Long Knives), when the SA's position as the major paramilitary formation of the NSDAP was taken over by the SS. It was made up of the most promising SA men drawn from SA units all over Germany. With headquarters in Berlin, it provided guard units for SA, State and Party Offices and as such was not a combat unit. Its units were stationed in Berlin, Krefeld, Hannover, Hattingen, Munich, Ruhr, Stettin and Stuttgart. It was one of the first units selected to enter Austria in March of 1938 during the Anschluss.

In September 1938, it was placed under the control of the Wehrmacht. In February 1939 the cadre of the unit was transferred to the Luftwaffe, forming the Luftlande-Regiment (glider infantry regiment) Feldherrnhalle, a part of the 7. Flieger-Division. The remainder of the regiment was transferred to the Heer, forming the 120. Infanterie-Regiment (mot) of the 60. Infanterie Division (mot) and 271. Infanterie-Regiment of the 93. Infanterie-Division. Thus the later Feldherrnhalle units were combat formations which drew manpower from the SA, tracing their history back to the days of the 1923 Beer Hall Putsch. As they were now in the Wehrmacht, the 'SA' was deleted from the emblem.

Material and Length Listing

PS-1 Adolf Hitler, 'Formal' Pattern	800	146 mm
PS-2 A H Napkin Ring	925	43 mm
PS-3 A H 'Informal' Pattern	800	185 mm
PS-4 A H, Curved 'AH',	800	148 mm
PS-5 A H, Runic	90	139 mm
PS-6 A H, Block	Alpacca	134 mm
PS-7 A H, Linked	90	210 mm
PS-8 Eva Braun, Baroque	46?	142 mm
PS-9 Eva Braun, Parfait Spoon	90	212 mm
PS-10 Herman Goering,	800	137 mm
PS-11 Goering, Ribbed	800	213 mm
PS-12 Goering, Reichsmarshall	800	145 mm
PS-13 Heinrich Himmler, Train	90	141 mm
PS-14 Heinrich Himmler,	18	138 mm
PS-15 Albert Speer,	60	140 mm
PS-16 Albert Speer	800	181 mm
PS-17 General Helmut Weidling	90	143 mm
PS-18 Bernard Rust,	90	210 mm
PS-19 Bernard Rust, DH	90	109 mm
PS-20 Dr. Robert Ley, DAF	90	216 mm
PS-21 Ernst Kaltenbrunner,	100	224 mm
PS-22 Fritz Sauckel,	90	213 mm
PS-23 Hans Frank, Personal	800	214 mm

PS-24	Hans Frank, Official	90	217 mm
PS-25	Bishop Ludwig Mueller	800	217 mm
PS-26	Martin Bormann	Al	112 mm
PS-27	Martin Bormann	Al	250 mm
PS-28	Joachim von Ribbentrop	925	208 mm
PS-29	Joachim von Ribbontrop	900	130 mm
PS-30	Rudolf Hess	800	112 mm
PS-31	Reinhard Heydrich	90	215 mm
PS-32	Reinhard Heydrich	100	144 mm
PS-33	General Gustav Scheel MD	100	215 mm
PS-34	General Hermann Breith	800	191 mm
OG-35	NSDAP-Fraktur	800	133 mm
OG-36	NSDAP, High Leader	800	141 mm
OG-37	NSDAP / SA Early Version	Al	211 mm
OG-38	NSDAP/SA fork, very early	90	210 mm
OG-39	SA Sturmabteilung	800	145 mm
OG-40	SA Sturmabteilung	800	143 mm
OG-41	RJV / German Youth	800	135 mm
OG-42	HJ Hitler-Jugend	800	132 mm
OG-43	HJ (HitlerYouth)	800	148 mm
OG-44	HJ - RFS Leadership School	90	213 mm

OG-45 HJ - Sportschule Braunau	90	212 mm
OG-46 DAF 1941	800	129 mm
OG-47 DAF Set of 7	90	NA
OG-48 DAF Cup	Alpacca	
OG-49 DAF / SdA Beauty of Work	RF	210 mm
OG-50 DAF / SdA I. G. Farben	RF	210 mm
OG-51 DAF / SdA Bra AG	RF	210 mm
OG-52 DAF / SdA, Borgward Auto	RF	142 mm
OG-53 Dh - alternate?	40	207 mm
OG-54 DLV German Aviation League	RF	183 mm
OG-55 DR - Deutsche Reichsbahn	800	140 mm
OG-56 DR / AH 205	800	210 mm
OG-57 DR / AH 205 detail	800	140 mm
OG-58 DR / 213	800	122 mm
OG-59 DR - Otto Dietrich 251	90	165 mm
OG-60 DR / Goering 243	90	216 mm
OG-61 DRK / Deutsche Rotes Kreuz	800	136 mm
OG-62 NSDStB / Student Federation	800	149 mm
OG-63 NSDStB / Student Federation	800	142 mm
OG-54 NSKK / Motor Korps - fork	90	178 mm
OG-65 NSKOV / Veterans Support	800	217 mm

OG-66 NSKOV, Basic	**800**	**139 mm**
OG-67 NSRL - Physical Fitness	**90**	**192 mm**
OG-68 NSV / NS People's Welfare	**800**	**144 mm**
OG-69 RAD / Labor Service 1936	**RF**	**217 mm**
OG-70 RAD / Mess Hall Fork, 1941	**RF**	**215 mm**
OG-71 RAD Wheat	**800**	**139 mm**
OG-72 RAD Knife H.M.Z. 37	**90**	**236 mm**
OG-73 RDB - German Civil Servants	**90**	**182 mm**
OG-74 RK - New Reich Chancellery	**800**	**210 mm**
OG-75 RKB / Colonial League	**800**	**138 mm**
OG-76 RLB, Air Raid Protection	**800**	**142 mm**
OG-77 RMJ, Ministry of Justice	**90**	**238 mm**
OG-78 RNS / Food Estate	**800**	**147 mm**
W-79 Army Eagle facing right 1942	**RF**	**141 mm**
W-80 Army Officer's Field Service	**RF**	**NA**
W-81 Army Field Service, Spork	**RF**	**NA**
W-82 Army Field Service 1943	**RF**	**NA**
W-83 Mystery - Army FBCM 41	**90**	**208 mm**

W-84 Army Mess, W.S.M.42. AL 212 mm

W-85 Army Mess, "WH" AL 210 mm

W-86 Army Mess, 'LGK&F 39 AL 209 mm

W-87 Army Mess, B.A. F. N. 39 AL 139 mm

W-88 Army 1944 Commemorative 800 142 mm

W-89 Army, JRS 41 RF 202 mm

W-90 Army H.U. - 1934 - fork Alpacca 127 mm
W-91 Army H.U. - 1938 - knife RF 240 mm
W-92 Army H.U. - Dug? Pot 153 mm

W-93 Army 5./89 Marksman Award 800 213 mm

W-94 Army Fuhrer Escort Brigade 90 138 mm

W-95 Army 107th Infantry Regiment 90 NA

W-96 Army 1st Mountain Division 800 145 mm

W-97 GTPp Mystery Solved 90 128 mm

W-98 Army Field Kitchen Can Opener NA

W-969Africa Corps D.AK 800 145 mm

W-100 Africa Corps D-AK, CA Krall 800 144 mm

W-101 Africa Corps, Denmark, No RM800 118 mm

W-102 Navy, Weimar Republic 90 215 mm

W-103 Navy Mess, HHL Rustfrei RF 212 mm
W-104 Navy Mess, Blancadur AL 144 mm
W-105 Navy Mess, No 'M', FWW 41 RF 211 mm

W-106 Navy Torpedo Testing Facility RF 202 mm

W-107 NTTF?, StVer RF 208 mm

W-108 Kriegsmarine Presentation 800 215 mm

W-109 Air Force Mess, Droop Tail RF 206 mm

W-110 Air Force Mess, Oxydex RF 210 mm

W-111 Air Force Mess, fork AL 208 mm

W-112 Air Force Eagle crosswise 90 205 mm

W-113 Air Force Officer's Service plate 209 mm

W-114 Air Force Officer's Service 90 207 mm

W-115 Air Force Officer's Service 800 142 mm

W-116 Air Force Officer's Service 800 174 mm

W-117 Fliegerhorst (airfield) Julich 10 152 mm

W-118 Fliegerhorst Staaken 90 147 mm

SS-119 Neusilber Alpacca 211 mm

SS-120 SS Knife & Fork Set 800 NA

SS-121 Allgemeine-SS, F.S. Cromagan 202 mm

SS-122 Allgemeine-SS 28 800 145 mm

SS-123 SS-VT Reich RF 180 mm

SS-124 Waffen-SS, DJC 800 208 mm

SS-125 Waffen SS, Alpacca Alpacca 149 mm

SS-126 1st SS Div. LSSAH, VSF 90 208 mm

SS-127 LSSAH, Becker 90 144 mm

SS-128 LSSAH, "1941", WMF 800 138 mm

SS-129 LSSAH, LW 800 136 mm

SS-130 LSSAH, K & B 800 133 mm

SS-131 2nd SS-Pz Div, "Reich" "XX" 800 140 mm

SS-132 SS-Reich, LSF 800 139 mm

SS-133 SS-Reich Lightening Bolt Alpaca 146 mm

SS-134 SS-Reich, textured RF 138 mm

SS-135 SS-Reich, Austria - fork RF 203 mm

SS-136 SS-Reich, China Silver CS 213 mm

SS-137 2nd SS Div-Reich 800 175 mm

SS-138 3rd SS-Div "Totenkopf" 800 141 mm

SS-139 4th SS Div "Polizei" 800 141 mm

SS-140	5th SS Div "Wiking"	RF	215 mm
SS-141	9th SS Div "Hohenstaufen"	800	133 mm
SS-142	10th SS Div "Frundsberg"	800	138 mm
SS-143	11th SS Div "Nordland"	800	145 mm
SS-144	12th SS Div "Hitlerjugend"	800	133 mm
SS-145	13th SS Regt Grp "Handshar"	800	125 mm
SS-146	15th Gren Div's 34th Reg	90	204 mm
SS-147	37th SS Cav. Div "Lutzow"	800	142 mm
SS-148	39th SS Div "Nibellungen"	800	138 mm
SS-149	SS - Raised SS	100	133 mm
SS-150	SS in a double circle	800	142 mm
SS-151	SS - Mocha Spoon	800	127 mm
SS-152	SS-Wewelsburg VIP	800	216 mm
SS-153	SS-Wewelsburg, RFS	20	211 mm
SS-154	SS-Wewelsburg, RFS	Alpacca	198 mm
SS-155	SS - W-burg, Mtg Hall	90	various
SS-156	Police, Reich	RF	211 mm
SS-157	SS/P - Police - GR	800	142 mm
SS-158	SS/P - Police - CB	800	137 mm

SS-159 SS/P - Breslau	Alpacca	213 mm
SS-160 SS/P - Kattowitz	RF	202 mm
SS-161 SS/P - Stegskopf	Alpacca	209 mm
SS-162 K. L. Buchenwald	RF	139 mm
SS-163 SS-Ostmark - fork	Alpacca	184 mm
SS-164 Helmwehr "Danzig"	800	140 mm
M-165 Berghof Cream Server	800	134 mm
M-166 Fuhrerbau Italian Service	800	278 mm
M-167 Reichswerke H. Goering	?	245 mm
M-168 Gastehaus Reichsparteitag	100	212 mm
M-169 Deutscher Hof Hotel	60	208 mm
M-170 Der Deutsche Hof	90	155 mm
M-171 Der Deutsche Hof soup taster	90	NA
M-172 Bayerischer Hof Hotel	30	128 mm
M-173 Hotel Post, Berchtesgaden	90	244 mm
M-174 Platterhof Hotel Creamer	90	NA
M-175 Dietrich Eckart Krankenhaus	90	213 mm
M-176 Dietrich Eckart knife	90	250 mm
M-177 U-47 Commemorative,	800	160 mm

M-178 Danziger Werft	**RF**	**210 mm**
M-179 Haus der Deutschen Arbeit,	**90**	**139 mm**
M-180 House of German Art, 1937	**90**	**110 mm**
M-181 HdDK informal	**90**	**various**
M-182 HdDK Iced Coffee Goblet	**Alpacca**	**NA**
M-183 HdDK Coffee Pot & Creamer	**Alpacca**	**NA**
M-184 Staatskasino - fork	**90**	**188 mm**
M-185 Kasino Lamsdorf	**Plate**	**213 mm**
M-186 Rabbit Breeders	**90**	**248 mm**
M-187 Danzig Andenken	**?**	**117 mm**
M-188 Nurnberg Andenken	**800**	**120 mm**
M-189 AVRO Tempelhof	**90**	**123 mm**
M-190 German Embassy - Paris	**RF**	**225 mm**
M-191 Gau Posen Welfare Office	**?**	**202 mm**
M-192 LZ 129 Hindenburg, No RM	**800**	**137 mm**
M-193 Danish Mystery	**800**	**122 mm**
M-194 Wellner of East German	**90**	**209 mm**
M-195 America's Swastikas		**various**
M-196 to 200 AH favorite?		**various**
M-201 NPEA	**100**	**252 mm**
M-202 Platterhof Hotel Tray		

Bibliography

Angolia, John R. and Schlicht, Adolf , *Uniforms & Traditions of the German Army 1933 - 1945* , Bender Publishing, Second Printing November 1992 in 3 volumes.

Borkin, Joseph. *The Crime and Punishment of I.G.Farben*, Barnes & Noble, 1978

Buchner, Alex, *The German Infantry Handbook 1939 - 1945,* Schiffer Military History, 1991

Cameron, Norman and Stevens, R. H., translators, *Hitler's Table Talk,* Enigma Books 1988

Coates, E.J., *The U-Boat Commanders Handbook,* Thomas Publications, 1989

D'Almeida, Fabrice. *High Society in the 3rd Reich*

Davis, Brian Leigh. *Badges & Insignia of the Third Reich*, Arms and /Armour, 1992

Degrelle, Leon, *Campaign in Russia*, Institute for Historical Review, 1985

Griffith, Mark D., *"Liberated" Adolf Hitler Memorabilia,* Ulric of England, 1986

Guido, Pietro. *Hitler's Berghof and the Tea-House,* 2010

Haddock, Chase with Snyder, Charles E., *Treasure Trove, The Looting of the Third Reich.*

Hamilton, Charles, *Leader's & Personalities of the Third Reich Volume 1, 2nd Edition Bender Publishing 1996*

Hamilton, Charles, *Leader's & Personalities of the Third Reich Volume 2, First Edition Bender Publishing 1996*

Hoess, Rudolf. *Commandant of Auschwitz,* Popular Library, 1961

Jeffreys, Diarmuid. *Hell's Cartel* (I G Farben), Metropolitan Books, 2008

Johnson, Aaron L., *Hitler's Military Headquarters*, Bender Publishing, 1999

Johnson, Paul Louis, *Horses of the German Army in World War II.* Schigger Military History, 2006

Keegab, John, *Waffen SS,* Ballentine Books, 1970

Lumsden, Robin, *The Allgemeine-SS,* Osprey Publishing, 2004

Lumsden, Robin, *Himmler's Black Order 1923-45. Sutton Publishing, 1997*

McCombs, Don & Worth, Fred *World War II, 4,139 Strange and Fascinating Facts.* Wings Books, 1983

MacLean, French L. *2000 Quotes From Hitler's 1000-Year Reich,* Schiffer, 2007

Megargee, Geoffrey P. *Inside Hitler's High Command.* University Press of Kansas, 2000

Mitchel, Samuel W. *German Order of Battle* Vol.3 Stackpole Books, 2007

Piekalkiewicz, Janusz, *The German National Railway in World War II*, Schiffer Military History 2008

Pool, James *Who Financed Hitler 1919 - 1933*, Pocket Books 1997

Pool, James, *Hitler and His Secret Partners, 1933-1945. Pocket Books, 1997*

Schroder, Christa, *He Was My Chief,* Frontline Books, The Memoirs of Adolf Hitler's Secrtary. 2009

Speer, Albert. *Inside the Third Reich*, Avon Books 1970

Toland, John, *Hitler, The Pictorial Documentary of His Life,* Doubleday, 1978

von Lang, Jochen, *The Secretary* (Martin Bormann), Random House, 1979

Waltczek, Beata & Marek Rasala. Firmenstempel auf Besteck 2007

Weitz, John, *Hitler's Diplomat* (von Ribbentrop), Ticknor & Fields, 1992

Windrow, Martin, *The Waffen-SS,* Osprey Publishing, 2004

Wistrich, Robert, *Who's Who in Nazi Germany*, Bonanza Books, 1982

Wikipedia <w> and the internet were a great help for research

Historical Addendum

Population comparison - 1939

Greater Germany	69 million
Russia	169 million
USA	131 million
UK	48 million

Military Reality

In 1933 Germany had a 100,000 man Military as prescribed by the Treaty of Versailles in 1920. The Wehrmacht was founded on 15Mar35 and the German military was expanded to 3,343,000 in 5 years under Hitler. Wehrmacht: 1Sep39 = 3,180,000, (with 2.7M Heer). Under the reintroduction of conscription in 1935, each service allotment of available recruits was: Heer 66%, Luftwaffe 25% and Kriegsmarine 9%. Actually, the Heer typically made up 75% of the Wehrmacht and within the Heer, 82% were Infantry Divisions. The Wehrmacht maxed at 9.5M (5.5M Heer) and on 9May45 still had 7.8 Million under arms with 5.3 million in the Heer).

As early as 9 November 1939, the German Army shortened their marching boots by 3 to 5 cm (1 to 2 inches) to save leather which was already in short supply. While production of the Army Officer's leather greatcoat was not prohibited until 29 February 1944.

Volkssturm's "people's army" (formed in 1944) of 6 million old men and boys armed with the true Volksgewehr / (peoples rifle) the Italian Carcano rifle confiscated from Italy when Italy withdrew from the war in 1943.

The War in the East

In 1941, prior to the June invasion of Russia: Germany had 3,500 tanks and German Intelligence estimated Russian tanks at 10,000. Russia actually had 24,000.

Note: On 4 August 1941, Hitler commented to Colonel General Heinz Guderian regarding his estimates of Russian tank strength: "If I had known that the figures for Russian tank strength which you gave in your book were in fact the true ones, I would not - I believe - ever have started this war."

German Air Intelligence estimated Russian A/C at 10,500. Russia actually had 18,000.

German Foreign Armies East estimated Red Army at 2 Million, with war level of 4M. Actual was 4.2 Million. By invasion day, 5 Million.

In the 51st day of the invasion, Gen. Halder reported that German intelligence originally estimated Russian Forces at 200 divisions and so far had identified 360!

Germany's surprise attack on The Soviet Union started on 22 June 1941 with 3.2 Million soldiers, 2,000 aircraft, 3,350 tanks, 7,184 pieces of artillery and 750,000 horses. In 10 days they had advanced 350 miles, started the Leningrad siege on 8 Sept. 41 took Minsk in August and Kiev in Sept, reached Moscow suburbs in December. By the end of 1941, almost 1 Million Soviet jews had been murdered, all before the "Final Solution" Wannsee Conference of Jan 42.

From the invasion of Russia (Operation Barbarosa) on 22 June 41 to 8 May 45, German Losses in the East were 1,015,000 dead, 4 Million wounded and 1.3 Million missing-in-action while the Red Army suffered 14 Million casualties with over 10 Million dead. The initial casualty rate was 16 Russians for every German. In 1941, German forces took 3.5 Million Russian POW's of a ultimate total of 5 Million, only 1.5 Million survived the war. Over 400,000 Russian died in the Battle for Berlin. Total estimated Russian civilian/ military killed in the East, 30 Million.

Prior to 1943, the standard German infantry division contained some 900 assorted gasoline powered vehicles consuming an average of 20 tons of fuel daily as well as 5,300+ horses consuming 58 tons of fodder daily.

Hitler

Versailles Treaty of 1919 - repudiated by Hitler. In 1935, Hitler renewed conscription, founded the Luftwaffe and started submarine production. In June 1936 renewed arms production, and remilitarized the Rhineland (Mar) , annexed Austria Mar 1938, annexed Sudetenland 30 Sep 38, Annexed Czechoslovakia 15 Mar 39 and finally declared war on Poland 1 Sep 39.

In Sept 1938, as a result of the "Munich Agreement" between Britain, France and Germany, the North Eastern Czechoslovakian Sudetenland was ceded to Germany, allegedly as Hitler's last territorial claim in Europe. The Sudetenland contained all the border fortifications established to protect Czechoslovakia from a German invasion. Thus Hitler had completely disarmed the Czech's without firing a shot. On 14 March 1939 the German army simply marched into what remained of Czechoslovakia, unopposed and established the German Protectorate of Bohemia & Moravia and the independent state of Slovakia which in reality was just a puppet state of the Germans.

Per Hitler: "All administration of justice is a political activity. Time honored commentaries have become wastepaper, the 'creative personality' of the National Socialist judge was liberated from the mortmain of the past. The whole body of previous interpretations of the statutes laboriously built up by German Jurists, no longer constituted precedents of value."

NAZI music: Hitler was equated to Wagner's hero Siegfried. Franz Liszt's 'Les Preludes' was always used to accompany film footage of dive bombers and also was the signature theme for the 'Sondermeldung' or "special announcements" that periodically interrupted normal radio programming to announce victories. In 1940-42, "We're Marching Against England" was the big hit. In 1944 "Dancing Together Into Heaven" was banned due to the success of allied bombing. Mozart's 'Requiem' banned as too depressing. "Fidelio' and 'William Tell' banned due to their themes of liberty triumphing over tyranny. Per Albert Speer's book '*Inside the Third Reich*', he quotes Hitler, " You'll hear that (Liszt's Les Preludes) often in the near future, because it is going to be our victory fanfare for the Russian Campaign". "For each of the previous campaigns Hitler had personally chosen a musical fanfare that preceded radio announcements of striking victories." His all time favorite was Tristan and Isolde followed closely by the third act of Aida, symphonies by Bruckner and Beethoven and the songs of Richard Strauss.

Hitler's yacht: Built by the Blohm & Voss shipyard of Hamburg and originally launched on 15 Dec 1934 as the Versuchboot Grille (Training Boat-Cricket), in 1935 it was re-designated as the "Aviso Grille". (Dispatch or advice / intelligence boat-Cricket), and became Adolf Hitler's personal state yacht harbored at Kiel. It had an overall length of 443 feet making it the largest yacht afloat. It had three, 22.7cm cannon, 6 antiaircraft guns and 2 or 3 machine guns and a capacity of carrying 280 mines. Hitler being, "landsinning", (land-minded), and subject to seasickness, only boarded the Aviso Grille on a few occasions and shortly after the outbreak of WW2 the Aviso Grille was utilized as an auxiliary mine sweeper in the Baltic and North seas. In the autumn of 1942 the Aviso Grille was posted to Norway as a floating Staff Headquarters for the German U-boat commander stationed in Narvik. Confiscated by the British at the end of the war the Aviso Grille was eventually privately purchased and used as a cruise ship in the Mediterranean for a period of time until it was finally scrapped in the USA in 1951. As noted by Army General of Infantry Gunther Blumentritt, "Only the admirals had a happy time in this war - as Hitler knew nothing about the sea, whereas he felt he knew all about land warfare."

Bandenweiler Marsch: Adolf Hitler's very own personal march played by his SS band, ONLY when Hitler was in the immediate vicinity. His 'Hail to the Chief'.

Although born a Catholic, Hitler despised religion as a crutch for the weak and believed that the idea of Christian equality protected the racially inferior of the world. (Germany was 1/ 3 Catholic and 2/ 3 rds Protestant.) Hitler privately declared that one could not be German and a Christian! Per famed psychologist Carl Jung...the decent and well-meaning German people are "intelligent enough not only to believe but to know that the God of the Germans is Wotan and not the Christian God."

Regarding the Treaty of Versailles: In 1922, Hitler said, "We do not pardon, we demand vengeance."

To manufacture the Volkswagon, Hitler had the town of Wolfsburg created. (None were ever delivered!) His nick name was Wolf, his sister was forced to change her name to "Wolf"!

Regarding his opposition: "Achievements which appear to strengthen the country do but increase their hatred. They are in permanent opposition. They are not filled with a desire to help the people, but rather by a hope which severs them from the people - the hope that the government may fail in its work for the people. They are for that reason never prepared to admit the benefit resulting from any act; rather they are filled with the determination to deny on principle every success and on every success to trace the failures and the weaknesses which may possibly ensue"

AH 13 July 1934 Reichstag.

As Hitler was the Reichskanzler, actually he was Germany's 23rd Chancellor, he had a Reichskanzlei at Bischofweisen, Bavaria starting in 1937 and the Neureichskanzlei or New Chancellery in Berlin.

As Bormann was enamored with the Obersalzberg area and to encourage Hitler's visits, he commissioned the construction of the Kehlsteinhaus (Eagle Nest) which took 13 months; its 4 mile access road cost the equivalent of $ 200 million and the 124 meter elevator, the lives of 12 construction workers. Given to Hitler for his 50th birthday.

From 1933, Hitler did not carry a pencil, pen or money.

Hitler favored Daimler-Benz as a result of its director-general Jacob Werlin's generosity in supplying him Benz's early on during the period of struggle when no one else would help either Hitler or the Party.

Nazi Swastika / Flags

The Swastika is a sanskrit word meaning "well being" and is an ancient symbol used by many cultures signifying the cycle of life as well as the sun. It was also a Nordic rune and pagan Germanic symbol for Thor, God of Adventurers. During WWI the swastika began to represent national and anti-semitic leanings in such organizations as the Thule society and other German nationalistic movements and later, assorted Freikorps groups. In the midsummer of 1920, Hitler adopted the swastika as the premier symbol of the NSDAP and in Mein Kampf, takes credit for the swastika's final presentation in red, black and white.

From Wikipedia: Nazi Flags: The Nazi party used a right-facing swastika as their symbol and the red and black colors were said to represent Blut und Boden (blood and soil). Black, white, and red were in fact the colors of the old North German Confederation flag (invented by Otto von Bismarck, based on the Prussian colors black and white). In 1871, with the foundation of the German Reich, the flag of the North German Confederation became the German Reichsflagge (Reich's flag). Black, white, and red became the colors of the nationalists through the following history (for example World War I and the Weimar Republic).

WWII Axis Powers:

Bulgaria	Croatia	Finland
Germany	Hungary	Italy
Japan	Romania	Slovakia

Ethnic Germans

Defined as considering themselves or others to be of German origin ethnically, not necessarily born or living within Germany. After WWI's dissolution of the Austrian-Hungarian Empire and the creation of Austria, the Treaty of Versailles forbid its integration into Germany. Hitler's move was to unite "all Germans". Some 6.9 million "ethnic " Germans from mostly eastern countries subsequently joined Germany's WWII effort and suffered 601,000 military deaths and 150,000 civilian deaths for a total of 751,000 or 10.8%

death rate. In Aug 1941, Russian law had banished all persons of German heritage to Siberia. After WWII, some 12 million ethnic Germans were expelled by Czechoslovakia, Hungary, Rumania, Yugoslavia, Russia and Poland.

WWII European Neutrals

War is dependent on money. To quote Cicero, 106-43 B.C. "Endless money forms the sinews of war." Germany spent an estimated $ 80 billion on their military buildup between 1933 and 1939. Some 170 Infantry Divisions were created during this period. let alone an air force. Since Germany was close to bankruptcy in 1939, the money 'Gold' was taken from the defeated countries. Nazi procedure was to offer conquered countries German currency in exchange for the countries gold reserves. Belgium refused and Germany simply confiscated their gold. This helped other countries to opt for exchange. The total gold from conquered countries was in the 100's of millions if not billions of dollars in monetary gold which was converted into war material from "neutral" countries. The five European countries that remained neutral during WWII were Ireland, Portugal, Spain, Sweden and Switzerland. Their contributions to the German war effort included: Vichy France (trucks), Switzerland (tools & ball bearings), Sweden (steel, iron ore & ball bearings), Rumania (oil), Spain (leather goods), Portugal (tungsten)), Turkey (chromium, being essentially the sole supplier to NAZI Germany of this key industrial metal and tobacco. By 1943, Germany had only 6 months supply of chromium). Without supplies from "neutrals", Germany could not have waged war beyond 1943! In addition, German coal paid for the problem free movement of German military equipment from Germany to Italy via the Swiss road and rail system. In 1942, Himmler stated, "The Swedes are parasites who have reaped the profits from two wars."

How the Swiss facilitated Germany's war effort

The laundering of money on a grand scale to finance a war: The Bank for International Settlements (BIS) based in Basel, Switzerland is an intergovernmental organization of central banks which "fosters international monetary and financial cooperation and serves as a bank for central banks." It is not accountable to any national government. The BIS was formed in 1930, the main actors were the then Governor of The Bank of England and his German colleague Hjalmar Schacht later Adolf Hitler's finance minister. BIS had unique status and privileges and virtual exemption from Swiss law. Regarding gold, BIS was charged with controlling its storage, and transfer of ownership for the central banks of the world and its charter provided that, 'the bank, its property and assets, and all deposits and other funds entrusted to it shall be immune in time of peace and in time of war from measure such as appropriation.' During the period 1933–45, the board of directors of the BIS included Walter Funk a prominent Nazi official, and Emil Puhl who were both convicted at the Nuremberg Trials after World War II, as well as Herman Schmitz the director of IG Farben and Baron von Schroeder, the owner of the J.H.Stein Bank, the bank that held the deposits of the Gestapo. Not surprisingly, there were allegations that the BIS had helped the Germans loot assets from occupied countries during World War II.

How the system worked: When Germany bought something from a neutral, a Letter of Credit was opened When the item was delivered the LOC and proof of delivery would be presented to the countries bank for payment. Early on, the documents could then be presented directly to the Reichsbank for payment although this was at times a less desirable option than having the countries central bank pass the documentation to BIS and the appropriate amount of German gold then would be transferred to the neutral countries central bank account and the neutral countries bank would in turn pay the vendor (after deducting its fee) in its local currency. This could be viewed as an international money laundering scheme that helped finance WWII in Europe. In any case, by 1942, Germany had confiscated all the gold in Europe and transferred much of it to its BIS account.

Nuremberg / Nurnberg War Crimes Trials

On 1 October 1946, death sentences were passed down at the Nuremberg trials for twelve of the 24 Nazi leaders tried. Goring had committed suicide on the 15th and Martin Bormann was in absentia. The remaining 10 were executed on 16 October 1946 in the following order: 1. Joachim von Ribbentrop, Nazi Minister of Foreign Affairs 1938-1945, 2. Field Marshal Wilhelm Keitel, Head of OKW 1938-1945, 3. Ernst Kaltenbrunner, Highest surviving SS leader of RSHA 1943-1945 Central Nazi Intelligence Organ, 4. Alfred Rosenberg, Minister of Eastern Occupied Territories, 5. Hans Frank, Reich Law Leader 1935-1945 and Governor General of Poland 1939-1945, 6. Wilhelm Frick, Minister of Interior 1933-1943 and Reich Protector of Bohemia-Moravia 1943-1945, 7. Julius Streicher, Gauleiter of Franconia 1922-1945 and publisher of "Der Sturmer", 8. Fritz Sauckel, Gauleiter of Thuringia 1927-1945 and Plenipotentiary of the Nazi slave labor program 1942-1945. 9. Colonel-General Alfred Jodl, 10, Arthur Seyss-Inquart, Reich Commissioner of the Occupied Netherlands 1940-1945

> Trivia: Field Marshall Keitel was the first professional soldier to be executed under the "new concept" of International law where by soldiers could no longer claim exemption due to "dutifully carrying out superior's orders".

IQ's of the tried were measured during their period of internment at Nuremberg prison.

- -

As an aside, my wife and I visit Germany every Spring, during white asparagus time. Having visited any number of antique shops in Germany, I can truthfully say that is no shortage of 3rd Reich period silverware and at very reasonable prices. To set up a small engraving operation to turn out 3rd Reich logo'd silverware would be a piece of cake except that the German authorities are quite against it. Unfortunately the same can not be said for Austria.

Special Note: *Collectible Spoons of the 3rd Reich* finished in 3rd place in London's Bookseller Magazine's 2009 contest for that years most unique book title. This news was carried world-wide from the NY Times to Reuters Africa, even in the Reader's Digest - twice! This, my first book was 224 pages and solely on spoons. My second book, *A Guide to 3rd Reich Cutlery* was expanded to include cutlery per se and ended with 374 pages. As you can see, this edition has expanded into the tableware area and came out with 495 pages and incidentally, some really interesting material to a collector. Also, in the interim, some earlier misconceptions have been clarified, identification of maker marks expanded as well as several outright misunderstandings rectified - in particular the earlier incorrect interpretation of the 'style' number to the correct identification as a 'Silver Gram Weight per individual piece' as explained on page 475. So the search goes on.

Some things that are to interesting to leave out

Army Regulation H.Dv.300/1, Truppenfuhrung (Troop Command), a pocket sized, (4 1/4" X 6") gray paperbound booklet of 319 pages affectionately called Tante Frieda / "Aunt Frieda", from its abbreviated title (T.F.) postulated the basic principles of march, attack, pursuit, defense and other military operations for German commanders. The 1936, Berlin edition was in Fraktur typeface!, see OG-30.

Tanks: Total German Production: I's = 1,500, II's = 2,000, III's 5,644 (with 5,000 destroyed), IV's = 7350 (main battle tank), V's = 6,000 and VI's = 487 for a total of 22,981!

Tanks in service on 1 September 1939: I's = 1,445, II's = 1,226, I Command Tanks = 215, III's = 98 and IV's = 211. Of the 3,195 tanks, 1,251 were outside the armored divisions. During September 1939 only 57 tanks were produced and only 45 IV's were produced in all of 1939.

The Tiger I's fuel capacity was 534 liters (141 gals) which was estimated to take it 100 Km (62 miles) on road travel at 20 Km per hour and 50 Km (31 miles) cross country.

The PzKw VI, the Tiger II King Tiger / Konigstiger: Reportedly, 487 were produced. Used by the Schwere Panzer Abteiling of the Wehrmacht and the Waffen-SS on the Russian Front, Normandy, Holland Ardennes and the Battle of the Bulge. Powered by a 12 cylinder Maybach diesel, producing 700 hp, it ate 2 gallons of fuel per mile. The Henshel turret stored 86 rounds for the 88 mm main gun. With its massive 180 mm (7 inches) of frontal armor, the Tiger was virtually impervious to any allied fire. According to historical accounts, the front armor on the Tiger II was never breached in battle.

The 1942 Panzer Division was composed of four battalions each with 80 tanks. By mid-1943 the tank quantity was reduced to two battalions each with 50 tanks and a third battalion of tank destroyers.

At the Battle of Kursk (5-22 July 1943) the German's 700,000 men with 2,700 tanks fought the 1,000,000 Russians with 3,600 tanks. In the following 50 days, Germany lost 500,000 men and 7 panzer division (1,500 tanks)

Note: The US produced some 49,000 M4 Sherman tanks, initially with 2" of front armor and a 75 mm gun. The M4's gun could penetrate 2" of armor while German tanks could penetrate 4" to 6" of armor. The M4 was nicknamed 'Ronson' as it "lights first time, every time" due to its gasoline fuel used by its aircraft engine. Russia produced 53,000 T-34 tanks with a 1944 run rate of 2,000 a month.

Halftracks (Spahpanzerwagon): a 7 ton vehicle able to run at 31 MPH, carried heavy machine guns and powered by a 6 cylinder Maybach engine. Some 14,000 were built.

Krauss-Maffei Sd Kfz0; 11.5 ton prime mover with a 6 cylinder Maybach HL 62TUK, water cooled engine with 140 hp moving this 22 1/2' long behemoth at 50 km/h (31 mph). 12,000+ built. Associated with the towed 88 mm FLAK gun (Flug Aberhr Kanone).

Third Reich Special Days:

1 January	Day of National Awakening
20 April	Hitler's Birthday
1 May	National Holiday of the German People
9 Nov	Day of the Fallen of the Movement

The "Blood Flag" (Blutfahne) was shown three times a year: Party Anniversary, Annual Party Rally and the 9 November 1923 Commemorative march.

Submachine Guns:

Pistol caliber submachine guns reached their zenith during WWII. The Soviet PPSh41 (PE-PE-SHA) was the dominant submachine gun with 5.5 million manufactured, the British produced 4 million Stens, the US made 1.4 million Thompson's and Germany produced 910,000 MP-40's. Within a few years, they were little more than a footnote in the arena of military small arms, having been replaced completely in concept by the intermediate size cartridge assault rifle (Sturmgewehr) introduced by Germany in the late years of the war.

Cigarets: Although they were forbidden in the Luftwaffe and Allgemeine-SS, the US military sent as many as 425 million cigarets overseas monthly. Every U.S. paratrooper carried 2 cartons of cigarets when they dropped into France on invasion day.

German Army (Heer) clothing seasons: The Winter season was from 15 September to 15 April.

Germany had 3 million deaths up till the last 9 months of the war, then 5 million more in the last 9 months for a total of 8 million.

The last Act: Did Hitler & Eva along with Goebbels & Magda end their lives in the Tristan and Isolde search for the realm of oneness, truth and reality, only to be achieved fully upon the simultaneous deaths of the lovers, did they call upon Death to make them one for ever?

Or

Did Hitler deliberately chose 30 April 1945? According to J.H. Brennam's observation that "The Dark Initiate had remained true to his black creed to the very last, had arranged his affairs so that even his suicide should be a sacrificial tribute to the Powers of Darkness. April 30 is the ancient Feast of Beltane, the day which blends into Walpurgis Night, It is perhaps the most important date in the whole calendar of Satanism."

In Appreciation

As an accumulator I rely on my sources as to the authenticity of the items purchased. I thank the following sources for their patience, the sharing of their expertise and delivering excellent besteck:

Baccardi, Ont, Canada
Brock's Inc., Decatur, Georgia
Collector's Guild Inc., Fredericton NB, Canada
Eberhardt, Matt, Nazareth, PA
Germania Int'l., Lakemont, GA
German War Booty, White Plains, NY
House of History, Seevetal, Germany
Patton, Terry, Acworth, GA
Relics of War, Kennesaw, GA
Snyder, Charles E.Jr., Bowie, MD
Thames Army Surplus, Groton, Conn
Third Reich CA, Sidney, BC Canada
Third Reich Depot, Conifer, CO
USMBOOKS.com, Rapid City, SD
Witte, David, Little Rock, AR
Wittman Militaria, NJ
WW2GermanMilitaria, Burnaby B. C. Canada

Special Note

The German War Graves commission founded in 1919 maintains some 800 graveyards in 43 countries for 1.9 million German military 'victims of war'. Some 1.5 million WWII German military dead have not been 'clarified'. Search is now focused in the EAST for the 250,000 German MIA's in the Stalingrad area as well as those in the areas of Kursk, Smolensk, the Ukraine, Poland, Estonia-Latvia-Lithuania, the Slovakian Republic etc.

Donations are not US tax deductible but can be sent to:

Volksbund Deutsche
Kriegsgraberfursorge e.V.
Bundesgeschaftsstelle
Werner-Hilpert-Str.2
34112 Kassel
Deutschland

This organization publishes illustrated brochures locating all German military cemeteries and assists in the specific location of the fallen for family members. The edition covering Germany is some 100 pages. A second edition covers France, Belgium, Luxembourg and the Netherlands. The cemeteries are located on detailed maps with specific directions, comments and number buried by WWI or WWII. Due to funding constraints, all documentation is in German only.

Film Comments

Metropolis - the film

Reference Air Base Starken W-118 and Fritz Lang's 1927 film Metropolis in which the ending message of the film is "the mediator between the head and the hand must be the heart". The film addresses the conflict between management and labor that can only be resolved by a mediator with a heart. Then reference PS-17, Dr. Ley - who under Hitler's direction, eliminated the unions and placed all employers and employees into the DAF achieved Hitler's vision of "all who create with head and hand" to be in a single organization. This goes a long way to explain why Hitler (the mediator with a heart?) thought Metropolis was the greatest film produced during his life time.

1933 Nuremberg Rally DVD

This DVD of the 1933 Party Rally at Nuremberg by Leni Riefenstahl titled 'Victory of Faith' (Der Sieg des Glaubens) could be best described as the first cut at her 1934 'Triumph of the Will'. As the A&M Productions description detailed, the film was premiered in Berlin on 1 December 1933 and had been financed by the NS Party and distributed by local Party film distributors and shown in over 5,000 German theaters at a rental price of 30RM per week. As Ernst Rohm was the head of the SA, with over 2.5 million members in 1934, (some 20 times larger that the Army) and as the heir apparent to control the NS Party, he played a large role in the movie. Particularly at the march by when he joined Hitler in his parade car and typically appeared on Hitler's right side throughout the movie. In June 1934, Hitler directed the assassination of Ernst Rohm and many of the top leaders of the SA. He then ordered that any existing photos and references to Ernst Rohm be obliterated from German history. How then did this record survive - In April of 1934, Leni Riefenstahl was invited to speak at major universities in Great Britain to discuss her innovative film techniques. It is now known that at least one copy of "Victory of Faith" was duplicated in Great Britain at that time. It was the most sought after film in history until its discovery in the 1980's.

Appendix

Hitler's Formal Service

With reference to PS-1, Hitler's "Formal" service from Bruckmann: as mentioned earlier, sets of Hitler's "formal" tableware were distributed to 6 locations. Each locations set size was believed to serve approximately 15 to 20 people. The cutlery (besteck) flatware pieces known to be manufactured by Bruckmann include:

Dinner spoon,	Dinner fork	Oyster fork,
Dinner knife	Luncheon spoon	Napkin ring
Luncheon fork	Luncheon knife	Coffee spoon
Demitasse spoon	Demitasse fork	Butter knife
Demitasse knife	Ice cream spoon	Butter spreader
Desert fork	Fruit knife	Grape scissors
Ice tea spoon	Fish fork	Cream Spoon
Fish knife	Lemon press	

Complimented by serving items such as: asparagus server, aspic server, pie server, sauce ladle, salad serving fork and spoon, gravy ladle, meat fork, serving spoon. pickle fork, butter knife, salt & pepper shakers etc. In addition from Wellner came serving vessels, coffee pots, tea pots, sugar bowls, creamers, casserole dish, roaster dish, gravy boat, bread plate, serving tray, warming plate, coasters, various sized serving trays. As an example, the 15 to 20 place settings at each location would typically have 6 serving vessels for such things as vegetables, mashed potatoes, stew etc. or the “Eintopf” or one-serving, compulsory meal served during the war years and therefore would need 6 serving spoons at each location for a total of 36 pieces which incidentally, were 10 inches long with a 2 inch wide bowl.

The mathematics are interesting! Bruckmann gifted 3,000 pieces of the formal ware to Hitler on his 50th birthday, 20 April 1939. Assuming each of the six locations received approximately 500 items and if a place setting could require a minimum of 20 different table items, as identified above, and with 20 place settings at each of the 6 locations equals 120 settings times 20 cutlery items equals 2,400 pieces of cutlery and 600 other items. Any additional cutlery items would add 120 to the cutlery total while reducing the servings total accordingly. This also suggests that Hitler’s use of his formal tableware was limited to relatively small, intimate groups and that the meals were ‘family style’. As an example, a post card of the period shows the Berghof speisesaal (dining) room table that sat 16! While in Christa Schroder’s book, *‘He Was My Chief’* her personal observation is, “The porcelain and silver were made to Hitler’s design. They bore the sovereignty symbol, the eagle with spread wings with right and left the initials ‘A’ and ‘H’ in the old script, the design on the porcelain in gold.” My own observation is that from anecdotal comments, reports that Hitler himself was disturbed by pilferage and between lost, damaged and as Hitler's private silver ware was in high demand as souvenirs during his life, attrition, these predictable losses must have led to orders for replacements which indicates that the 3,000 quantity was the base number for this service. Some knowledgeable dealers estimate actual quantity at 6,000!

The Tee House Controversy

Thanks to Matthew Sollis, a serious fellow collector, below is listed an acquisition for Hitler's "Tea House" / Kehlstein. This service for 36 was contracted 29 July 1938 and totaled some 854 pieces and is believed to have been ready for his 50th birthday on 20 April 1939? There is some confusion as to whether this service was actually for the Teehaus which was built in 1937 or for the nearby Kehlsteinhaus ("Eagles Nest") as the Eagles Nest was also a 50th birthday present, compliments of Martin Bormann and was some times also referred to as the tea house. In Germany, a tea house is called Teehaus). See PS-1 for more on Adlerhorst!

The cutlery items bought in quantities of 36 each were:

Tafelloeffel / Dinner Spoon
Tafelgabel / Dinner Fork
Tafelmesser / Dinner Knife
Dessertloeffel/ Dessert Spoon
Dessertgabel / Dessert Fork
Dessertmesser/ Dessert Knife
Fischmesser / Fish Knife
Fischgabel / Fish Fork
Mokkaloeffel / Demi-Tasse spoon
Eisloeffel / Ice Cream Spoon
Kuchengabel / Pastry Fork
Obstgabel / Fruit Fork
Obstmesser / Fruit Knife

Service items:

Quantity 10 Pfefferstreuer / Pepper Shakers
Salzstreuer / Salt Shakers

Quantity 8: Eisvorleger / Ice Server
Tortenspaten / Cake / Tart Server
Konfektgabel / Sweets Server
Zuckerzangen / Sugar Tongs
Traubenscheren / Grape Scissors
Kuchenvorlegegabeln / Cake Serving Fork
Sahnevorleger / Cream Server
Limonadenloeffel / Lemonade / Ice Tea Spoon

Quantity 6: Saucenloeffel / Gravy Ladle
Fleischgabeln / Meat Fork
Gemueseloeffel / Vegetable Serving Spoon
Kompottloeffel / Applesauce / Fruit Serving Spoon

Quantity 4 Spargelheber / Asparagus Server
Fischvorlegebesteck / Fish Serving Set
Salatbesteck / Salad Serving Set
Kaesemesser / Cheese Knife
Kuchenmesser / Cake Knife
Zitronenpresser / Lemon Press

Quantity 2 Teesieb m. Unterschale / Tea Strainer with Tray
Zahnstocherbehaelter / Tooth Pick Holder

Interestingly, in addition, there were also 72 Kaffeeloeffel ordered with a eye toward the inevitable souvenir attrition associated with these smaller and easily pocketed after dinner tea spoons. Even today, quality German cutlery sets differentiate between Teeloeffel (Teaspoon) and the smaller Kaffeeloeffel (After dinner tea spoon) while still listing the even smaller Espresso-/Mokkaloeffel (Demi-Tasse spoon). To expand on the Teehaus issue, besides his Berghof home in the Bavarian Alps, undoubtedly Hitler's favorite place on the Obersalzberg was his cozy Tea House (Teehaus) built in 1937 on the northern boundary of the area, just below the Mooslahnerkopf hill, overlooking the Berchtesgaden valley below. Hitler's tea house was a cylindrical structure built in the woods where Hitler, his close friends, party colleagues and secretaries used to have their daily afternoon walk followed by tea. Tea was Adolf Hitler's favorite drink. Having a separate tea house was a cultural statement in many countries in Europe. Most of Hitler's stays at the Berghof included a daily afternoon walk to this Teehaus. This pleasant walk often became the scene for important political decisions, but Hitler preferred to relax, and even nap, in the Teehaus itself, surrounded by his closest friends and associates. The Teehaus was apparently undamaged by the 1945 bombing, but was mostly destroyed ca. 1951, due to its association with Hitler. The ruins remained in the woods behind the Gutshof golf course, until they were removed in 2006. (Note - the 1937 architectural plans for the Teehaus as well as captions in Eva Braun's photo albums spell the name "Moslanderkopf," but it is generally given as "Mooslahnerkopf" today, and that is the spelling found on period maps of the area.) The Mooslahnerkopf Teehaus, was completely separate from the more famous Kehlsteinhaus ("Eagles Nest"), high on the ridge above.

The Kehlsteinhaus was also called "Diplomatenhaus"

(Diplomat's House) by the Nazis as well as "Teahouse at the Kehlstein". The great dining room table sat 14 on a side and 2 at each end for a total of 32 seats. The facility was designed for meetings, had no beds and was only visited by Hitler from 10 to 20 times although it was used by Eva Braun frequently, including for her sister's wedding in 1944.
So, the mystery as to where these 36 place settings (854 pieces) went and in what pattern remains unanswered. The dinning capacity of the Teehouse is unknown to me. In Pietro Guido's book *Hitler's Berghof and the Tea-House*, he does not include a floor plan nor any mention of dining arrangements. Hitler's "curved" pattern PS-4 was reportedly used in the Obersalzberg and thus at either all or some of the 3 locations the Berghof, the Teehaus, and/or the Kehlsteinhaus.

Conclusion: The teahouse built in 1937 would have already been supplied with cutlery plus it was small, probably hosting a maximum of 12 for K&K (Kaffee and Kochen). The Eagles Nest presentation to AH in 1939 coincides with the delivery of the service. Also the seating at the Eagles Nest is in harmony with the quantity purchased. Based on the above, I believe the 854 pieces went to the Eagles Nest. In addition, I propose that Bormann would have directed the purchase and that knowing the Bruckmann "Formal' pattern to be presented to AH on his 50th, that Bormann directed a simplified 'informal' version that focused solely on the AH Adler.

Note: to repeat, per a fellow collector (Br.) James Teets BSG, Canon; regarding AH 'formal' and 'informal' patterns: The terms origin is unknown. German sources indicate that there was no such thing as formal or informal. The terms "formal" and "informal" have been retained, despite their inaccuracies, due to widespread collector acceptance."

An English Service

In our 'modern' era, the opulent life styles of the wealthy of earlier years has been in large part forgotten. The style in the Olde World regarding cutlery was one to be viewed today as excessive. As an example, in 1920, an English service for 12 could be described as "a silver 213-piece "Old English Bead" pattern canteen of cutlery, made in Sheffield, by William Hutton and Sons Ltd. having a total weight of silver, excluding all pieces with loaded handles and steel blades of 189 troy oz. (5,877g)." It was hand fitted into a felt-lined seven-draw antique oak cutlery box. The set was composed of 12 each: Soup Spoons, Table Knives, Table Forks, Fish Knives, Fish Forks, Dessert Knives, Dessert Forks, Dessert Spoons, Fruit Knives, Fruit Forks, Oyster Forks, Escargot Forks, Grapefruit Spoons, Tea Spoons, Demitasse Spoons. Plus: 6 Serving Spoons, 3 Salt Spoons, 2 Fish Servers, 2 Salad Servers, 2 Fruit Servers, 2 Sauce Ladles, 1Soup Ladle, 1 Pair of Grape Scissors, 1 Pair of Nut Crackers, 1 Basting Spoon, 1 Pair of Asparagus Servers, 1 Cake Server, 1 Cake Spatula, 1 Pie Server, 1 Jam Spoon, 1 Caddy Spoon, 1 Mustard Spoon,1 Sardine Server, 1 Cocktail Fork, 1 Olive Spoon, 1 Pair of Sugar Tongs and 1 Butter Knife.

Notes

1. Although they are of one piece, they are listed as one pair of 'asparagus servers' and 'nut crackers'.

2. Reference the Luftwaffe Nutcracker W-117. The English refer to this device, fastened so that they will work toward each other in the plural. This is not the case in the U.S. or Germany where we refer to the two handled, opposed nut cracker as a nutcracker vs its description as a nutcrackers in England. Other two handled devices that operate toward each other that we all pluralize are scissors, shears and pliers.

3. Style comment: I have recently seen an 'AH' nutcracker identical to W-117 with same silver gram weight of 3 but in his case, with 90 silver plate.

Contemporary Cutlery Measurements

Contemporary spoon sizes per Villeroy & Boch are recorded in length.

Typical European lengths:

Tafelloeffel / Dinner Spoon	205 mm / 8"
Dessertloefel / Dessert Spoon	184 mm / 7.25"
Teeloeffel / Teaspoon	156 mm / 6.1"
Kaffeeloeffel / Coffee spoon	139 mm / 5.5"
Mokkaloeffel / Demitasse spoon	111 mm / 4.4"
Eisloeffel / Ice Cream Spoon	135 mm / 5.3"

Typical US volume measurements:

Tablespoon = 14.8 ml
Teaspoon = 4.9 ml
Dessert Spoon = 11.8 ml

Demitasse spoon length = 3 to 4 inches / 7.62 - 10.16 cm

Typical silver weight of '800' pieces:

Teaspoon	1.0 Oz X .8 = .8 Oz Ag
Tablespoon	2.5 Oz X .8 = 2 Oz Ag

Reference W-94, Hitler's Flag: Both eagles face left, both symbolize the NAZI party. One eagle is the Presidential Eagle symbolizing the Head of State (an elected office) and the other is the Reichskanzlar or Chancellor's eagle - the head of the Government (typically appointed by the elected Head of State. Himself was both!

Roneusil / Roching Ref SS-156

Röchling-Gruppe was founded in 1826 and entered the coal and later iron production in western Germany and France. The company logo of three stick figures was used as a result of the company recognizing the 3 sons of Carl Rochling by renaming itself Gebruder Rochling in the late 1800's when it became specialized in high quality steel production. Its many innovations in steel production led to massive growth prior to and during WWI After WWI, all holdings in France were lost as well as management problems with those in the Saarland.. Between the wars, Herman Rochling took over management. As a very early Nazi supporter, he became Reich Minister of War Industries in 1938 and ultimately became infamous as being possibly the only German national to survive convictions as a war criminal in both WWI and WWII! Roneusil is not necessarily the brand of the company that produced the spoon but it's sort of a registered trademark of the material that spoon is made of which was Rochling stainless steel (rostfrei). In this case, the Gebruder Rochling and the shield are both Rochling maker marks.

Symbolism: Oak is the sacred tree of the Teutons.
Lorbeerkranz - laurel wreath (symbolic of victory)

Quality indicator: When the logos on tableware are proportional to the size of the piece, this indicates a higher quality product.

Reference W-96 Heer 1st Mountain Division and SS-145 Handshar Div: There were nine army mountain divisions and six W-SS mountain divisions.

Deutsche Reichsbank 1 Kilo Gold Bar

The 1 kilogram bar seen below used to finance the war was produced by the Deutsche Reichsbank in the period 1942-1943 and measures 4" X 1 3/4" X 1/2". For comparison, the US standard dimensions for the 1 Kilo (32.15 Oz) bar is 4 5/8" X 2 1/8" X 5/16". These would most probably have ended up in the Bank of International Settlements, Basel

Reich Mark rate to the US $

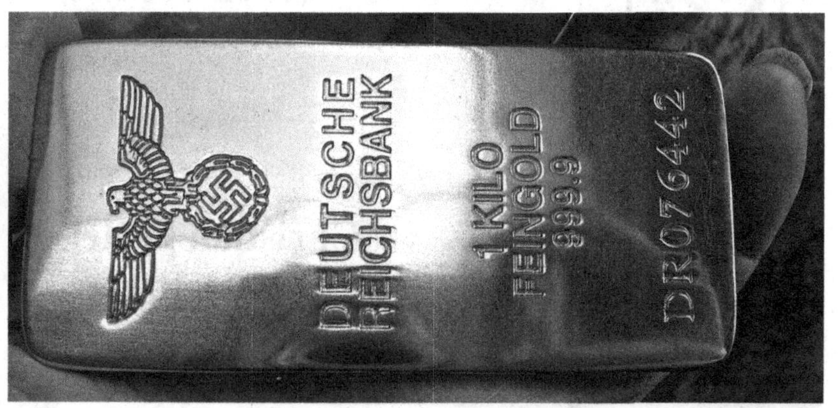

1 Jan

1926	4.18	1930	4.2	1934	2.61	1938	2.49
1927	4.2	1931	4.2	1935	2.45	1939	2.49
1928	4.21	1932	4.24	1936	2.48	1940	2.5
1929	4.20	1933	4.2	1937	2.48		

Special thanks to Shawn Bernhardt whose friendship has developed out of my earlier books and our love for 3rd Reich tableware. Shawn not only identified W-97 but also was kind enough to part with M-190. Thanks Shawn!

	**Peter R. Hinnerup** (1840-1863)
	**Simon Groth** (1863-1904)
	**Christian F. Heise** (1904-1932)
	**Jens Sigsgaard** (1932-1960)

Danish Assayer Marks 1840 - 1960

Danish Assayer Marks 1840 - 1960

Regarding W-101, M-192 & M-193, With thanks to “Online Encyclopedia of Silver Marks” and regarding Danish Makers' Marks: “ The ‘Three Tower Mark’ was instituted in 1608 as the official city mark of Copenhagen. Other Danish cities had their own marks until 1893 when the Copenhagen Three Towers became the national mark for Denmark. This mark guarantees a silver purity minimum of 826/1000 (unless a higher standard mark is indicated). Each year the design of the mark was slightly changed - making it unique, the numbers below indicate the year (four digits were used until 1771, two digits after, with a few exceptions). The Three Towers were always marked in conjunction with the initial mark of the Assay Master (Stadtsguardein), it was he who took final responsibility of guarantee. The use of both marks was discontinued by 1977.”

Since 1888, Danish silver could either carry the fineness in thousandths and a maker's mark or it could carry the Copenhagen assay mark (3 towers above date) and the Assayer's initials indicating 826 silver purity.

In our case:

W-101 German Africa Corps has the 3 towers over 53 for 1853? assayer mark of Peter R. Hinnerup for 826 min AND the German fineness of 800 but no RM.

M-192 LZ 129 with 3 Towers over '33' for 1933 and Assayer mark of Jens Sigsgaard + German 800 but no RM

M-193 Danish Mystery with 3 towers over '23' and assayer mark of C.F. Heise and German 800 but no RM

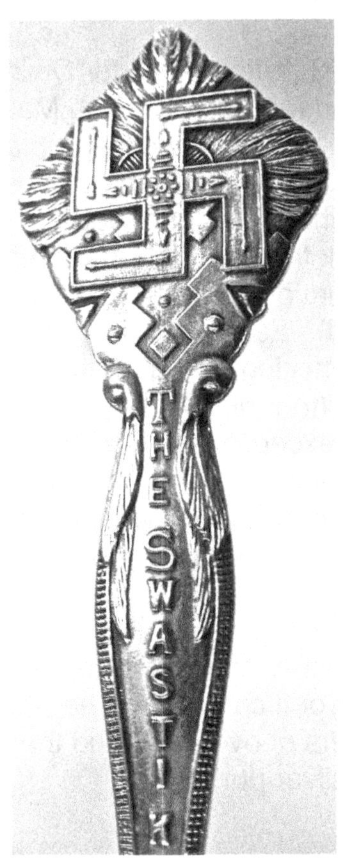

M-195 America's "Andenken" & Our Swastika

During a lull in 3rd Reich cutlery collecting and in a hot flash of collectors enthusiasm, I weakened and bought a mystery mix of 24 unidentified U.S. spoons to while away the time. This has led to this brief look at rise and fall of America's interest in souvenir spoons The souvenir era was in the period from about 1890 to the 1920's. Having started in Europe, moved to England by returning tourists and finally immigrating to the U.S.A., again by returning tourists from

England, the acquisition of souvenir spoons became a mania. This mania for collecting souvenir spoons in the United States began about 1890; the "souvenir spoon craze," as it was called in the newspapers at the time, lasted for nearly 30 years. With the depression, there was little capacity for holiday travel and less for souvenirs. Your first question is, What has this got to do with the 3rd Reich. Actually, nothing but included in my 24 were a 6 Swastika spoons. As it turns out, the American indians were using the swastika way before the 3rd Reich. For almost 1000 years the American Indians of the Southwest used the swastika as a symbol of good luck. The swastika was a respected symbol of Native America, long before it was co-opted by the Nazis. Native Americans called this symbol the whirling log or rolling log and it represented the four seasons, the four sacred mountains, and the four corners of the earth. These spoons and all of the other non-German swastika spoons were made long before Hitler adopted the swastika as the symbol of his regime. Our perception today is based upon the terrible things that were done by the NAZI's. The American spoons date to the late 19th to early 20th Century, and are remarkably well preserved, with a little tarnish and usage marks to be expected in potentially 100 year old spoons. Of particular interest besides the 6 "Swastika" spoons are the patriotic spoons focused on famous military events and personalities, particularly the spoons recognizing the Spanish America War, the Boer War and WWI. Specifically, 3 ea. Commodore Dewey, in bowl 'Flagship Olympia, Battle of Manila, May 1, 1898, 3 ea. Defender's of U.S. Freedom & War Declared April 6, 1917, 2 ea. Pershing, Wilhelm II, General Miles 1898, commanding U.S. Army. Of course, local specific spoons were also in high demand such as Boston's Old State House & Minute Man spoon. With the exception of the 7 sterling silver spoons, they are very inexpensive. Recently on the internet I saw 9 presidential spoons available for $ 5 and $ 6

shipping. Unlike the European andenken spoons, the U.S. spoons are virtually color free and more for mass production and consumption with little regards to artistic quality. Fordism seen clearly here. There was even a Sheffield sterling silver spoon in my 24.

On the left, counter clockwise

On the right 'Good Luck" with horse shoe

The AmericanSwastika Spoons

Note: The left spoon had "Eureka Springs, Ark" engraved in the bowl. This was the final home location of Gerald K. Smith. He founded the America First Party a national socialist organization preaching nationalism and a fear of a "Jewish conspiracy." Smith, an ordained minister, was also a prominent member of the pro Nazi organization, Silver Shirts. He also created the "Christ of the Ozarks" statue which still draws thousands to Eureka Springs.

Still Searching for these

Personality

Bormann, Martin
Frick, Wilhelm
Goebbels, Josepf
Jodl, Colonel-General Alfred
Keital, Field Marshall Wilhelm
Seyss-Inquart, Arthur

Government Orgnizations

D.D.A.C., "Der Deutsche Automobil-Club"
(The German Automobile Club)

Instituted in September 1933 by N.S.K.K. Korps Führer Adolf Hühnlein as an independent organization that was similar to the American Automobile Association. The club consisted of personnel who owned a car, and who were not members of the N.S.K.K.

German Embassies

Joachim von Ribbentrop approved this logo for the use at all German Embassies. The German Reich Eagle over the world. Each embassy personalized the logo.

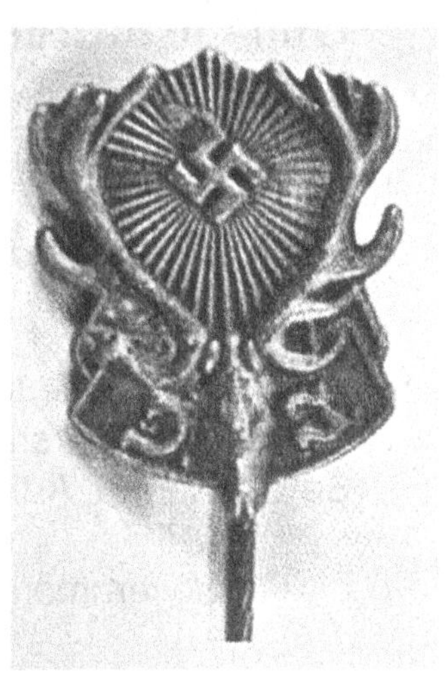

DJ - Deutsche Jagerschaft
(German Hunting
Association)

The form of a deer's skull with antlers, between which is a mobile swastika with rays radiating out from it. Flanking the skull to the base is "D" and "J,"

NSBO,Nationalsozialische Betriebszellen Organisierung (National-socialist Trade-cells Organization

RBA"Reichsbetriebszellenabteilung" (National-trade-cells department), was founded in January of 1931 and was renamed the NSBO, "Nationalsozialische Betriebszellen Organisierung" (National-socialist Trade-cells Organization), in March of that year. This organization acted as the NSDAP's alternative to labor unions and communist worker groups in industrial factories. Officially a national organization, the NSBO was concentrated in the heavy industrial centers, with very little representation outside these areas. The NSBO was absorbed into the DAF, "Deutsche Arbeitsfront" (German Labor-front), in October of 1934, and ceased to exist in March of 1935

NSFK,
"Nationalsozialistisches Fliegerkorps"
(National-Socialist Flying-corps),

Originally instituted in January of 1932,
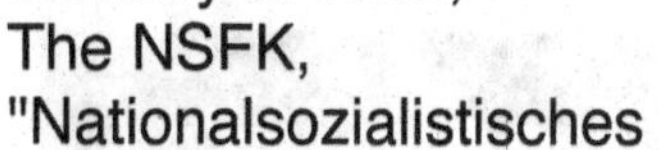
The NSFK, "Nationalsozialistisches Fliegerkorps" (National-socialist Flying-corps), was soon absorbed into the DLV, "Deutscher Luftsport Verband" (German Air-sports Association). In April of 1937 the NSFK was re-established, and, at the same time, the DLV was disbanded. The NSFK was mainly a voluntary organization, with a small cadre of paid personnel, whose mandate was to train its members in the flying of powered aircraft, gliders, and balloons. The NSFK Deutschlandflug was an annual national competition that was established in 1933 and awards were issued in gold, silver and bronze for 1ST, 2ND and 3RD place respectively.

Affiliated organizations (Angeschlossene Verbaende der NS DAP).
NS Women's Organization (NS Frauenschaft
NS University Teachers' Bund (Deutscher Dozentenbund).
NS Bund for, German Technology (Bund Deutscher Technik).
NS Physicians' Bund (Deutscher Aerztebund).
NS Teachers' Bund (Lehrerbund).
NS League of Legal Officials (Rechtswahrerbund).
A group of organizations that was officially Known as supervised organizations (Betreute Organisationen der NSDAP).
These included the following:
German Women's Work (Deutsches Frauenwerk).
German Students' Society (Deutsche Studentenschaft).

Rd No 554107
Rd No 350586

Sheffield's "Gentleman in Kharki", 1899 Boer War.

A comparison of source information available for English tableware vs 3rd Reich tableware is astonishing. Compared to the 3rd Reich, the English have been able to maintain astounding records. When I identified this spoon as English, I got on the internet and within a day, had received a response explaining the RD, the 'g' the RD numbers with comment. Fantastic!

Included in this bulk buy was my 1st ever Sheffield spoon, "A Gentleman in Kharki". The Anglo-Boer War's most famous picture showing a British soldier with a bandaged head holding a rifle ready to face the enemy, was from the painting titled 'A Gentleman in Khaki' by British artist Richard Caton Woodville. Thought to have inspired Kipling's poem The Absent-minded Beggar, the image became so popular that it was used on cups, saucers and copper plaques and in many other forms throughout the war. The spoon itself carries the W.W.Harrison & Co. trefoil. Also the sheffield crown and a lion and a 'g', the date letter for 1899. The other 2 numbers are design registration numbers and therein lies a bit of a mystery. RD NO (D and N are superscript) mean "registered [design] number". The number on the bowl "350386" was issued in 1899 which ties in very nicely with the hallmark date and the Boer War. However 551107 was not issued until 1909. Having two separate RD NO's and with no evidence of rework makes for an interesting sterling silver piece. Background on the two main suppliers of cutlery to 3rd Reich principles and organizations. The dominant supplier by quantity was Wellner dealing mostly with silver plate while the most prestigious supplier was Bruckmann dealing mostly in silver product.

Bruckmann & Wellner - the Big Guys

Bruckmann's tie with Hitler was its strong suite. They not only supplied him his trade mark 'formal' cutlery but also his 'informal'. Bruckmann specialized in raised (repousse) decorations and silver product while Wellner produced mostly machine engraved, plated flat product.

BRUCKMANN

Peter Bruckmann & Söhne AG, Heilbronn was founded in 1805 by the Paris educated silversmith Georg Peter Bruckmann (born 1778, died 1850). At that time Heilbronn was responsible to the Emperor and there fore applied the Reichsadler (Eagle of the Emporium) coat of arms. After 1918, the Reichsadler was retained without the symbols of the former Monarchy (Crown, Collar, Breast shield with the Prussian Arms). This left the black eagle with one head, facing to the right, with open wings. Peter Bruckmann (1865-1937), grandson and one of the co-owners of Peter Bruckmann & Söhne AG, after an intensive Art education, assumed responsibility for the organization in 1887. The firm trained its own designers, silversmiths, chasers and engravers. Peter Bruckmann was the first chairman of the Deutscher Werkbund. The period of the German 'Jugendstil' (Art Nouveau) was one of Bruckmann company's famous "high noon" periods. In 1937 Peter Bruckmann died and with the World in a depression, 90 gram plated silver was the "high end standard". After WWII, Bruckmann was acquired by GERO N.V. which went bankrupt in 1973 ending both GERO N.V. and Bruckmann.

note: GERO, the Maker Mark for Gerofabriek, Zeist, Holland is on the M-189 AVRO Tempelhof andeneken with 90 and GZ, an acronym for Gero-zilver, found on Gerofabriek's silver plated wares with a nickel silver base metal. First used in 1917.

During the 3rd Reich period, Bruckman used four styles of Maker Marks.

The premier MM was its Prussian Eagle with spread wings and legs (without the Emperors insignia that was deleted from the original after WWI) applied to 800 silver product:

	Page	Material
AH Formal, raised	27	800
AH Napkin Ring, raised	29	925
AH Informal, raised	31	800
DR 205, raised	137	800
DR 213, raised	141	800
RK, raised	173	800
SS, raised	278	800
Berghof	361	800
F Bau, raised	363	800

A 2nd MM for silver is 'Bruckmann' in an oblong reserve, the Prussian Eagle and 800.

U-47	385	800

A 3rd MM is the Locomotive 90 for plated flatware (adopted around1855).

Himmler	51	90
DR243, raised	145	90

A 4th MM with 'Bruckman 90' in an oblong reserve for plated flatware.

Saukel, raised	69	90
Kunst, raised	391	90

WELLNER

Wellner & Sons - The "Säch. Metallwarenfabrik Aug. Wellner Söhne" was founded 1850 in Aue, Germany by August Wellner. Wellner tableware and cutlery was produced for the Kempinski Hotel in Berlin, the Titanic and the Hapag-Liner “Imperator“. Peter Behrens and Joseph Maria Olbrich worked for Wellner in the 1910 to 20´s. As an example, in 1911 annual production was 36 million cutlery items in 122 different models and 222 different hotel services. Charles Augustus Wellner selected the companies symbolic figures: Elephant for Force, the 3 Dwarves and the Cube for Happiness and Diversity. Wellner produced mostly machine engraved, silver plated and alpacca flatware. The most prolific maker from 1854 to 1958. From 1958 to 1992 it was renamed ABS (Auer Besteck and Silver Works).

Wellner		Page		Material	Grams
	Hitler, block	37		alpacca	
D	Hitler, linked	39		90	30
D	Speer	55		60	?
D	Weidling	59		90	21
D	Ley	65		90	45
	Kaltenbrunner	67		100	24
	Heydrich	87	P	90	45
D	Heydrich	89		100	18
	General Scheel	91		100	50
	Otto Dietrich	143		90	
	NSRL	159	P	90	4
	RMJ	179	P	90	3
	89th Inf	213		800	
	GOWE = "GOttfried WEllner.				
	D.AK	225		800	
	AWS = August Wellner & Son (1928-41)				
	Luftwaffe crosswise	251	P	90	45
	Luftwaffe nut cracker	261		10	3

	Waffen-SS	281		alpacca	
	34th Gren Reg	323		90	
	SS Breslau	349		alpacca	
	SS Stegskopf	353		alpacca	
	WS = Wellner & Son				
	SS Ostmark	357		alpacca	
	Reichswerke	365		alpacca	
	wello (Vello was their Italian factory)				
	Gastehaus	367		100	50
	Hotel Deutscher Hof	369		60	
	Wellner Soehne				
	Dietrich Eckart	381	P	90	45
		383			
D	Haus Arbeit	389		90	16
	Haus German Art	395, 396, 397		alpacca	
	Rabbit Breeder	403		90	
	Paris Embassy	411		alpacca	
	East Germany	419		90	45
D	M-196	481		90	45
	M-197	482	P	90	45

D - Die (Cube) leads markings on reverse
P - Patent
Note: Another Wellner MM is FHW = FHWellner

With special focus on the ‘grams’ column above, Joerg Mueller-Daehn addressed this matter in great detail in his article entitled “Numerical Marks on German & French Silverplate”. Below is an abbreviated German portion:

“Germany The production of silver plated cutlery on an industrial level began in Germany in the middle of the 19th Century. Engineers achieved the best results if they used a small bath, put one dozen table spoons and one dozen table forks in it , used 90 grams of fine silver and then immersed the pieces until the silver anodes were dissolved and the silver firmly settled on the cutlery. Using 12 + 12 pieces as described above and 90 grams of fine silver became the standard in Germany. To document this, the '90' was punched on the pieces. If companies wanted to produce cheaper cutlery, they used less silver, 60 grams, 40 grams or more 100 grams and punched the pieces accordingly "60", "40" or "100" etc. When plated cutlery became more affordable and more customers bought it, they began to ask how much pure silver their flatware actually 'contained'. Manufacturers realized they could use the answer as a method to promote sales and started punching a further mark that roughly provided the actual gram weight of the silver that coated the specific piece. Unfortunately they used two different systems:

1. Pieces that usually came in a dozen (table-forks / -spoons / -knives, -coffee spoons etc.) are punched with the weight of silver used for plating a dozen pieces. So table spoons and table forks were marked with a "45". smaller

pieces were punched a lower figure (e.g. "30", as less silver was needed to give them the same thickness of plating.

2.Pieces that usually came singly or in pairs (serving pieces) were punched with the weight of silver on a single piece.

Examples: If you have a spoon marked “90” and “45” it means: the standard process as described above was used, on one spoon roughly 1/12 of 45 grams (ca. 3.75 Grams) of fine silver were spread. If you have a sugar tong marked “90” and “2” it mens: again the standard process was used, 2 grams of fine silver were used to coat the piece. If you have a pair of salad servers, each piece marked “90” and “4”

it means: again the standard process was used, on each piece 4 grams of fine silver were used.

This German system of silver plate marking has been adopted by other European countries, and is sometimes seen on Dutch, Danish and Austrian silver plate.”

When Hitler became Reich’s Chancellor in 1933 and secretly began re-armament, to conceal what was going on in the German arms and allied industries, manufacturers were assigned code numbers. Ordnance coding by letters began in 1938 and continued to the last days of the war. Wellner’s letter code was ‘gn’, associated with its manufacture of small-arms ammunition & anti-aircraft shells from 1943 on. Wellner’s participation in the manufacture of 7.92 X 57 rifle ammunition was as a Plating Firm (galvanisieranstalten). Their code was “y” which would appear at the head stamp’s 3 o’clock position.

F. H. WANI
GOLDSCHMIEDE
MÜNCHEN DORFEN
ADALBERTSTR. 70/III
TELEFON: 372386
Mitglied Bayr. Kunstgewerbeverein
u. Münchner Künstlergenossenschaft

München, 29. Juli 1938.

An das

Architekturbüro Professor Fick

Herrn Architekt Michaelis

M ü n c h e n .

Betr. Silberlieferung Teehaus Kehlstein.

LIEFERSCHEIN

36 Tafellöffel
36 Tafelgabeln
36 Tafelmesser
36 Dessertlöffel
36 Dessertgabeln
36 Dessertmesser
36 Fischmesser
36 Fischgabeln
72 Kaffeelöffel
36 Moccalöffel
36 Eislöffel
36 Kuchengabeln
36 Obstgabeln
36 Obstmesser
6 Saucenlöffel
4 Spargelheber
4 Fischvorlegebestecke
6 Fleischgabeln
4 Salatbestecke
4 Käsemesser
6 Gemüselöffel
6 Kompottlöffel
8 Eisvorleger
8 Tortenspaten
4 Kuchenmesser
8 Konfektgabeln

8 Zuckerzangen
8 Traubenscheren
8 Kuchenvorlegegabeln
8 Sahnevorleger
8 Limonadelöffel
2 Teesiebe m. Unterschale
10 Flaschenkorke
2 Zahnstocherbehälter

2 Zigarrenabschneider
4 Zigarettenkästen
2 Zigarrenkasten
4 Leuchter
4 Zündholzbehälter

In versilbert:
36 Bierglasuntersetzer
4 Bierglasträgertabletts
10 Salzstreuer
10 Pfefferstreuer
4 Zitronenpresser

Diese 750 Einzelteile wurden verpackt in 2 Kisten und 1 Karton von der Firma Thomas Geiger, München zum Transport nach Obersalzberg in Empfang genommen.

114

Again, Thanks to Matthew Sollis for the above,

My Last Word on Hitler's "Informal"

Opposite is a copy of the order for the Kehlstein teahouse silver ware placed 29 July 1938. The quantity of 36 fits the Eagles Nest seating requirements. This 'informal;' design is also in harmony with the use of the Eagles Nest for luncheons as there were no overnight accommodation available, no beds were ever placed there with the exception of a cot for Eva Braun's visits indicating that its use was for day time only. An overriding concern would have been the motor access to the elevator which would be prohibited during the winter as well as at night as the road is dangerous at all times but particularly when wet or at night. I propose that Hitler's use of the Eagles Nest focused on the informal luncheons at best and that an 'informal' service suited this accordingly. The 'formal' ware would not have been in adequate quantity to service the 32 place settings at the table and in any case would have been overkill. Placing the informal at the Eagles Nest also complies with the generally accepted estimates of less that 1,000 in quantity and the date of the order would indicate the service was to be in place for the opening of the Eagles Nest on Hitler's 50th birthday - 20 April 1939. Bruckmann made both services - a Hitler favorite!. The ultimate destination for the service is unknown but I propose that its first destination was the Eagles nest.

Note: At least one source states that Speer was involved with the design of the AH formal / informal cutlery.

HITLERS's Favorite Monogram?

As I was putting the final touches on this book, I was in communication with Charles E. Snyder, Jr. who wrote the best and most comprehensive book on 3rd Reich personal collectibles entitled *Treasure Trove - The Looting of the Third Reich* and a must for every collector. In any case, Mr. Snyder allowed that he had a selection of AH pieces with the monogram of interest and was kind enough to send them along for my viewing. He said the provenance of the items can be traced to the acquisition of some 1,000 pieces by 1st Lt D C Watts that were sequestered in the storage rooms underneath the Plattenhof Hotel. Lt. Watts was "famous" for his diligence in acquiring collectibles from the Obersalzburg area. One photo in Snyder's book shows the Lt. with a large footlocker on his shoulder, reportedly full of collectibles, leading a procession of troops down the hill from the Berghof. Mr.Snyder recalls showing several of the monogramed pieces to Albert Speer, also in his book, who stated that this was indeed a favorite AH pattern.

This would explain why the outlined curved linked 'AH" with pointed 'A' cross bar above and linked to the "H" monogram as seen on PS-7 is available on different pattern cutlery from different makers. The remarkable resemblance of this monogram to Speer's PS-16 may not be mere coincidence, but could indicate that not only did Speer design Eva Braun's monogram but that we could hypothesize Speer and AH collaborating on this monogram. Extending this thought - to assure a favorable reception, it could very easily have been the recommended monogram (via Bormann?) to companies in the preparation of gift sets for AH on either their own behalf or customers. Reassuringly, the monograms are all proportional to the individual pieces.

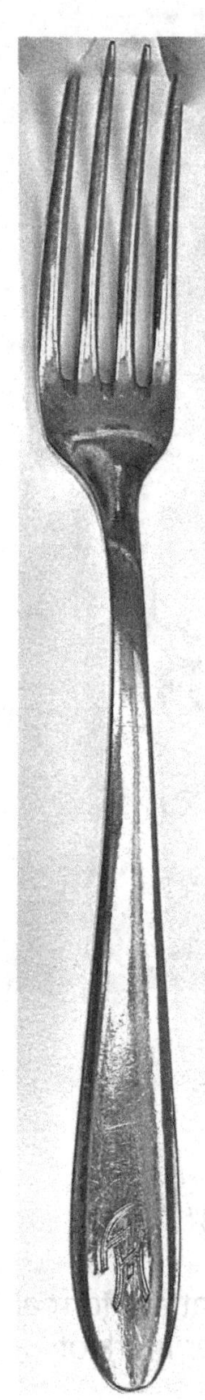

M-196

L = 210 mm / 8 1/4"

After PS-7, a Wellner fork variation, pattern plain with monogram, reverse maker mark of the Die (cube) WELLNER 90 45.

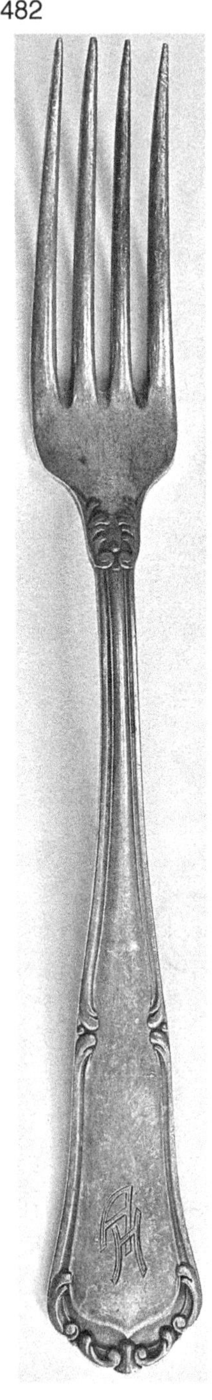

M-197

L = 210 MM / 8 1/4"

2rd variation, a Wellner fork pattern formal with monogram, reverse maker mark of WELLNER PATENT 90 45.

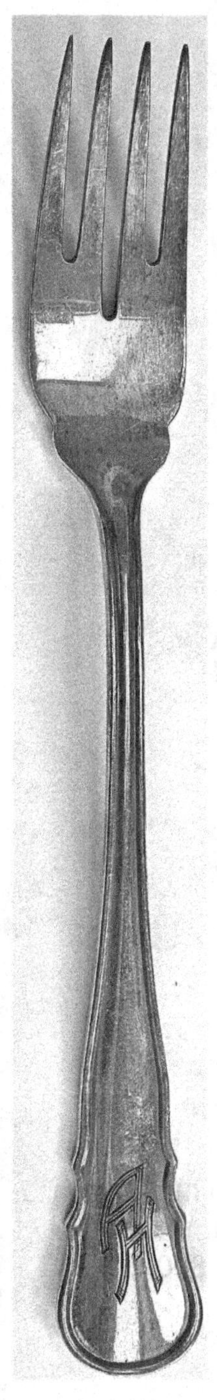

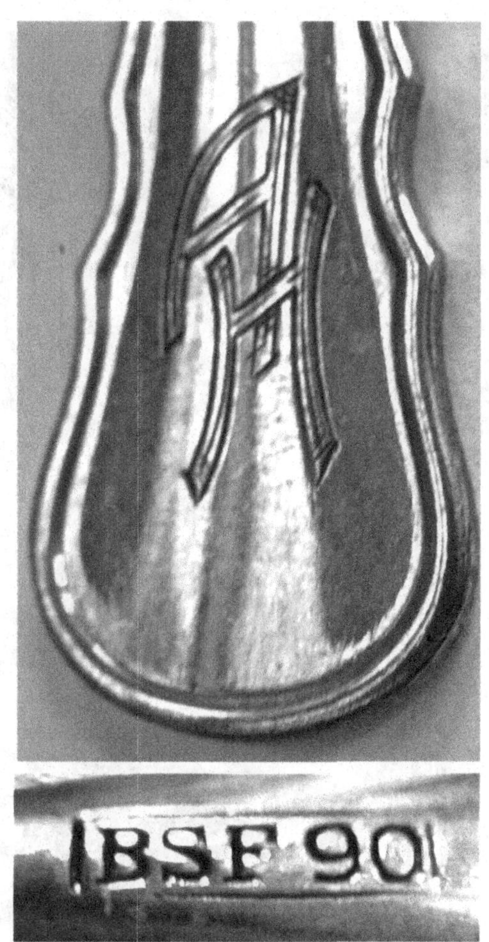

M-198

L = ‘180 mm / 7 1/8”

3rd variation, Salad Fork pattern scolloped with monogram, reverse maker mark BSF (Bremer Silberwarenfabrik AG., Bremen-Sebaldsbrueck) 90 in an oblong reserve.

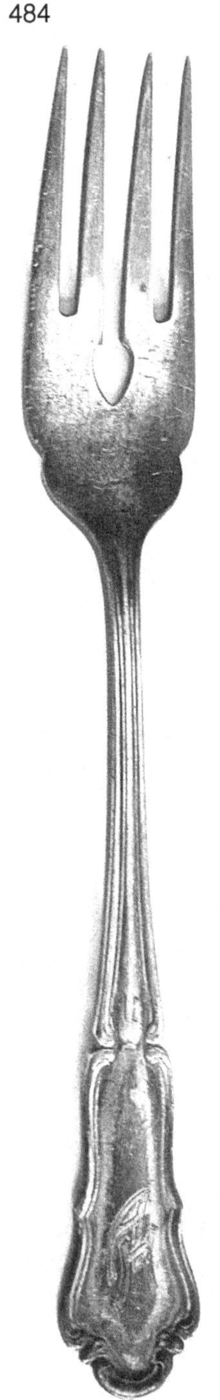

M-199

L = 182 mm / 7 3/16"

4th variation, Fish Fork with monogram, reverse maker mark of M. H. Wilkens & Sons, Bremen-Hemelingen, 800, RM.

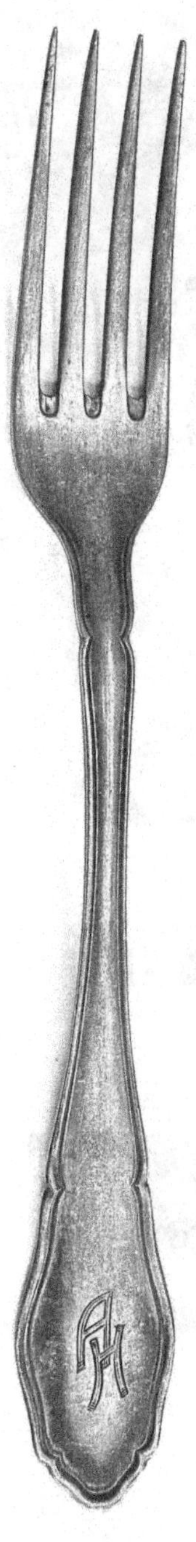

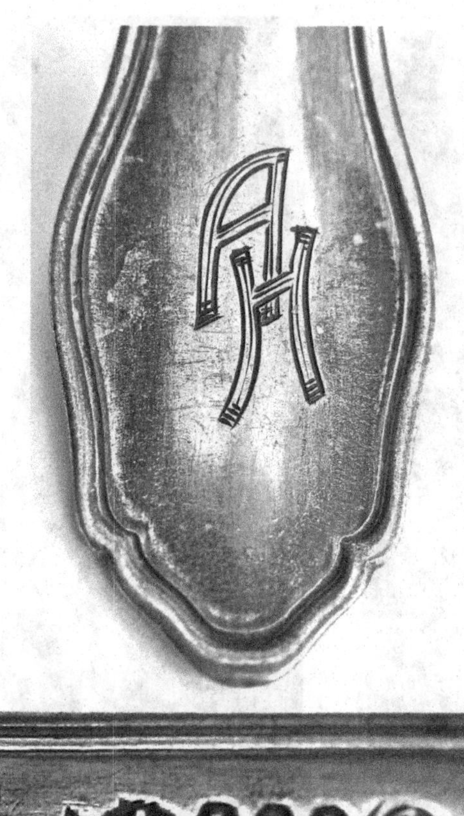

M-200

L = 182 mm / 7 3/16"

5th variation, Fork, with monogram, reverse maker mark of RM, 800, GR (Gebrueder Reiner), Krumbach i. Bayern)

M-201
L = 252 mm / 9 15/16”

M-201 NPEA Ploen - Nationalpoltische Erziehungsanstalt
(National Political Educational Institute)

Table Knife: Obverse handle with Ploen and below it a shield with NPEA at the top over a mobile swastika. The blade carries the makers mark of Fr. Burberg & Co. AG of Mettmann, with Feinstahl over Solingen and Rostfrei. Reverse handle carries the same makers mark over 100.

In April 1933, Dr Bernard Rust, Minister for Science, Education and Culture, set up the first of a number of special residential institutions to train the future Nazi elite, the NPEA. Three schools were opened in 1933, with the Ploen being the very first. Favorite locations were old Army cadet schools, requisitioned monasteries and refurbished castles. The motto of the NPEA was "Mehr sein als scheinen" which translated means "Be modest but always excel". The training was designed to prepare the Nazi elite with the necessary skills and ideology to act as a leader in state departments or the Army. Each school enrolled about 400 students, of which about only 100 students were successful. Education covered a strong academic curriculum with a strong emphasis on physical training. In addition to the political curriculum, instruction was given in marksmanship, boxing, sailing, horsemanship, gliding and military science. Age of students was from 10 to 18 years old. Supervision of the NPEA (or NAPOLA) school system was placed in the hands of the SS.

Special Note: As this book was about to be sent to my publisher, Brian McAvoy, a fellow collector, was kind enough to send this knife to me for my appraisal. We subsequently discussed the piece and to my surprise and delight, Brian offered to part with the knife. This is what collecting is all about - a fellow collector who graciously shared his good fortune with another collector! Thanks Brian!

GEBRÜDER HEPP
PFORZHEIM

M-202

L = 24 cm / 9 1/2" vs
W = 18.5 cm / 7 1/4"

M-202 Platterhof Hotel Serving Tray

This small serving tray measures about 9½ inches at the ovals long side, and about 7 1/4 inches across the center. The tray has a rim on it, and would have been the size that would have been used to serve a cup of coffee or tea, with perhaps a little room for a creamer pitcher. The tray is stamped on the bottom side near the rim with the oval logo of the Platterhof Hotel. It consists of a woman in peasant costume standing in front of the Bavarian mountains. The tray is also marked on the lower section with the full name of the producer and the town where they were located, “Gebrüder Hepp/Pforzheim”. It came with a 3-page letter written by the veteran that brought this silvered piece home, and he mentions in the letter that he liberated some silvered pieces from the Platterhof Hotel.

More on the Obersalzberg Complex: The main area of Nazi occupation in Berchtesgaden was on the Obersalzberg, a quiet mountain retreat two miles east of Berchtesgaden and some 1200 feet higher in elevation.

Architect Albert Speer, the fourth member of the Nazi hierarchy (Hitler, Goering, Bormann) had a house and a spacious architectural studio built to Speer's design in 1939 to facilitate intercourse with AH.

To supply Hitler's vegetarian diet, Bormann had a huge, 2 tier, greenhouse (Gewächshaus) built,

To supply the power needs of the Obersalzberg complex, a coal storage bunker was built in 1940. This huge stone and concrete edifice could hold over 3500 tons of coal and was set on fire in early May 1945 and burned until October!

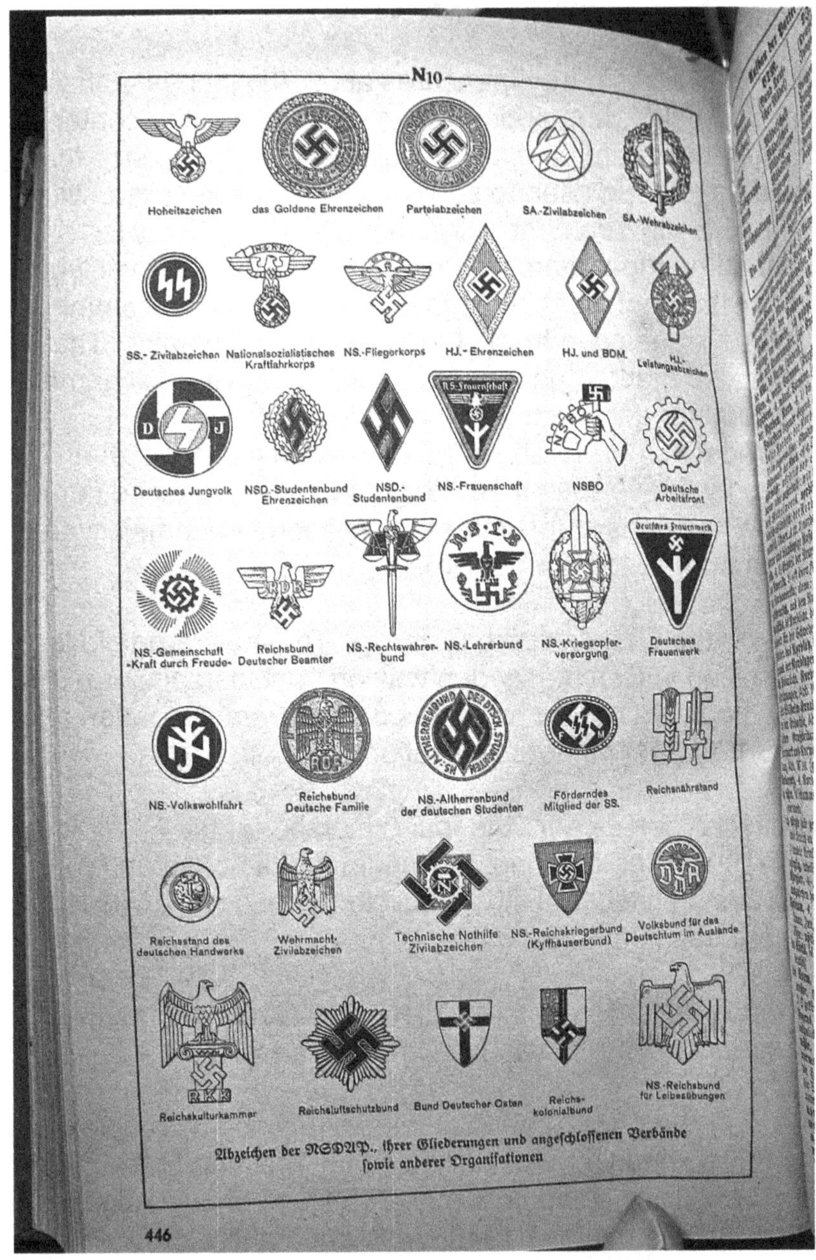

Der Sprach-Brockhaus, Leipzig dated 1940

Opposite page: Der Sprach-Brockhaus, Leipzig dated 1940 and a copy date of 1935 with 762 pages had on page 446 these illustrations of the various Nazi Abzeichen der NSDAP (Badges/Emblems of the NSDAP). This edition used Fraktur typeface which was shortly to be outlawed in 1941. You will find representations of 21 of these organizations in this book.

Contemporary 1933 guidance regarding official 3rd Reich cutlery: "Each of the collections had been commissioned by a special high ranking officer. The collections had the name of the personality who commissioned it. A distinct pattern was created for them and then a monogram was designed to identify it as a personal collection."

Thanks to USMBooks.com copies of the 1935 "Original Wellner Haupt-Musterbuch" (General Line Pattern Book) and a separately bound price list are now available. Pages 5 to 36 of the catalog depict over 350 original Wellner service items along with the product number of each. There are Indices of items by both name and number in the back. Pages in the 32-page Price List (Property of Sächsische Metallwarenfabrik August Wellner Söhne AG) explain the various markings on the backs and bottoms of Original Wellner tableware items and the weight of the silver used in the plating. The Price List is divided into sections for Hotel Silver and Table Service for Consumer Use. Some pieces (designs) are offered in a dozen or more sizes and various finishes, platings, etc. Every one of them has a price in each size! The Price List is alphabetically indexed in the back. If collectors studied original literature of this sort they would be far less likely to buy the myriad fakes and phantoms that flood the market today. Unfortunately, the catalog does not cover cutlery items.

Your Comments??

Additions, corrections and comments, please send to my publisher for forward to me:

Trafford Publications
9045 North River Road
Suite 400
Indianapolis, Indiana 46240

Please pass to: James A. Yannes
The Collector's Guide to 3rd Reich Tableware
Manuscript # 329254

First of all, thanks for buying this book and especially for actually getting to the end.

As you may know, this is my 5th book. The others were:

Astonishing Investment Facts and Wisdom
Astonishing Conservative Thoughts, Facts and Humor
Collectible Spoons of the 3rd Reich
A Guide to 3rd Reich Cutlery

And it is time, again, to thank my beloved wife Gerda for her saintly patience and tireless assistance with both the research and editing of the books.

"A great war leaves the country with three armies - an army if cripples, an army of mourners, and an army of thieves." (German Proverb)

ENDE

NOTES

Special Offer / Request: If you have any 3rd Reich metal tableware that is not in this book and would like to sell it to me for inclusion in my next book, please contact me at:

jimandgerda@verizon.net

or

508 655-5957

Should you wish to having the piece attributed to your self, that would be enthusiastically accommodated!

NOTES

Notes